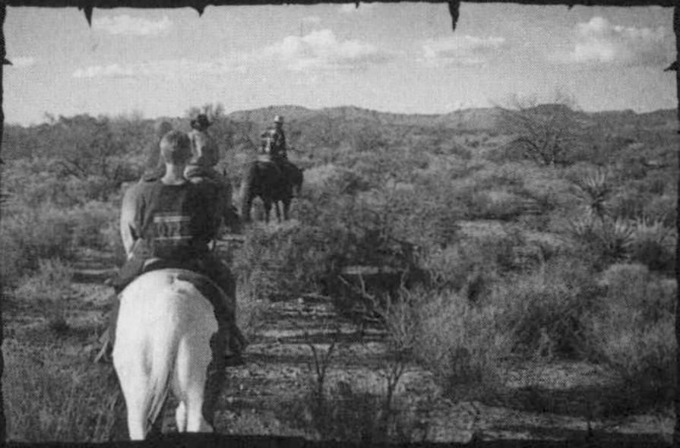

*I rode on a horse. It was the first time ever, but somehow, it was awesome. Clippety-clop, clippety-clop for about two hours. I stared up at the vast sky, thought about what lay beyond the horizon, dodged a spray of urine from the horse in front—everything was a precious experience. When it was all said and done, I couldn't make use of my trip in this story, but I know that this experience will surely come in handy someday. Let's head out again. Yup.*

—NOBUHIRO WATSUKI, 2001

Nobuhiro Watsuki earned international accolades for his first major manga series, *Rurouni Kenshin*, about a wandering swordsman in Meiji Era Japan. Serialized in Japan's *Weekly Shonen Jump* from 1994 to 1999, *Rurouni Kenshin* quickly became a worldwide sensation, inspiring a spin-off short story ("Yahiko no Sakabato"), an animated TV series, and several animated movies. Watsuki's latest series, *Buso Renkin*, also available in English from VIZ Media, began publication in *Weekly Shonen Jump* in June 2003.

# GUN BLAZE WEST VOL.2
The SHONEN JUMP ADVANCED Manga Edition

STORY AND ART BY
NOBUHIRO WATSUKI

Translation **JN Productions**
Touch-up Art & Lettering **HudsonYards**
Design **Courtney Utt**
Editor **Ian Robertson**

Editor in Chief, Books **Alvin Lu**
Editor in Chief, Magazines **Marc Weidenbaum**
VP of Publishing Licensing **Rika Inouye**
VP of Sales **Gonzalo Ferreyra**
Sr. VP of Marketing **Liza Coppola**
Publisher **Hyoe Narita**

Printed in the U.S.A.

Published by VIZ Media, LLC
P.O. Box 77010
San Francisco, CA 94107

SHONEN JUMP ADVANCED Manga Edition
10 9 8 7 6 5 4 3 2 1
First printing, July 2008

www.viz.com          www.shonenjump.com

SHONEN JUMP ADVANCED

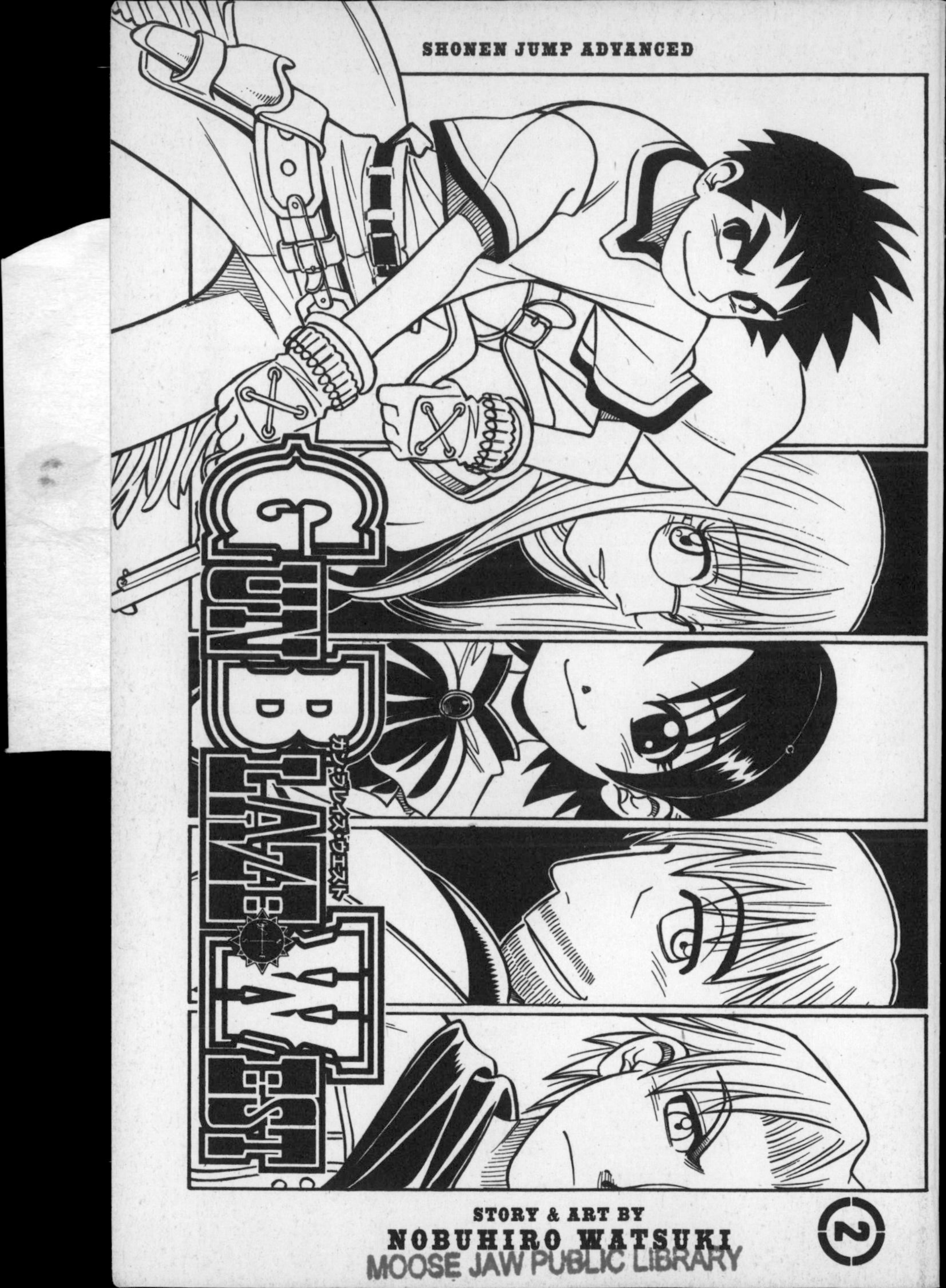
GUN BLAZE WEST

STORY & ART BY

**NOBUHIRO WATSUKI**

2

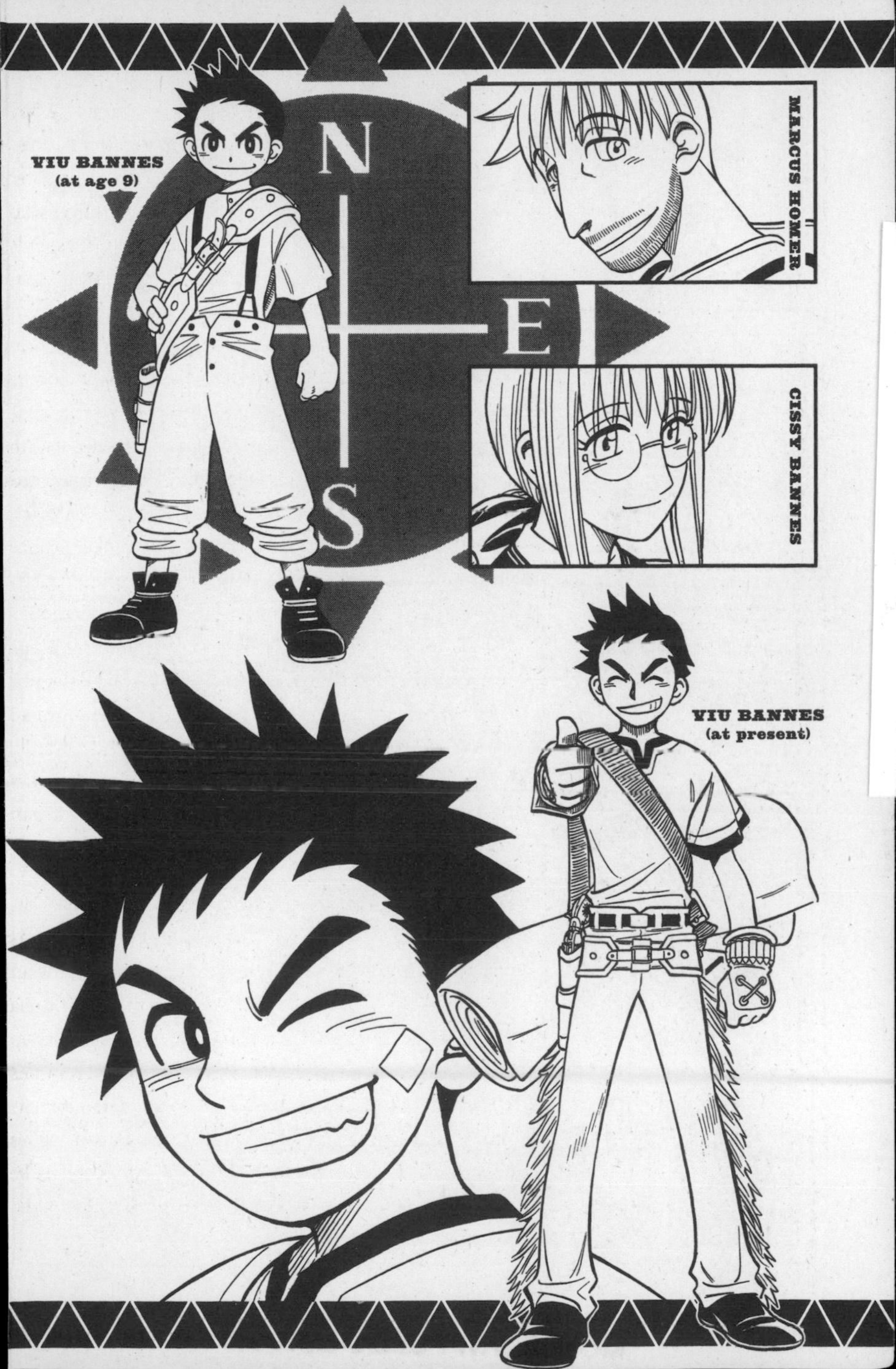
MARCUS HOMER
CISSY BANNES
VIU BANNES (at age 9)
VIU BANNES (at present)

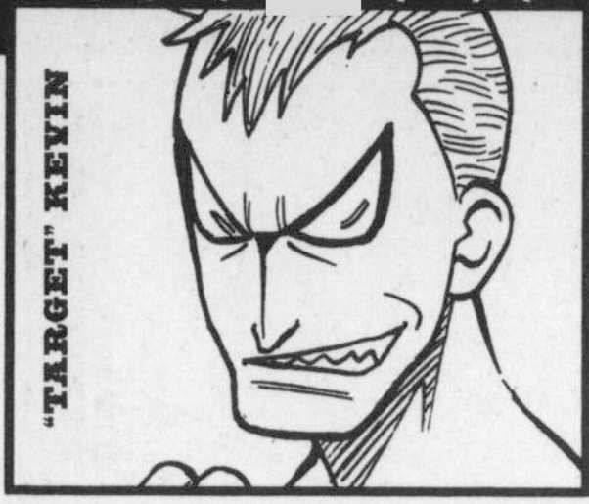
"TARGET" KEVIN

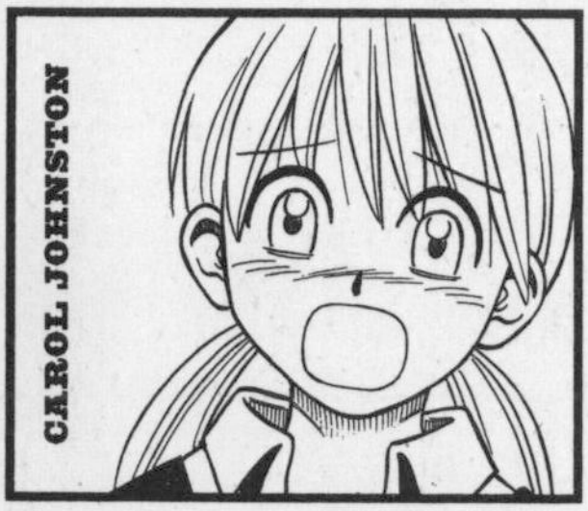
CAROL JOHNSTON

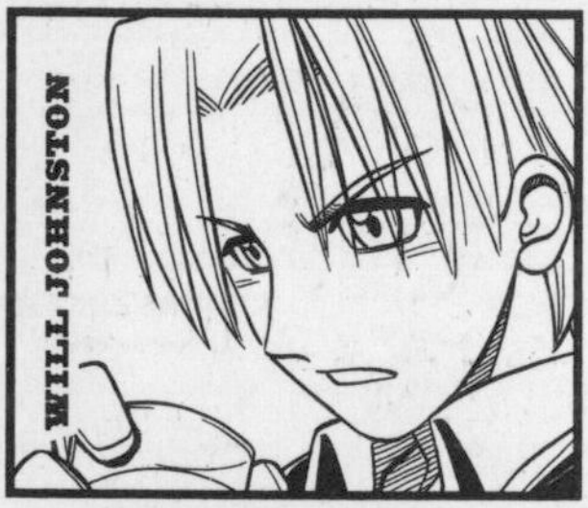
WILL JOHNSTON

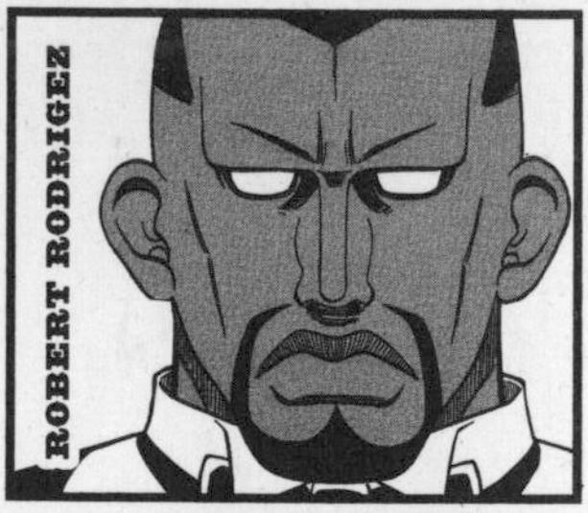
ROBERT RODRIGEZ

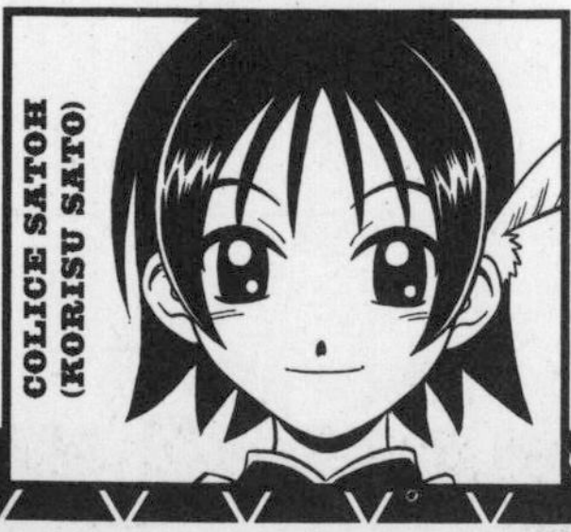
COLICE SATOH
(KORISU SATO)

America in the 19th century. Viu, a young boy who dreams of becoming a gunslinger, lives in Winston Town, Illinois, with his older sister Cissy. One day, Viu meets Marcus Homer, a gunslinger who scurried away from the West. With Marcus's help, Viu stands up against two outlaws and manages to apprehend them despite getting badly beaten up. When Viu tells Marcus, "I want to become stronger," Marcus makes up his mind to resume his quest for "Gun Blaze West," a promised land he once dreamt of—a place where only the strong who are confident of their skills are allowed to set foot. The two vow to join together and head toward their goal. When it is learned that the outlaws were scouts for the heinous Kenbrown Gang, the town prepares for attack. A volunteer defense force guards the west trail where they anticipate the gang will pass through... When Viu and Marcus approach the guard outpost during their training, Kenbrown's gang attacks. Marcus restrains Viu from charging in and then takes a desperate risk, challenging the leader, Kenbrown, to a man-to-man duel. Marcus, however, falls to a bullet from the cowardly Kenbrown's gun. Marcus entrusts his gun to Viu, who takes on the gang without giving an inch, finally managing to gun down Kenbrown.

Five years later, Viu, now 14, heads west. He starts by visiting the city of St. Louis, the "Gateway to the West." Viu is invited into a shabby saloon by a young girl named Carol but is harassed by a bouncer named Kevin from the Bella Donna saloon across the street. Carol's older brother Will shows up just as a fight is about to start inside the saloon and restrains Viu and Kevin with his magnificent rope technique. The situation calms when Carlo, the owner of Bella Donna, makes his appearance. Viu stays the night at Will's place, where he learns that Will too seeks Gun Blaze West. But that night, Kevin sets fire to Will's house…!

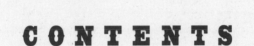

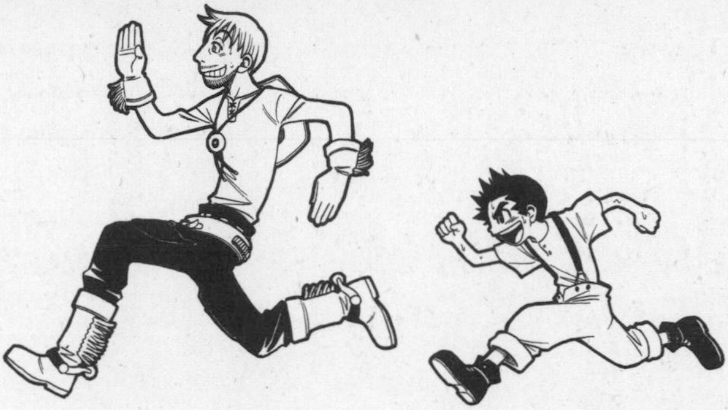

# CONTENTS

# CHAPTER 8: STANCE

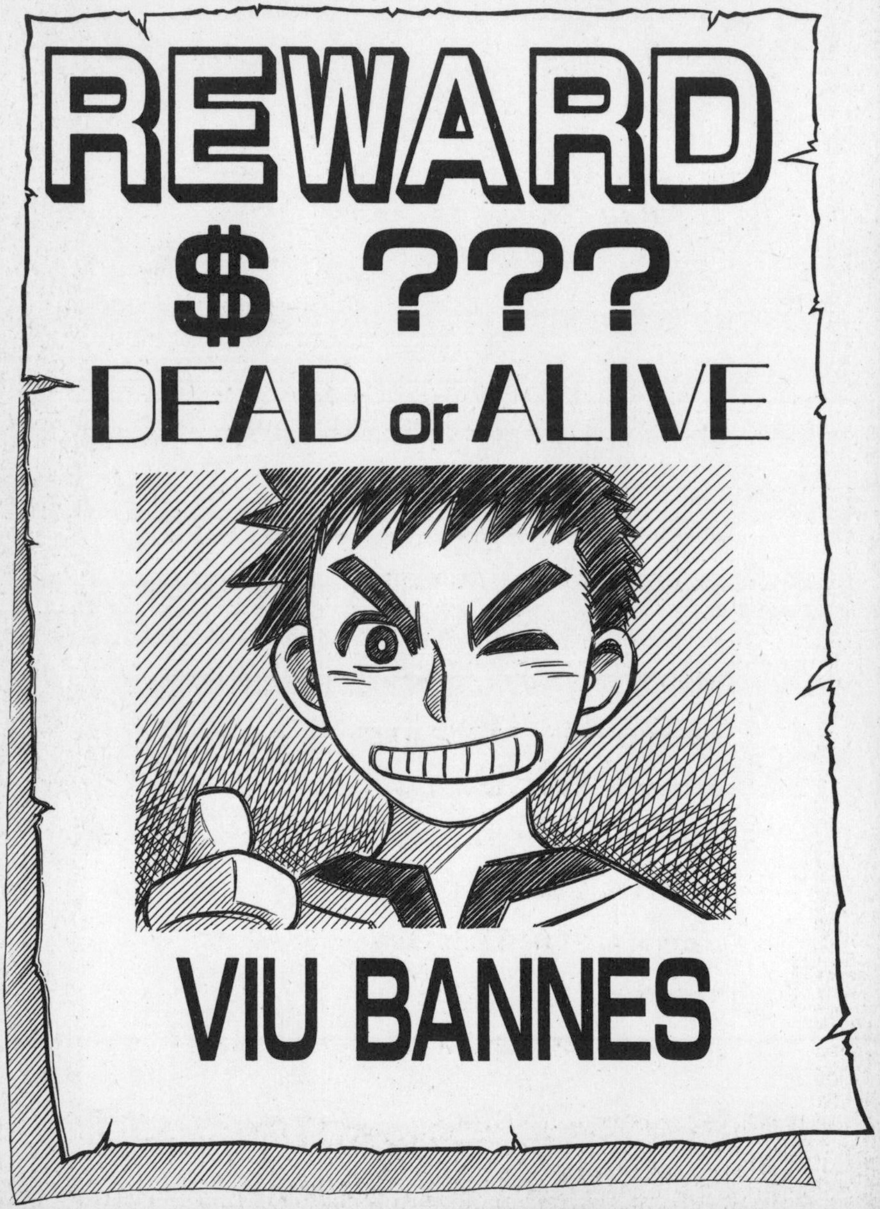
REWARD
$ ???
DEAD or ALIVE
VIU BANNES

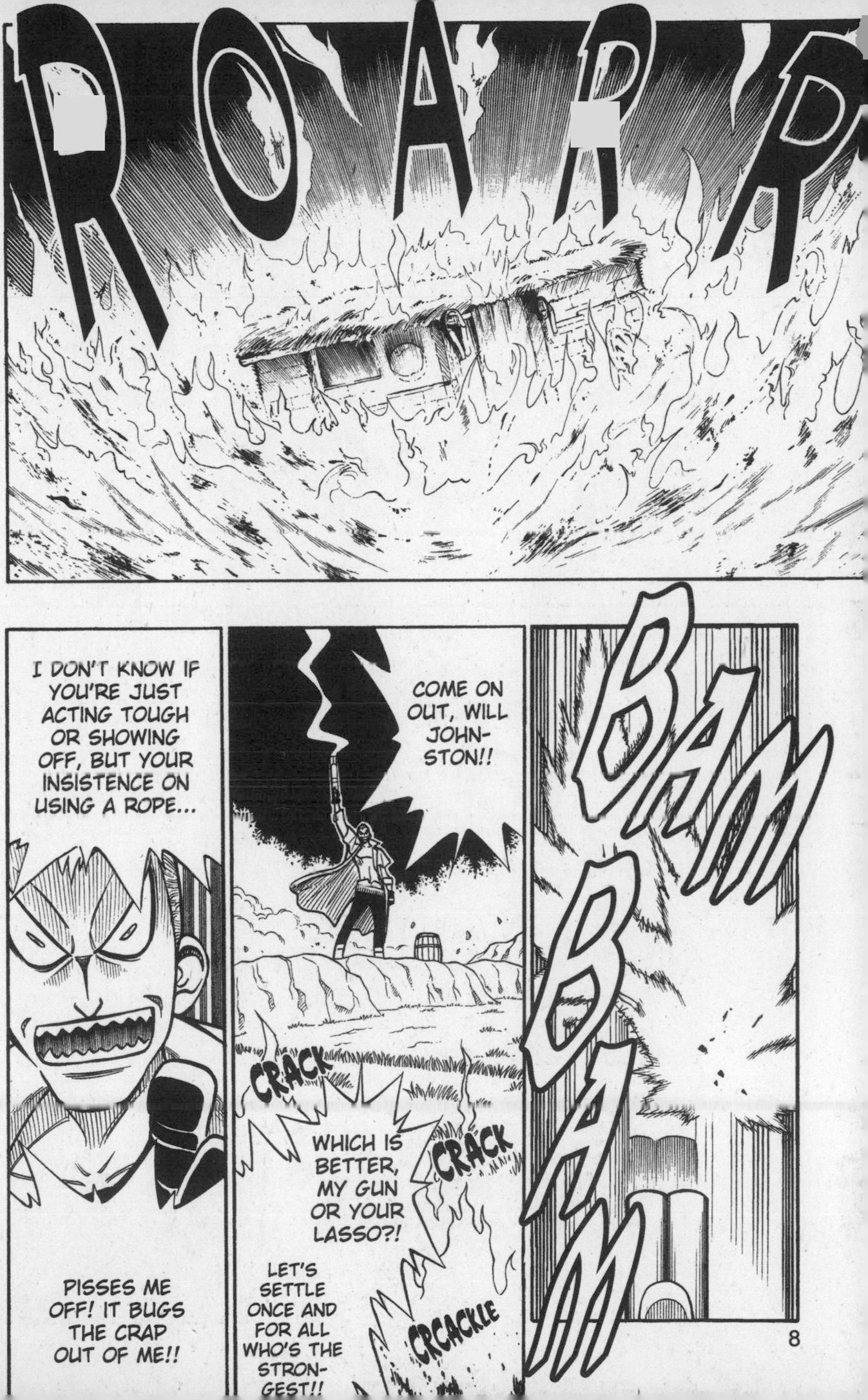
ROARR
BAM
BAM
COME ON OUT, WILL JOHN-STON!!
CRACK
WHICH IS BETTER, MY GUN OR YOUR LASSO?!
CRACK
LET'S SETTLE ONCE AND FOR ALL WHO'S THE STRON-GEST!!
CRCACKLE
I DON'T KNOW IF YOU'RE JUST ACTING TOUGH OR SHOWING OFF, BUT YOUR INSISTENCE ON USING A ROPE...
PISSES ME OFF! IT BUGS THE CRAP OUT OF ME!!

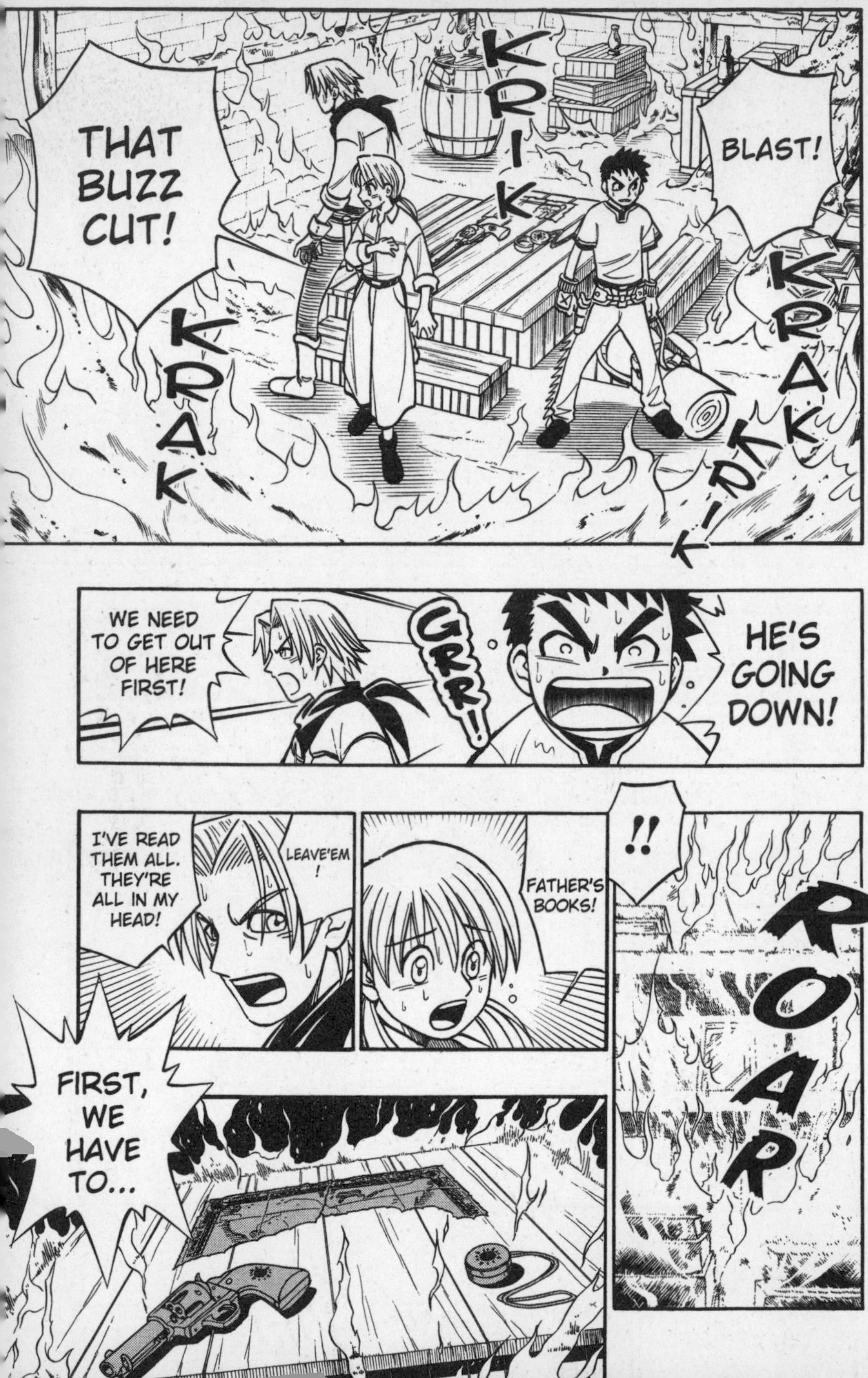
BLAST!
KRIK
THAT BUZZ CUT!
KRAK
KRIK
KRAK
HE'S GOING DOWN!
GRR!
WE NEED TO GET OUT OF HERE FIRST!
!!
ROAR
FATHER'S BOOKS!
LEAVE'EM!
I'VE READ THEM ALL. THEY'RE ALL IN MY HEAD!
FIRST, WE HAVE TO...

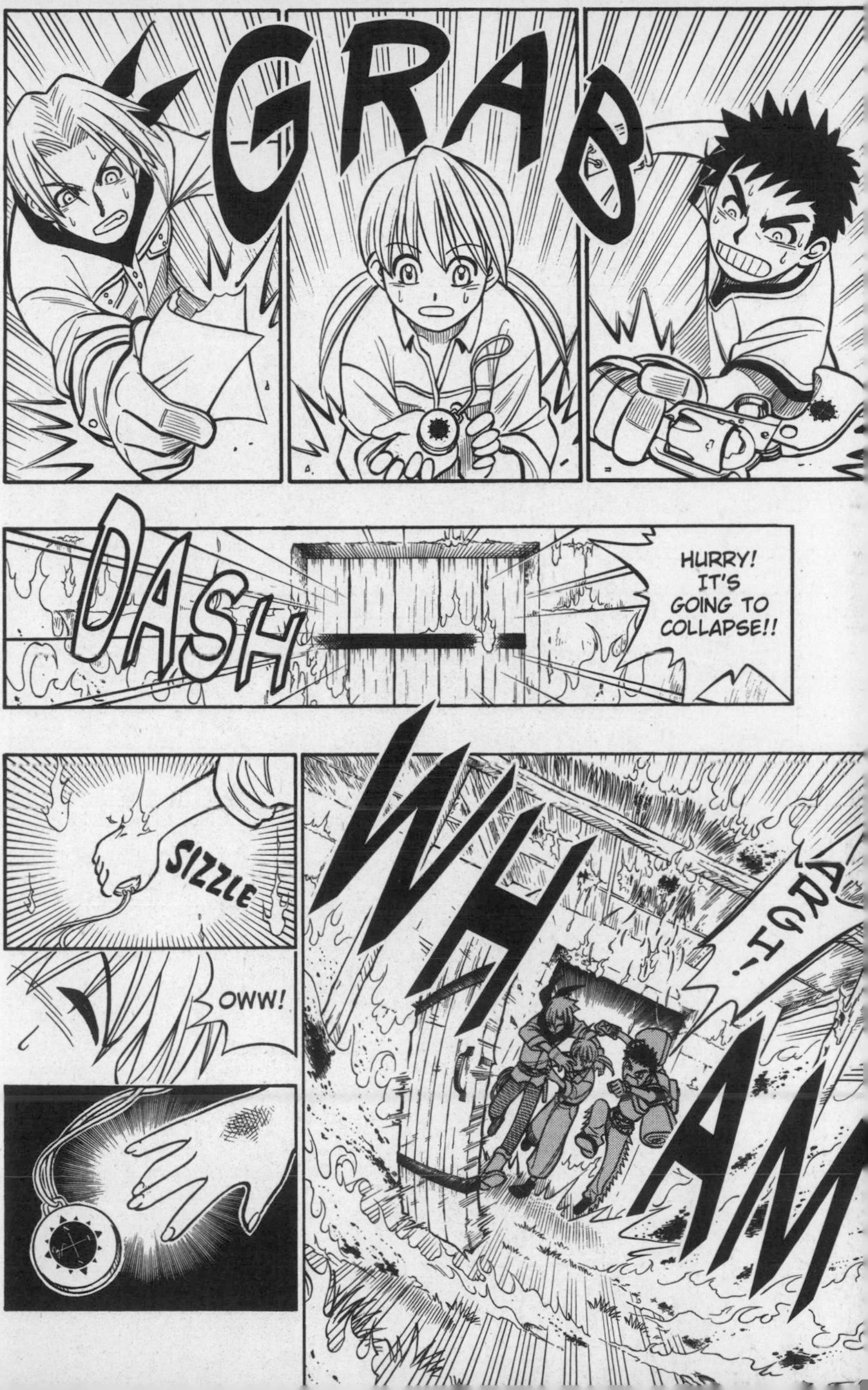
GRAB
HURRY! IT'S GOING TO COLLAPSE!!
DASH
ARGH!
WHAM
SIZZLE
OWW!

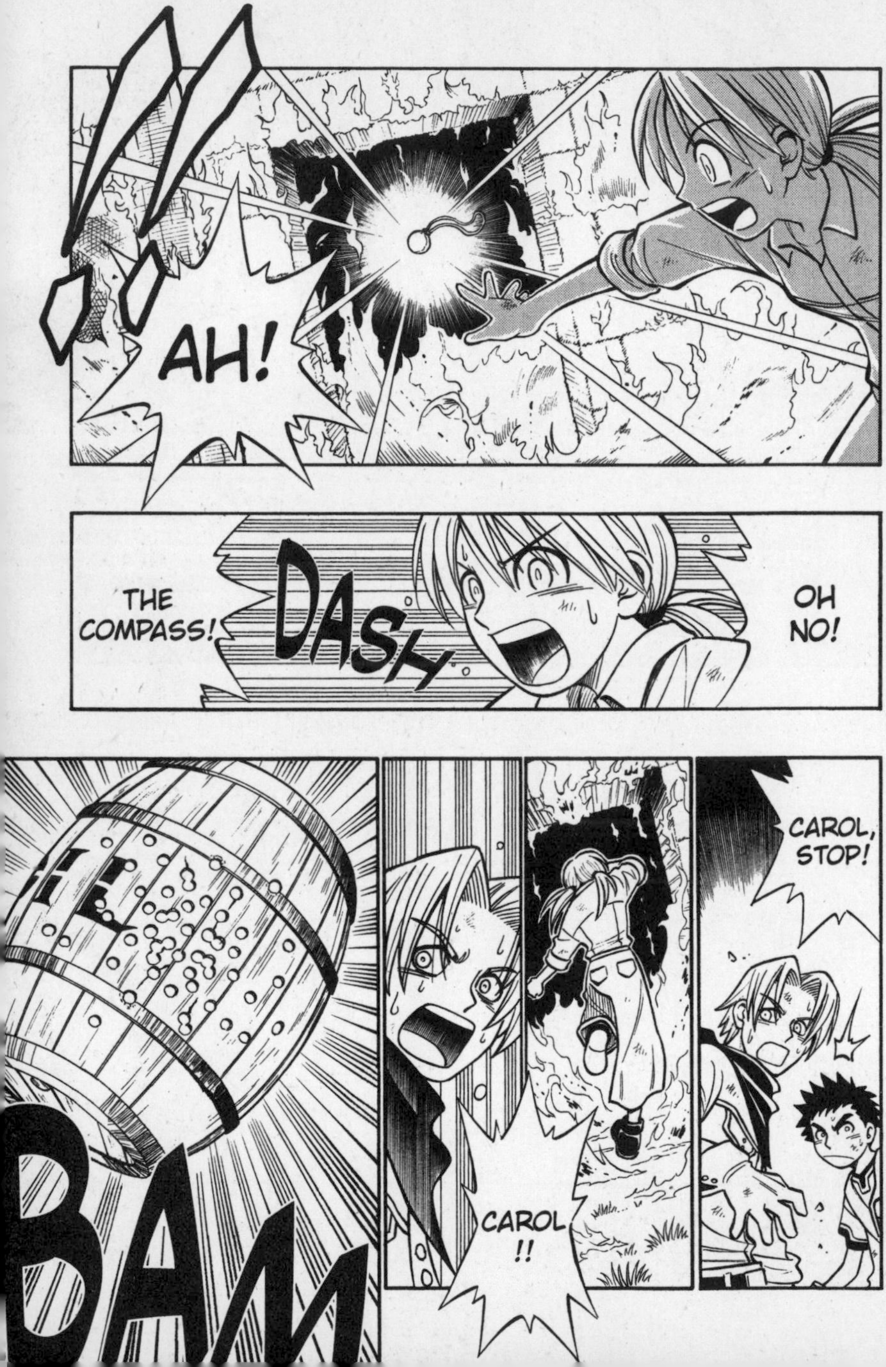
AH!
OH NO!
DASH
THE COMPASS!
CAROL, STOP!
CAROL !!
BAM

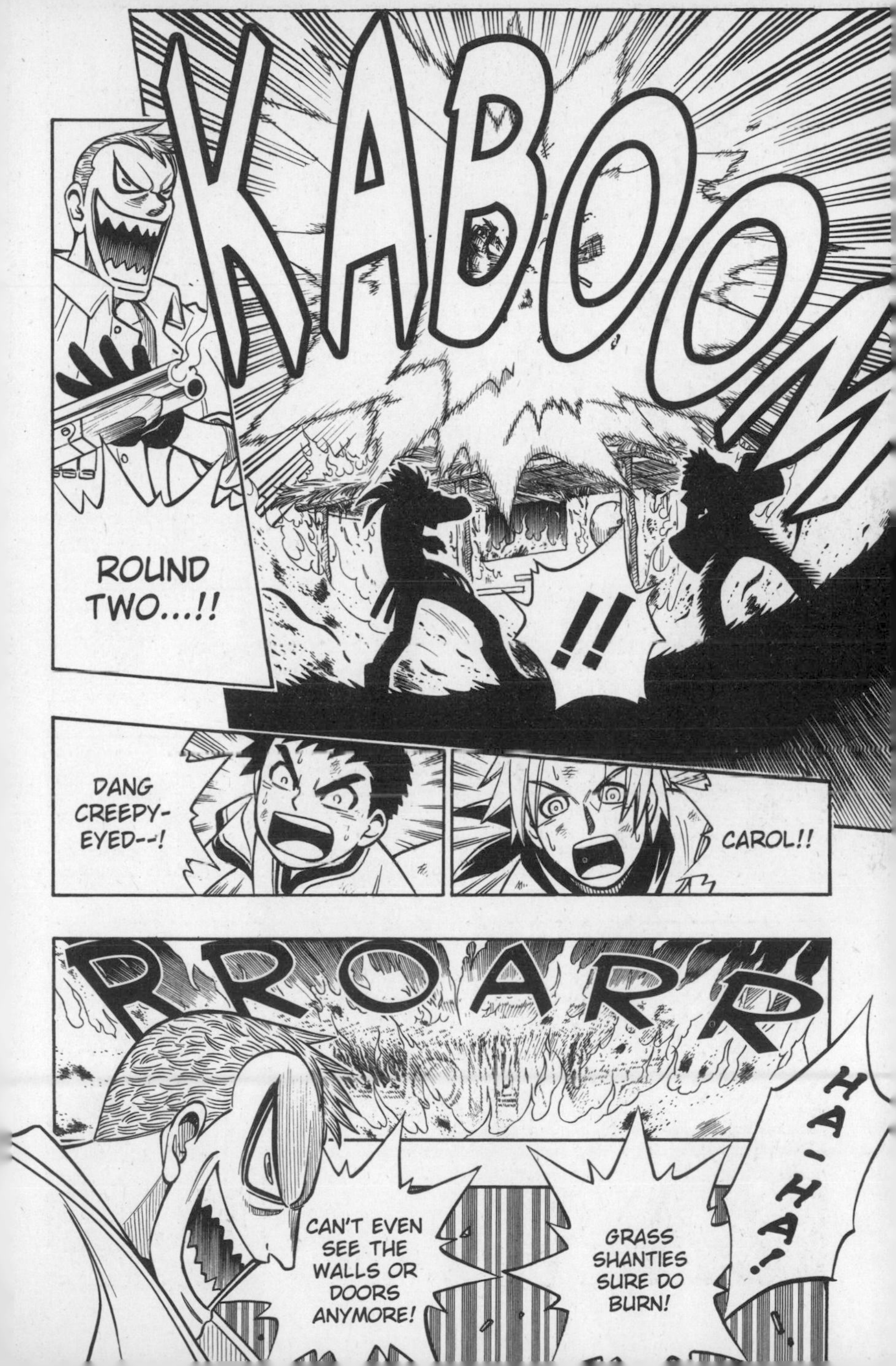
KABOOM
!!
ROUND TWO...!!
CAROL!!
DANG CREEPY-EYED--!
RROARR
HA-HA-HA!
GRASS SHANTIES SURE DO BURN!
CAN'T EVEN SEE THE WALLS OR DOORS ANYMORE!

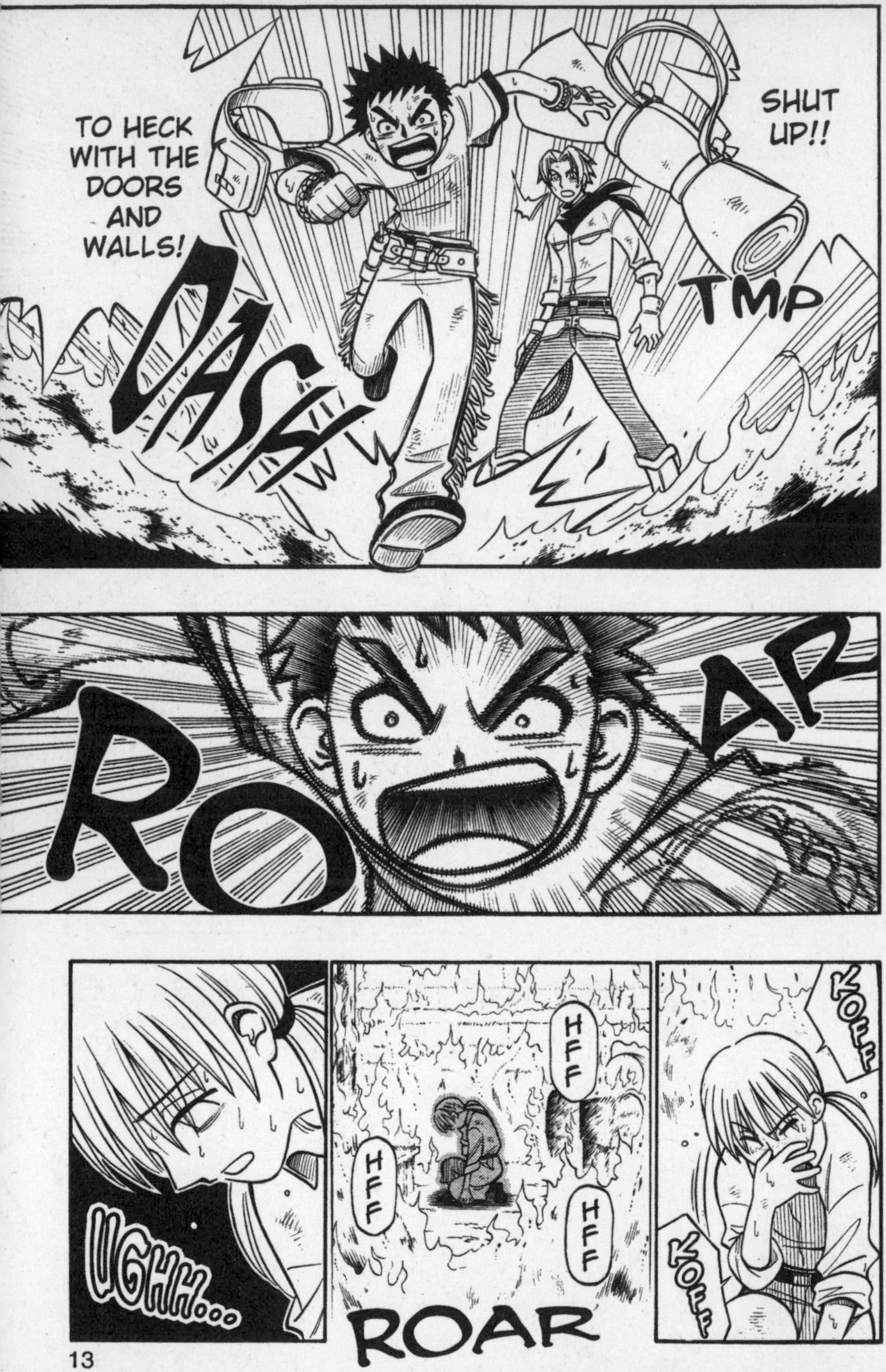
SHUT UP!!
TO HECK WITH THE DOORS AND WALLS!
TMP
DASH
ROAR
KOFF
KOFF
HFF
HFF
HFF
ROAR
UGHH...

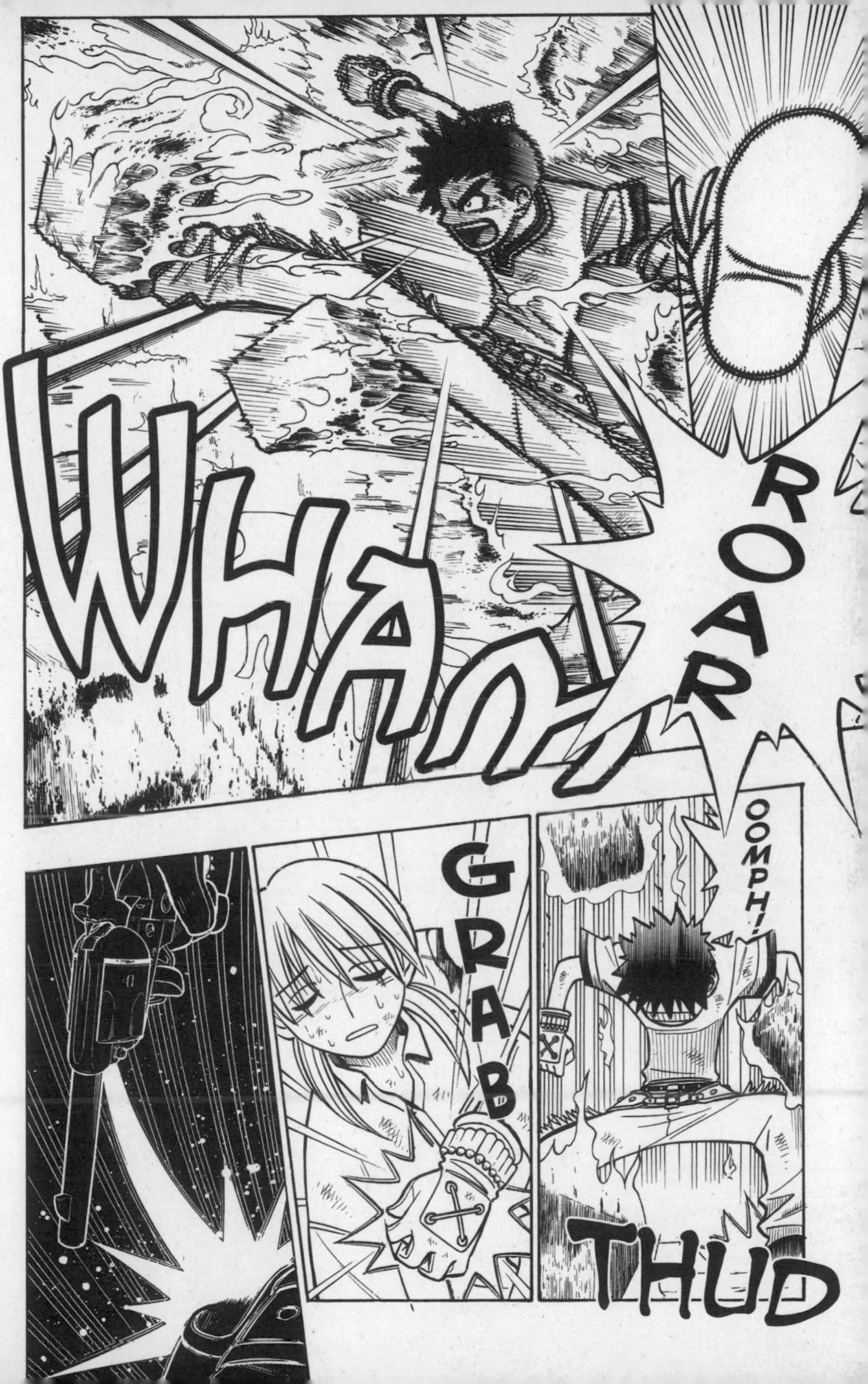
ROAR
WHAM
OOMPH!
THUD
GRAB

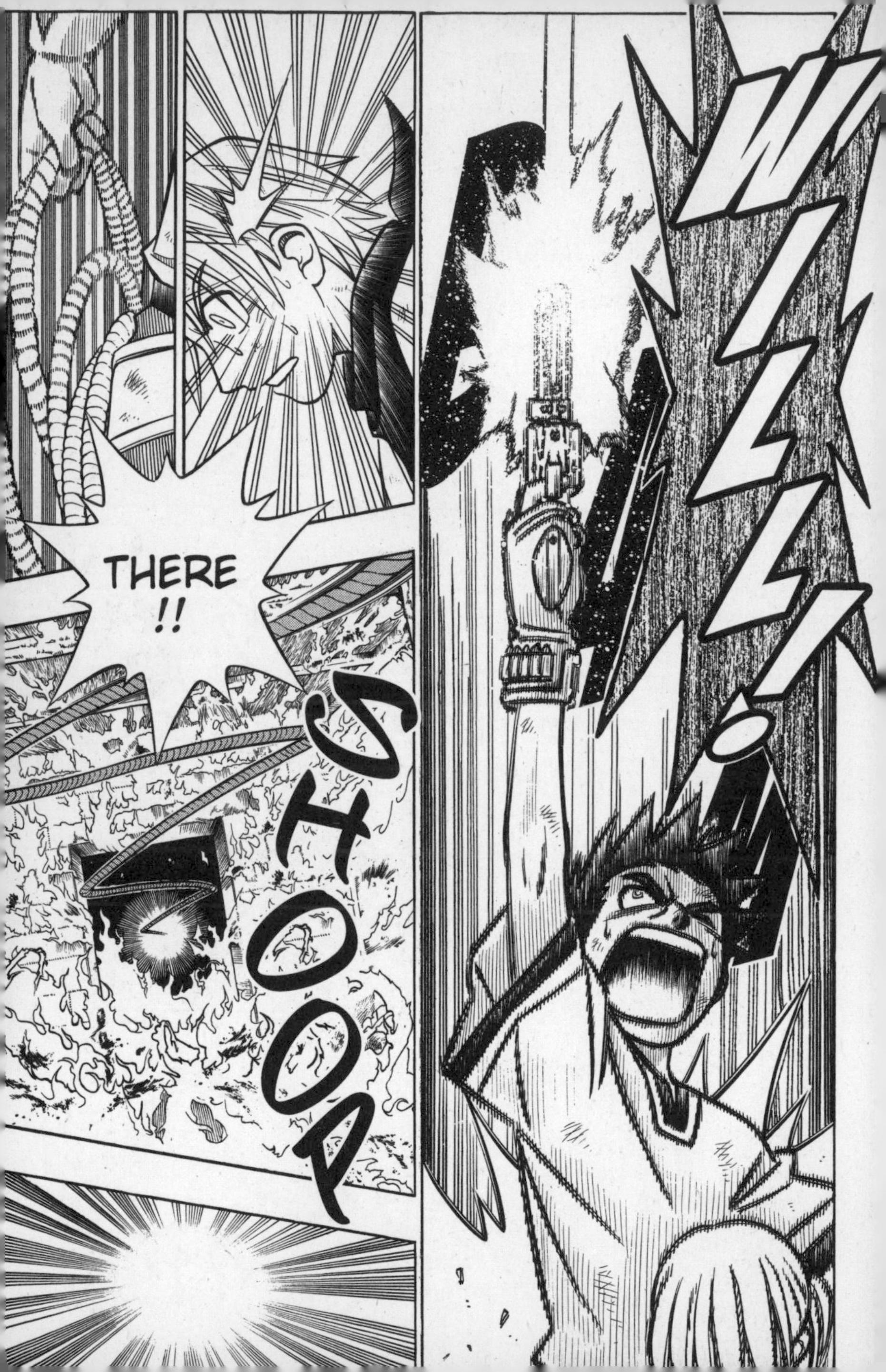
THERE !!
SHOOP

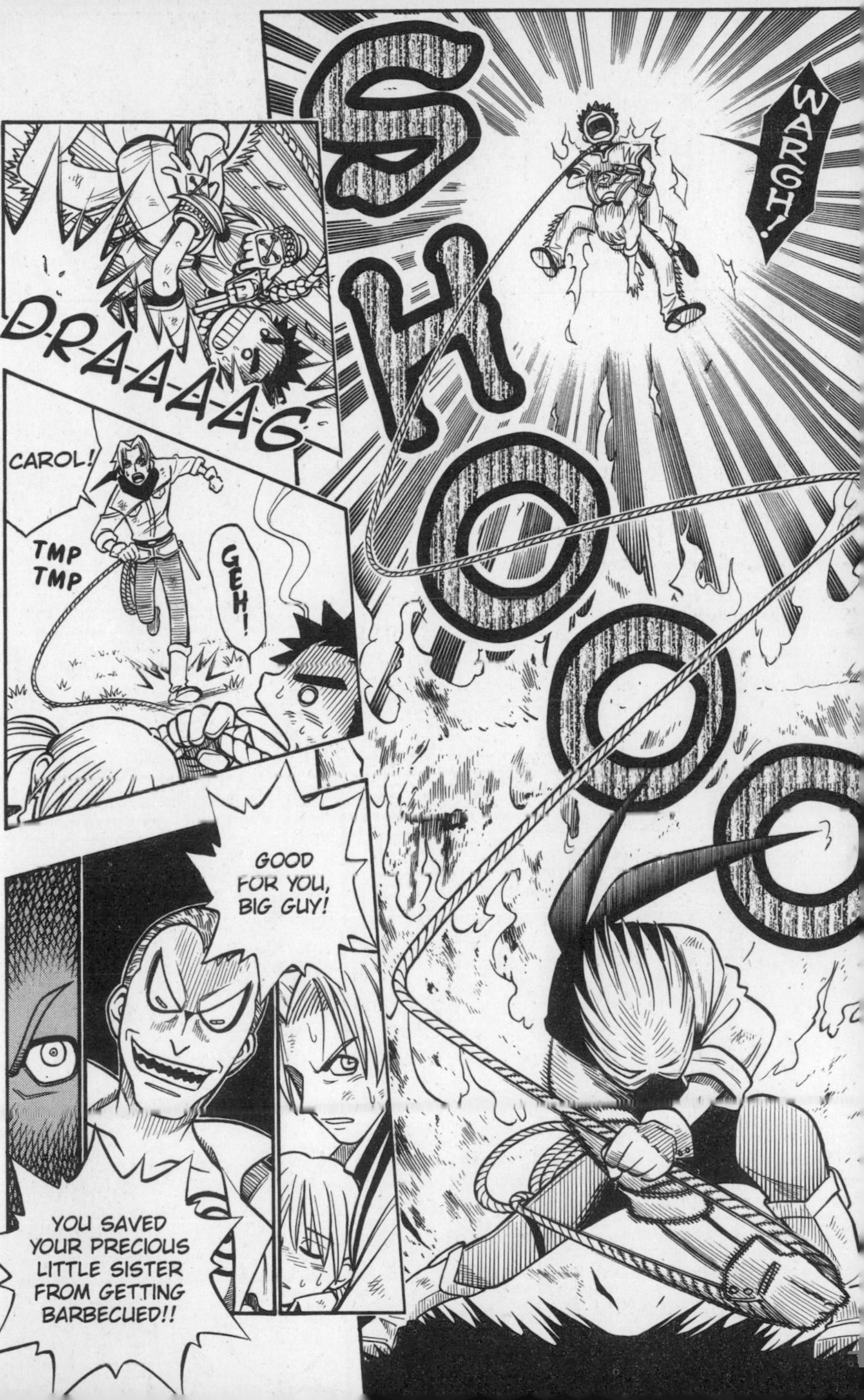
WARGH!
SHOOOOO
DRAAAAAG
CAROL!
TMP TMP
GEH!
GOOD FOR YOU, BIG GUY!
YOU SAVED YOUR PRECIOUS LITTLE SISTER FROM GETTING BARBECUED!!

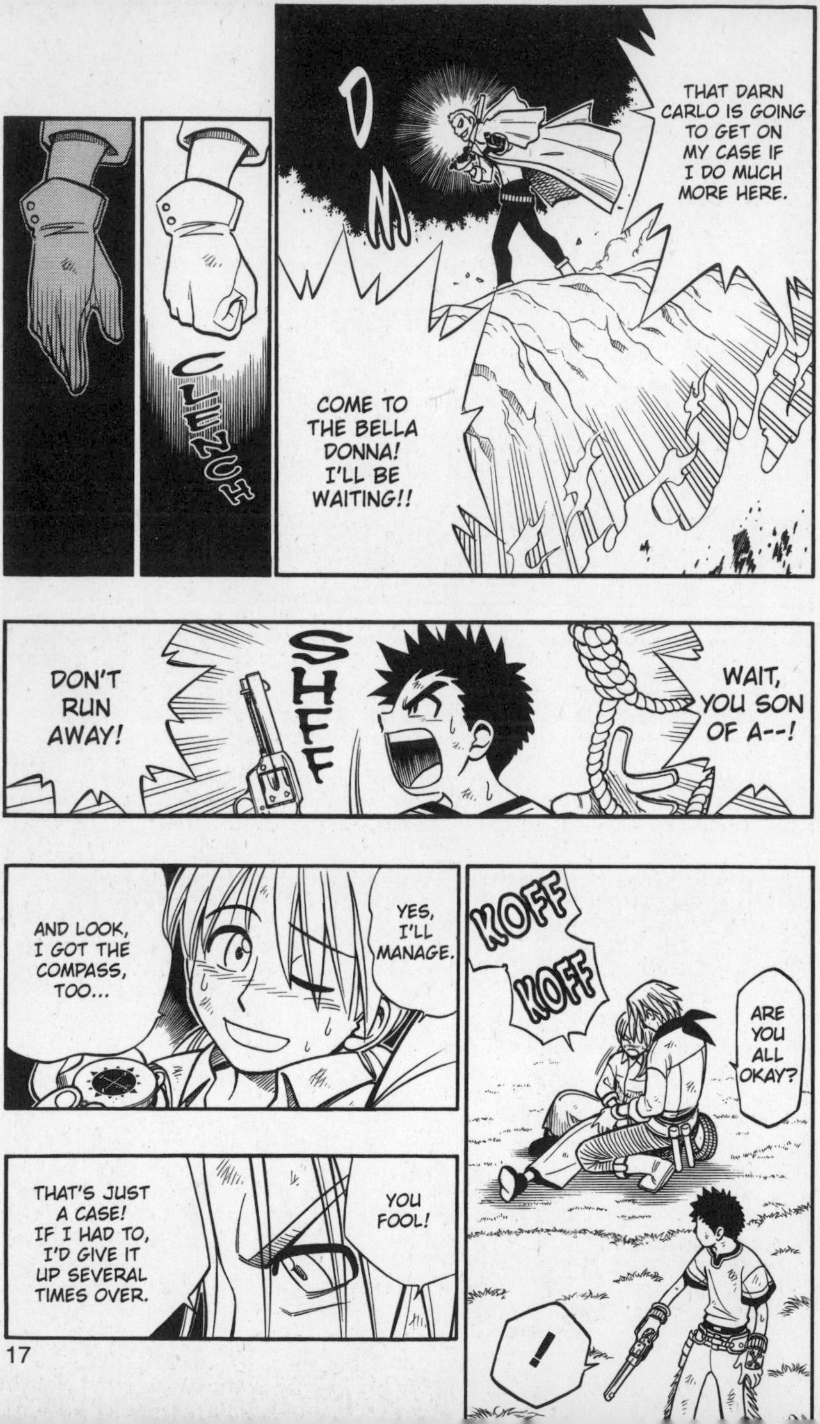

THAT DARN CARLO IS GOING TO GET ON MY CASE IF I DO MUCH MORE HERE.
COME TO THE BELLA DONNA! I'LL BE WAITING!!
CLENCH
WAIT, YOU SON OF A--!
SHFF
DON'T RUN AWAY!
KOFF
KOFF
ARE YOU ALL OKAY?
!
YES, I'LL MANAGE.
AND LOOK, I GOT THE COMPASS, TOO...
YOU FOOL!
THAT'S JUST A CASE! IF I HAD TO, I'D GIVE IT UP SEVERAL TIMES OVER.

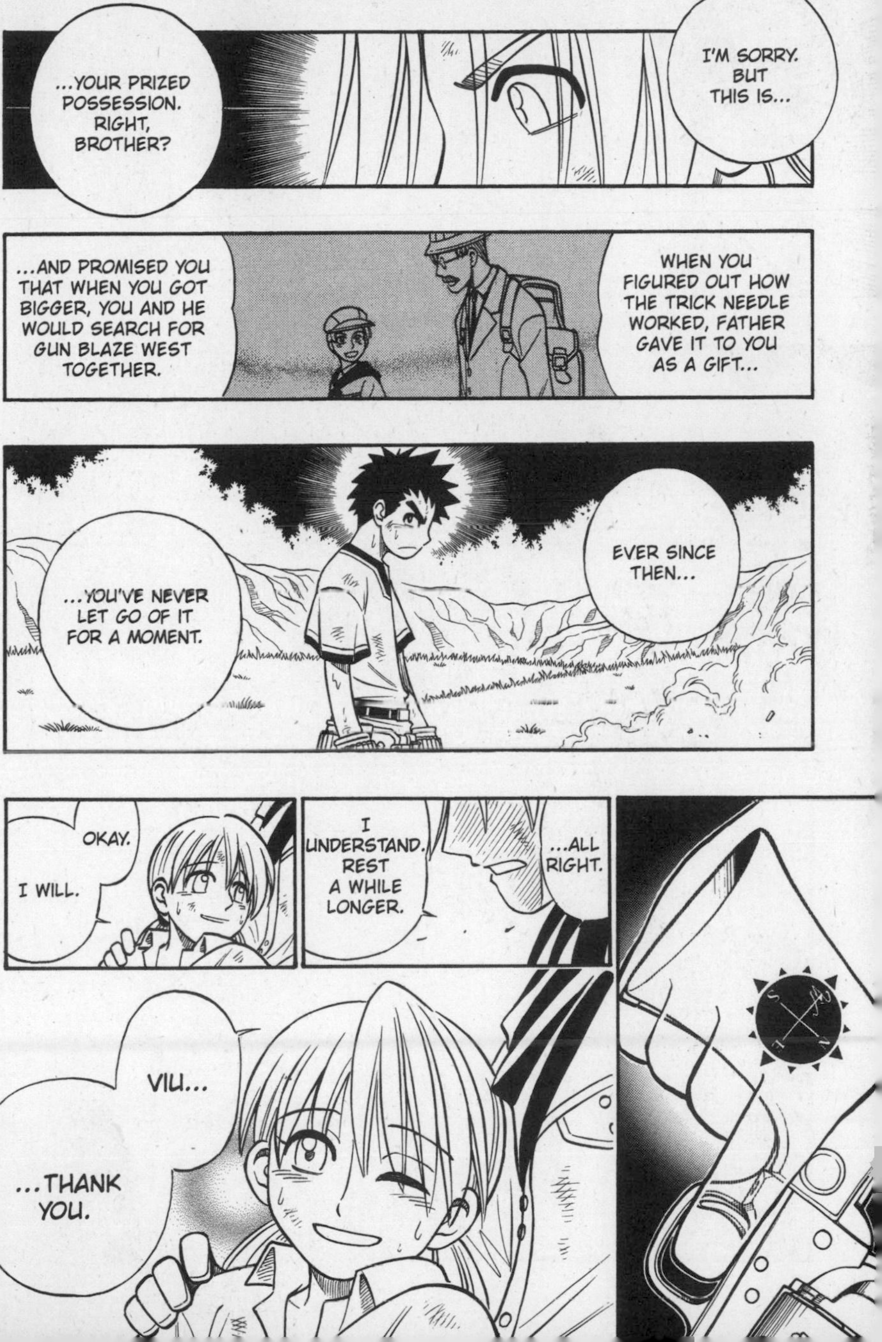
I'M SORRY. BUT THIS IS...
...YOUR PRIZED POSSESSION. RIGHT, BROTHER?
WHEN YOU FIGURED OUT HOW THE TRICK NEEDLE WORKED, FATHER GAVE IT TO YOU AS A GIFT...
...AND PROMISED YOU THAT WHEN YOU GOT BIGGER, YOU AND HE WOULD SEARCH FOR GUN BLAZE WEST TOGETHER.
EVER SINCE THEN...
...YOU'VE NEVER LET GO OF IT FOR A MOMENT.
...ALL RIGHT.
I UNDERSTAND. REST A WHILE LONGER.
OKAY.
I WILL.
VIU...
...THANK YOU.

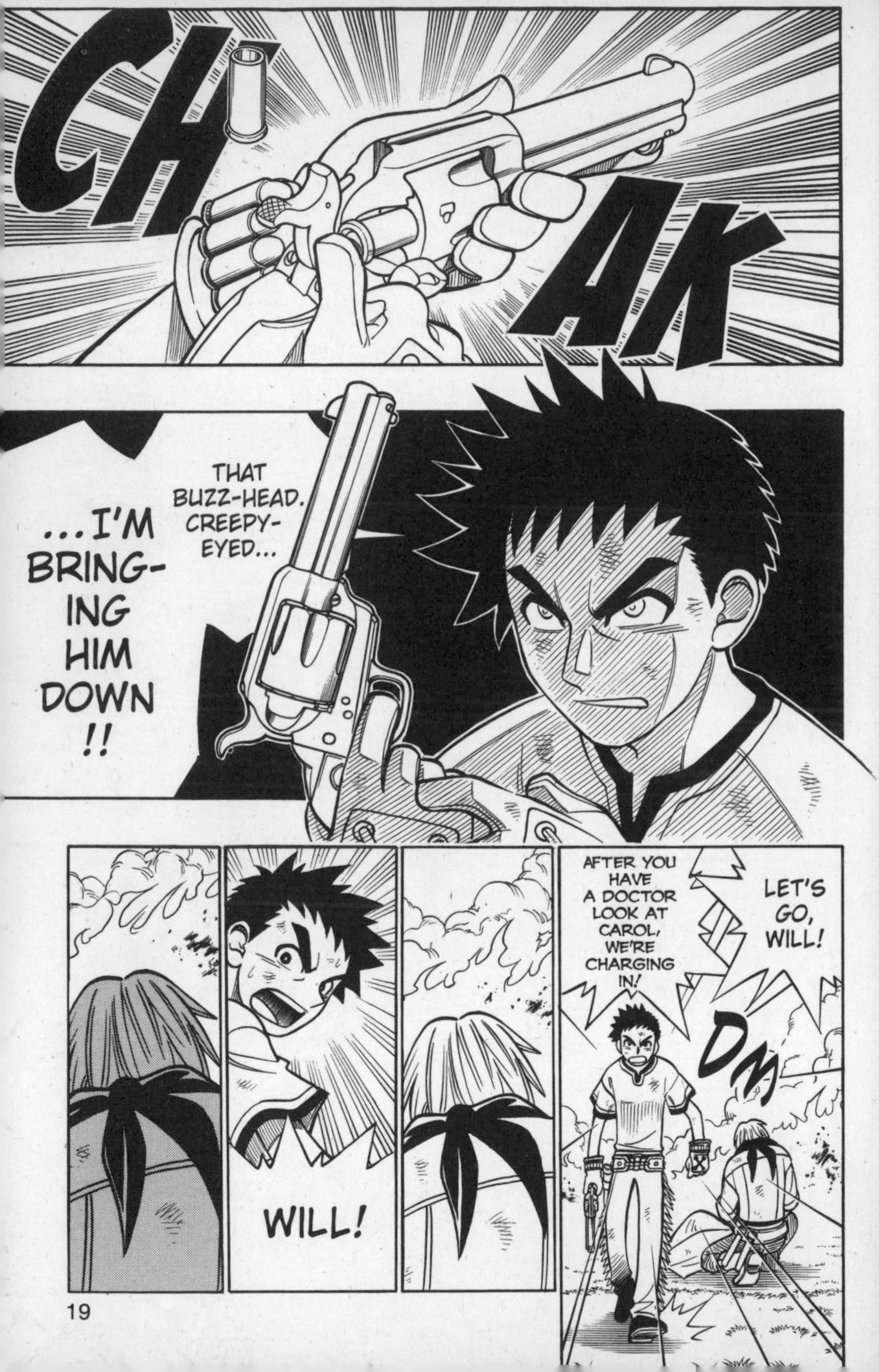
CHAK
THAT BUZZ-HEAD. CREEPY-EYED...
...I'M BRINGING HIM DOWN!!
LET'S GO, WILL!
AFTER YOU HAVE A DOCTOR LOOK AT CAROL, WE'RE CHARGING IN!
DM
WILL!

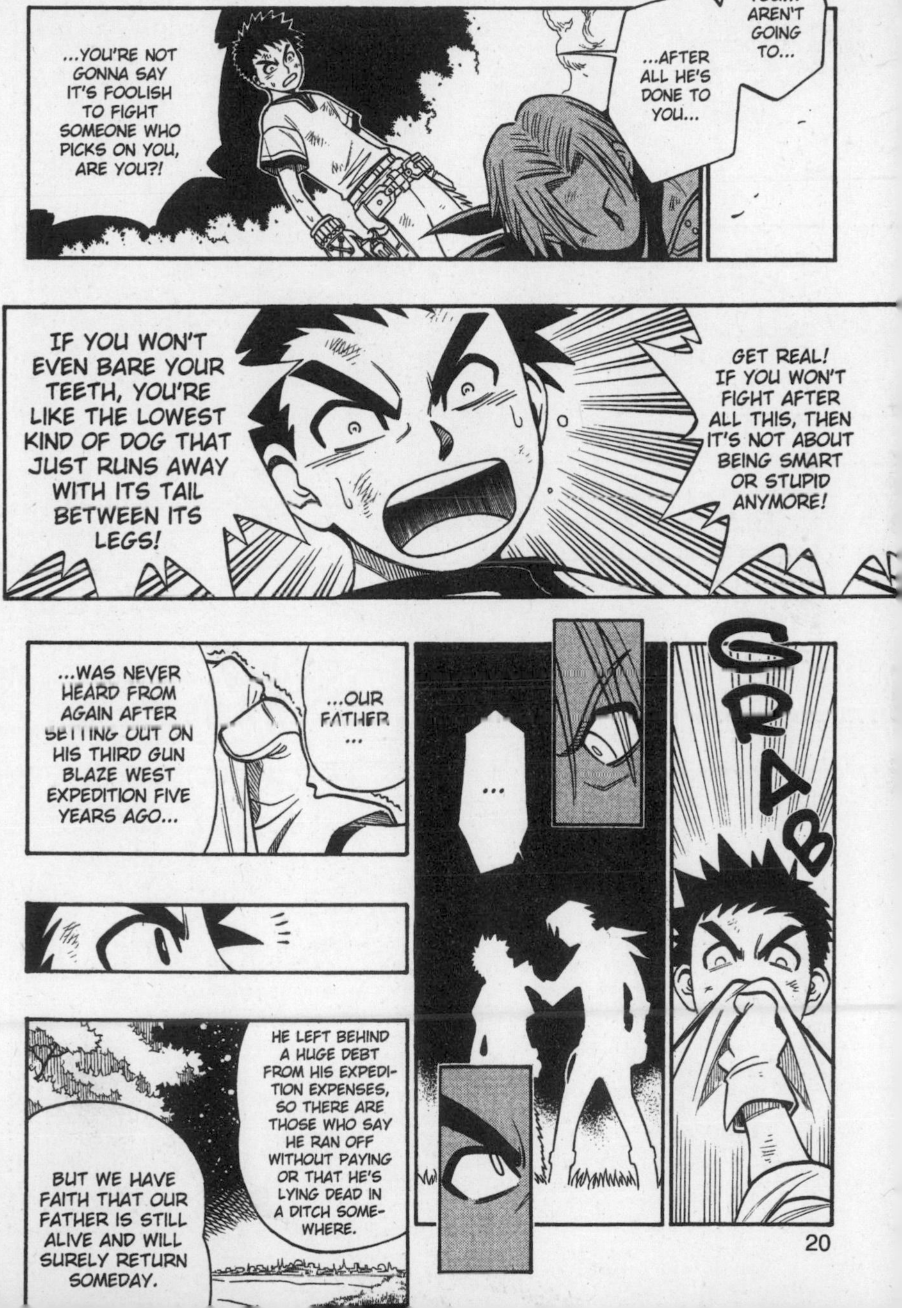

YOU... AREN'T GOING TO...
...AFTER ALL HE'S DONE TO YOU...
...YOU'RE NOT GONNA SAY IT'S FOOLISH TO FIGHT SOMEONE WHO PICKS ON YOU, ARE YOU?!
GET REAL! IF YOU WON'T FIGHT AFTER ALL THIS, THEN IT'S NOT ABOUT BEING SMART OR STUPID ANYMORE!
IF YOU WON'T EVEN BARE YOUR TEETH, YOU'RE LIKE THE LOWEST KIND OF DOG THAT JUST RUNS AWAY WITH ITS TAIL BETWEEN ITS LEGS!
GRAB
...
...OUR FATHER ...
...WAS NEVER HEARD FROM AGAIN AFTER SETTING OUT ON HIS THIRD GUN BLAZE WEST EXPEDITION FIVE YEARS AGO...
HE LEFT BEHIND A HUGE DEBT FROM HIS EXPEDITION EXPENSES, SO THERE ARE THOSE WHO SAY HE RAN OFF WITHOUT PAYING OR THAT HE'S LYING DEAD IN A DITCH SOMEWHERE.
BUT WE HAVE FAITH THAT OUR FATHER IS STILL ALIVE AND WILL SURELY RETURN SOMEDAY.

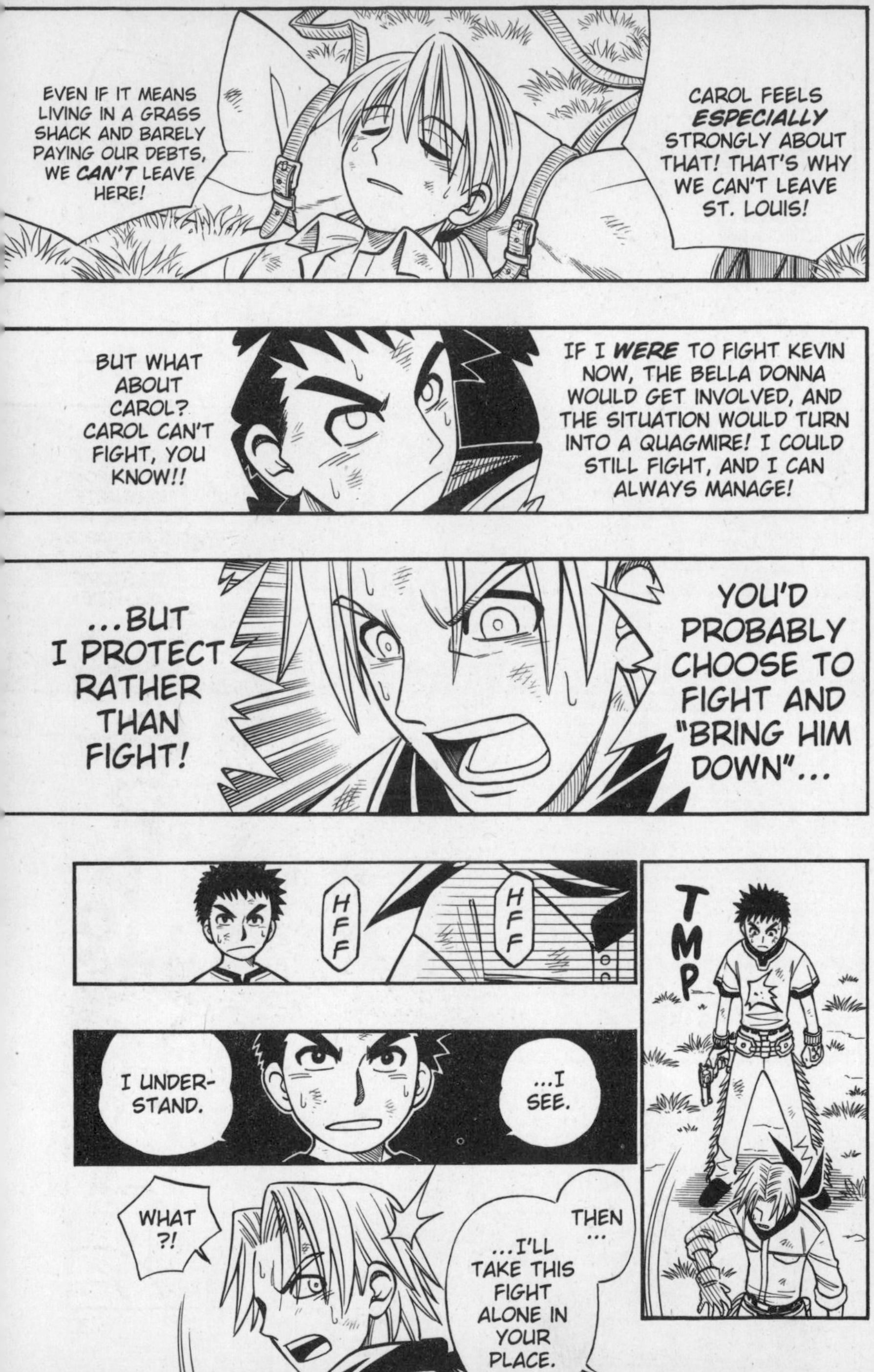
CAROL FEELS ESPECIALLY STRONGLY ABOUT THAT! THAT'S WHY WE CAN'T LEAVE ST. LOUIS!
EVEN IF IT MEANS LIVING IN A GRASS SHACK AND BARELY PAYING OUR DEBTS, WE CAN'T LEAVE HERE!
IF I WERE TO FIGHT KEVIN NOW, THE BELLA DONNA WOULD GET INVOLVED, AND THE SITUATION WOULD TURN INTO A QUAGMIRE! I COULD STILL FIGHT, AND I CAN ALWAYS MANAGE!
BUT WHAT ABOUT CAROL? CAROL CAN'T FIGHT, YOU KNOW!!
YOU'D PROBABLY CHOOSE TO FIGHT AND "BRING HIM DOWN"...
...BUT I PROTECT RATHER THAN FIGHT!
TMP
HFF
HFF
...I SEE.
I UNDER-STAND.
THEN...
...I'LL TAKE THIS FIGHT ALONE IN YOUR PLACE.
WHAT?!

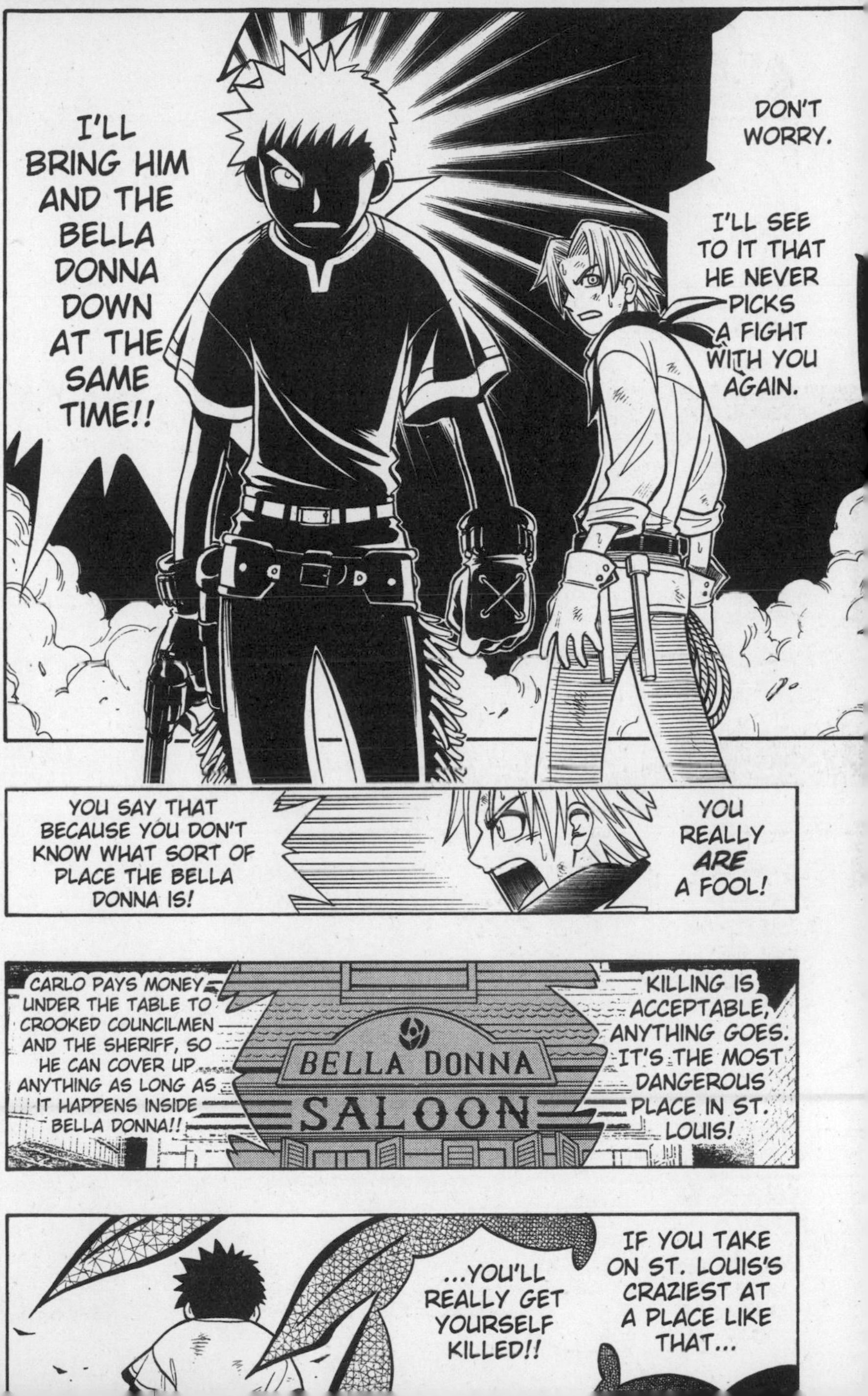
DON'T WORRY.
I'LL SEE TO IT THAT HE NEVER PICKS A FIGHT WITH YOU AGAIN.
I'LL BRING HIM AND THE BELLA DONNA DOWN AT THE SAME TIME!!
YOU REALLY *ARE* A FOOL!
YOU SAY THAT BECAUSE YOU DON'T KNOW WHAT SORT OF PLACE THE BELLA DONNA IS!
KILLING IS ACCEPTABLE, ANYTHING GOES. IT'S THE MOST DANGEROUS PLACE IN ST. LOUIS!
BELLA DONNA
SALOON
CARLO PAYS MONEY UNDER THE TABLE TO CROOKED COUNCILMEN AND THE SHERIFF, SO HE CAN COVER UP ANYTHING AS LONG AS IT HAPPENS INSIDE BELLA DONNA!!
IF YOU TAKE ON ST. LOUIS'S CRAZIEST AT A PLACE LIKE THAT...
...YOU'LL REALLY GET YOURSELF KILLED!!

READ THIS WAY

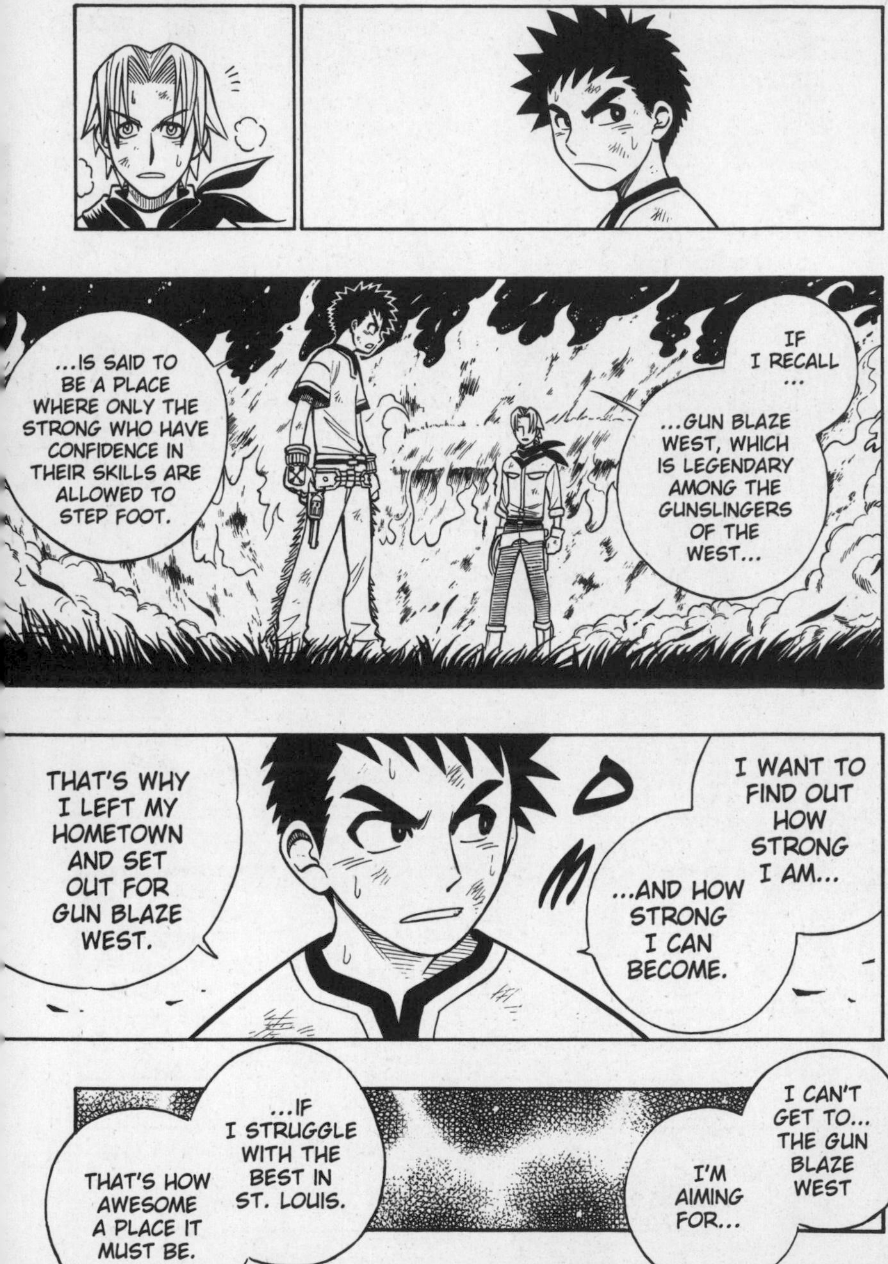

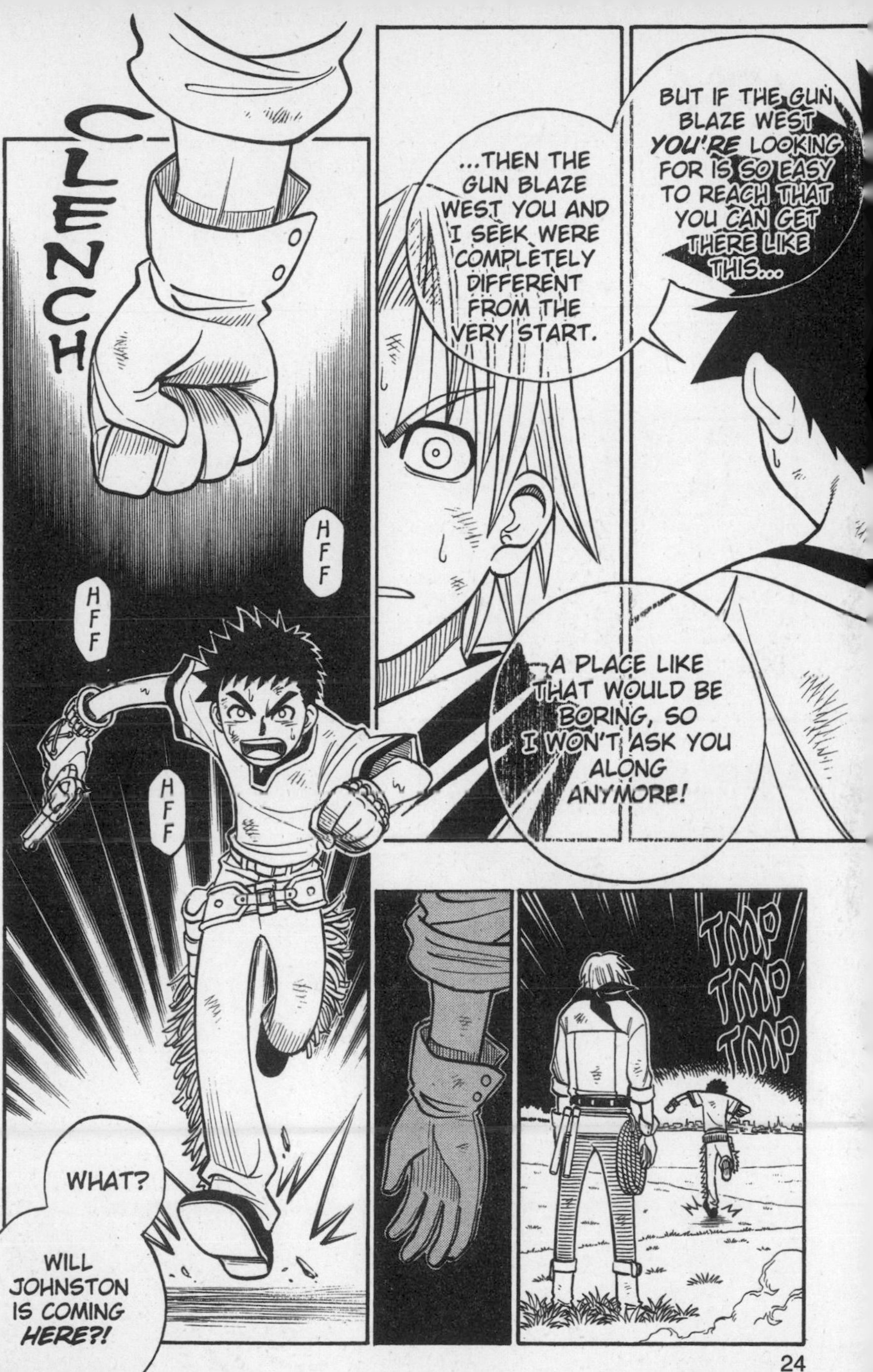
BUT IF THE GUN BLAZE WEST *YOU'RE* LOOKING FOR IS SO EASY TO REACH THAT YOU CAN GET THERE LIKE THIS...
...THEN THE GUN BLAZE WEST YOU AND I SEEK WERE COMPLETELY DIFFERENT FROM THE VERY START.
A PLACE LIKE THAT WOULD BE BORING, SO I WON'T ASK YOU ALONG ANYMORE!
TMP TMP TMP
CLENCH
HFF
HFF
HFF
WHAT?
WILL JOHNSTON IS COMING *HERE?!*

READ THIS WAY

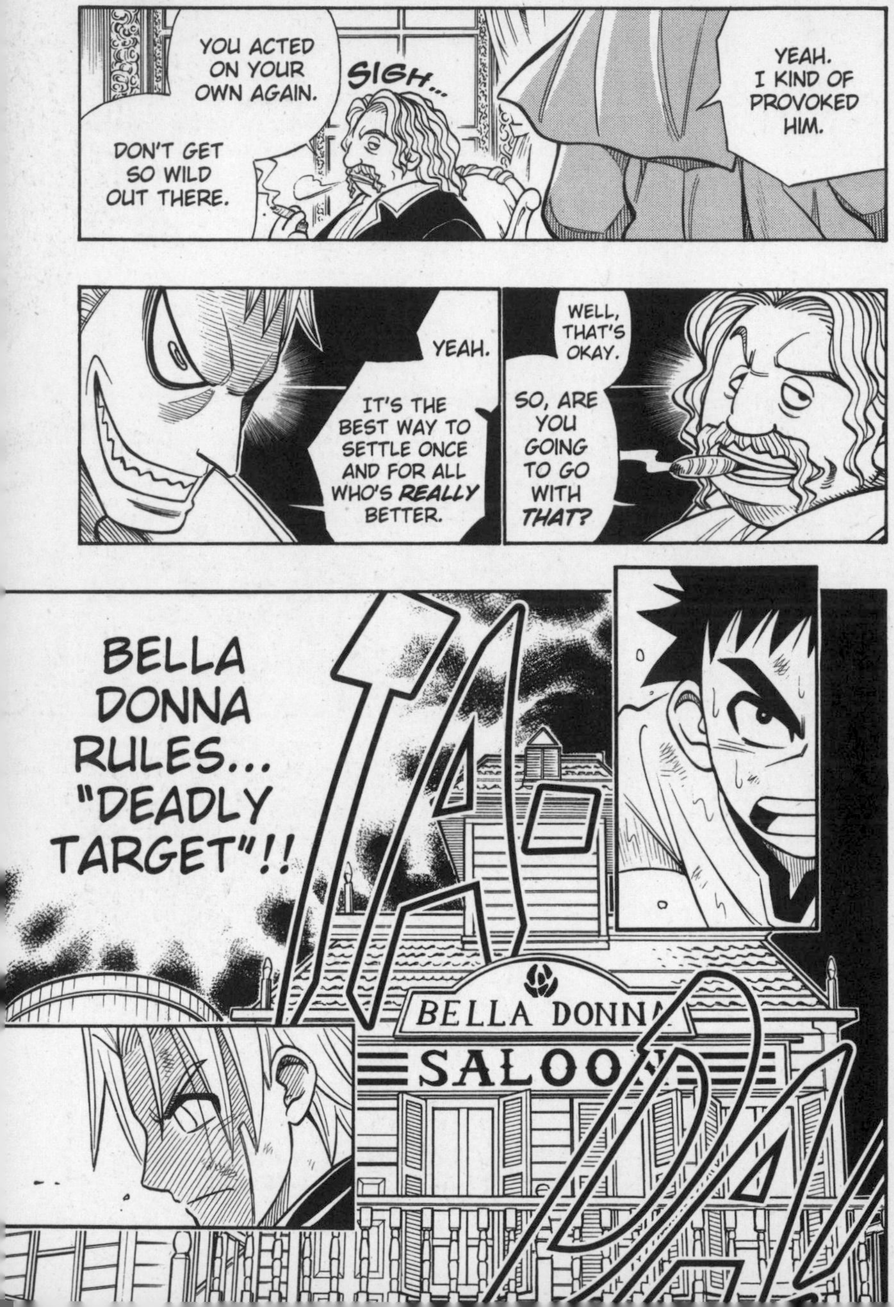
YEAH. I KIND OF PROVOKED HIM.
SIGH...
YOU ACTED ON YOUR OWN AGAIN.
DON'T GET SO WILD OUT THERE.
WELL, THAT'S OKAY.
SO, ARE YOU GOING TO GO WITH *THAT?*
YEAH.
IT'S THE BEST WAY TO SETTLE ONCE AND FOR ALL WHO'S *REALLY* BETTER.
BELLA DONNA RULES... "DEADLY TARGET"!!
BELLA DONN
SALOO

AND SO, DESPITE SOME DISAPPROVING LOOKS FROM THOSE INVOLVED, HERE IS THE USUAL COMICS BONUS CORNER, PRESENTED WITH A FEW CHANGES IN FORMAT.

IN THIS BOOK, I GAVE TOP PRIORITY TO "THIS IS THE SORT OF CHARACTER I WANT TO DRAW!" AND ELIMINATED WHAT I WOULD CALL MOTIFS TO THE GREATEST EXTENT POSSIBLE, TRYING HARD TO KEEP IT LIMITED TO AN "IMAGE ZONE." AS FOR WHETHER OR NOT THAT ATTEMPT WENT WELL, LOOKING AT THE RESULTS, QUITE FRANKLY, I FEEL IT WENT PRETTY BADLY.

FROM HERE ON, WITH APOLOGIES, I'D LIKE TO COMPRISE THIS CORNER OF THREE MAIN ASPECTS: CONCEPT, IMAGE ZONE AND DESIGN.

FIRST, THE MAIN CHARACTER: VIU BANNES.

CONCEPT: VIU CAME ABOUT FROM MY STRONG WISH TO DO A SHONEN-TYPE MAIN CHARACTER.

## CHARACTER FILE #01

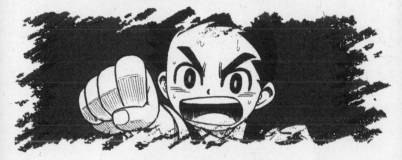

## VIU BANNES

HOWEVER, I STRUGGLED MIGHTILY BECAUSE IT APPEARED THAT MY SENSIBILITIES WERE WAY OFF FOR A SHONEN TITLE. (WHEN YOU REALLY THINK ABOUT IT, MY PREVIOUS WORK, *RUROUNI KENSHIN*, WAS WAY OFF WITH A THIRTY-ISH MAIN CHARACTER, KENSHIN, WHO HAD ALREADY BEEN MARRIED.) AS I SQUIRMED MY WAY THROUGH THAT SERIES, I WAS FORCED TO JUMP INTO THE NEXT SERIES WITH HARDLY ANY PREPARATION BECAUSE THE SCHEDULE FOR THE NEXT SERIAL HAD ALREADY BEEN SET. (I TOUCH ON THE CIRCUMSTANCES IN THE EPILOGUE OF THE NEXT AND FINAL VOLUME. WITHOUT DOING SO, IT WOULD BE IMPOSSIBLE TO WRAP UP *GUN BLAZE WEST*.) AFTER THAT, I FOUND MYSELF JUST FRANTICALLY FILLING UP PAGES WITHOUT KNOWING WHAT I WAS DOING. QUITE FRANKLY, IN THE END, THE STORY CONCLUDED WITH ME HAVING LOST SIGHT OF VIU'S CHARACTER TO THE VERY END. IT WAS EXTREMELY UNFORTUNATE.

I HOPE TO ONE DAY REVIVE THE CHARACTER, GIVING SERIOUS THOUGHT TO VIU BANNES AND WHAT I WANTED TO DO THROUGH HIS CHARACTER AND WHAT IT IS I WANTED TO DRAW.

# CHAPTER 9: DEADLY TARGET

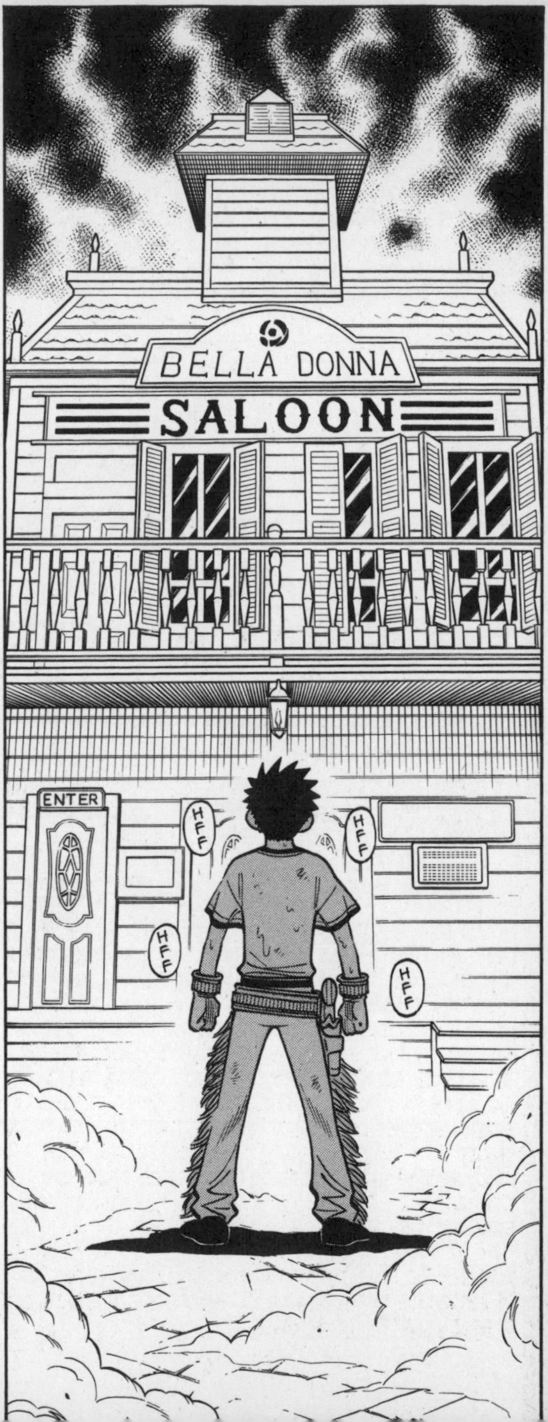
BELLA DONNA
SALOON
ENTER
HFF
HFF
HFF
HFF

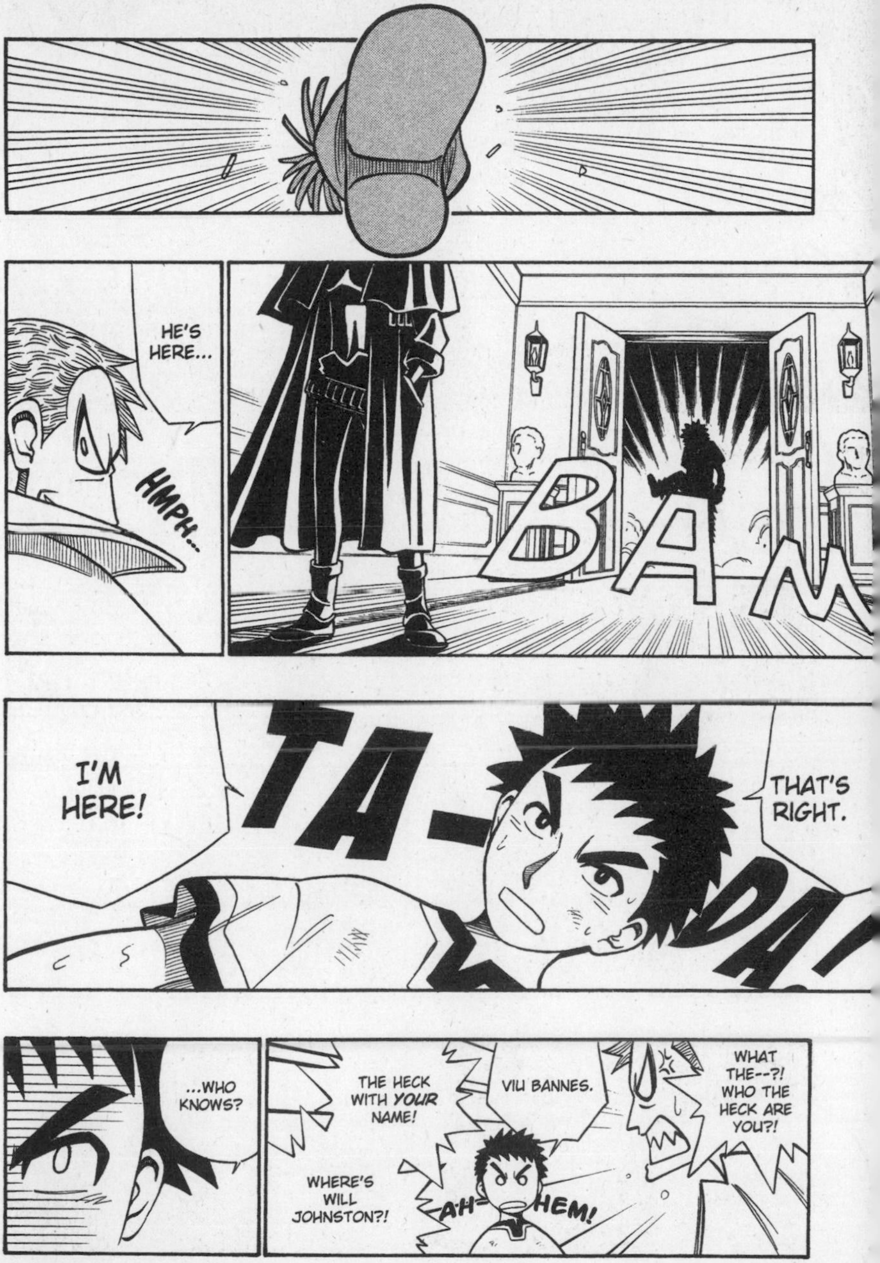
BAM
HE'S HERE...
HMPH...
THAT'S RIGHT.
TA-DA
I'M HERE!
WHAT THE--?! WHO THE HECK ARE YOU?!
VIU BANNES.
THE HECK WITH *YOUR* NAME!
WHERE'S WILL JOHNSTON?!
AH-HEM!
...WHO KNOWS?

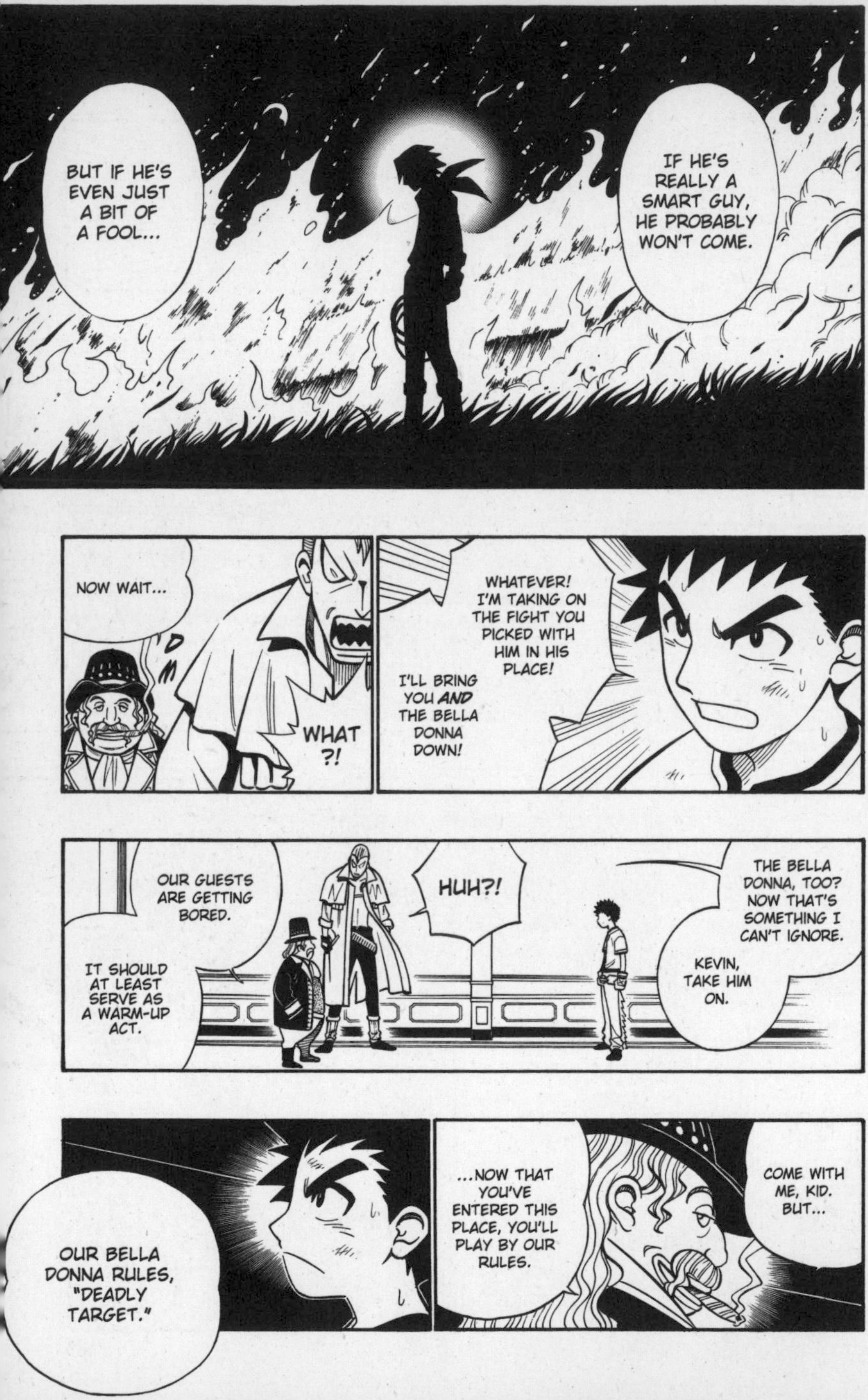
IF HE'S REALLY A SMART GUY, HE PROBABLY WON'T COME.
BUT IF HE'S EVEN JUST A BIT OF A FOOL...
WHATEVER! I'M TAKING ON THE FIGHT YOU PICKED WITH HIM IN HIS PLACE!
I'LL BRING YOU AND THE BELLA DONNA DOWN!
WHAT ?!
NOW WAIT...
THE BELLA DONNA, TOO? NOW THAT'S SOMETHING I CAN'T IGNORE.
KEVIN, TAKE HIM ON.
HUH?!
OUR GUESTS ARE GETTING BORED.
IT SHOULD AT LEAST SERVE AS A WARM-UP ACT.
COME WITH ME, KID. BUT...
...NOW THAT YOU'VE ENTERED THIS PLACE, YOU'LL PLAY BY OUR RULES.
OUR BELLA DONNA RULES, "DEADLY TARGET."

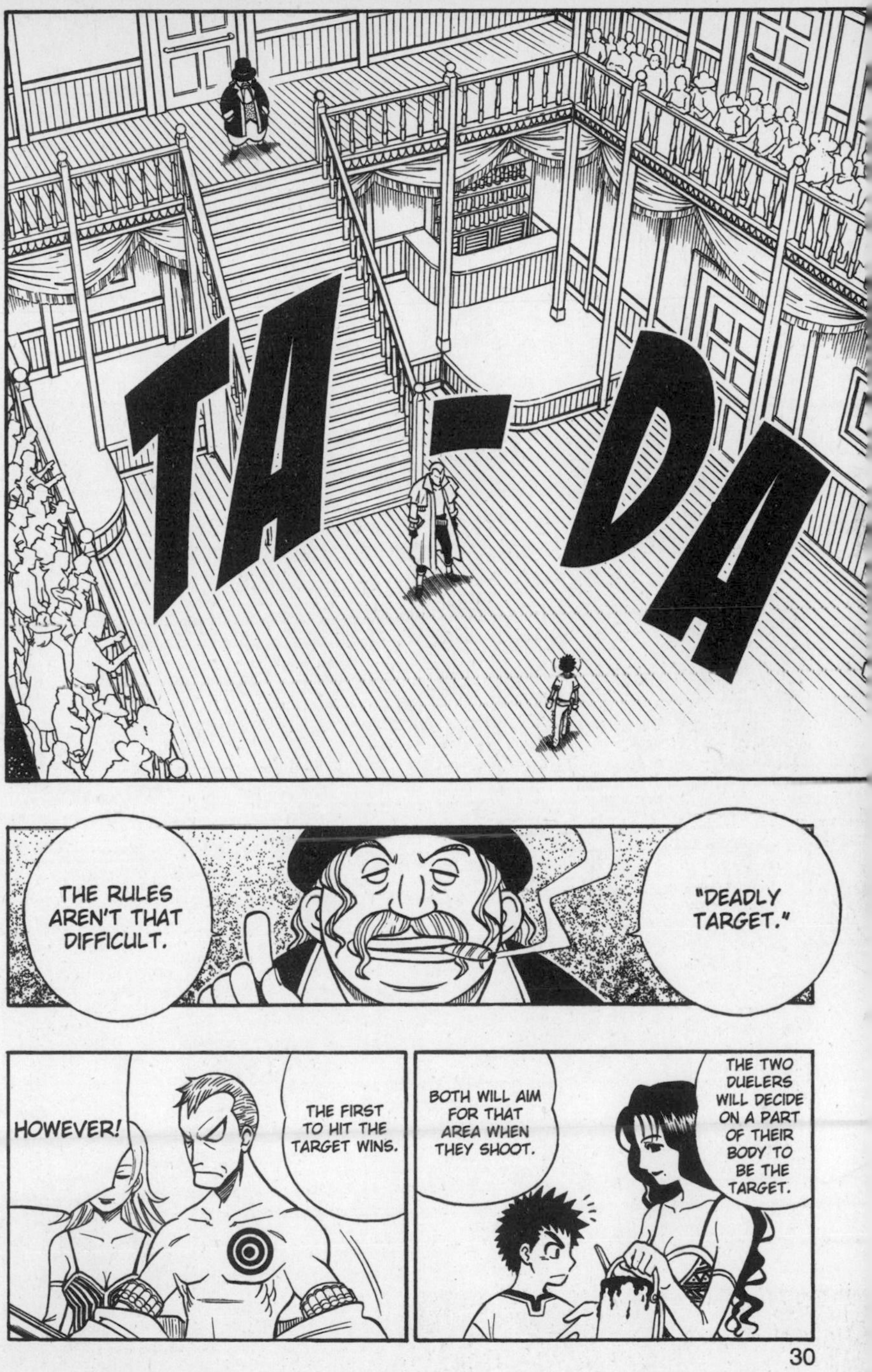
TA-DA
"DEADLY TARGET."
THE RULES AREN'T THAT DIFFICULT.
THE TWO DUELERS WILL DECIDE ON A PART OF THEIR BODY TO BE THE TARGET.
BOTH WILL AIM FOR THAT AREA WHEN THEY SHOOT.
THE FIRST TO HIT THE TARGET WINS.
HOWEVER!

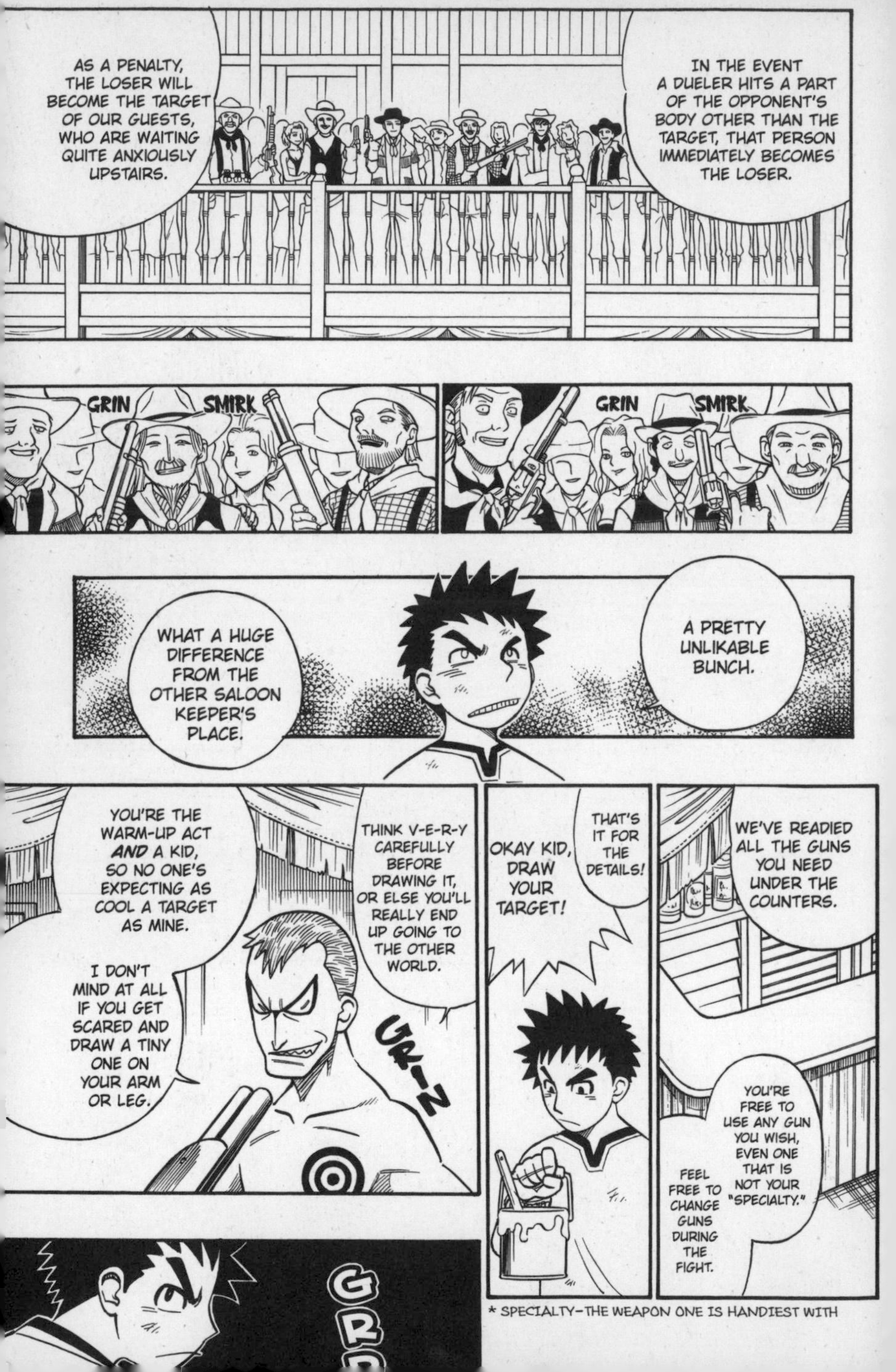
IN THE EVENT A DUELER HITS A PART OF THE OPPONENT'S BODY OTHER THAN THE TARGET, THAT PERSON IMMEDIATELY BECOMES THE LOSER.
AS A PENALTY, THE LOSER WILL BECOME THE TARGET OF OUR GUESTS, WHO ARE WAITING QUITE ANXIOUSLY UPSTAIRS.
GRIN
SMIRK
GRIN
SMIRK
A PRETTY UNLIKABLE BUNCH.
WHAT A HUGE DIFFERENCE FROM THE OTHER SALOON KEEPER'S PLACE.
WE'VE READIED ALL THE GUNS YOU NEED UNDER THE COUNTERS.
YOU'RE FREE TO USE ANY GUN YOU WISH, EVEN ONE THAT IS NOT YOUR "SPECIALTY."
FEEL FREE TO CHANGE GUNS DURING THE FIGHT.
THAT'S IT FOR THE DETAILS!
OKAY KID, DRAW YOUR TARGET!
THINK V-E-R-Y CAREFULLY BEFORE DRAWING IT, OR ELSE YOU'LL REALLY END UP GOING TO THE OTHER WORLD.
YOU'RE THE WARM-UP ACT *AND* A KID, SO NO ONE'S EXPECTING AS COOL A TARGET AS MINE.
I DON'T MIND AT ALL IF YOU GET SCARED AND DRAW A TINY ONE ON YOUR ARM OR LEG.
GRIN
GR


* SPECIALTY—THE WEAPON ONE IS HANDIEST WITH

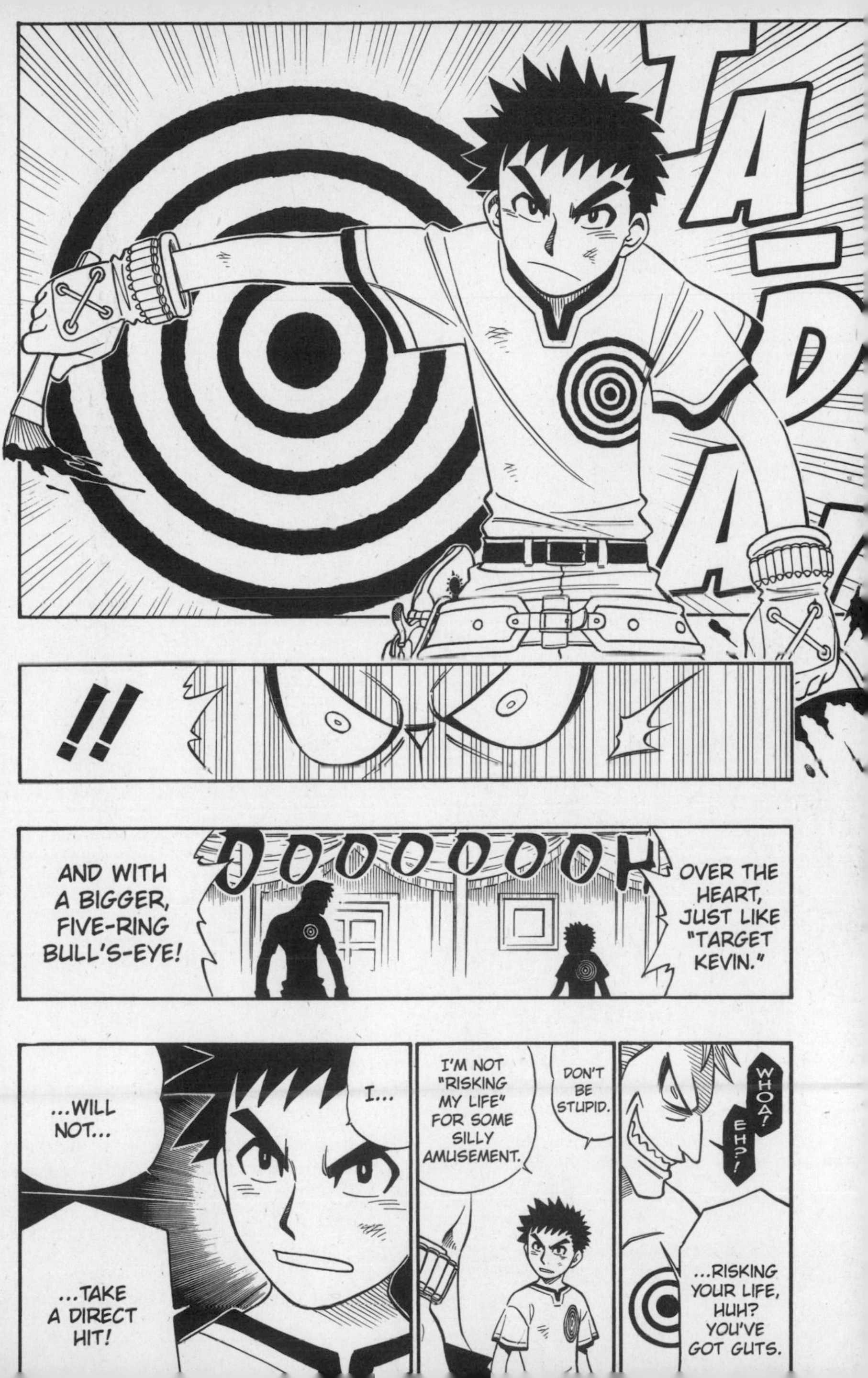

TA-DA
!!
OVER THE HEART, JUST LIKE "TARGET KEVIN."
OOOOOOOH
AND WITH A BIGGER, FIVE-RING BULL'S-EYE!
WHOA!
EH?!
...RISKING YOUR LIFE, HUH? YOU'VE GOT GUTS.
DON'T BE STUPID.
I'M NOT "RISKING MY LIFE" FOR SOME SILLY AMUSEMENT.
I...
...WILL NOT...
...TAKE A DIRECT HIT!

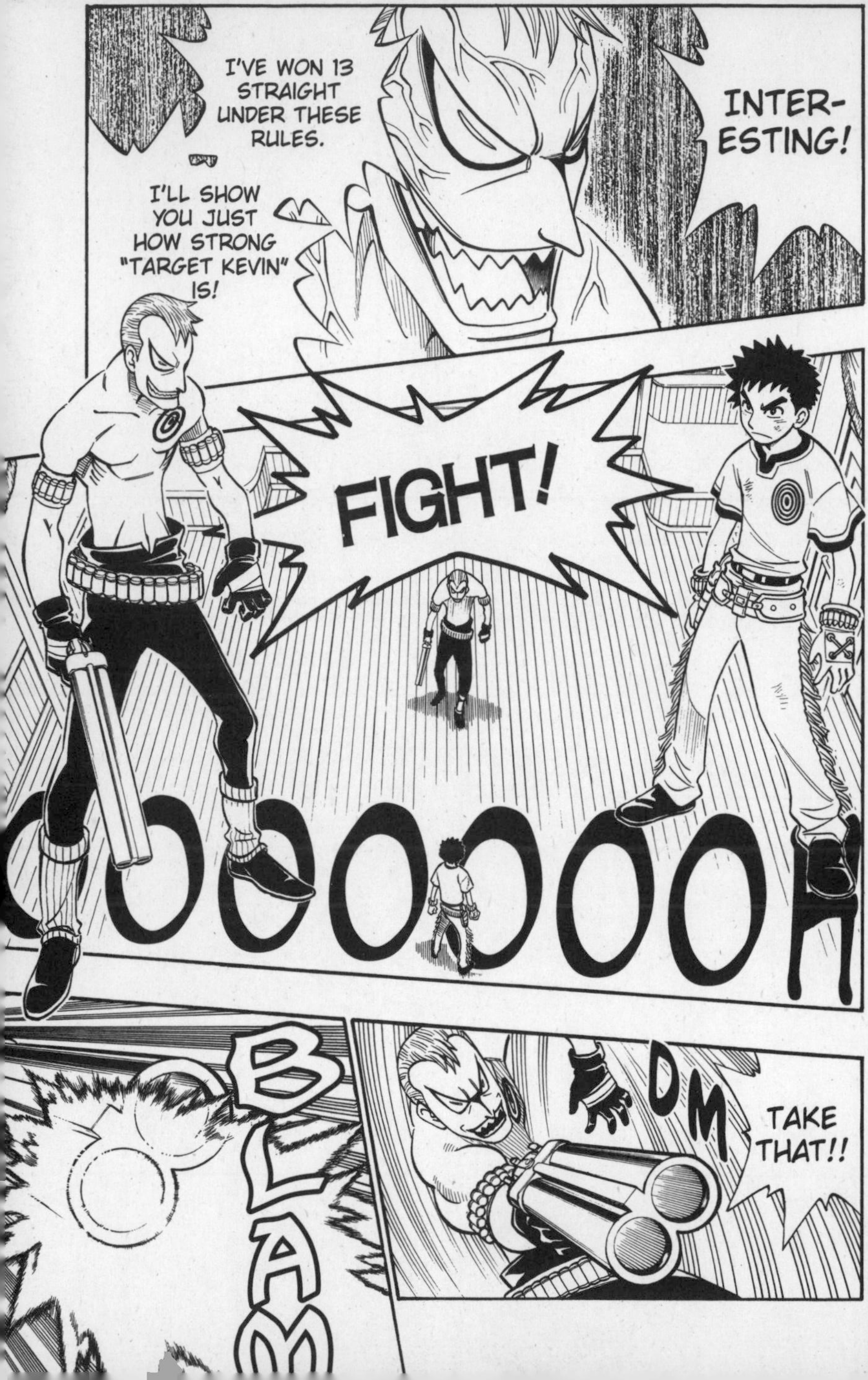
INTER-ESTING!
I'VE WON 13 STRAIGHT UNDER THESE RULES.
I'LL SHOW YOU JUST HOW STRONG "TARGET KEVIN" IS!
FIGHT!
OOOOOOH
TAKE THAT!!
DM
BLAM

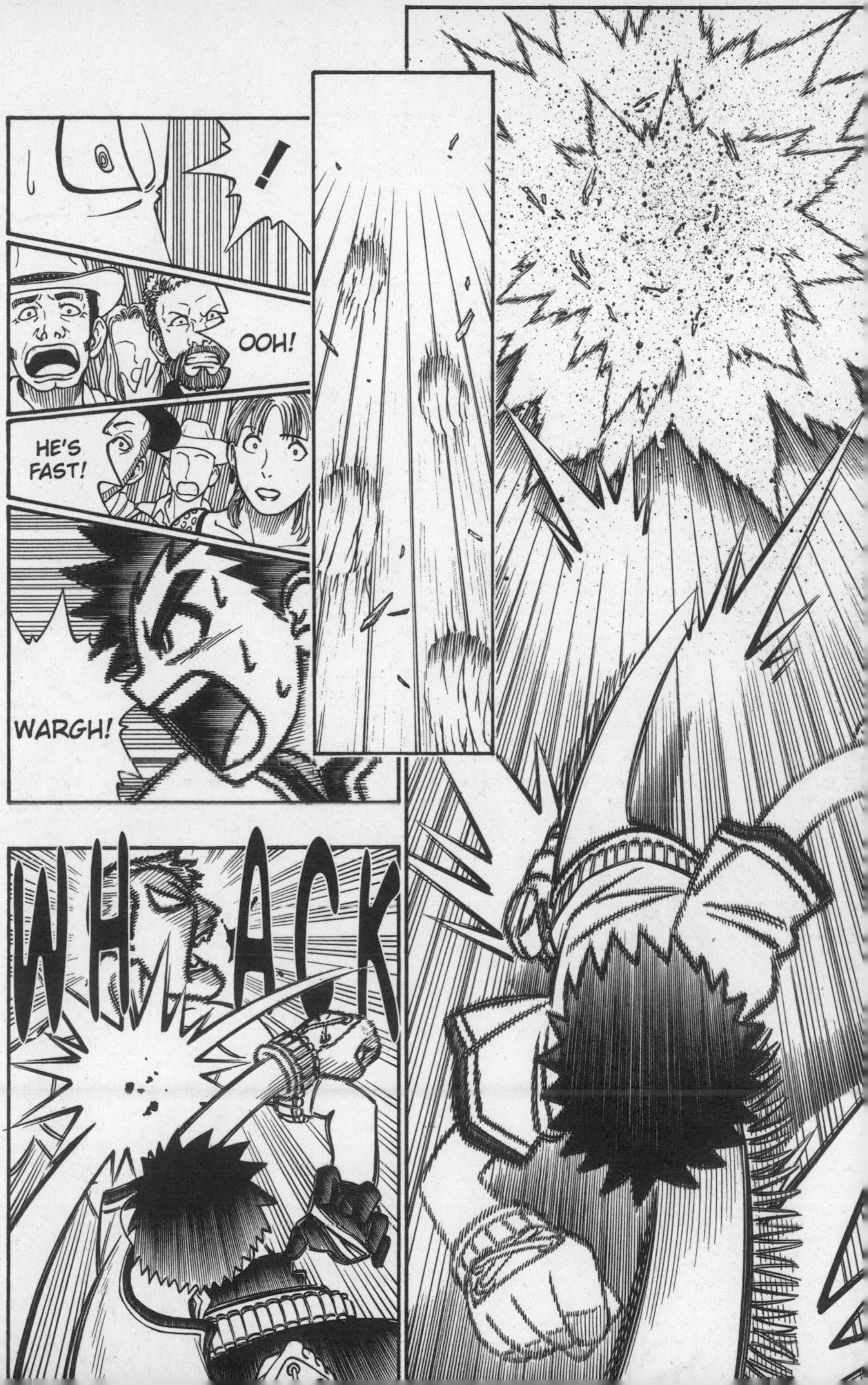
!
OOH!
HE'S FAST!
WARGH!
WHACK

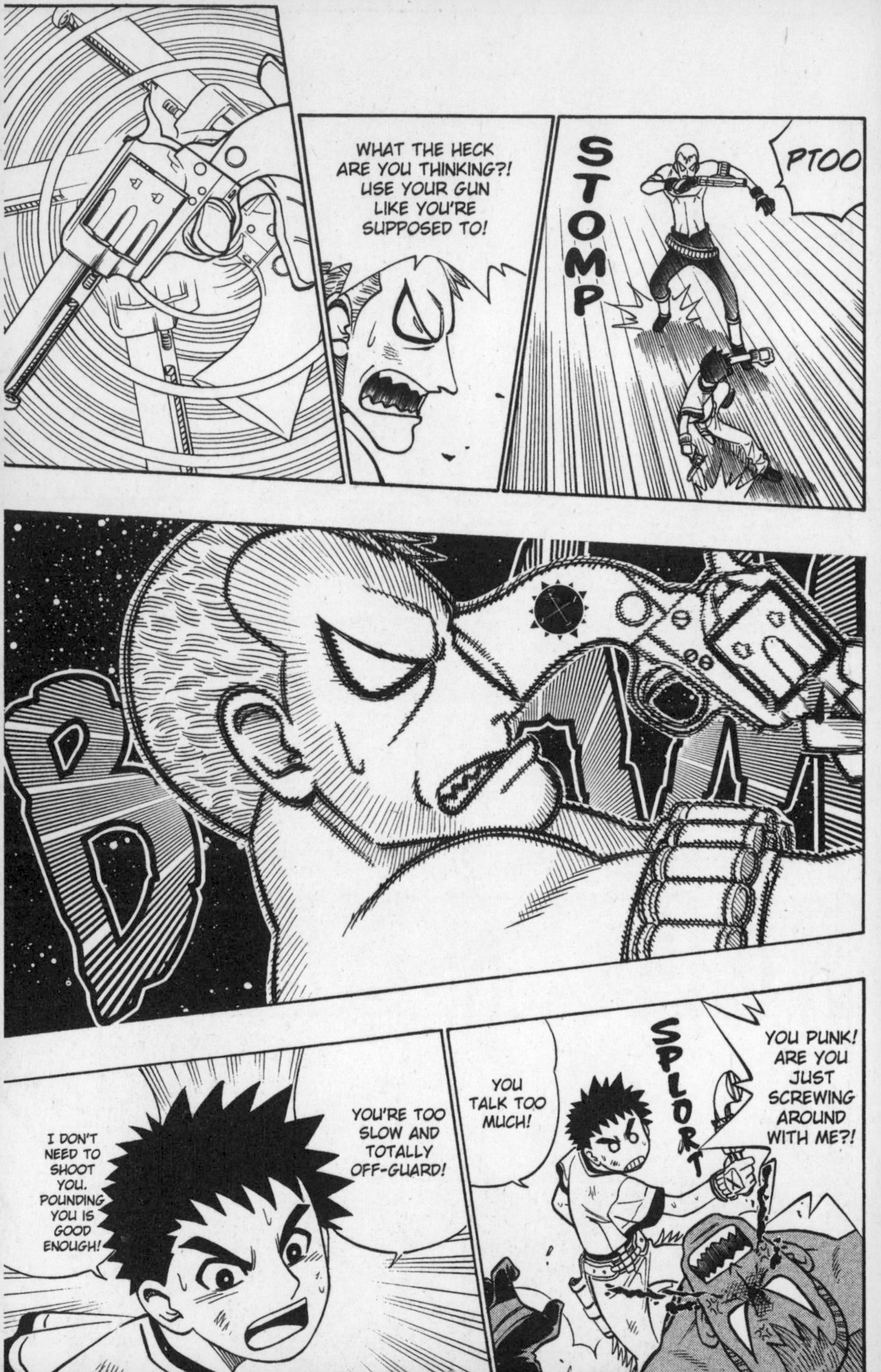
PTOO
STOMP
WHAT THE HECK ARE YOU THINKING?! USE YOUR GUN LIKE YOU'RE SUPPOSED TO!
YOU PUNK! ARE YOU JUST SCREWING AROUND WITH ME?!
SPLORT
YOU TALK TOO MUCH!
YOU'RE TOO SLOW AND TOTALLY OFF-GUARD!
I DON'T NEED TO SHOOT YOU. POUNDING YOU IS GOOD ENOUGH!

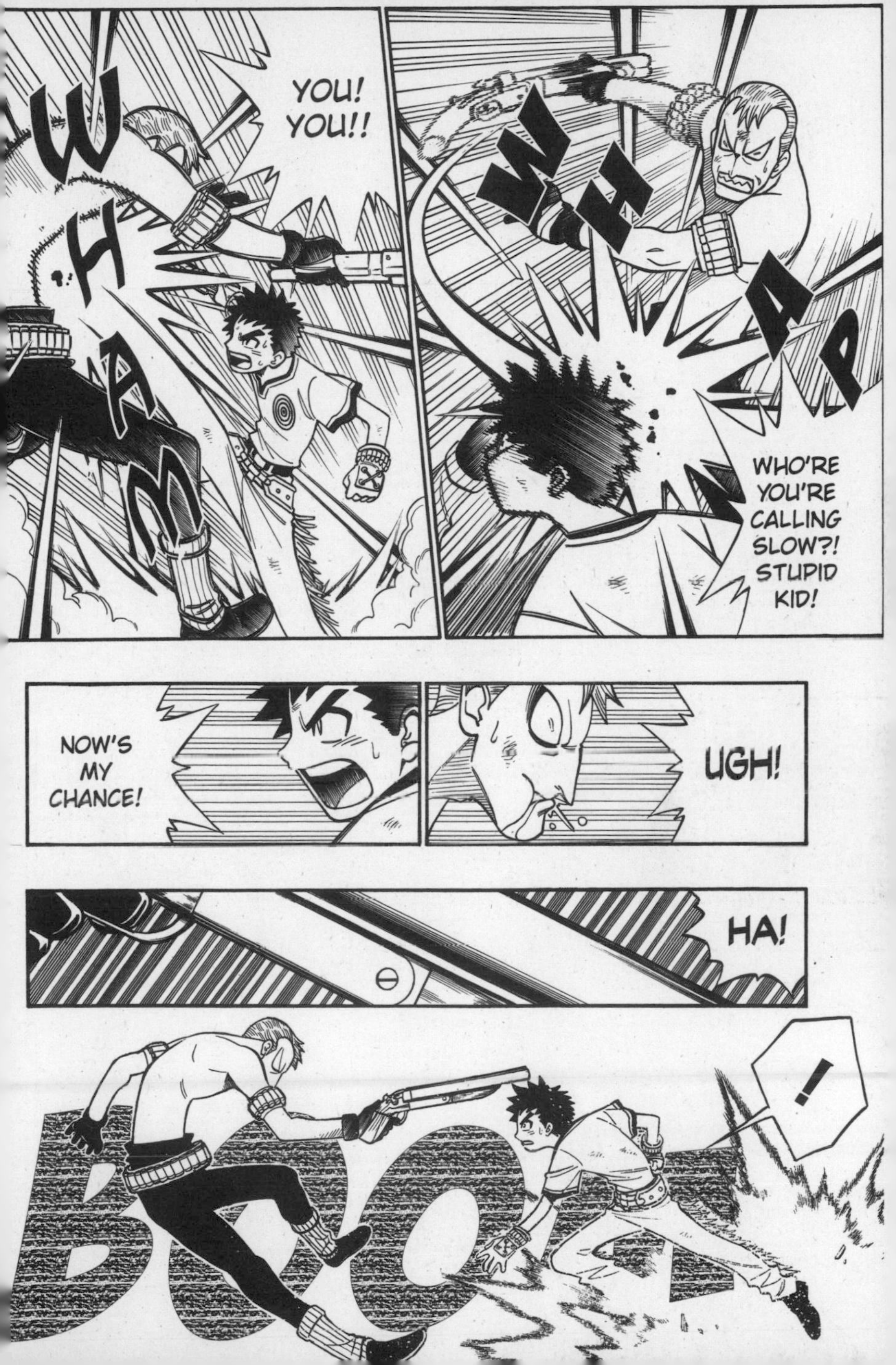
WHAP
WHO'RE YOU'RE CALLING SLOW?! STUPID KID!
YOU! YOU!!
WHAM
UGH!
NOW'S MY CHANCE!
HA!
!
BOO

READ THIS WAY

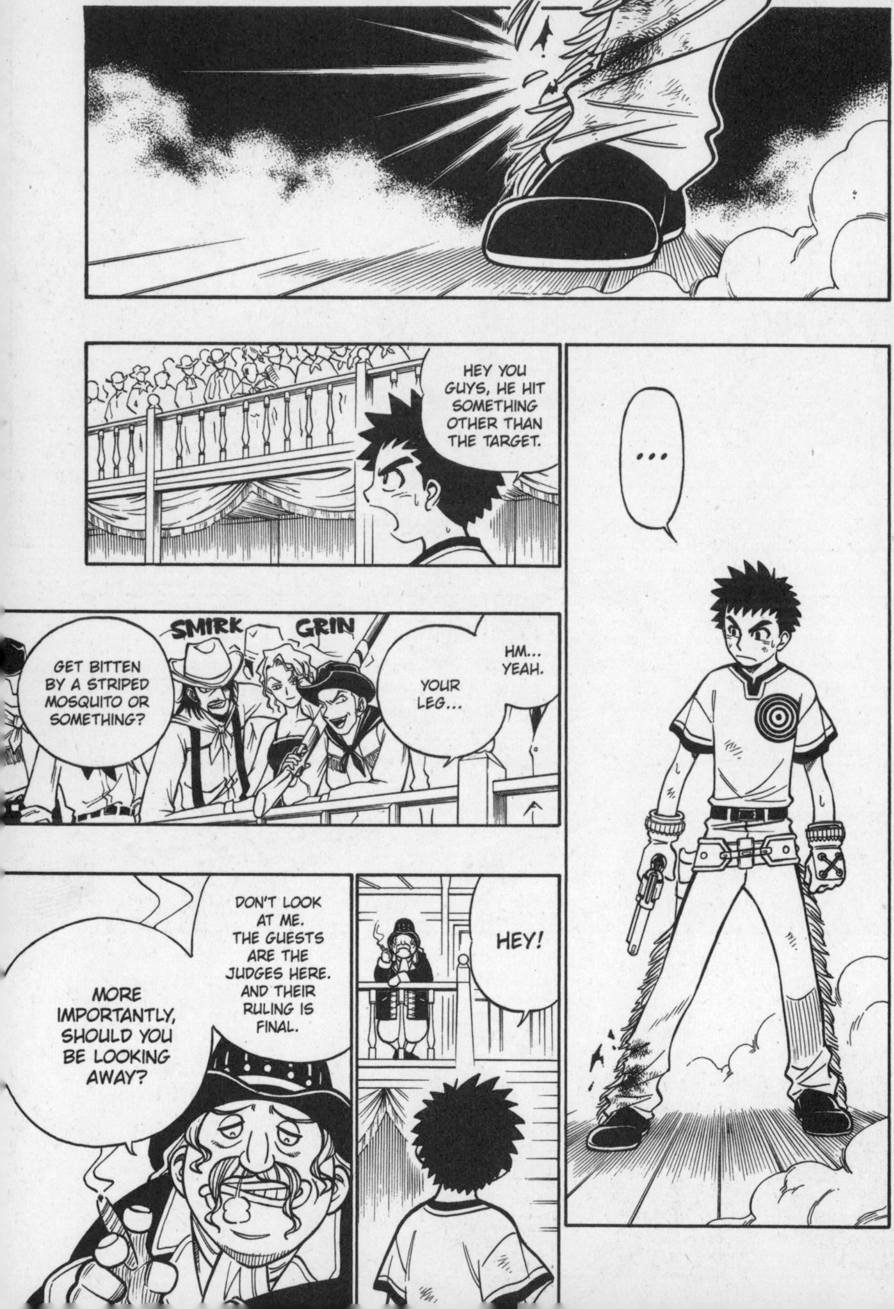
...
HEY YOU GUYS, HE HIT SOMETHING OTHER THAN THE TARGET.
GRIN
SMIRK
HM... YEAH.
YOUR LEG...
GET BITTEN BY A STRIPED MOSQUITO OR SOMETHING?
HEY!
DON'T LOOK AT ME. THE GUESTS ARE THE JUDGES HERE. AND THEIR RULING IS FINAL.
MORE IMPORTANTLY, SHOULD YOU BE LOOKING AWAY?

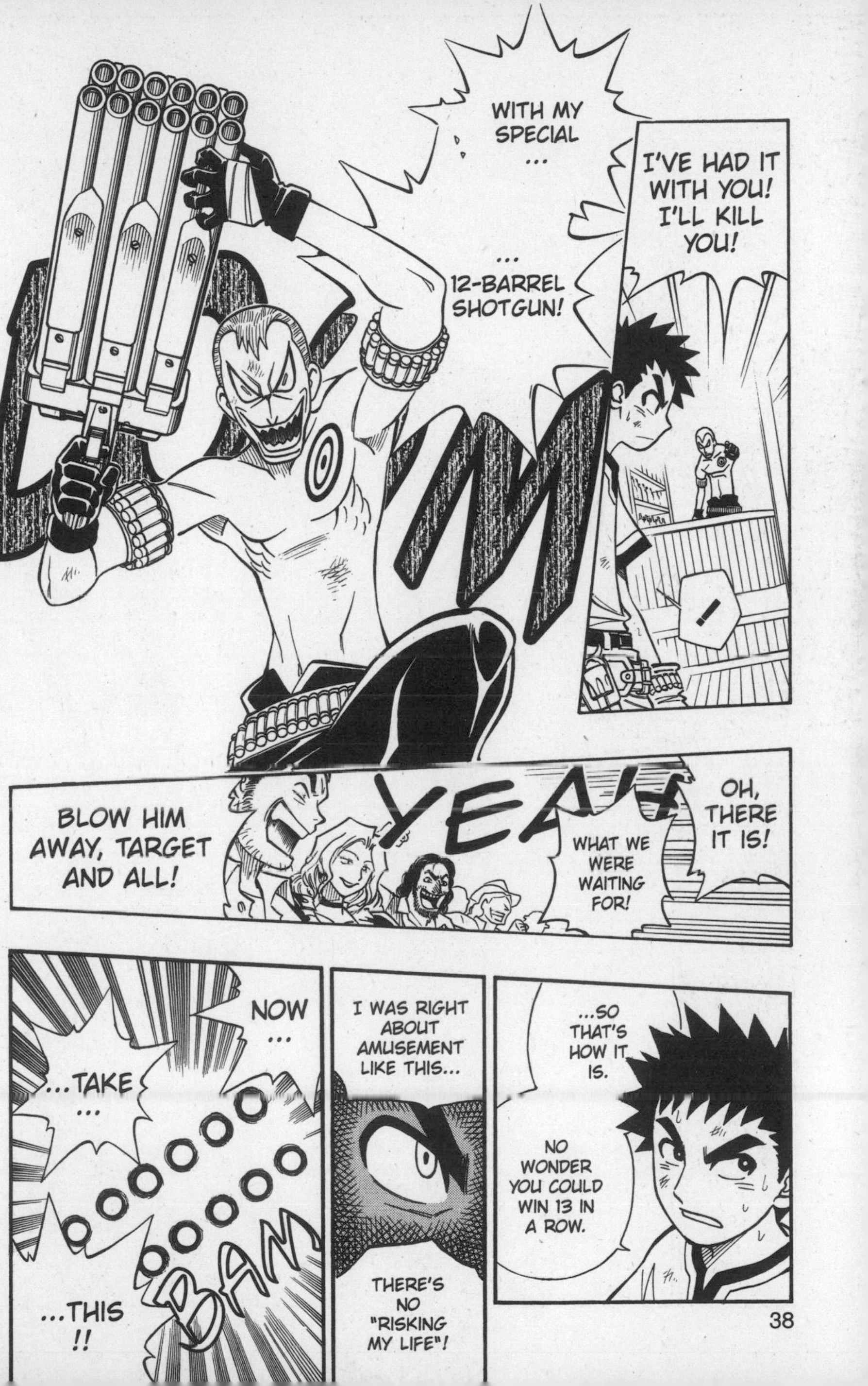
I'VE HAD IT WITH YOU! I'LL KILL YOU!
WITH MY SPECIAL ...
... 12-BARREL SHOTGUN!
!
OH, THERE IT IS!
WHAT WE WERE WAITING FOR!
YEA
BLOW HIM AWAY, TARGET AND ALL!
...SO THAT'S HOW IT IS.
NO WONDER YOU COULD WIN 13 IN A ROW.
I WAS RIGHT ABOUT AMUSEMENT LIKE THIS...
THERE'S NO "RISKING MY LIFE"!
NOW ...
...TAKE ...
...THIS !!
BAM

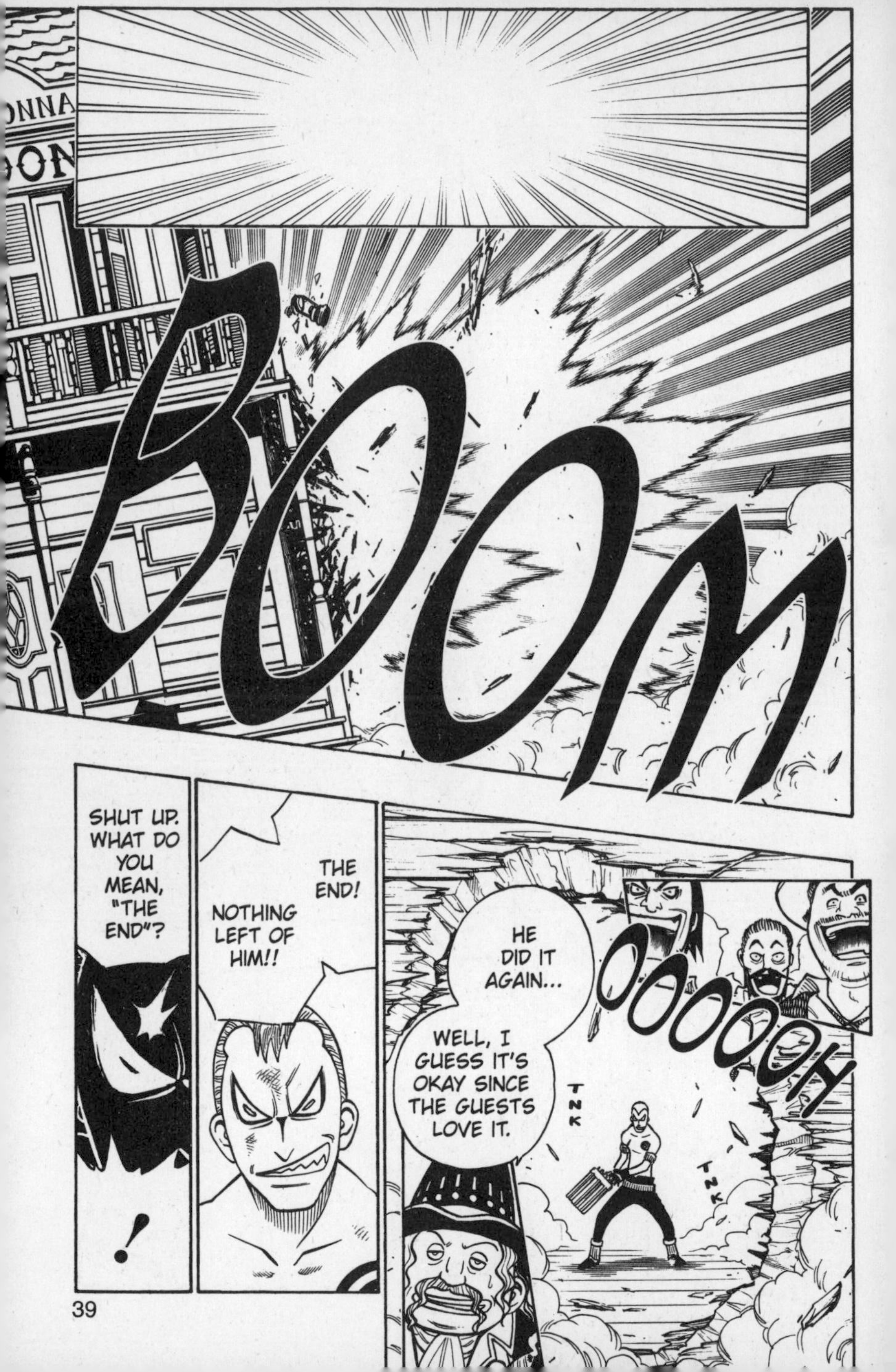
BOOM
OOOOOOH
HE DID IT AGAIN...
WELL, I GUESS IT'S OKAY SINCE THE GUESTS LOVE IT.
TNK
TNK
THE END!
NOTHING LEFT OF HIM!!
SHUT UP. WHAT DO YOU MEAN, "THE END"?
!

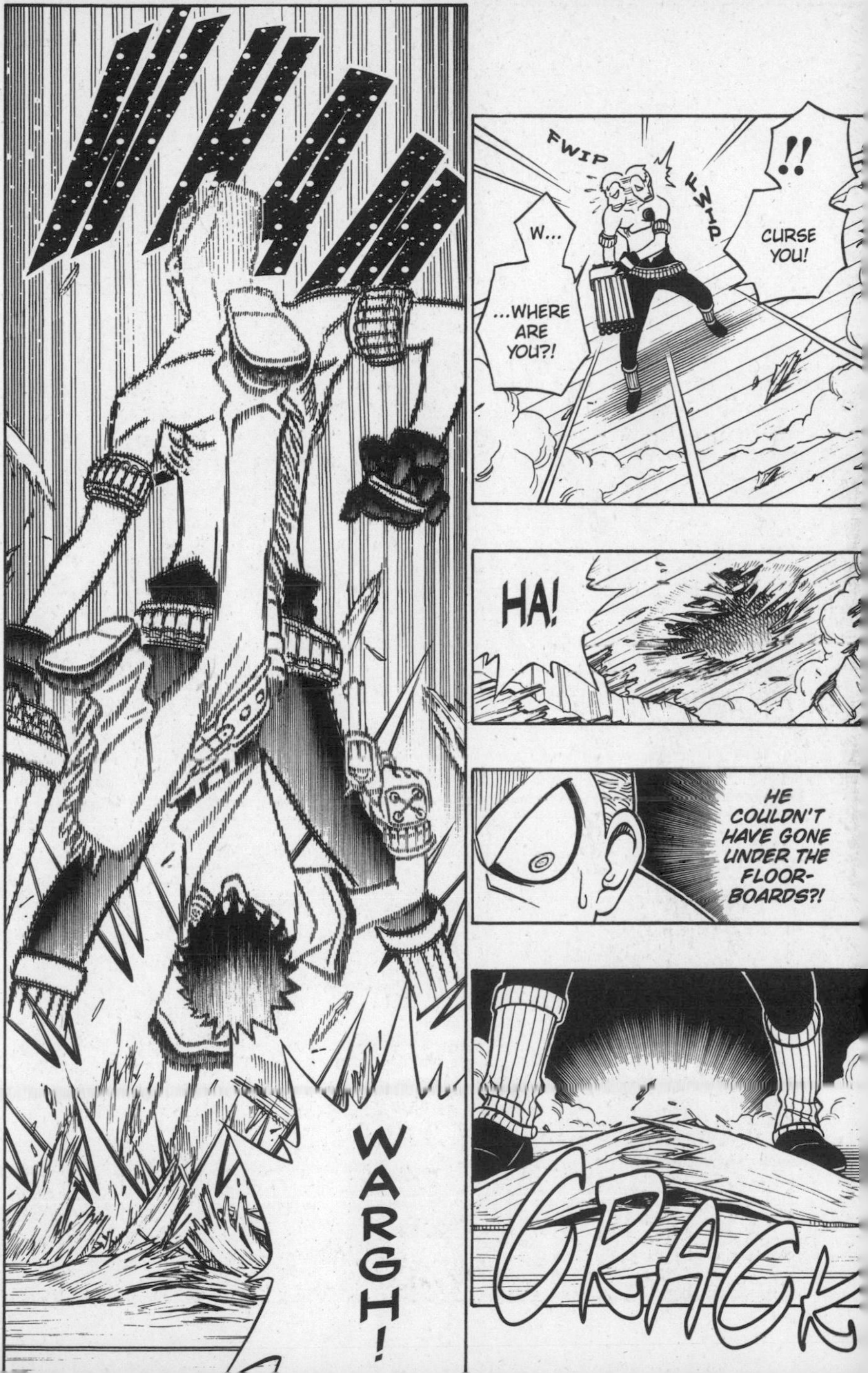
!!
CURSE YOU!
FWIP
FWIP
W...
...WHERE ARE YOU?!
HA!
HE COULDN'T HAVE GONE UNDER THE FLOOR-BOARDS?!
CRACK
WHAM
WARGH!

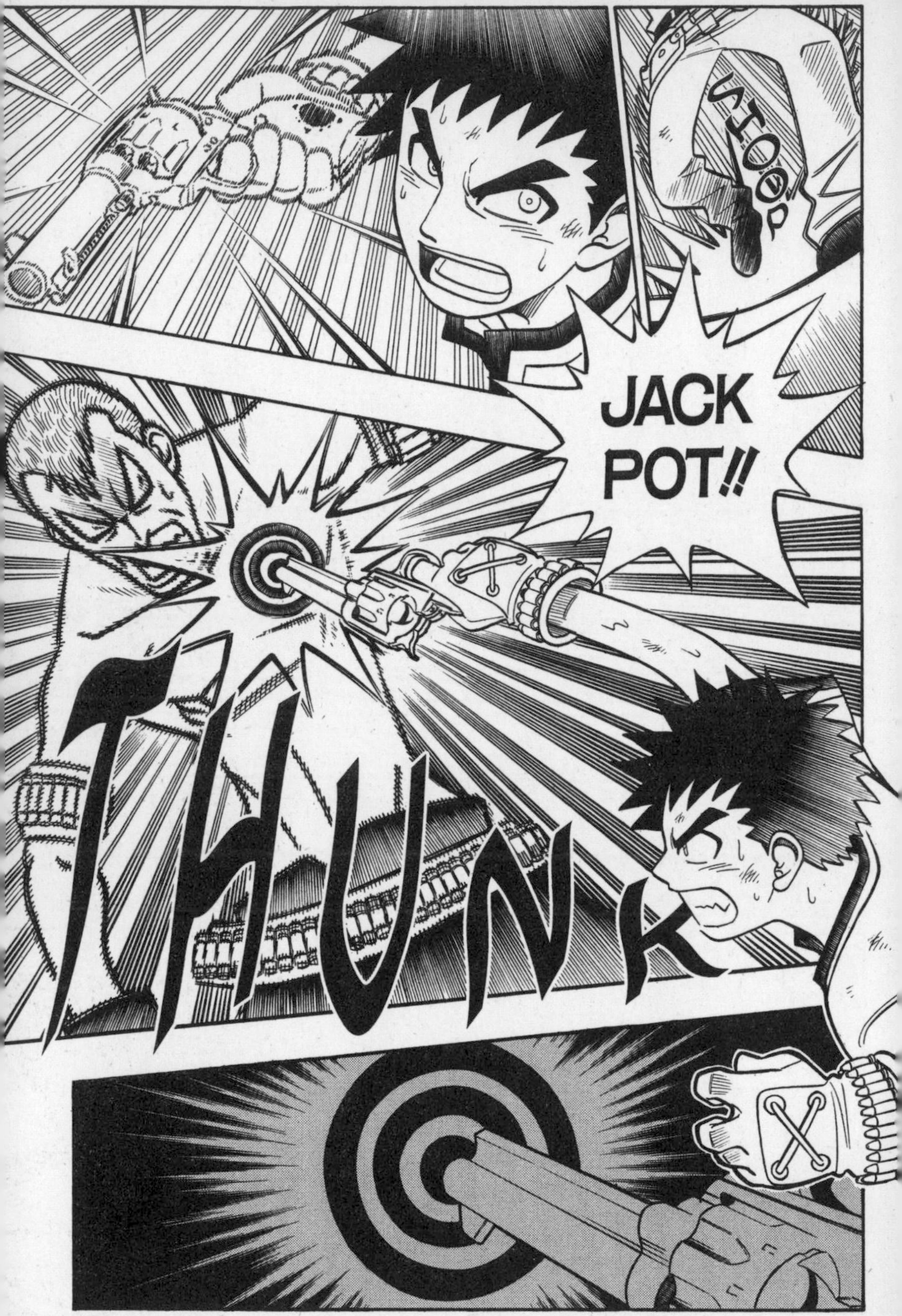
JACK POT!!
THUNK

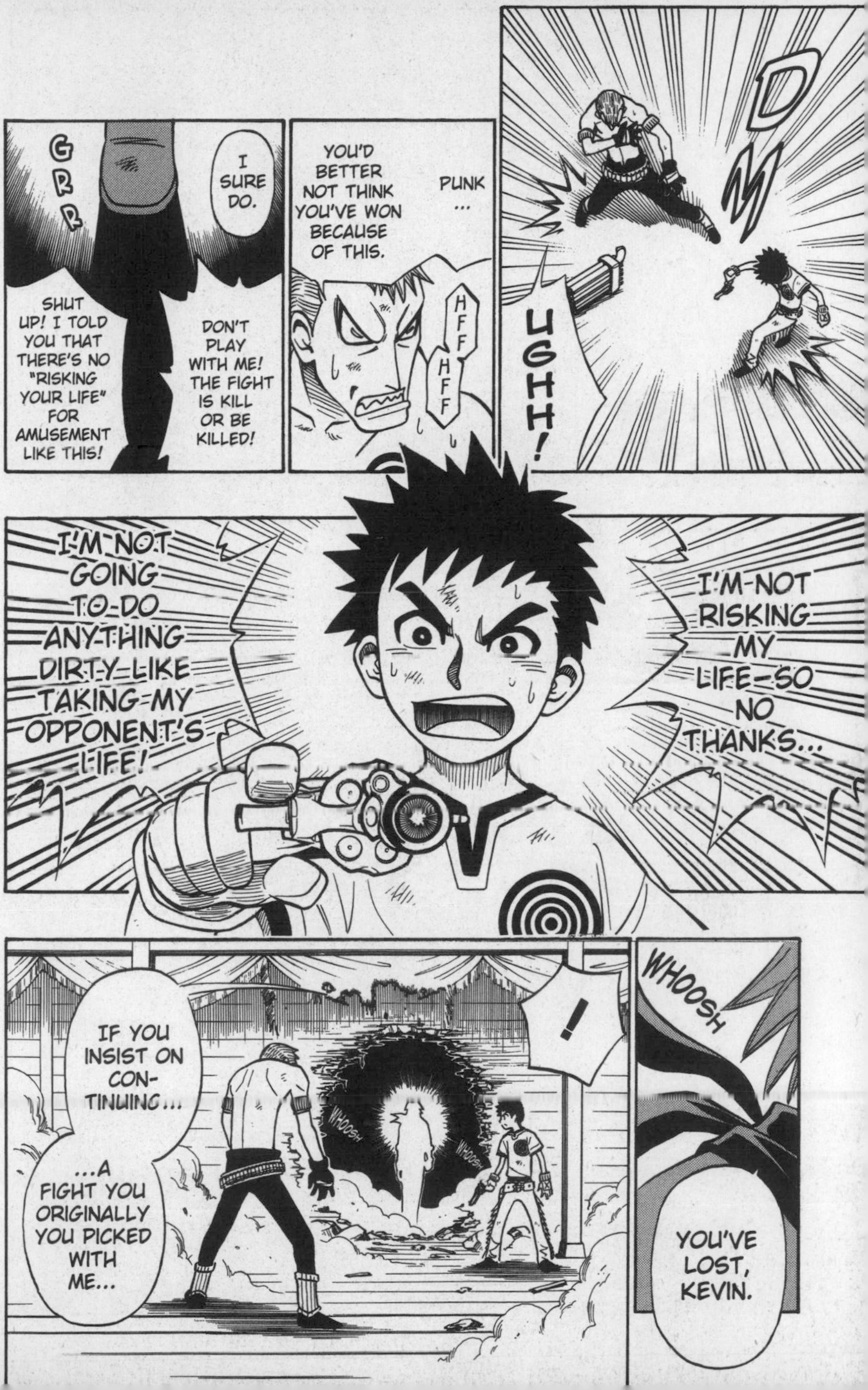
DM
UGHH!
PUNK...
YOU'D BETTER NOT THINK YOU'VE WON BECAUSE OF THIS.
HFF HFF
I SURE DO.
GRR
DON'T PLAY WITH ME! THE FIGHT IS KILL OR BE KILLED!
SHUT UP! I TOLD YOU THAT THERE'S NO "RISKING YOUR LIFE" FOR AMUSEMENT LIKE THIS!
I'M NOT RISKING MY LIFE SO NO THANKS...
I'M NOT GOING TO DO ANYTHING DIRTY LIKE TAKING MY OPPONENT'S LIFE!
WHOOSH
YOU'VE LOST, KEVIN.
!
IF YOU INSIST ON CON-TINUING...
...A FIGHT YOU ORIGINALLY YOU PICKED WITH ME...
WHOOSH
WHOOSH

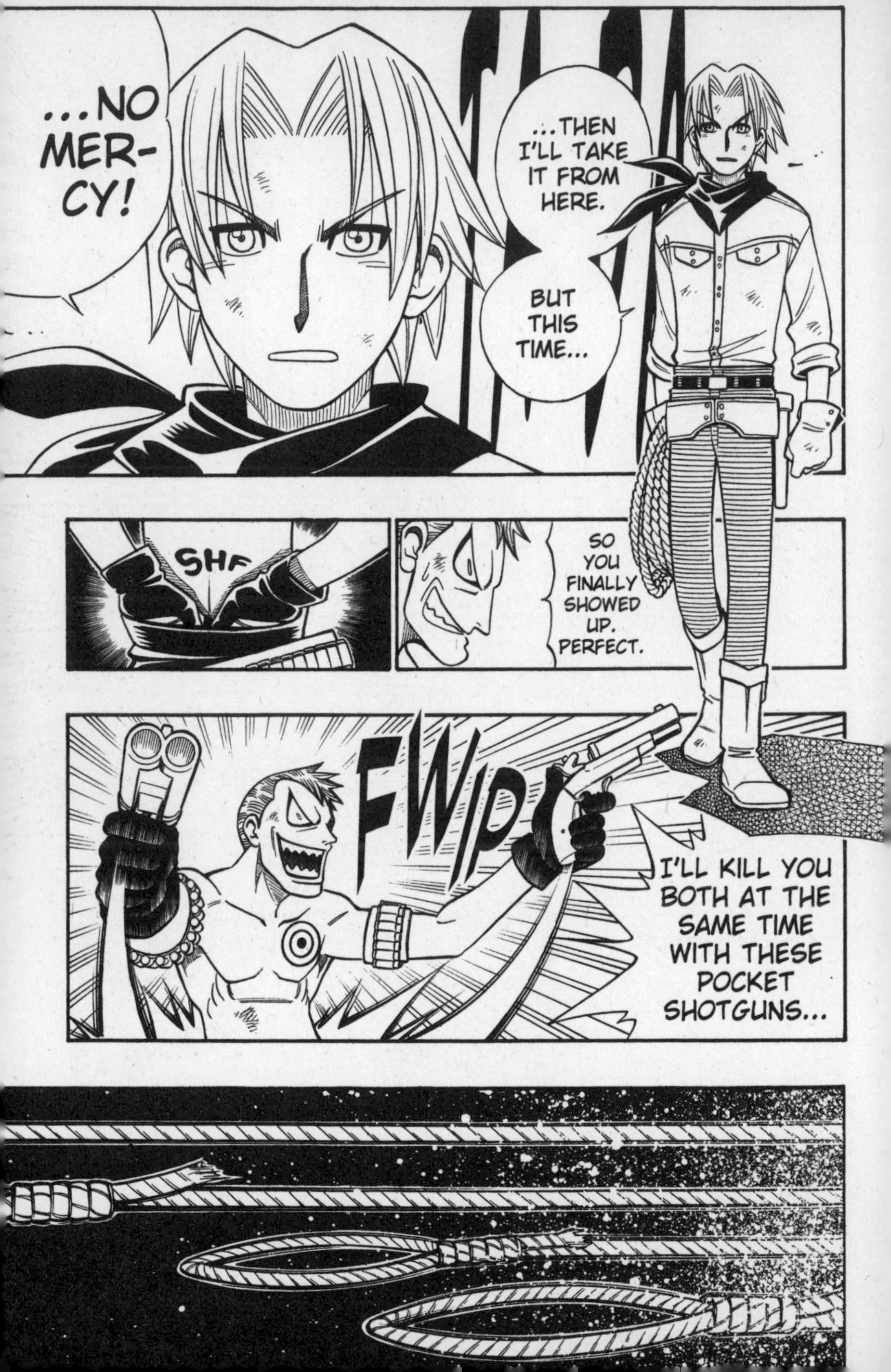
...THEN I'LL TAKE IT FROM HERE.
BUT THIS TIME...
...NO MER-CY!
SO YOU FINALLY SHOWED UP. PERFECT.
SHF
I'LL KILL YOU BOTH AT THE SAME TIME WITH THESE POCKET SHOTGUNS...
FWIP

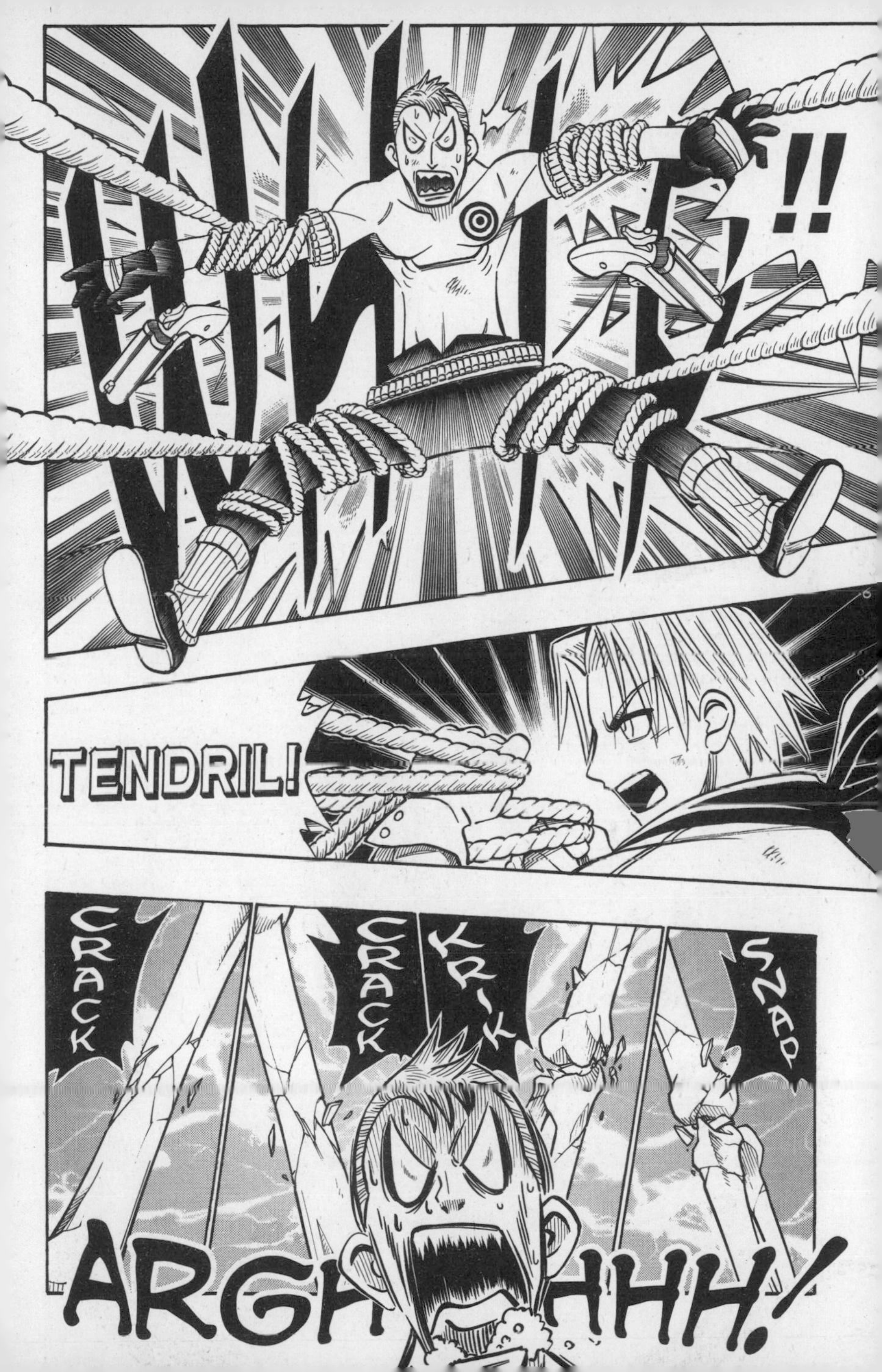
!!
TENDRIL!
SNAP
KRIK
CRACK
CRACK
ARGHHHH!

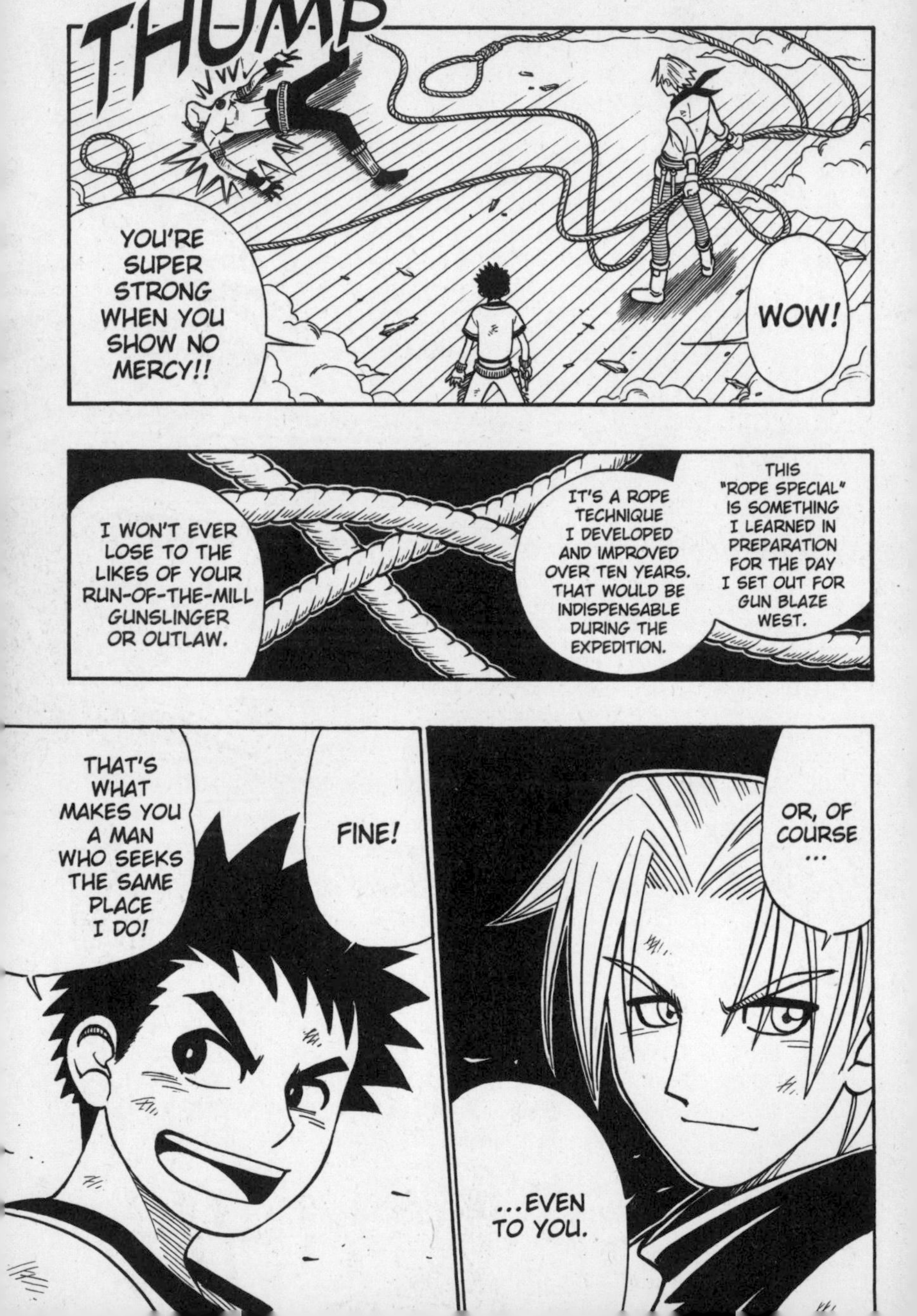
THUMP
WOW!
YOU'RE SUPER STRONG WHEN YOU SHOW NO MERCY!!
THIS "ROPE SPECIAL" IS SOMETHING I LEARNED IN PREPARATION FOR THE DAY I SET OUT FOR GUN BLAZE WEST.
IT'S A ROPE TECHNIQUE I DEVELOPED AND IMPROVED OVER TEN YEARS. THAT WOULD BE INDISPENSABLE DURING THE EXPEDITION.
I WON'T EVER LOSE TO THE LIKES OF YOUR RUN-OF-THE-MILL GUNSLINGER OR OUTLAW.
OR, OF COURSE ...
...EVEN TO YOU.
FINE!
THAT'S WHAT MAKES YOU A MAN WHO SEEKS THE SAME PLACE I DO!

SOURCE OF THE IMAGE: FRANKLY, THERE WAS NONE FOR VIU. AFTER ALL, THE SITUATION WAS AS I DESCRIBED ON PAGE 26...

HOWEVER, THERE WAS ONE FOR VIU AS A KID (HEREAFTER LITTLE VIU). THERE WAS A LOT OF CONJECTURE, BUT THE IMAGE SOURCE FOR KID VIU WAS THE YOUNG LAD JOHNNY BOY WHO APPEARED IN A PROVIDER O COMMERCIAL THAT WAS SHOWING ON TV AT THE TIME.

IN INSTALLMENTS 1 THROUGH 5 WHICH COMPRISED THE PROLOGUE, THE REASON THERE WERE SO MANY SCENES WHERE VIU DOES NOTHING BUT RUN IS BECAUSE I WAS INFLUENCED BY THE STRANGE AND WONDERFUL SCENE FROM A COMMERCIAL WHERE JOHNNY BOY, WITH A DONUT IN HIS MOUTH, AND HIS DAD RUN AWAY. "LISTEN, JOHNNY BOY, THINK OF ANYONE WHO TRIES TO MAKE YOU PAY, EVEN THE PRESIDENT, AS YOUR ENEMY!"

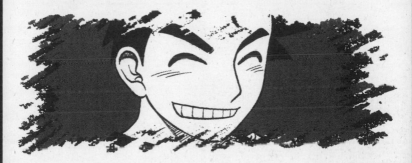

DESIGN: I HAD SET IT FROM THE START THAT HIS HAIR BE SHORT AND SHOW HIS EYEBROWS. HOWEVER, BECAUSE THE SITUATION WAS AS DESCRIBED ON PAGE 26, IT WAS MOSTLY A DESIGN CREATED OFF THE TOP OF MY HEAD.

THE MAIN CHARACTER IS USUALLY DRAWN AND REFINED OVER AND OVER BEFORE SERIALIZATION TO BECOME FAMILIAR WITH IT, BUT THAT PROCESS WAS COMPLETELY NONEXISTENT, SO DID VIU'S HAIR EVER CHANGE. TOWARD THE END, I GAVE UP AND SAID, "I DON'T CARE ALREADY IF HIS BANGS HANG OVER." SORRY.

THAT'S HOW IT WAS WITH VIU, BUT I REALLY LIKE THE DESIGN OF HIS GLOVES. BUT WHO KNOWS, IT COULD BE A FAULTY, DANGEROUS-TO-THE-EXTREME DESIGN THAT WOULD LET HIS ENTIRE ARM GET BLOWN OFF IF THE GUN EVEN PARTIALLY MISFIRED.

ON A SIDE NOTE, THE ENGLISH SPELLING OF VIU'S NAME, VIU BANNES, WAS SOMETHING I HAD A FRIEND WHOM I MET DURING MY TRAVELS ACROSS AMERICA COME UP WITH. THANK YOU, MR. R.

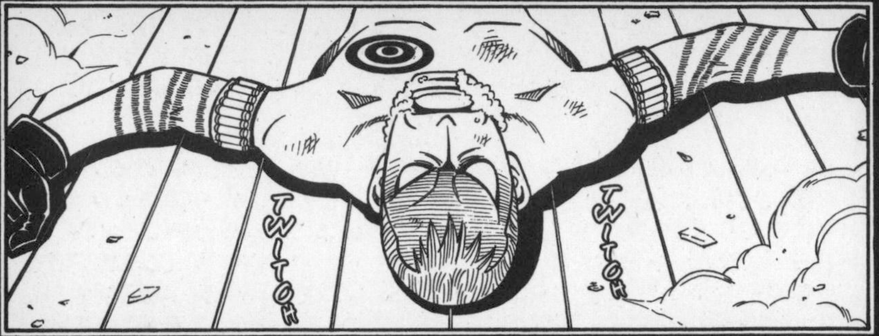
TWITCH
TWITCH

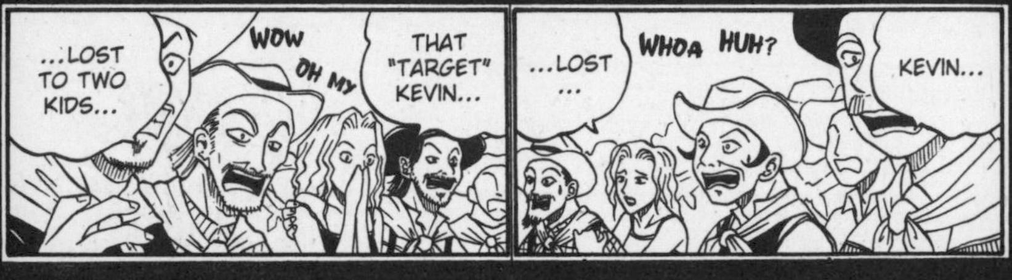
KEVIN...
HUH?
WHOA
...LOST ...
THAT "TARGET" KEVIN...
OH MY
WOW
...LOST TO TWO KIDS...

# CHAPTER 10: WILL RISING

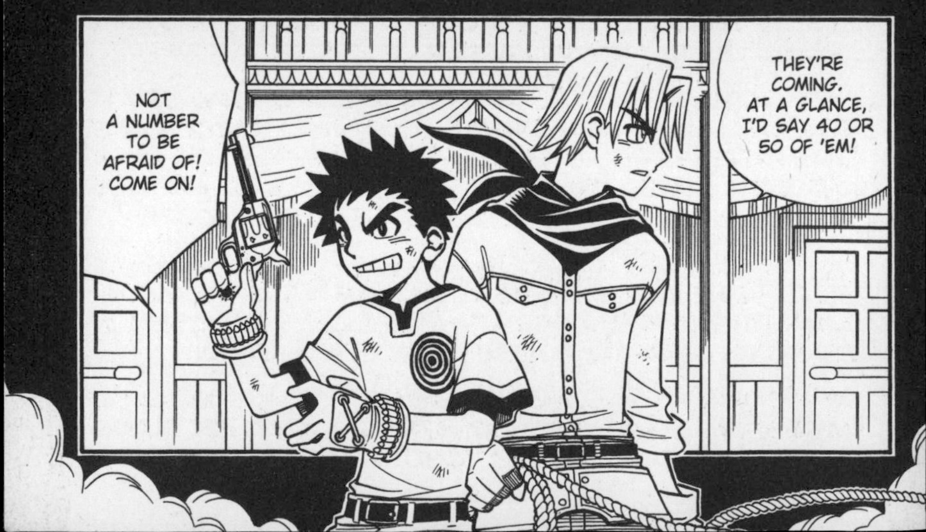
THEY'RE COMING. AT A GLANCE, I'D SAY 40 OR 50 OF 'EM!
NOT A NUMBER TO BE AFRAID OF! COME ON!

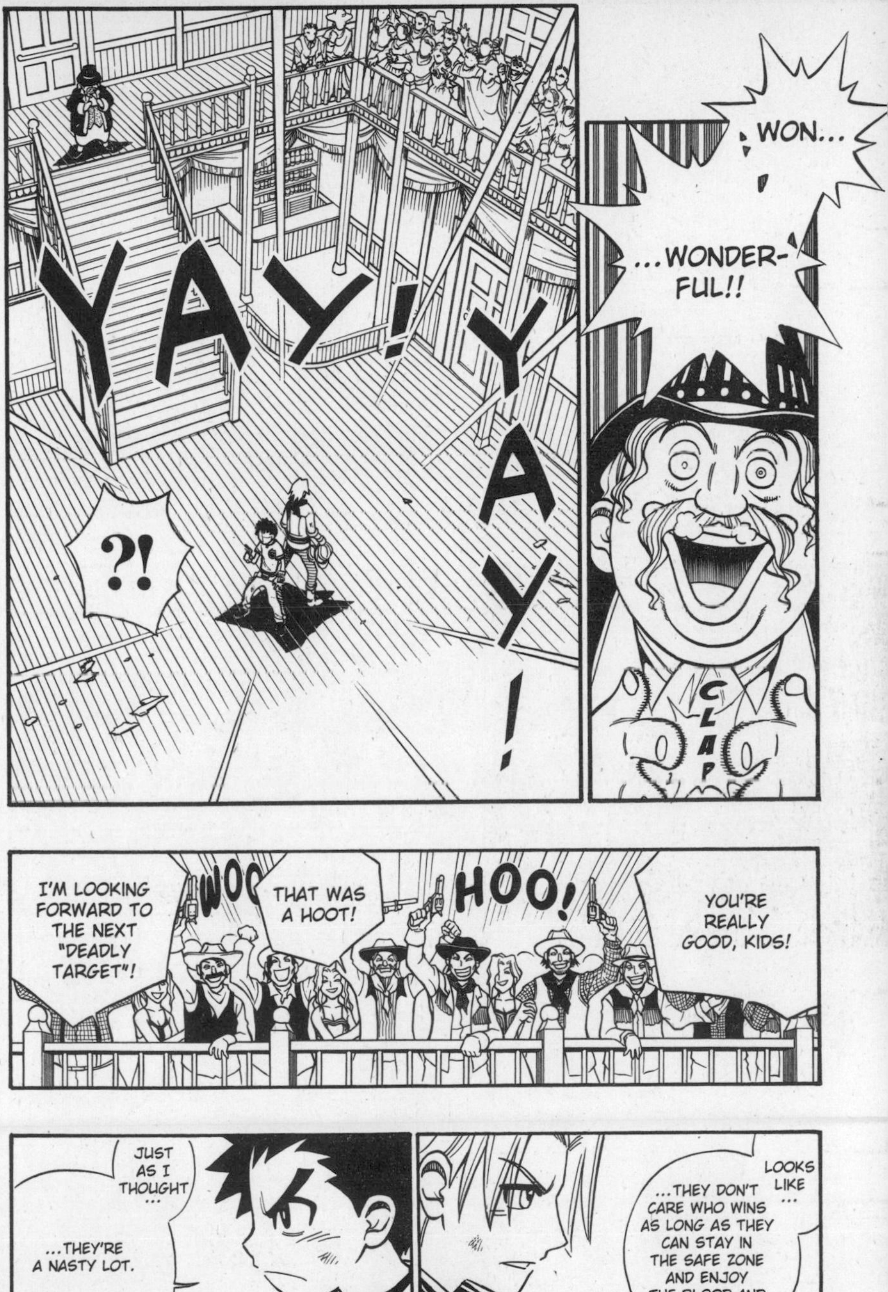
WON...
...WONDER-FUL!!
CLAP
YAY! YAY!
?!
YOU'RE REALLY GOOD, KIDS!
HOO!
THAT WAS A HOOT!
WOO
I'M LOOKING FORWARD TO THE NEXT "DEADLY TARGET"!
LOOKS LIKE...
...THEY DON'T CARE WHO WINS AS LONG AS THEY CAN STAY IN THE SAFE ZONE AND ENJOY THE BLOOD AND GUNSHOTS.
JUST AS I THOUGHT...
...THEY'RE A NASTY LOT.

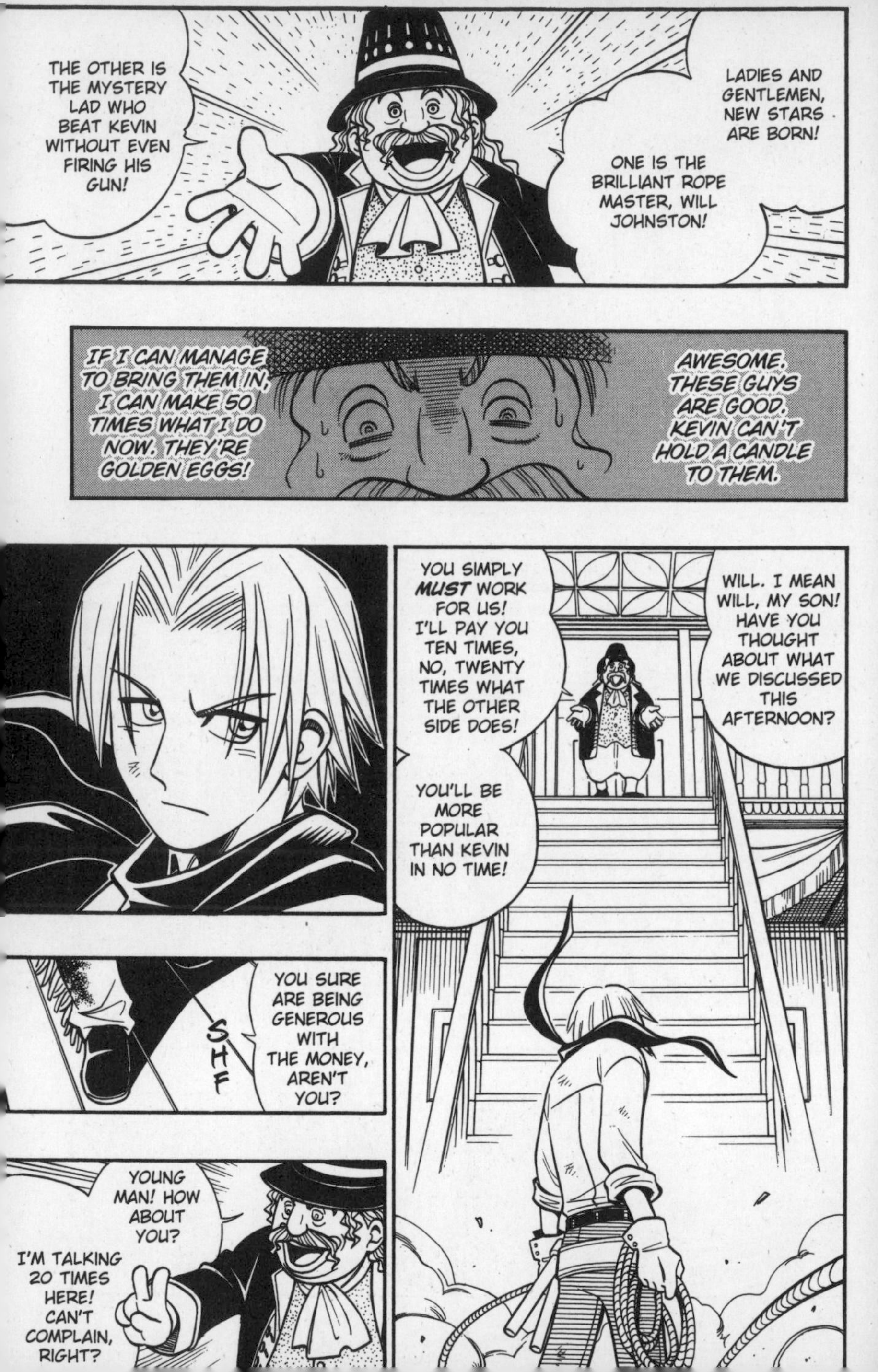
LADIES AND GENTLEMEN, NEW STARS ARE BORN!
ONE IS THE BRILLIANT ROPE MASTER, WILL JOHNSTON!
THE OTHER IS THE MYSTERY LAD WHO BEAT KEVIN WITHOUT EVEN FIRING HIS GUN!
AWESOME. THESE GUYS ARE GOOD. KEVIN CAN'T HOLD A CANDLE TO THEM.
IF I CAN MANAGE TO BRING THEM IN, I CAN MAKE 50 TIMES WHAT I DO NOW. THEY'RE GOLDEN EGGS!
WILL. I MEAN WILL, MY SON! HAVE YOU THOUGHT ABOUT WHAT WE DISCUSSED THIS AFTERNOON?
YOU SIMPLY *MUST* WORK FOR US! I'LL PAY YOU TEN TIMES, NO, TWENTY TIMES WHAT THE OTHER SIDE DOES!
YOU'LL BE MORE POPULAR THAN KEVIN IN NO TIME!
SHF
YOU SURE ARE BEING GENEROUS WITH THE MONEY, AREN'T YOU?
YOUNG MAN! HOW ABOUT YOU?
I'M TALKING 20 TIMES HERE! CAN'T COMPLAIN, RIGHT?

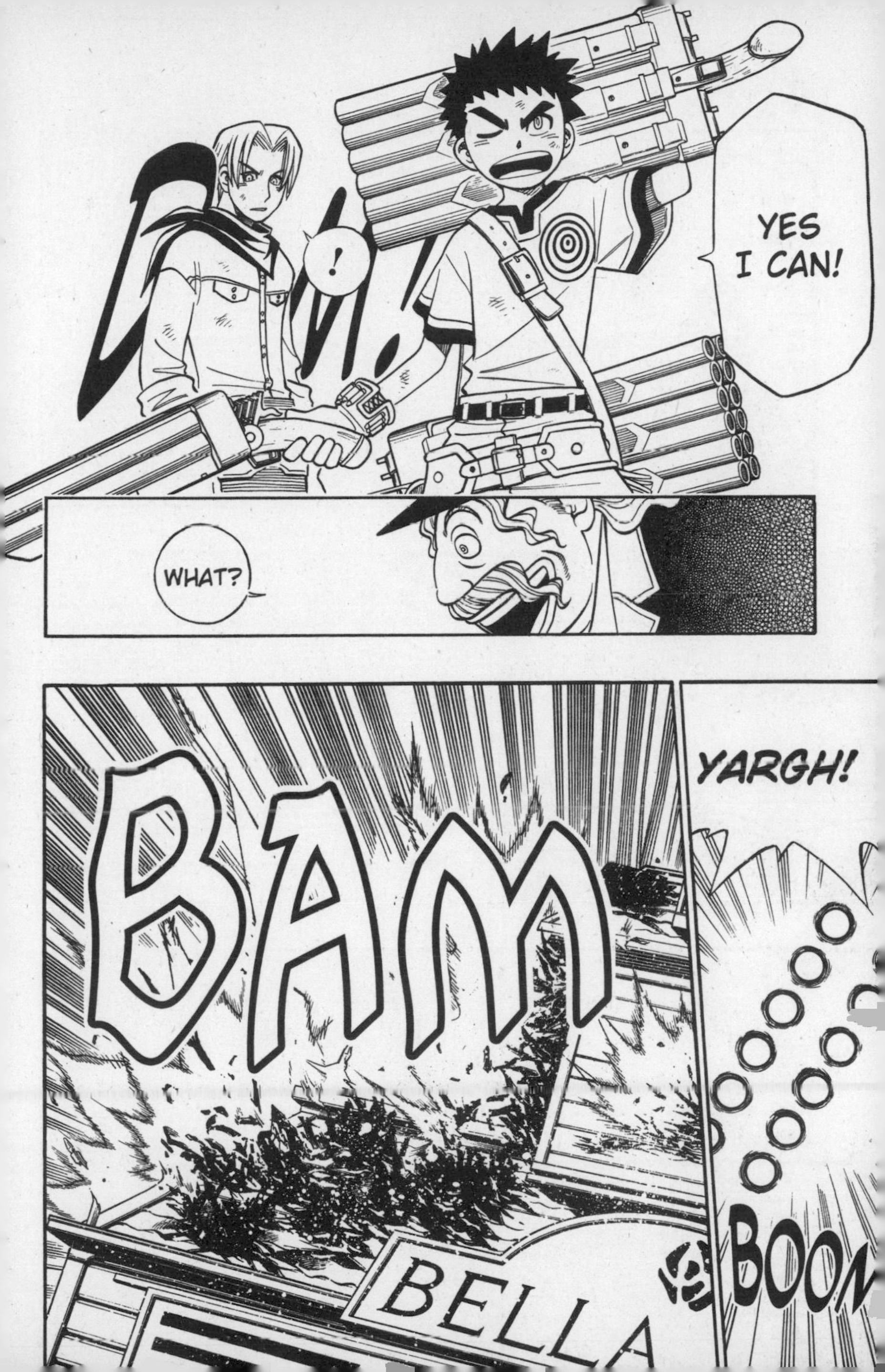
YES I CAN!
!
WHAT?
YARGH!
BOO
BAM
BELLA

READ THIS WAY

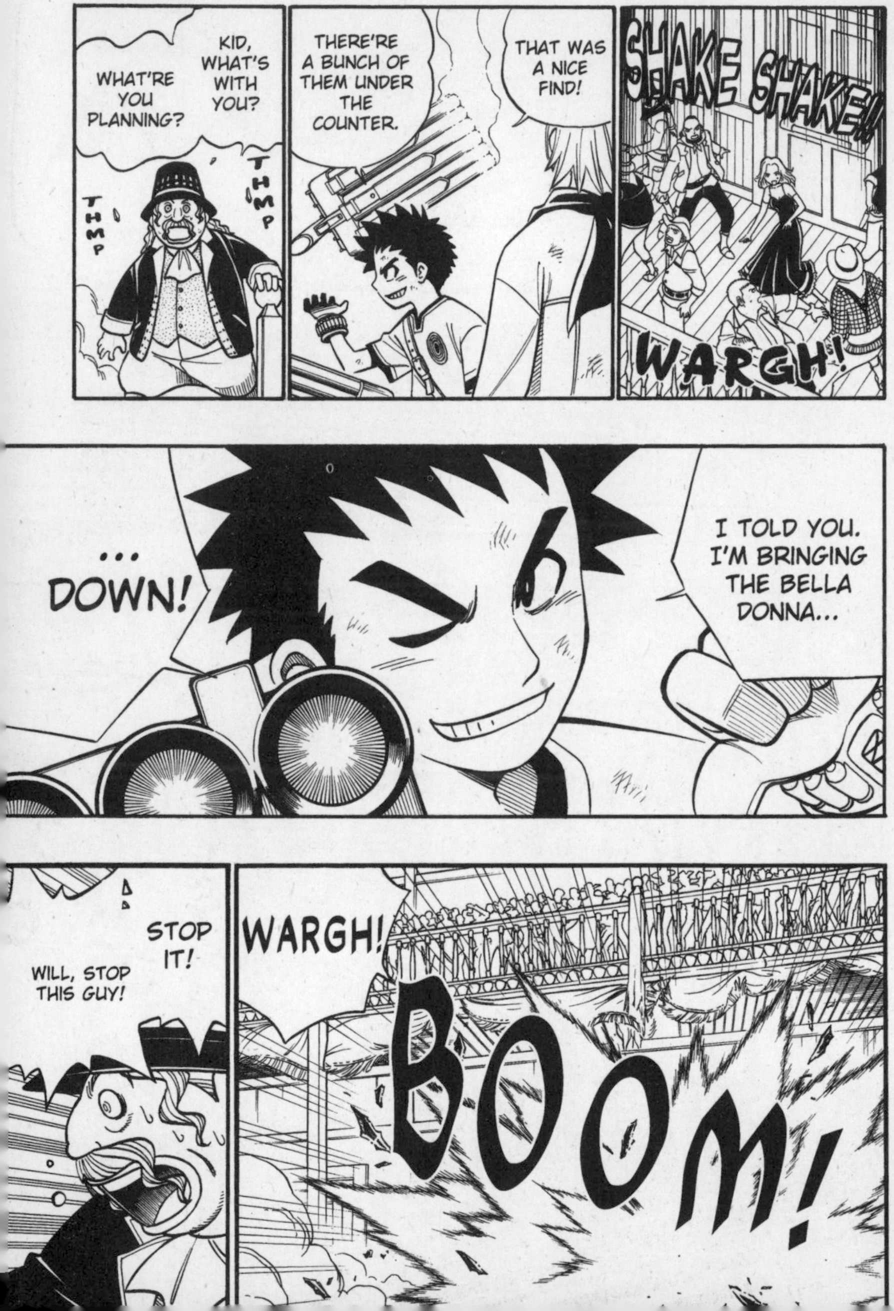
SHAKE SHAKE!!
WARGH!
THAT WAS A NICE FIND!
THERE'RE A BUNCH OF THEM UNDER THE COUNTER.
KID, WHAT'S WITH YOU?
WHAT'RE YOU PLANNING?
THMP
THMP
I TOLD YOU. I'M BRINGING THE BELLA DONNA...
... DOWN!
WARGH!
BOOM!
STOP IT!
WILL, STOP THIS GUY!

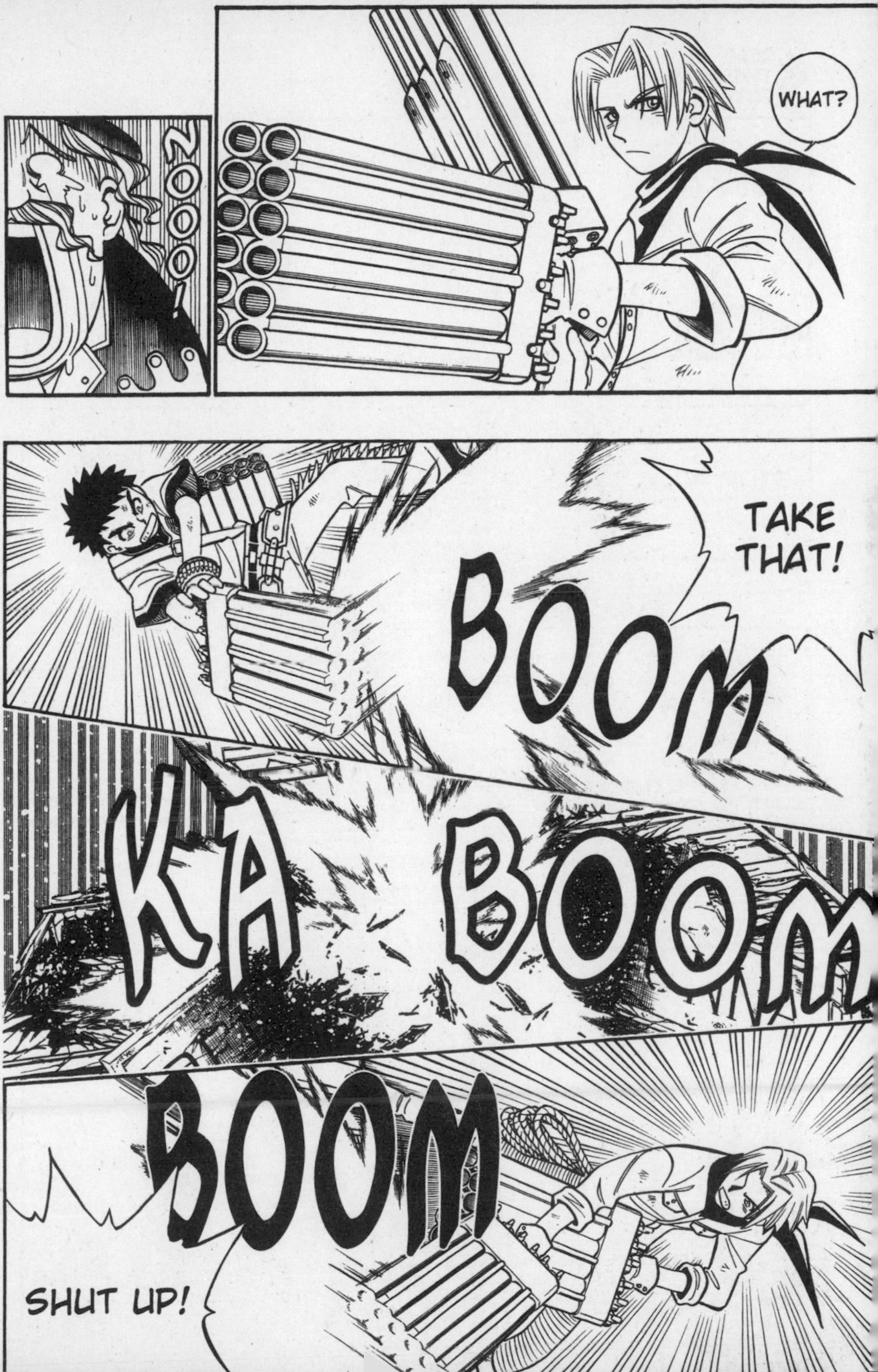
WHAT?
NOOOO!
TAKE THAT!
BOOM
KA BOOM
BOOM
SHUT UP!

READ THIS WAY

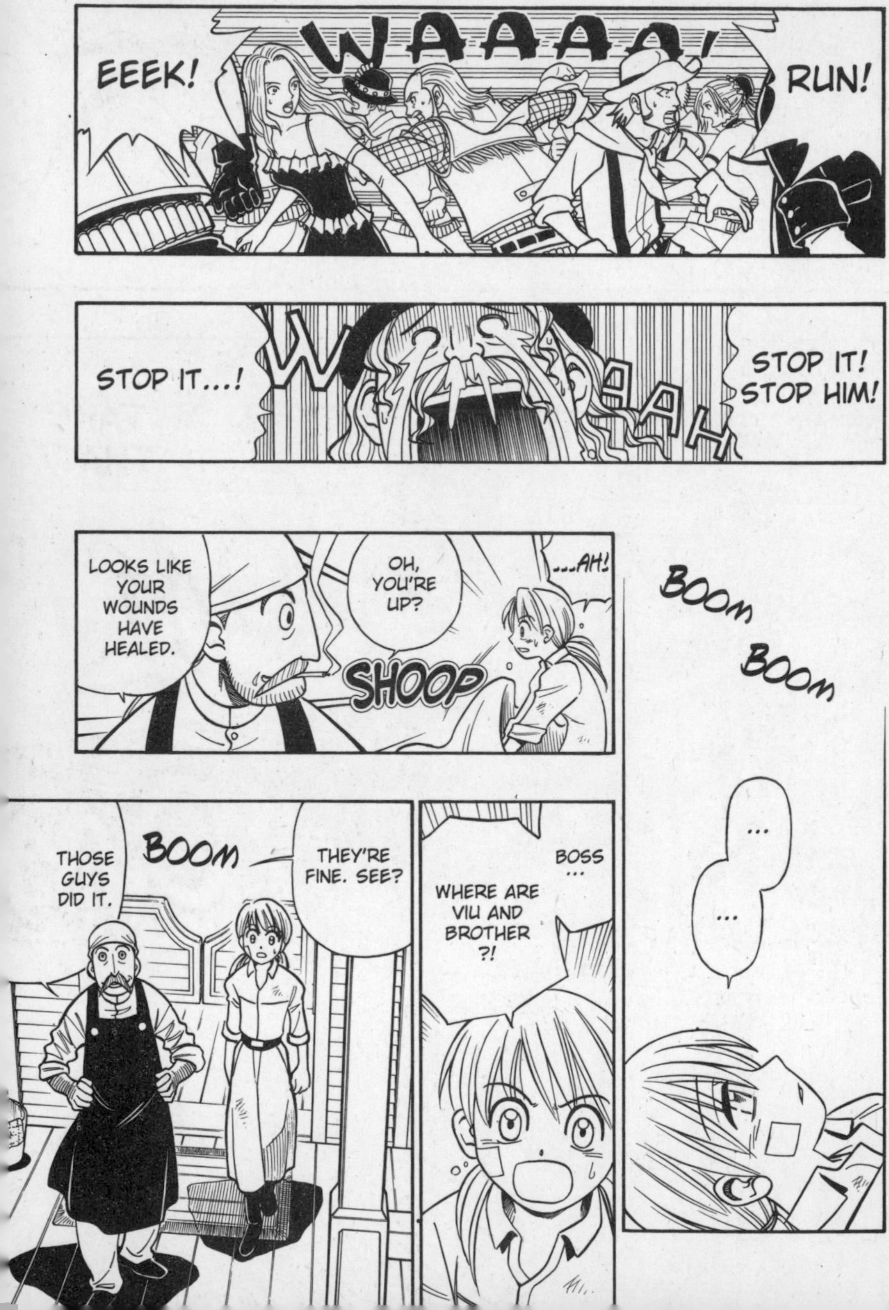
RUN!
WAAAA!
EEEK!
STOP IT! STOP HIM!
WAAAH
STOP IT...!
BOOM
BOOM
...
...
...AH!
OH, YOU'RE UP?
SHOOP
LOOKS LIKE YOUR WOUNDS HAVE HEALED.
BOSS...
WHERE ARE VIU AND BROTHER ?!
THEY'RE FINE. SEE?
BOOM
THOSE GUYS DID IT.

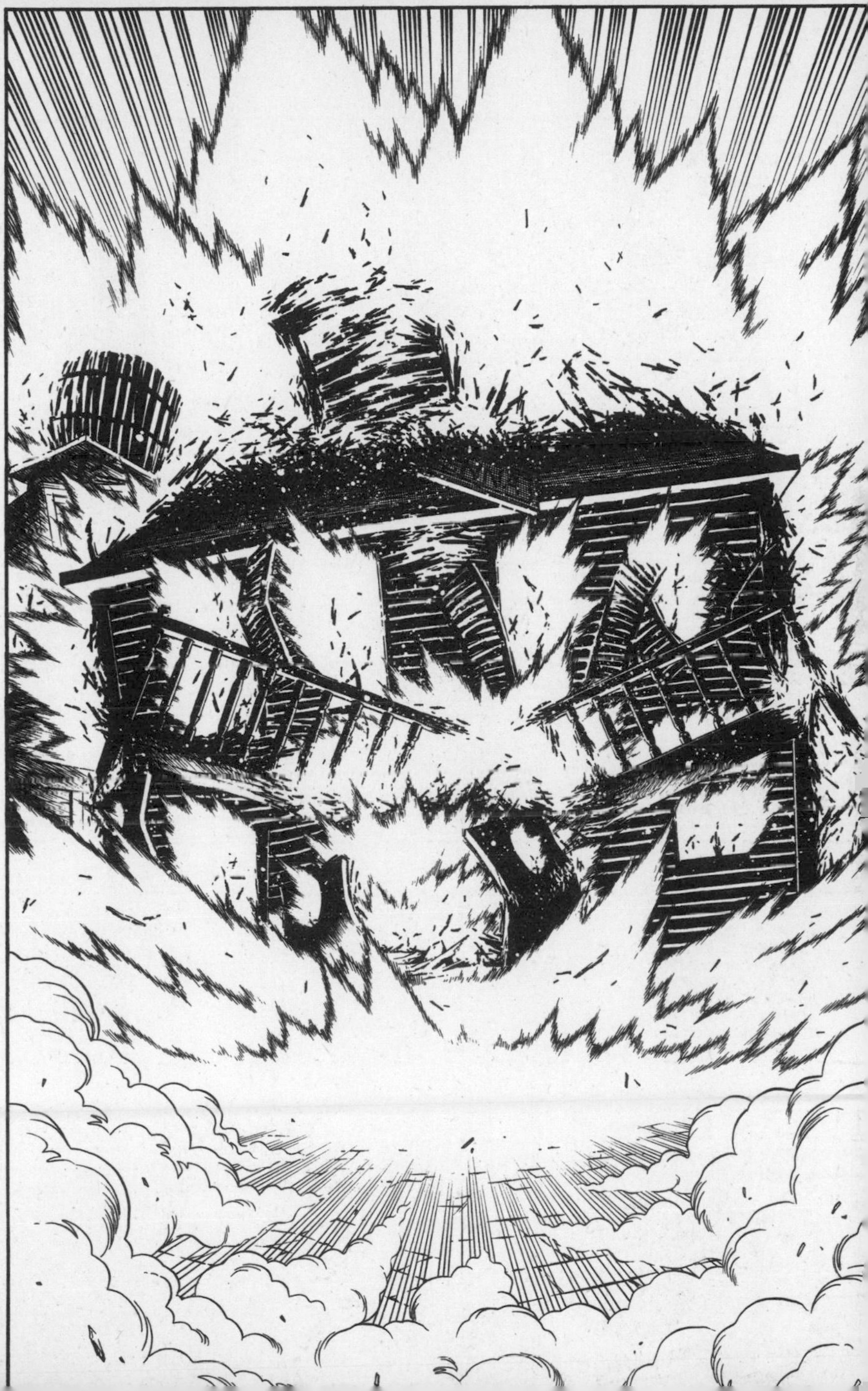

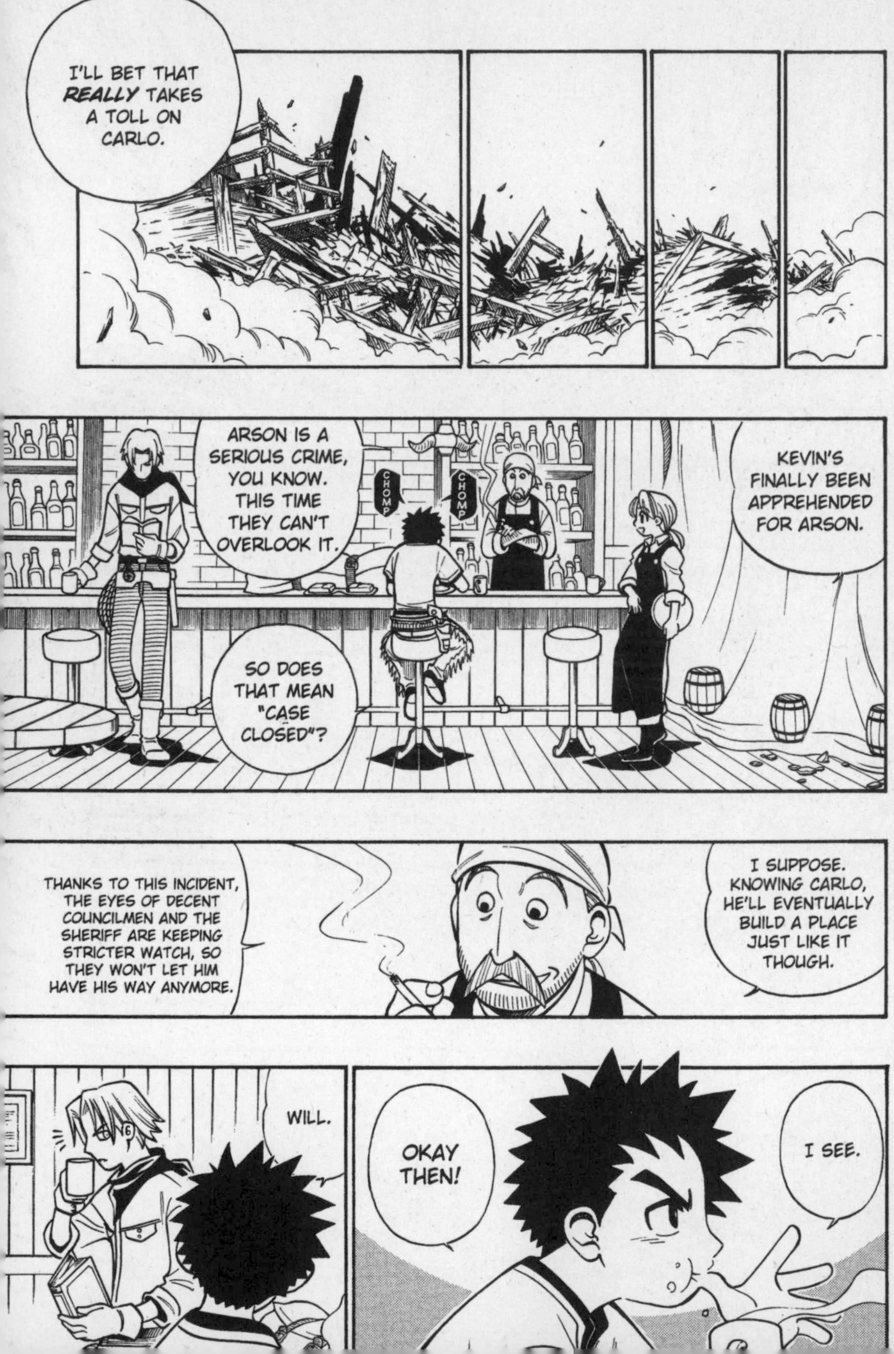
I'LL BET THAT *REALLY* TAKES A TOLL ON CARLO.
KEVIN'S FINALLY BEEN APPREHENDED FOR ARSON.
ARSON IS A SERIOUS CRIME, YOU KNOW. THIS TIME THEY CAN'T OVERLOOK IT.
CHOMP
CHOMP
SO DOES THAT MEAN "CASE CLOSED"?
I SUPPOSE. KNOWING CARLO, HE'LL EVENTUALLY BUILD A PLACE JUST LIKE IT THOUGH.
THANKS TO THIS INCIDENT, THE EYES OF DECENT COUNCILMEN AND THE SHERIFF ARE KEEPING STRICTER WATCH, SO THEY WON'T LET HIM HAVE HIS WAY ANYMORE.
I SEE.
OKAY THEN!
WILL.

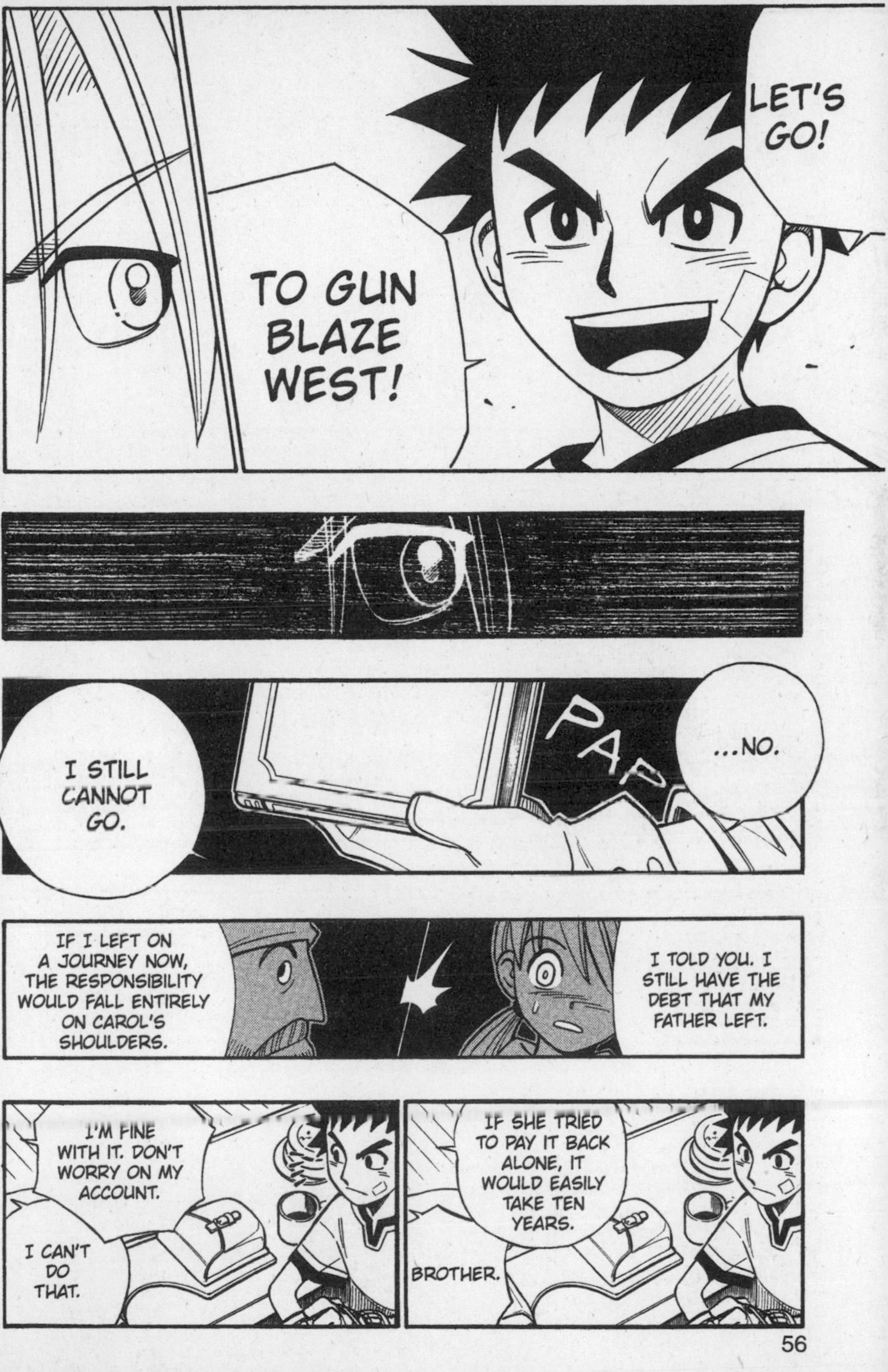
LET'S GO!
TO GUN BLAZE WEST!
...NO.
PAP
I STILL CANNOT GO.
I TOLD YOU. I STILL HAVE THE DEBT THAT MY FATHER LEFT.
IF I LEFT ON A JOURNEY NOW, THE RESPONSIBILITY WOULD FALL ENTIRELY ON CAROL'S SHOULDERS.
IF SHE TRIED TO PAY IT BACK ALONE, IT WOULD EASILY TAKE TEN YEARS.
BROTHER.
I'M FINE WITH IT. DON'T WORRY ON MY ACCOUNT.
I CAN'T DO THAT.

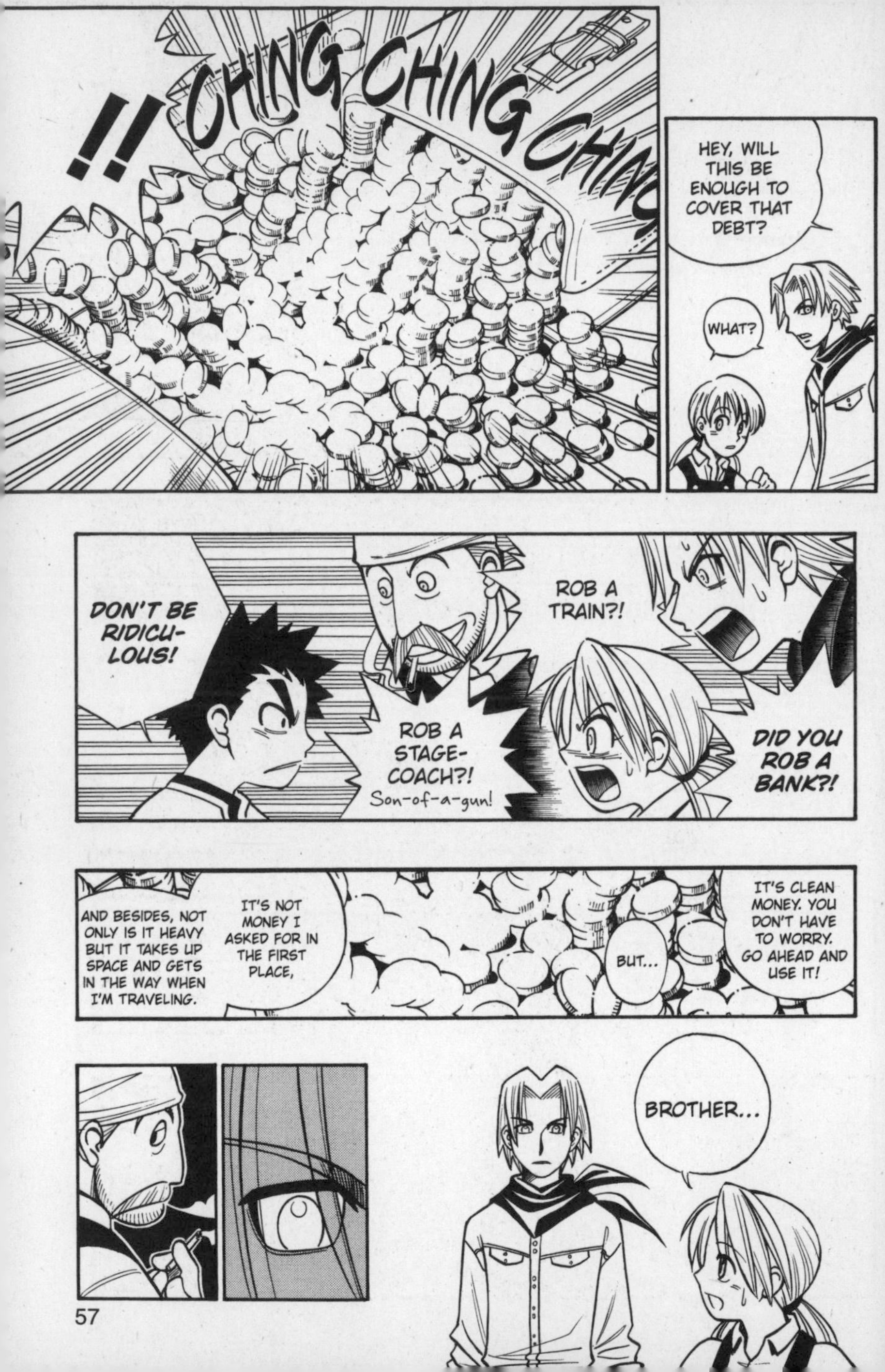
HEY, WILL THIS BE ENOUGH TO COVER THAT DEBT?
WHAT?
!!
CHING CHING CHING
DID YOU ROB A BANK?!
ROB A TRAIN?!
ROB A STAGE-COACH?!
Son-of-a-gun!
DON'T BE RIDICULOUS!
IT'S CLEAN MONEY. YOU DON'T HAVE TO WORRY. GO AHEAD AND USE IT!
BUT...
IT'S NOT MONEY I ASKED FOR IN THE FIRST PLACE,
AND BESIDES, NOT ONLY IS IT HEAVY BUT IT TAKES UP SPACE AND GETS IN THE WAY WHEN I'M TRAVELING.
BROTHER...

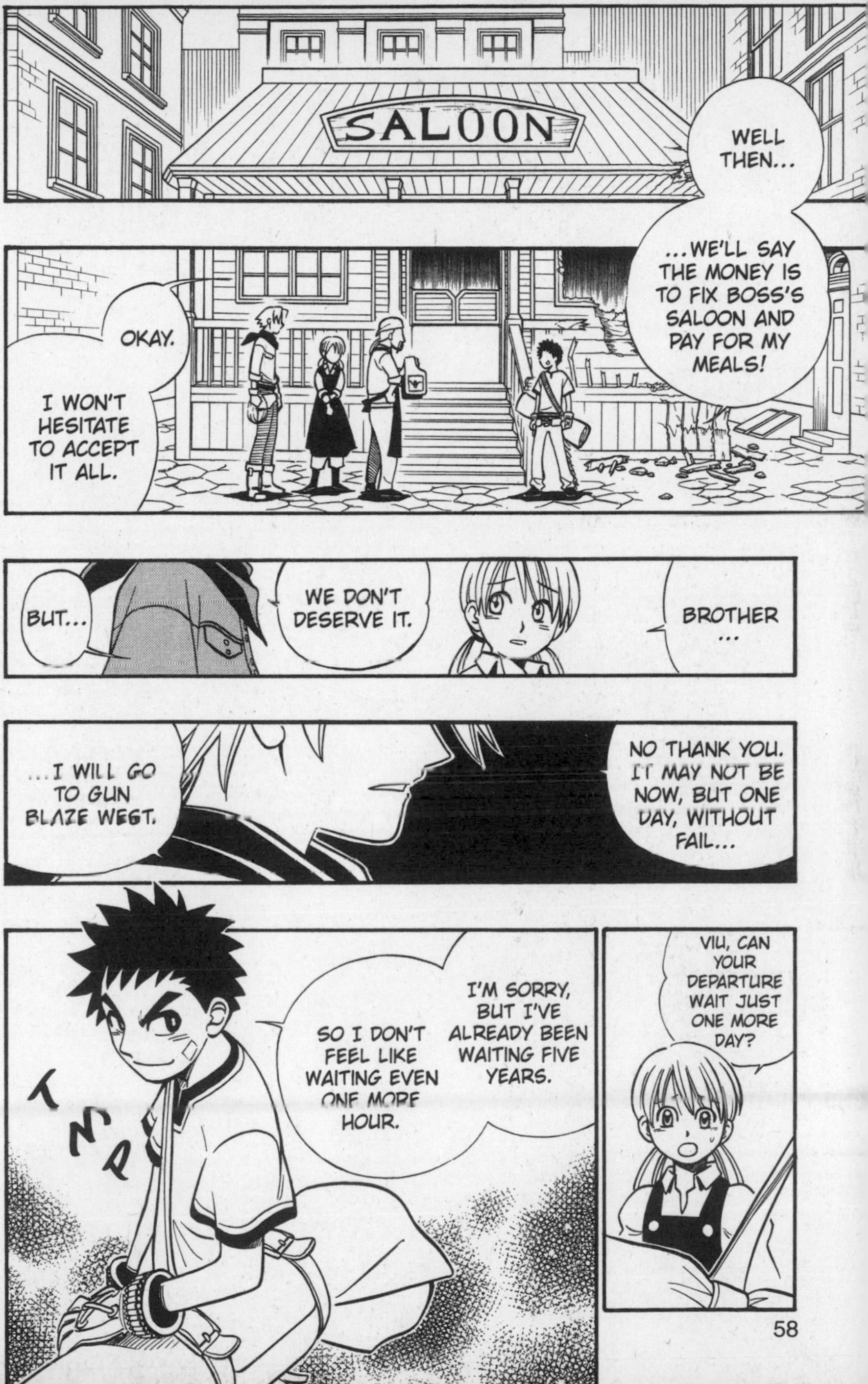
SALOON
WELL THEN...
...WE'LL SAY THE MONEY IS TO FIX BOSS'S SALOON AND PAY FOR MY MEALS!
OKAY.
I WON'T HESITATE TO ACCEPT IT ALL.
BROTHER ...
WE DON'T DESERVE IT.
BUT...
NO THANK YOU. IT MAY NOT BE NOW, BUT ONE DAY, WITHOUT FAIL...
...I WILL GO TO GUN BLAZE WEST.
VIU, CAN YOUR DEPARTURE WAIT JUST ONE MORE DAY?
I'M SORRY, BUT I'VE ALREADY BEEN WAITING FIVE YEARS.
SO I DON'T FEEL LIKE WAITING EVEN ONE MORE HOUR.
TMP

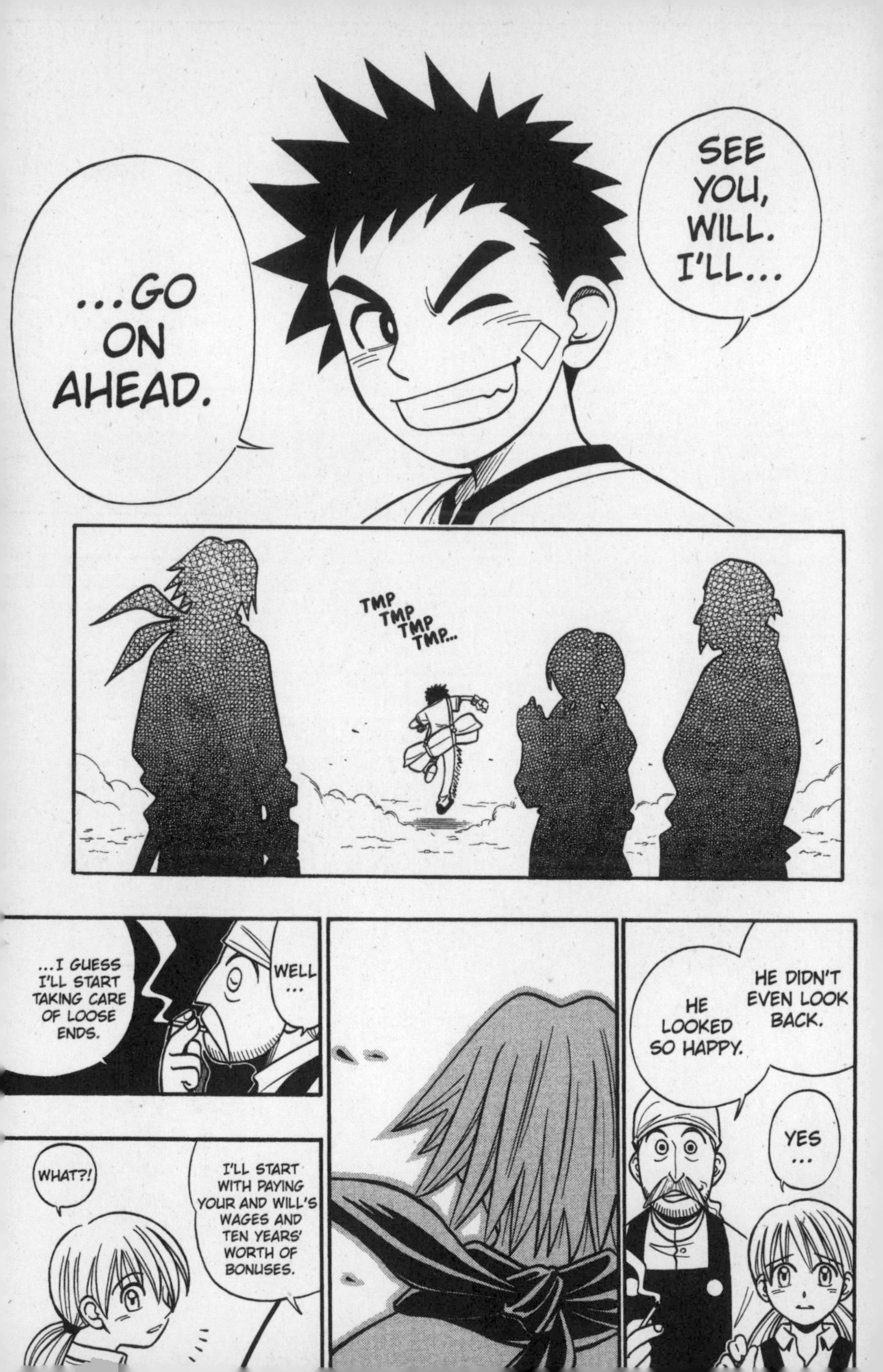
SEE YOU, WILL. I'LL...
...GO ON AHEAD.
TMP TMP TMP TMP...
HE DIDN'T EVEN LOOK BACK.
HE LOOKED SO HAPPY.
YES...
WELL...
...I GUESS I'LL START TAKING CARE OF LOOSE ENDS.
I'LL START WITH PAYING YOUR AND WILL'S WAGES AND TEN YEARS' WORTH OF BONUSES.
WHAT?!

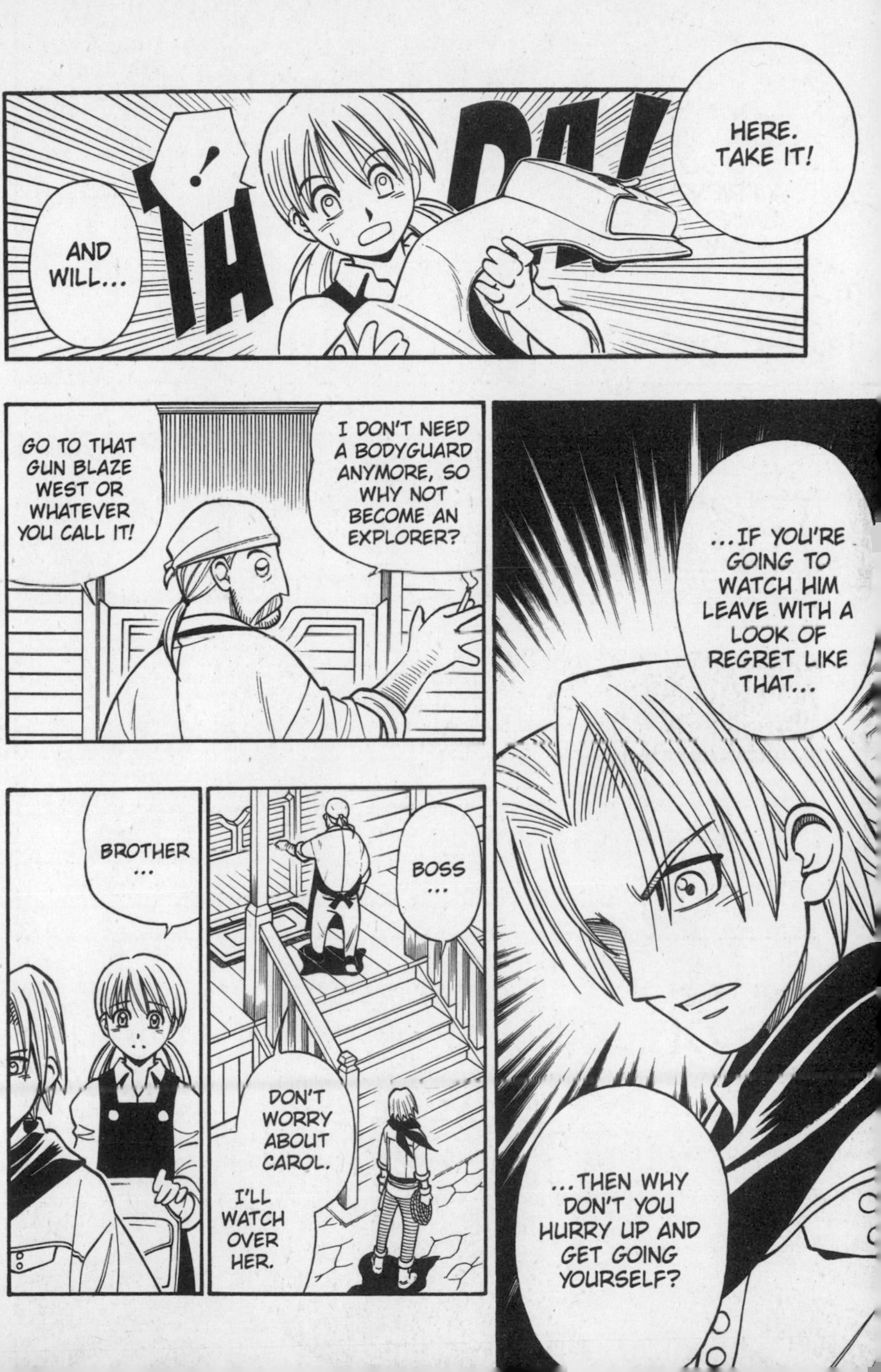
HERE. TAKE IT!
TA DA!
!
AND WILL...
...IF YOU'RE GOING TO WATCH HIM LEAVE WITH A LOOK OF REGRET LIKE THAT...
...THEN WHY DON'T YOU HURRY UP AND GET GOING YOURSELF?
I DON'T NEED A BODYGUARD ANYMORE, SO WHY NOT BECOME AN EXPLORER?
GO TO THAT GUN BLAZE WEST OR WHATEVER YOU CALL IT!
BOSS ...
DON'T WORRY ABOUT CAROL.
I'LL WATCH OVER HER.
BROTHER ...

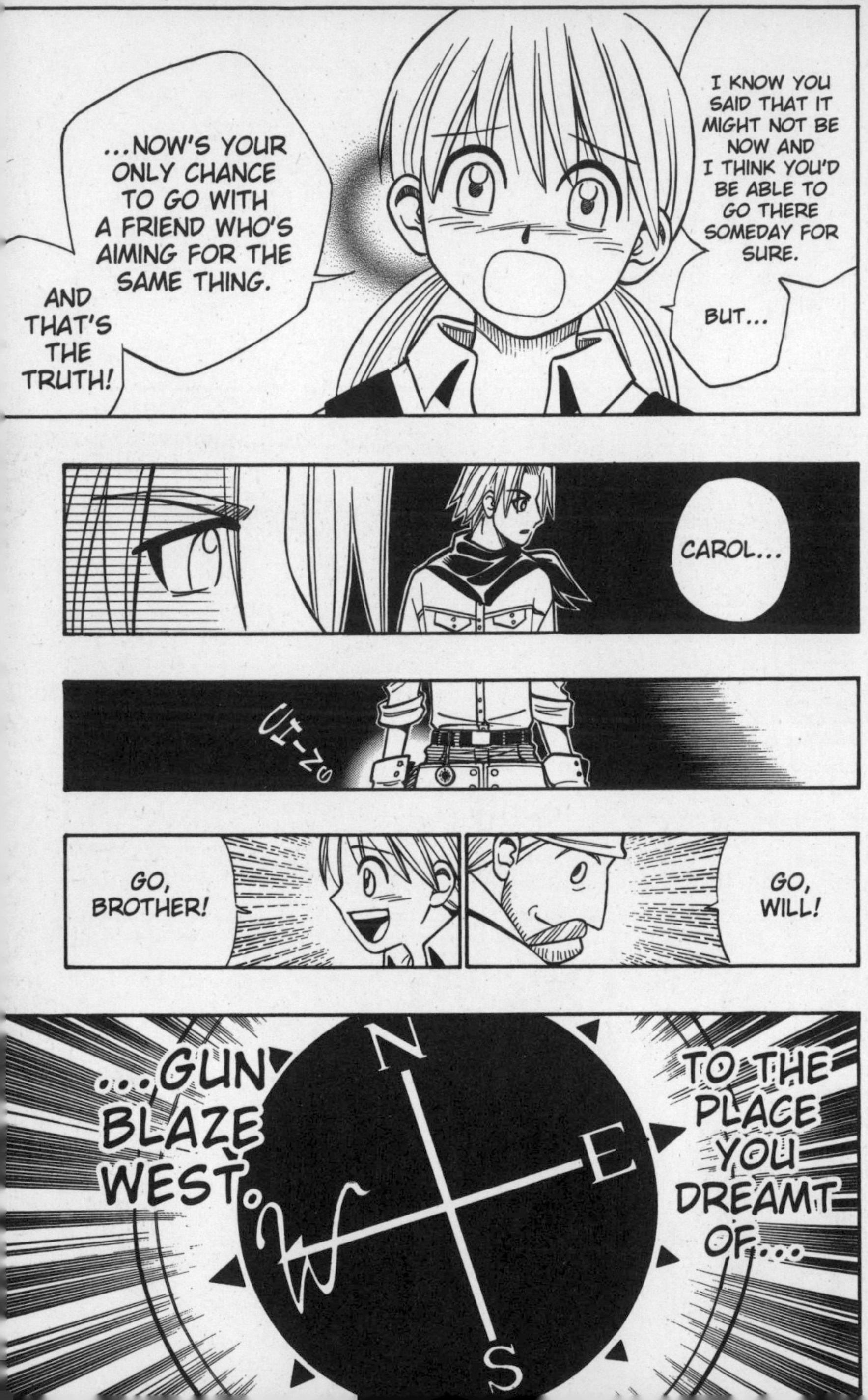

I KNOW YOU SAID THAT IT MIGHT NOT BE NOW AND I THINK YOU'D BE ABLE TO GO THERE SOMEDAY FOR SURE.
BUT...
...NOW'S YOUR ONLY CHANCE TO GO WITH A FRIEND WHO'S AIMING FOR THE SAME THING.
AND THAT'S THE TRUTH!
CAROL...
GO, WILL!
GO, BROTHER!
TO THE PLACE YOU DREAMT OF...
...GUN BLAZE WEST.
N
E
S
W

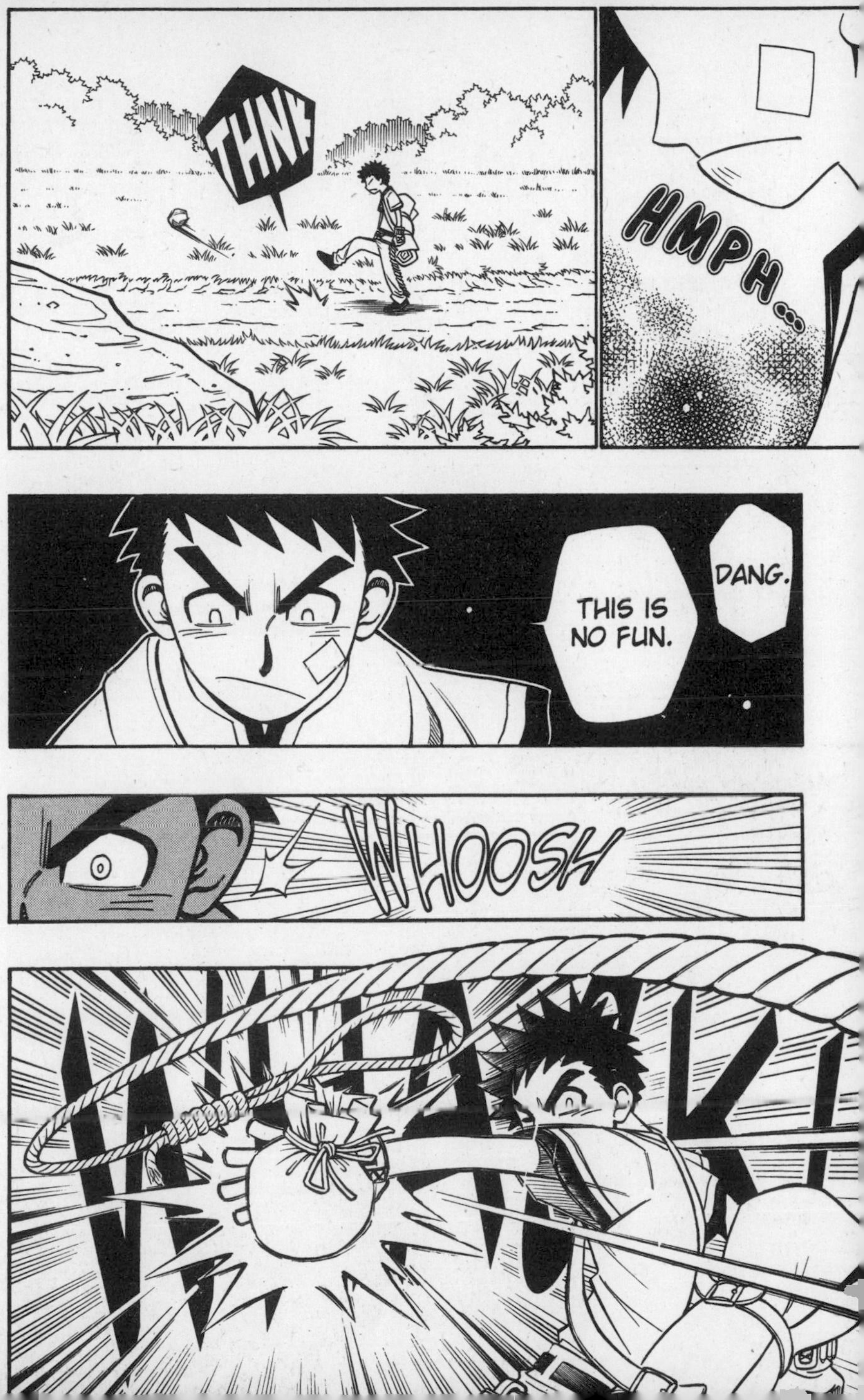
HMPH...
THNK
DANG.
THIS IS NO FUN.
WHOOSH

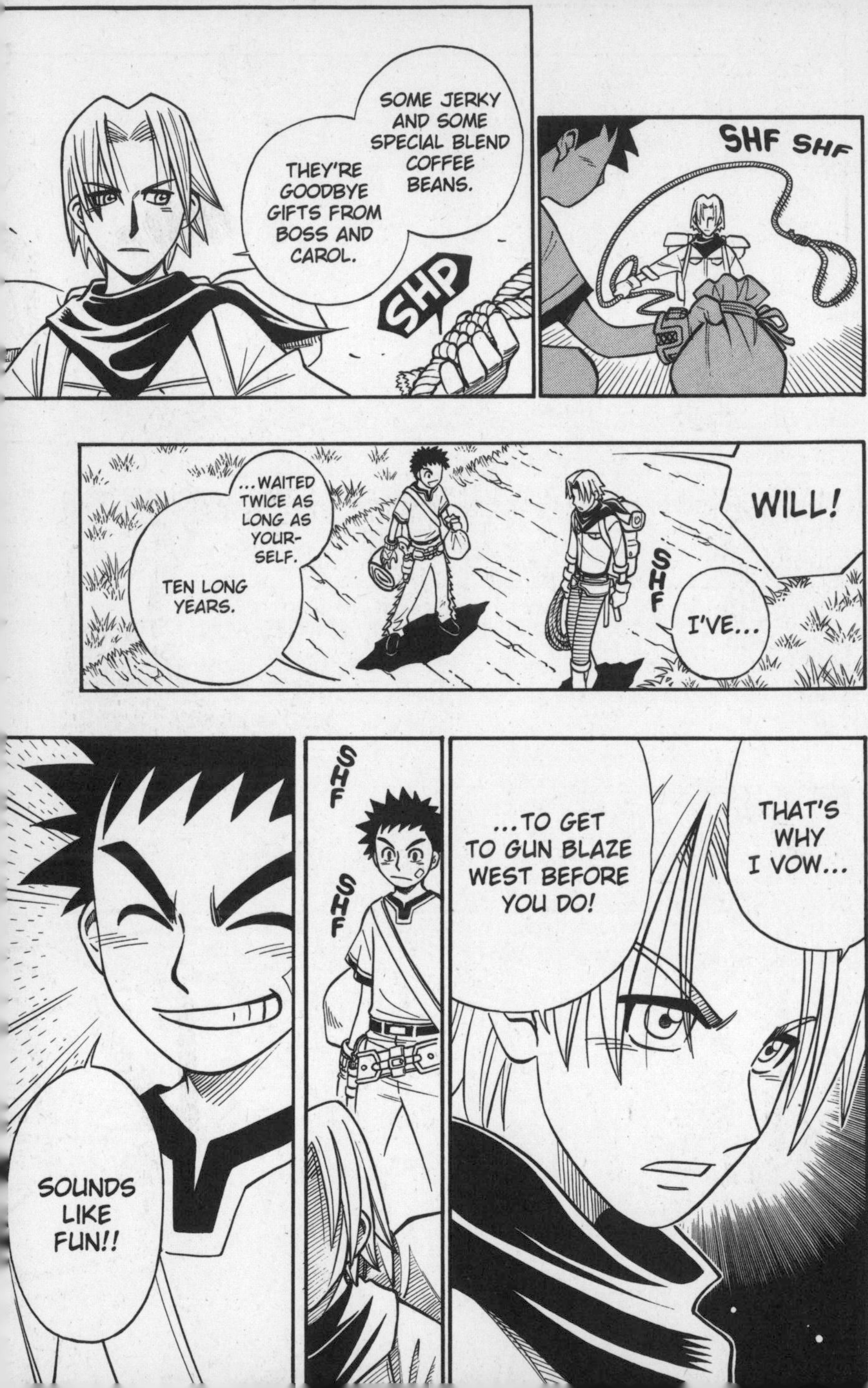
SHF SHF
SOME JERKY AND SOME SPECIAL BLEND COFFEE BEANS.
THEY'RE GOODBYE GIFTS FROM BOSS AND CAROL.
SHP
WILL!
I'VE...
SHF
...WAITED TWICE AS LONG AS YOUR-SELF.
TEN LONG YEARS.
THAT'S WHY I VOW...
...TO GET TO GUN BLAZE WEST BEFORE YOU DO!
SHF
SHF
SOUNDS LIKE FUN!!

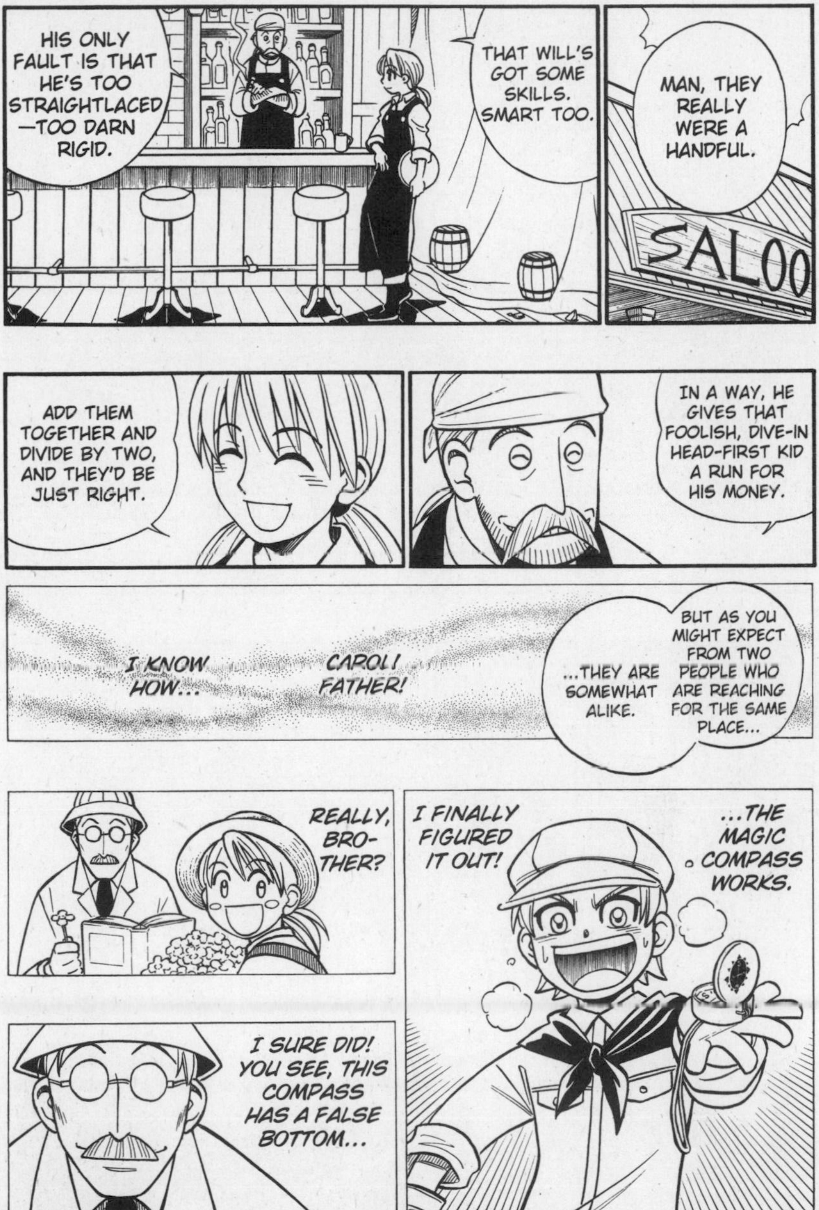
MAN, THEY REALLY WERE A HANDFUL.
SALOO
THAT WILL'S GOT SOME SKILLS. SMART TOO.
HIS ONLY FAULT IS THAT HE'S TOO STRAIGHTLACED—TOO DARN RIGID.
IN A WAY, HE GIVES THAT FOOLISH, DIVE-IN HEAD-FIRST KID A RUN FOR HIS MONEY.
ADD THEM TOGETHER AND DIVIDE BY TWO, AND THEY'D BE JUST RIGHT.
BUT AS YOU MIGHT EXPECT FROM TWO PEOPLE WHO ARE REACHING FOR THE SAME PLACE...
...THEY ARE SOMEWHAT ALIKE.
CAROL! FATHER!
I KNOW HOW...
...THE MAGIC COMPASS WORKS.
I FINALLY FIGURED IT OUT!
REALLY, BROTHER?
I SURE DID! YOU SEE, THIS COMPASS HAS A FALSE BOTTOM...

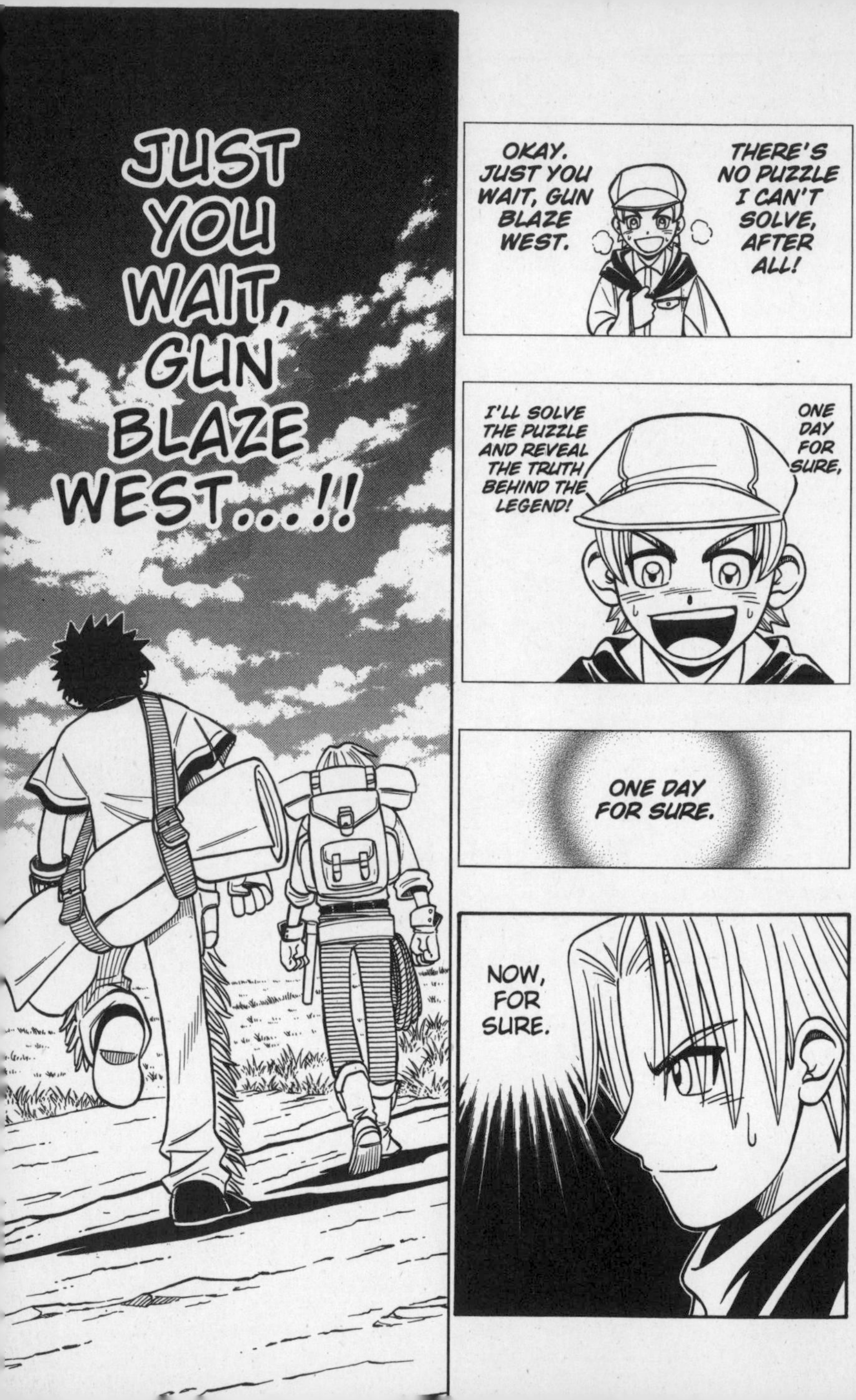
THERE'S NO PUZZLE I CAN'T SOLVE, AFTER ALL!
OKAY. JUST YOU WAIT, GUN BLAZE WEST.
ONE DAY FOR SURE,
I'LL SOLVE THE PUZZLE AND REVEAL THE TRUTH BEHIND THE LEGEND!
ONE DAY FOR SURE.
NOW, FOR SURE.
JUST YOU WAIT, GUN BLAZE WEST...!!

CONCEPT: IN TANDEM WITH MY INTENTION TO MAKE VIU A SHONEN-TYPE MAIN CHARACTER, I THOUGHT OF MAKING MARCUS A PATHETIC UNDERDOG, WHO LOOKED LIKE A LOSER, WASN'T STRONG, AND WHO WAS MORE OR LESS A CHARACTER UNLIKE THOSE IN SHONEN STORIES.

ALTHOUGH THE BASICS FOR AN ADULT CHARACTER IN HIS POSITION IS SOMEONE COOL AND STRONG ENOUGH FOR THE MAIN CHARACTER TO ADMIRE AND ASPIRE TO BECOME, SOMEHOW FOR MARCUS, THAT WAS THE IMAGE THAT POPPED INTO MY MIND FROM THE VERY START. AN ADULT THAT ACTS LIKE A CHILD AND A CHLD THAT ACTS LIKE AN ADULT--THAT WAS THE RELATIONSHIP BETWEEN VIU AND MARCUS THAT I WANTED TO PORTRAY.

PERSONALLY, MARCUS IS A CHARACTER I REALLY LIKE, AND I'D LIKE, IN SOME WAY OR FORM, TO BRING HIM BACK SOMEHOW.

IMAGE SOURCE: AS WAS THE CASE WITH LITTLE VIU, THE IMAGE SOURCE FOR MARCUS WAS JOHNNY BOY'S DAD, WHO APPEARED IN THE PROVIDER O COMMERCIALS. HE SEEMED TOTALLY GOOD FOR NOTHING, BUT HE GOT ALONG WITH HIS CHILDREN AND NEVER SPOILED THEM. SOMEHOW, I THINK THAT'S GREAT.

# CHARACTER FILE #02

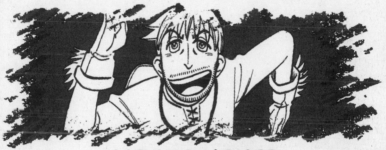

# MARCUS HOMER

ANYWAY, I REALLY LOVED THE PROVIDER O COMMERCIALS. I SHOULD HAVE RECORDED THEM. TOO BAD. I REGRET IT NOW.

DESIGN: AIMING FOR THE LOOK OF A LOSER, I CHOSE THE ONE THAT HAD THE MOST INTERESTING FLAVOR FROM AMONG ABOUT FOUR DESIGNS.

THE SCRUFFY BEARD, HUNCHED SHOULDERS, LONG TRUNK, SHORT LEGS AND BOWLEGGED STANCE MAKE IT A DESIGN FEMALE READERS WOULD LIKELY SHY AWAY FROM, BUT IT WAS QUITE WELL-RECEIVED AMONG MY FRIENDS AND ACQUAINTANCES. I ALSO LIKED IT A GREAT DEAL AS WELL.

WHILE MARCUS'S ATTIRE WAS SLIGHTLY DIFFERENT FROM TYPICAL GUNSLIN-GER WEAR, HE LOOKED LIKE A GUNSLINGER--THAT WAS WHAT I STROVE FOR AND CREATED BY STUDYING MANY RESOURCES. THE FOCUS IS ON THE FRONT THIGH POCKETS WHICH LOOK LIKE SOMETHING ONE MIGHT EXPECT, BUT DON'T SEE, ON TODAY'S WEAR.

ON A SIDE NOTE, AS I OPEN UP MY SKETCHBOOK TO THE FIRST DRAWINGS OF MARCUS, I NOTICE HE LOOKS A BIT LIKE SOMEONE I AM DEEPLY INDEBTED TO. (THE ACTUAL PERSON IS NOT A LOSER OF A MAN LIKE MARCUS. IN FACT, HE IS THE EXACT OPPOSITE: A NEAT GUY.)

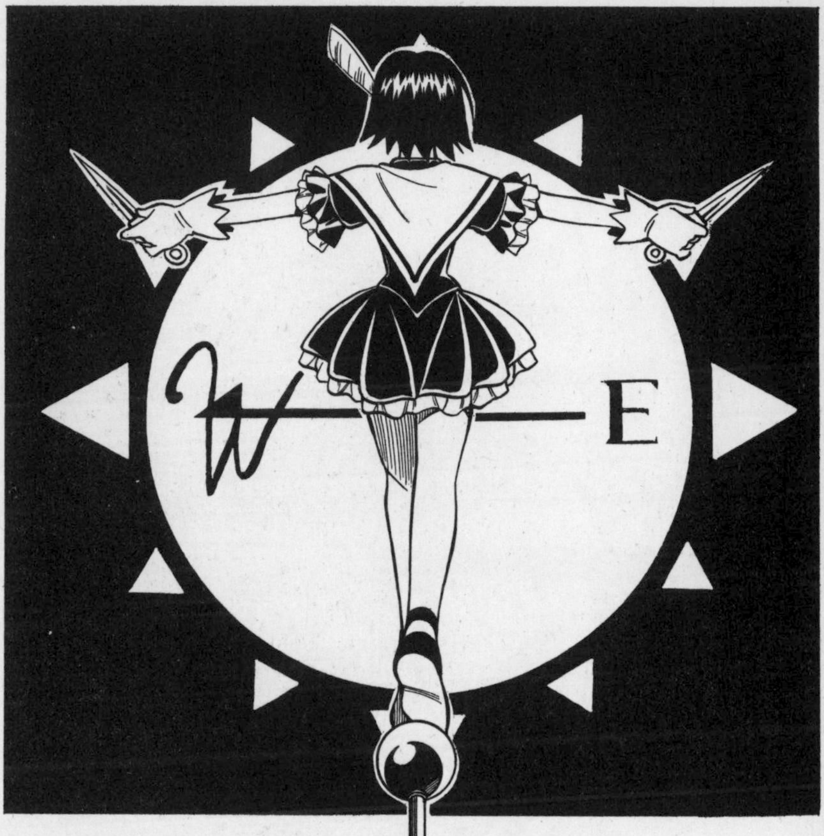
W
E

# CHAPTER 11: CIRCUS WONDER

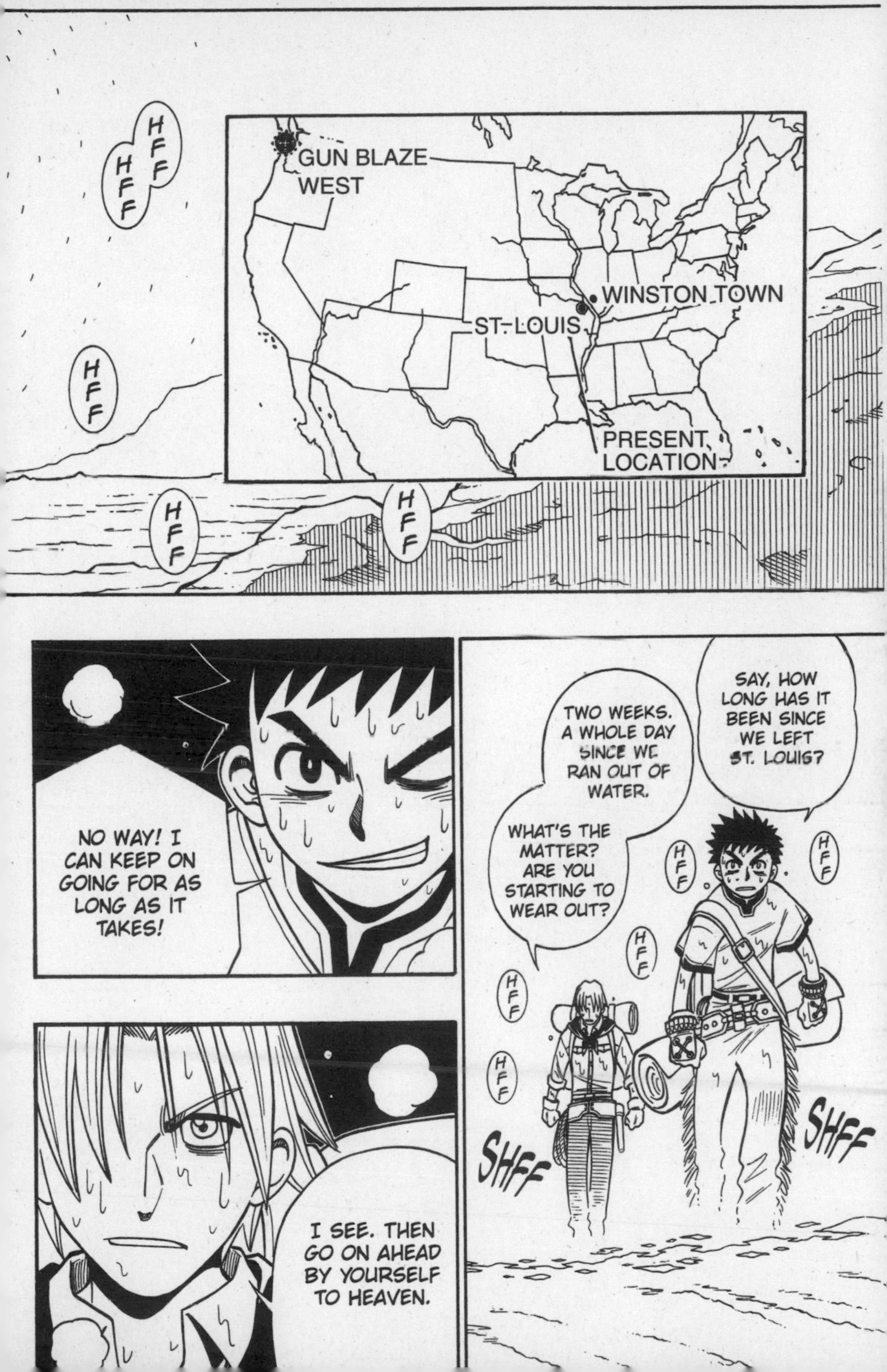
HFF HFF
HFF
GUN BLAZE WEST
WINSTON TOWN
ST. LOUIS
PRESENT LOCATION
HFF
HFF
SAY, HOW LONG HAS IT BEEN SINCE WE LEFT ST. LOUIS?
TWO WEEKS. A WHOLE DAY SINCE WE RAN OUT OF WATER.
WHAT'S THE MATTER? ARE YOU STARTING TO WEAR OUT?
HFF
HFF
HFF
HFF
HFF
SHFF
SHFF
NO WAY! I CAN KEEP ON GOING FOR AS LONG AS IT TAKES!
I SEE. THEN GO ON AHEAD BY YOURSELF TO HEAVEN.

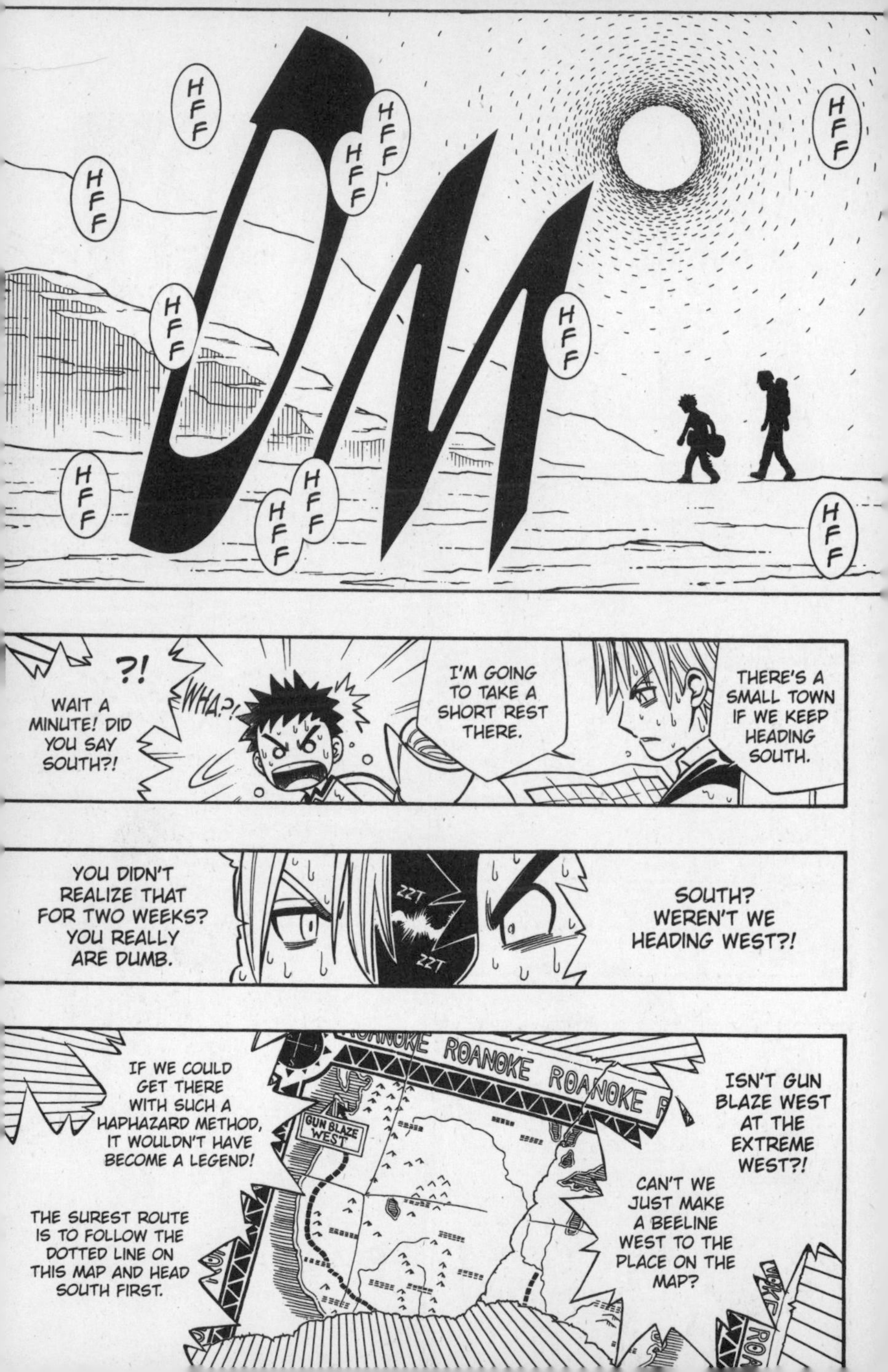
HFF
HFF
HFF
HFF
DM
HFF
HFF
HFF
HFF
HFF
HFF
HFF
HFF
THERE'S A SMALL TOWN IF WE KEEP HEADING SOUTH.
I'M GOING TO TAKE A SHORT REST THERE.
WHA?!
?!
WAIT A MINUTE! DID YOU SAY SOUTH?!
SOUTH? WEREN'T WE HEADING WEST?!
ZZT
ZZT
YOU DIDN'T REALIZE THAT FOR TWO WEEKS? YOU REALLY ARE DUMB.
ISN'T GUN BLAZE WEST AT THE EXTREME WEST?!
CAN'T WE JUST MAKE A BEELINE WEST TO THE PLACE ON THE MAP?
ROANOKE ROANOKE ROANOKE
GUN BLAZE WEST
IF WE COULD GET THERE WITH SUCH A HAPHAZARD METHOD, IT WOULDN'T HAVE BECOME A LEGEND!
THE SUREST ROUTE IS TO FOLLOW THE DOTTED LINE ON THIS MAP AND HEAD SOUTH FIRST.

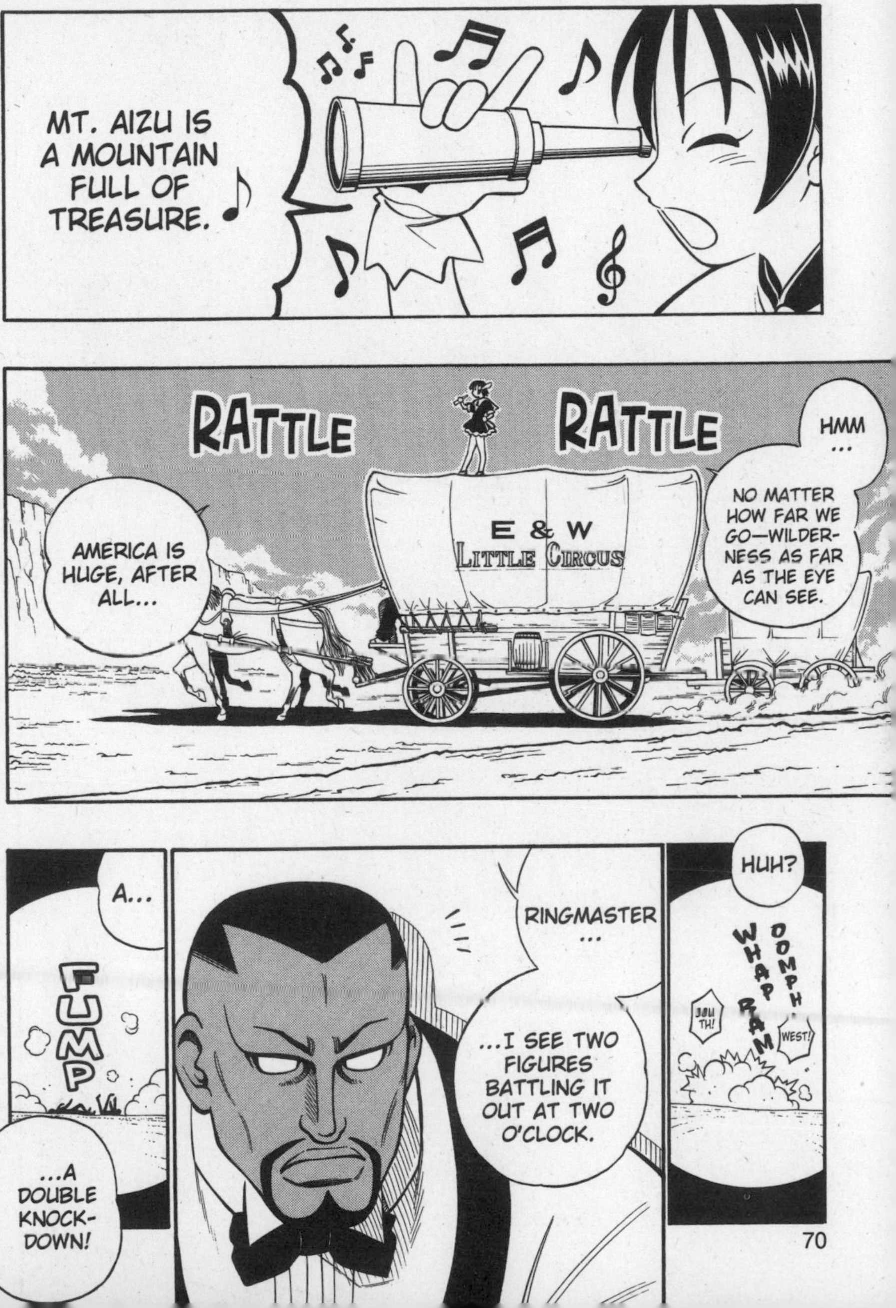
MT. AIZU IS A MOUNTAIN FULL OF TREASURE.
HMM...
NO MATTER HOW FAR WE GO—WILDER-NESS AS FAR AS THE EYE CAN SEE.
RATTLE
RATTLE
E & W LITTLE CIRCUS
AMERICA IS HUGE, AFTER ALL...
HUH?
OOMPH
WHAP
BAM
WEST!
RINGMASTER...
...I SEE TWO FIGURES BATTLING IT OUT AT TWO O'CLOCK.
A...
FUMP
...A DOUBLE KNOCK-DOWN!

READ THIS WAY

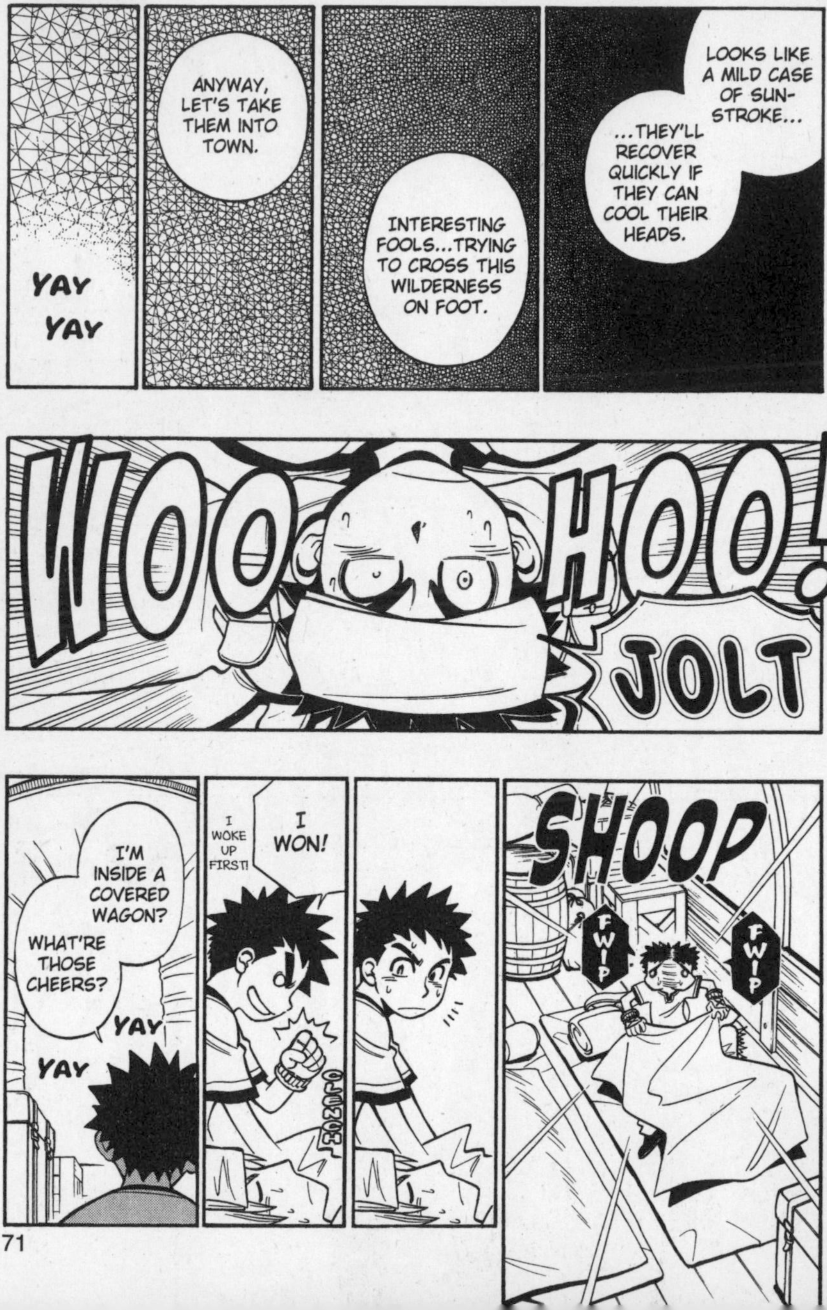
LOOKS LIKE A MILD CASE OF SUN-STROKE...
...THEY'LL RECOVER QUICKLY IF THEY CAN COOL THEIR HEADS.
INTERESTING FOOLS...TRYING TO CROSS THIS WILDERNESS ON FOOT.
ANYWAY, LET'S TAKE THEM INTO TOWN.
YAY
YAY
WOO HOO!
JOLT
SHOOP
FWIP
FWIP
I WON!
I WOKE UP FIRST!
CLENCH
I'M INSIDE A COVERED WAGON?
WHAT'RE THOSE CHEERS?
YAY
YAY

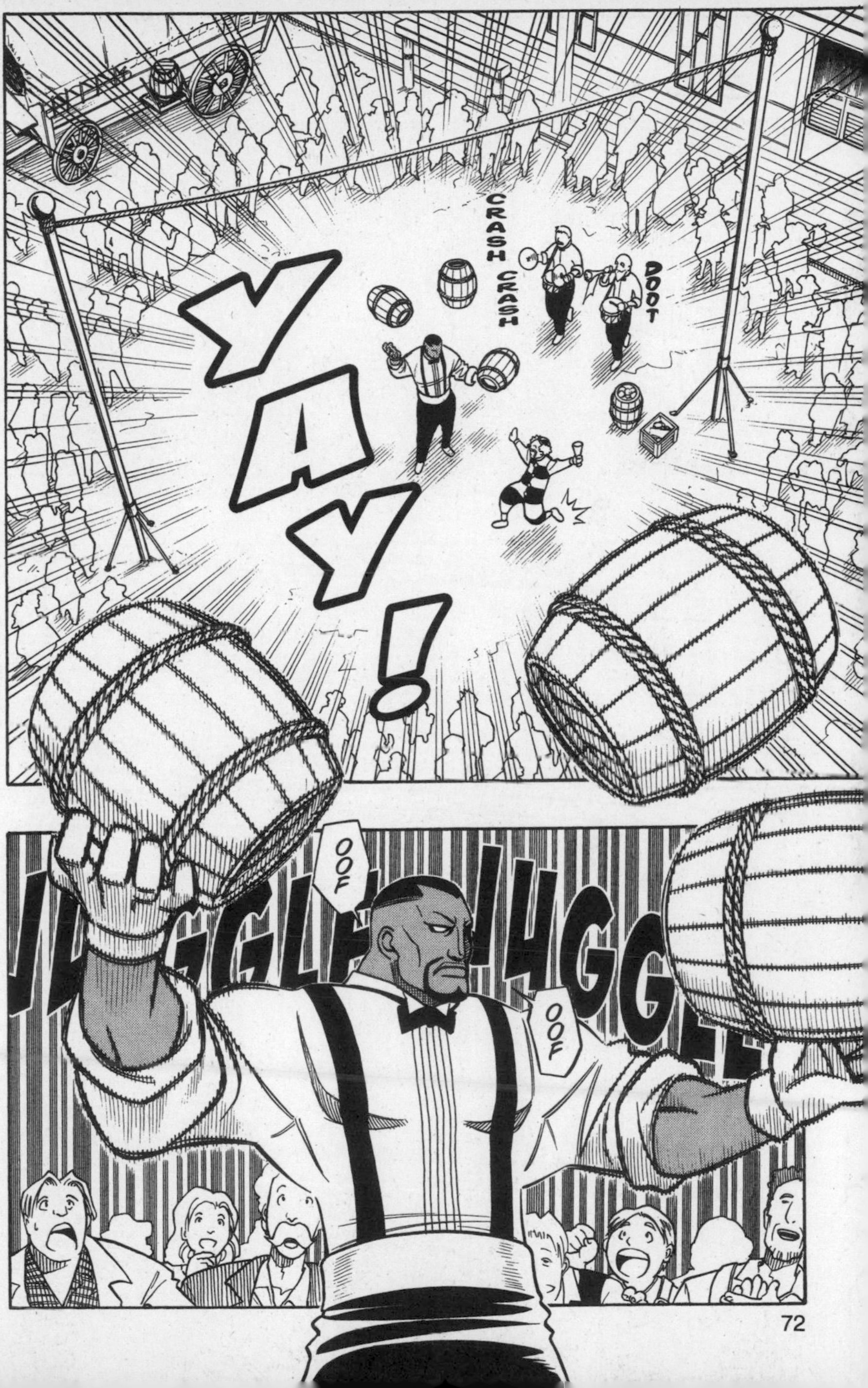
DOOT
CRASH CRASH
YAY!
OOF
OOF

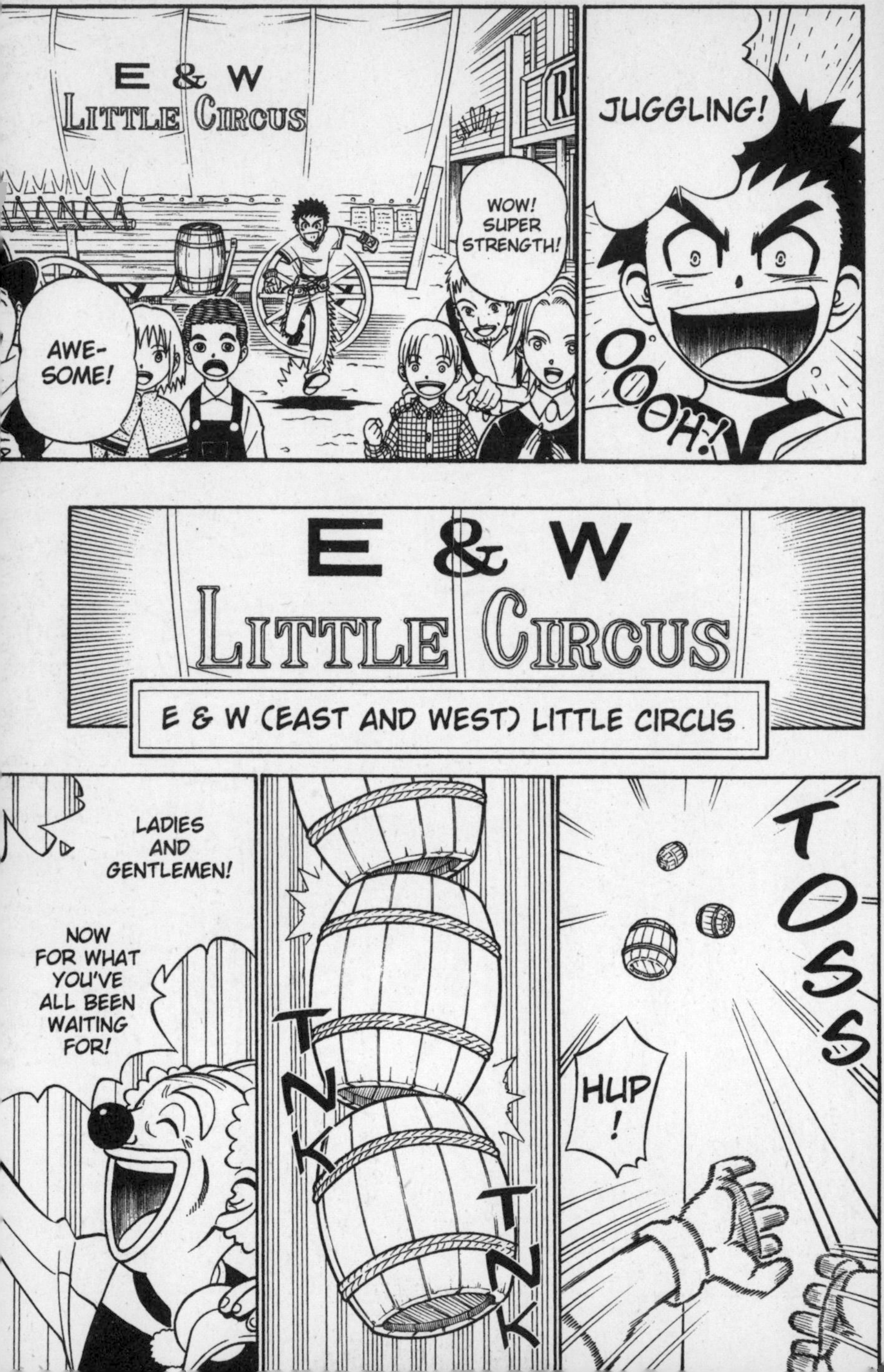
E & W
LITTLE CIRCUS
WOW! SUPER STRENGTH!
AWE-SOME!
JUGGLING!
OOOOH!
E & W
LITTLE CIRCUS
E & W (EAST AND WEST) LITTLE CIRCUS
LADIES AND GENTLEMEN!
NOW FOR WHAT YOU'VE ALL BEEN WAITING FOR!
TNK
TNK
HUP!
TOSS

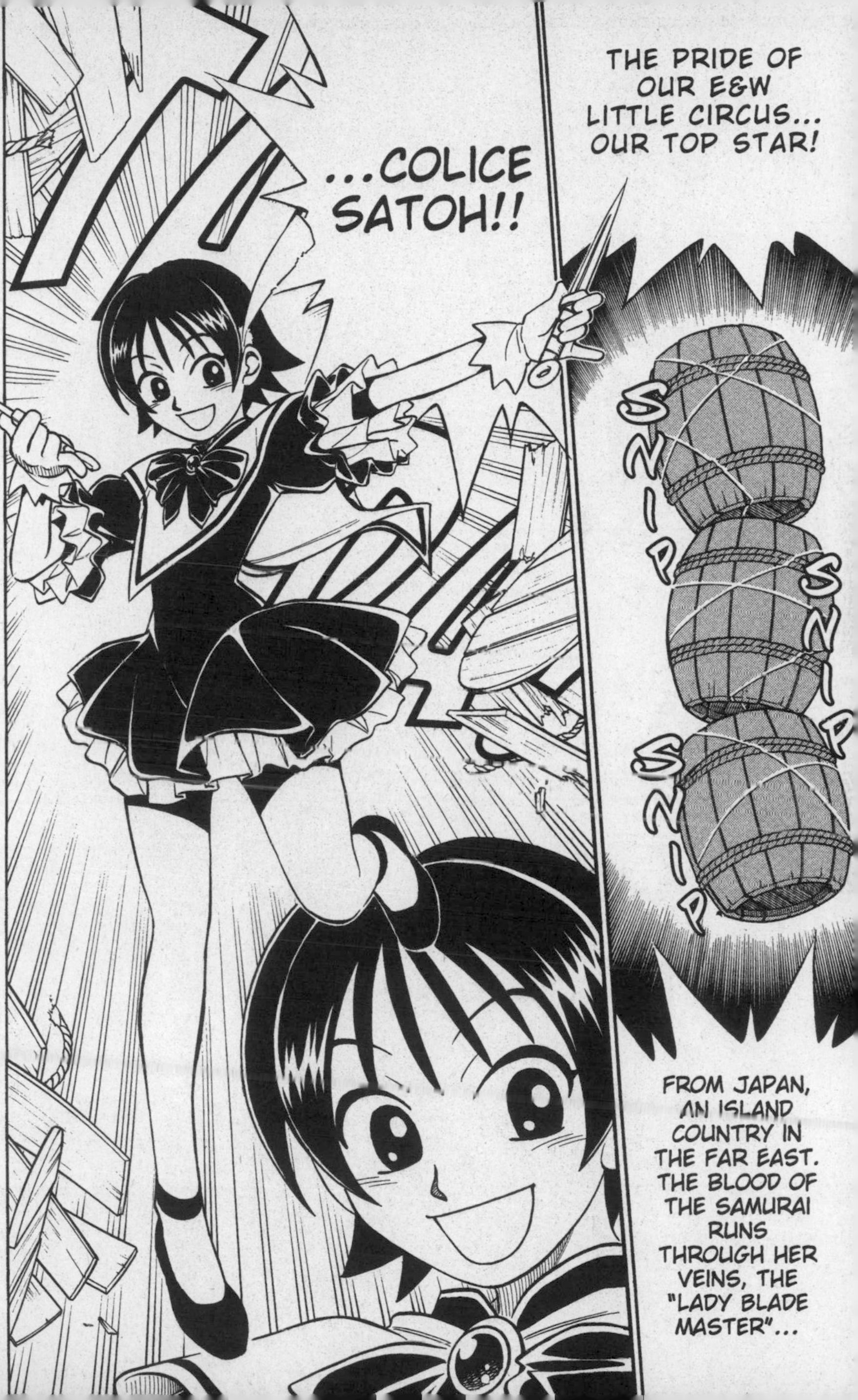
THE PRIDE OF OUR E&W LITTLE CIRCUS... OUR TOP STAR!
SNIP
SNIP
SNIP
FROM JAPAN, AN ISLAND COUNTRY IN THE FAR EAST. THE BLOOD OF THE SAMURAI RUNS THROUGH HER VEINS, THE "LADY BLADE MASTER"...
...COLICE SATOH!!

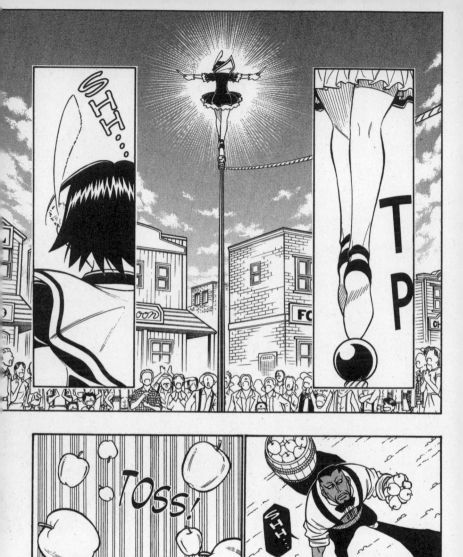

SHH...

T
P

TOSS!

SHH...

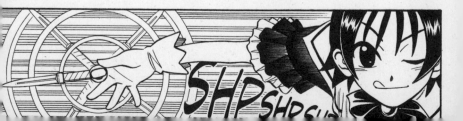

SHP SHP SHP

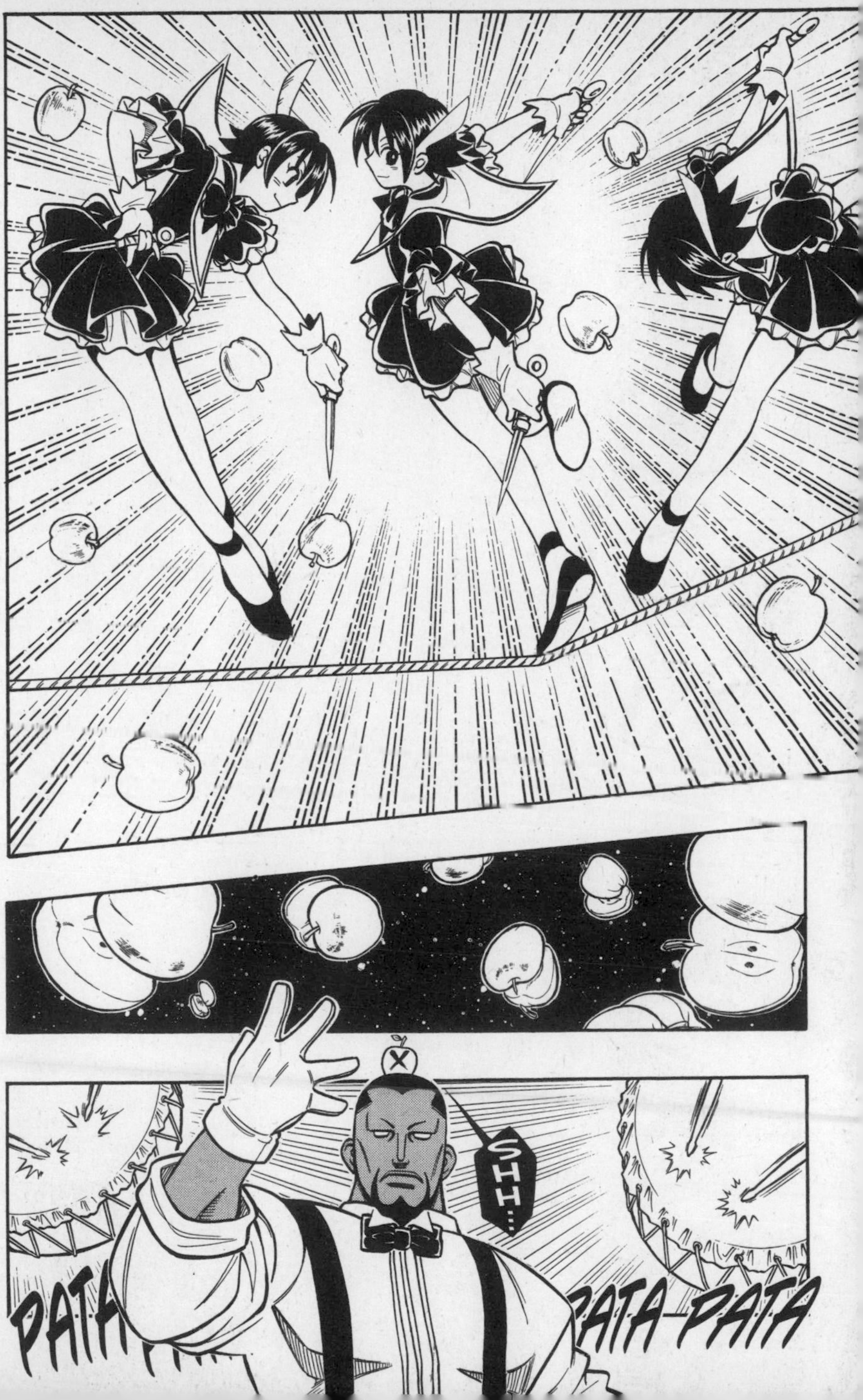
SHH...
PATA-PATA
PATA...

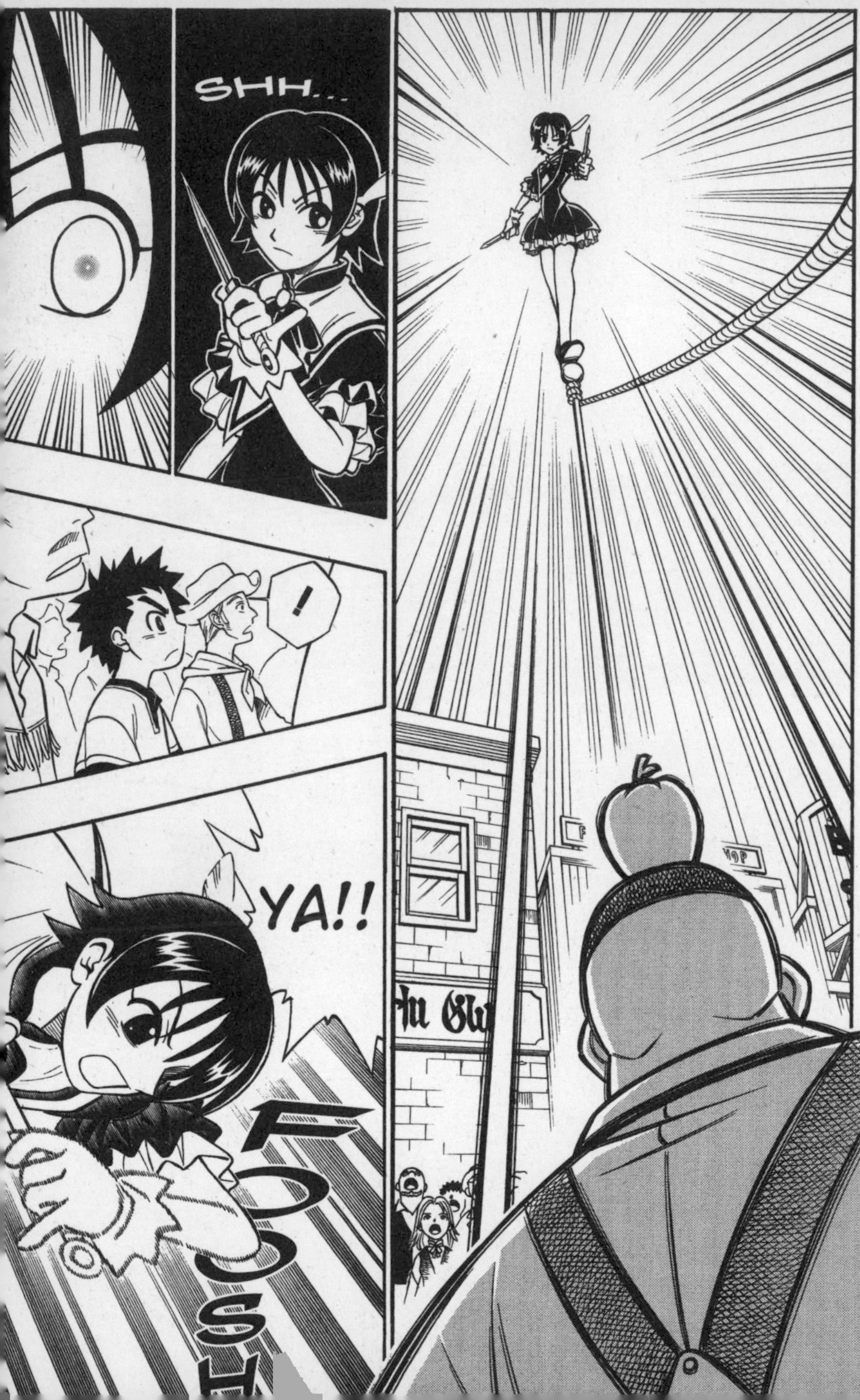
SHH...
!
YA!!
FOOSH

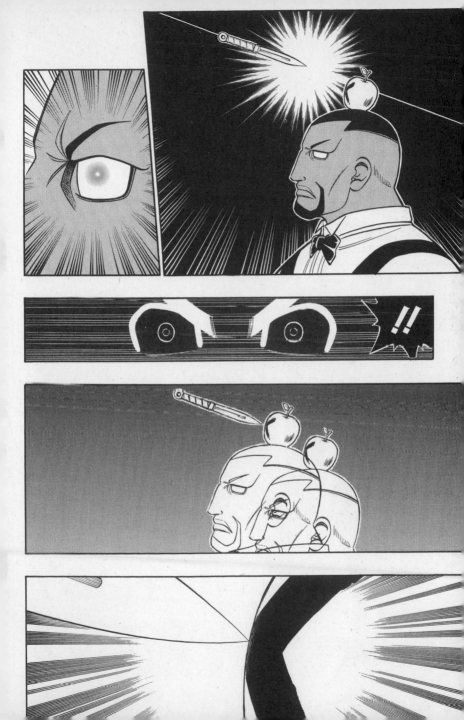

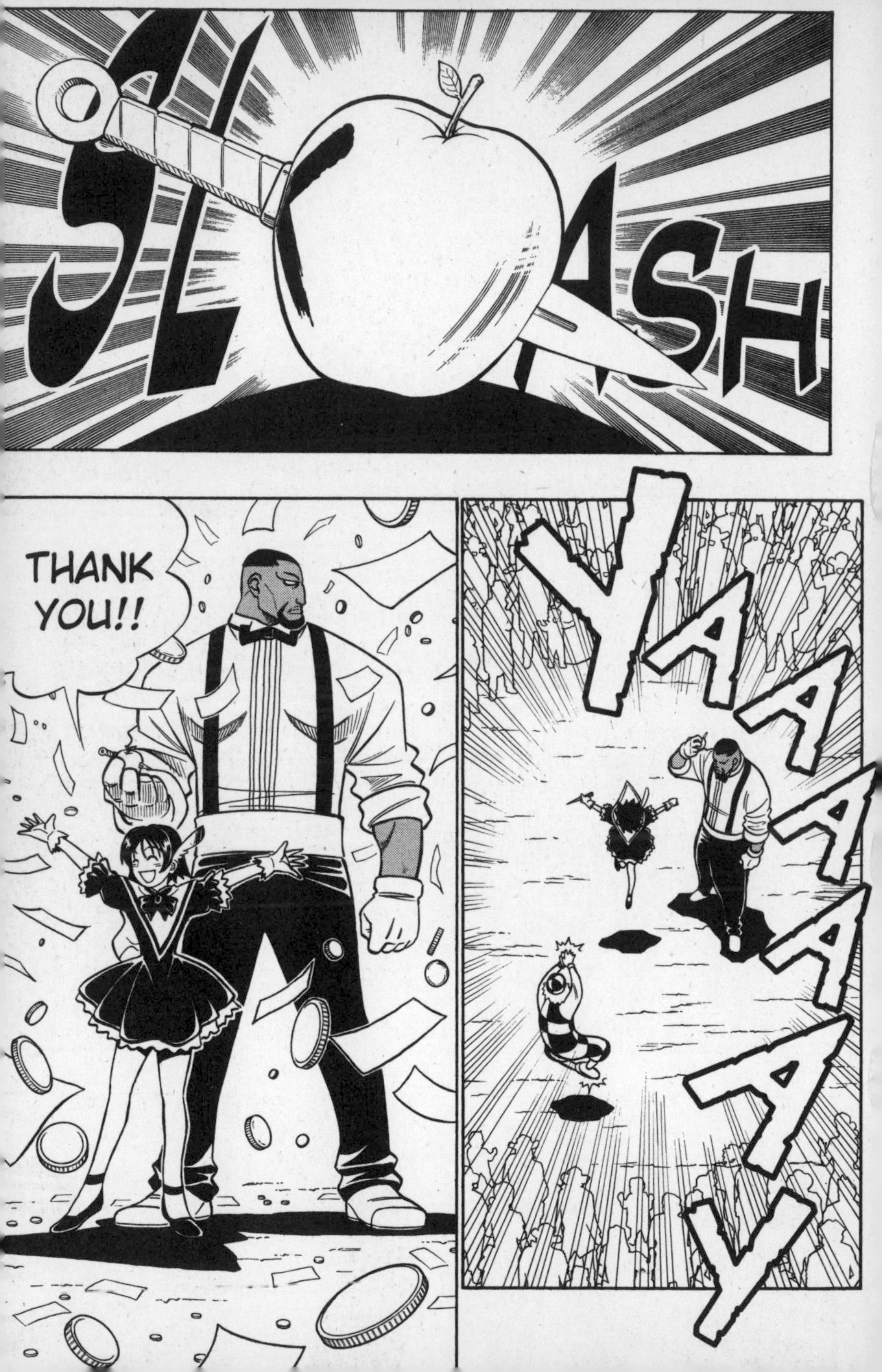
SLASH
YAAAAAY
THANK YOU!!

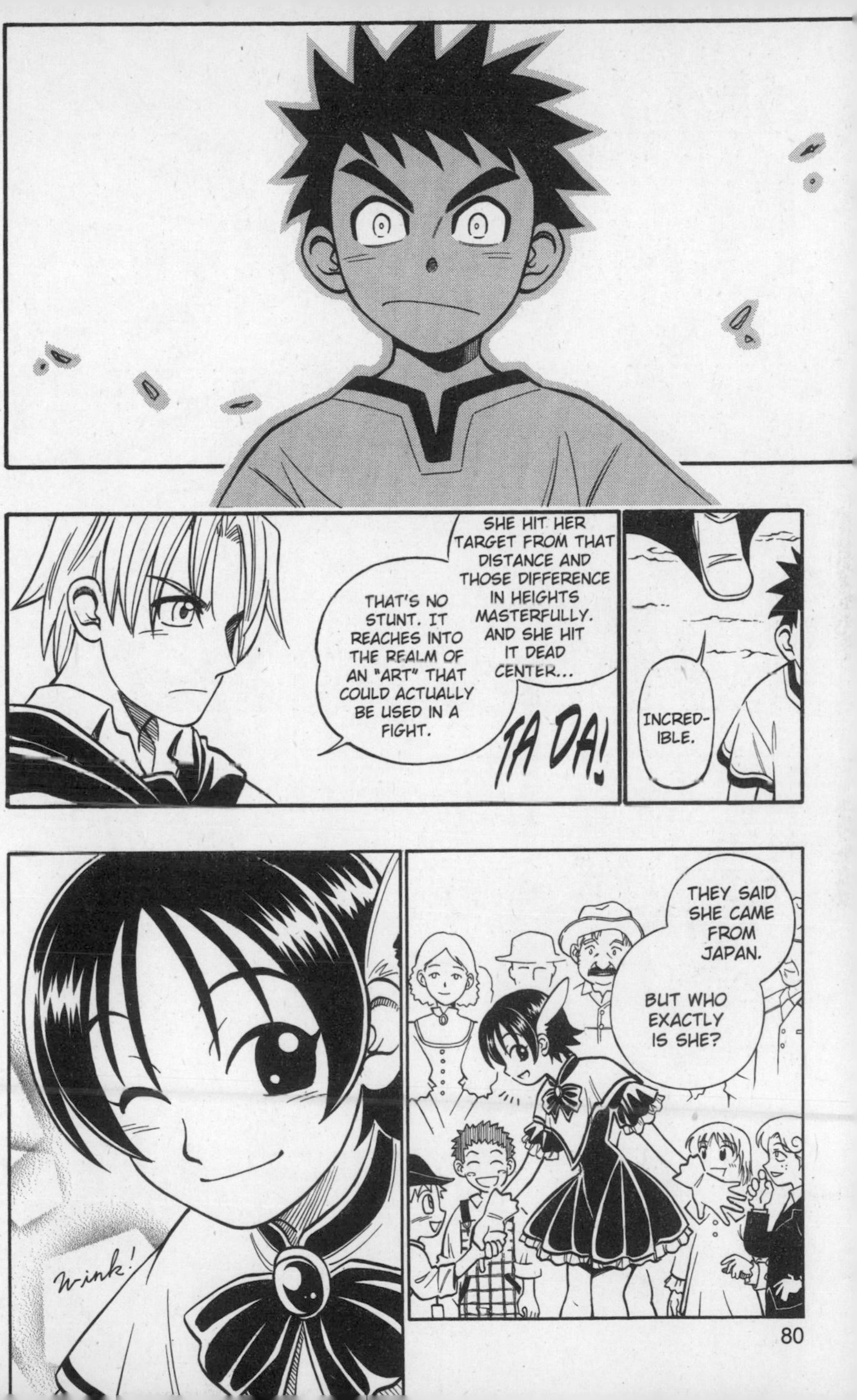
INCRED-IBLE.
SHE HIT HER TARGET FROM THAT DISTANCE AND THOSE DIFFERENCE IN HEIGHTS MASTERFULLY. AND SHE HIT IT DEAD CENTER...
THAT'S NO STUNT. IT REACHES INTO THE REALM OF AN "ART" THAT COULD ACTUALLY BE USED IN A FIGHT.
TA DA!
THEY SAID SHE CAME FROM JAPAN.
BUT WHO EXACTLY IS SHE?
Wink!

READ THIS WAY

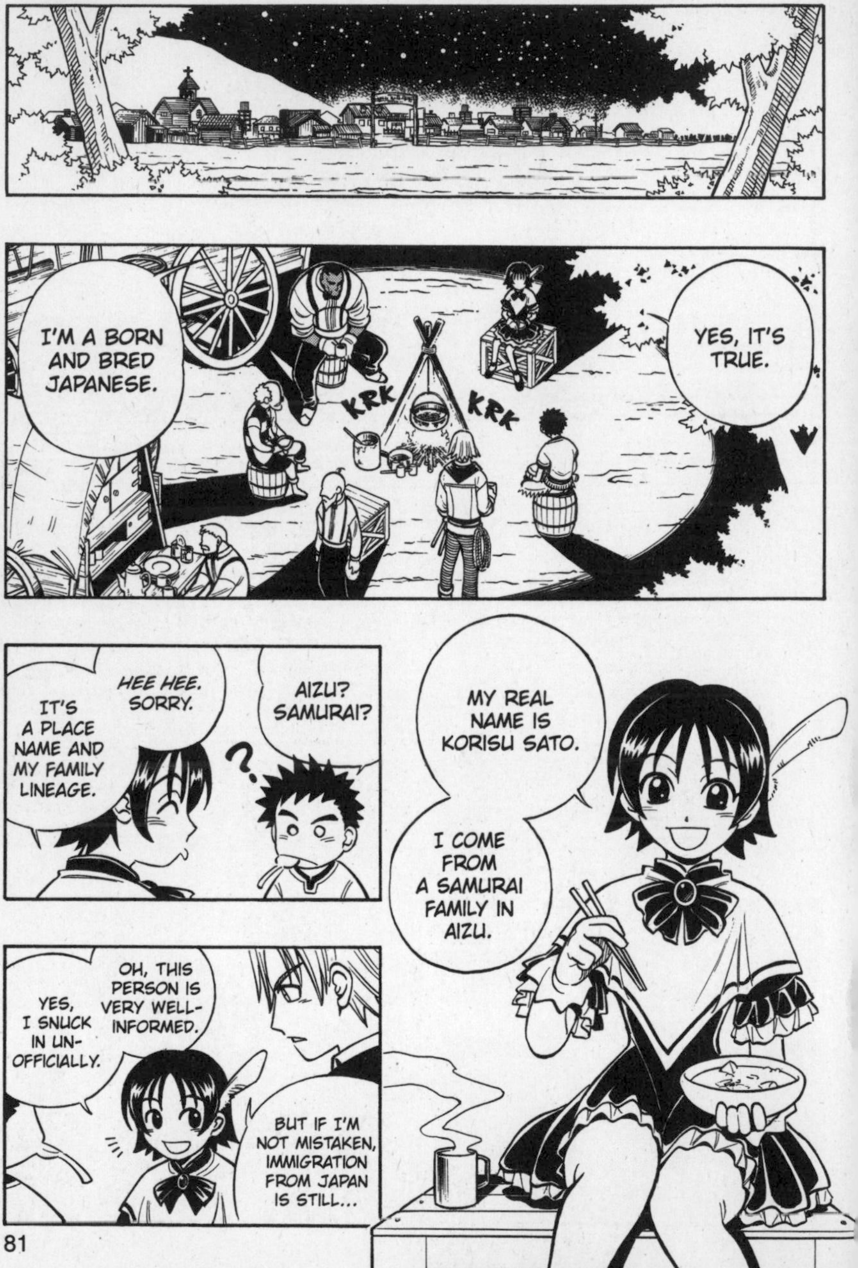
YES, IT'S TRUE.
I'M A BORN AND BRED JAPANESE.
KRK
KRK
MY REAL NAME IS KORISU SATO.
I COME FROM A SAMURAI FAMILY IN AIZU.
AIZU? SAMURAI?
HEE HEE. SORRY.
IT'S A PLACE NAME AND MY FAMILY LINEAGE.
BUT IF I'M NOT MISTAKEN, IMMIGRATION FROM JAPAN IS STILL...
OH, THIS PERSON IS VERY WELL-INFORMED.
YES, I SNUCK IN UN-OFFICIALLY.

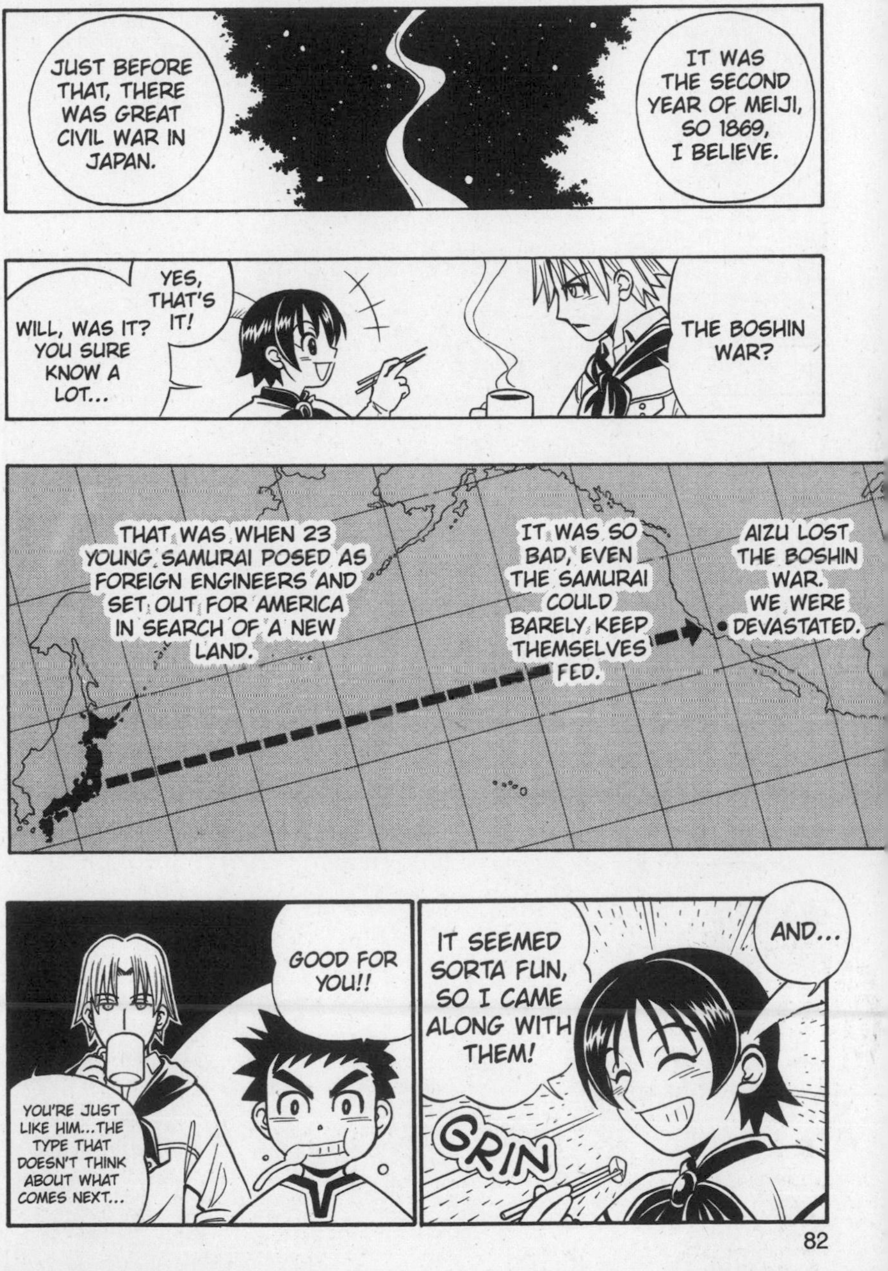
IT WAS THE SECOND YEAR OF MEIJI, SO 1869, I BELIEVE.
JUST BEFORE THAT, THERE WAS GREAT CIVIL WAR IN JAPAN.
THE BOSHIN WAR?
YES, THAT'S IT!
WILL, WAS IT? YOU SURE KNOW A LOT...
AIZU LOST THE BOSHIN WAR. WE WERE DEVASTATED.
IT WAS SO BAD, EVEN THE SAMURAI COULD BARELY KEEP THEMSELVES FED.
THAT WAS WHEN 23 YOUNG SAMURAI POSED AS FOREIGN ENGINEERS AND SET OUT FOR AMERICA IN SEARCH OF A NEW LAND.
AND...
IT SEEMED SORTA FUN, SO I CAME ALONG WITH THEM!
GRIN
GOOD FOR YOU!!
YOU'RE JUST LIKE HIM...THE TYPE THAT DOESN'T THINK ABOUT WHAT COMES NEXT...

READ THIS WAY

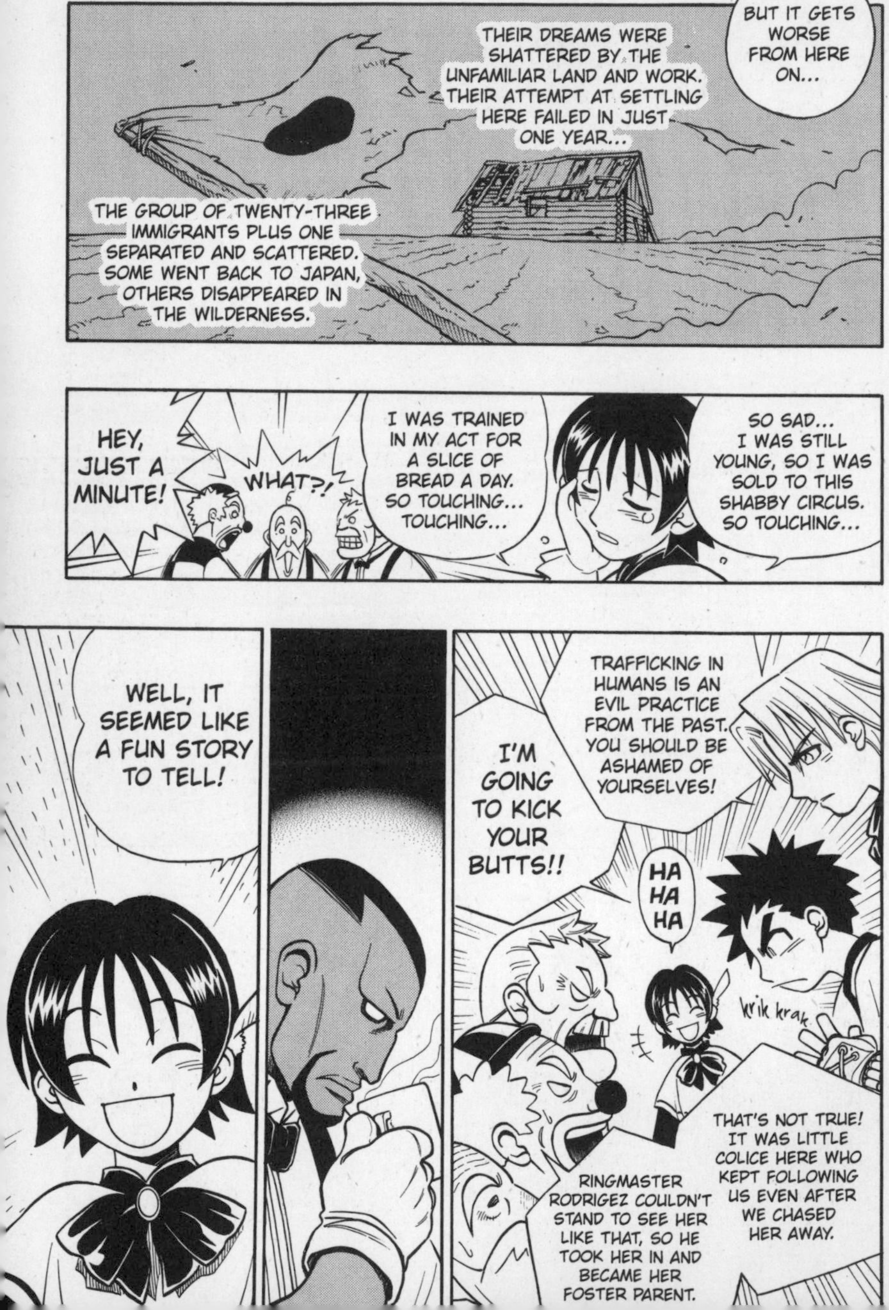
BUT IT GETS WORSE FROM HERE ON...
THEIR DREAMS WERE SHATTERED BY THE UNFAMILIAR LAND AND WORK. THEIR ATTEMPT AT SETTLING HERE FAILED IN JUST ONE YEAR...
THE GROUP OF TWENTY-THREE IMMIGRANTS PLUS ONE SEPARATED AND SCATTERED. SOME WENT BACK TO JAPAN, OTHERS DISAPPEARED IN THE WILDERNESS.
SO SAD... I WAS STILL YOUNG, SO I WAS SOLD TO THIS SHABBY CIRCUS. SO TOUCHING...
I WAS TRAINED IN MY ACT FOR A SLICE OF BREAD A DAY. SO TOUCHING... TOUCHING...
WHAT?!
HEY, JUST A MINUTE!
TRAFFICKING IN HUMANS IS AN EVIL PRACTICE FROM THE PAST. YOU SHOULD BE ASHAMED OF YOURSELVES!
I'M GOING TO KICK YOUR BUTTS!!
HA HA HA
krik krak
THAT'S NOT TRUE! IT WAS LITTLE COLICE HERE WHO KEPT FOLLOWING US EVEN AFTER WE CHASED HER AWAY.
RINGMASTER RODRIGEZ COULDN'T STAND TO SEE HER LIKE THAT, SO HE TOOK HER IN AND BECAME HER FOSTER PARENT.
WELL, IT SEEMED LIKE A FUN STORY TO TELL!

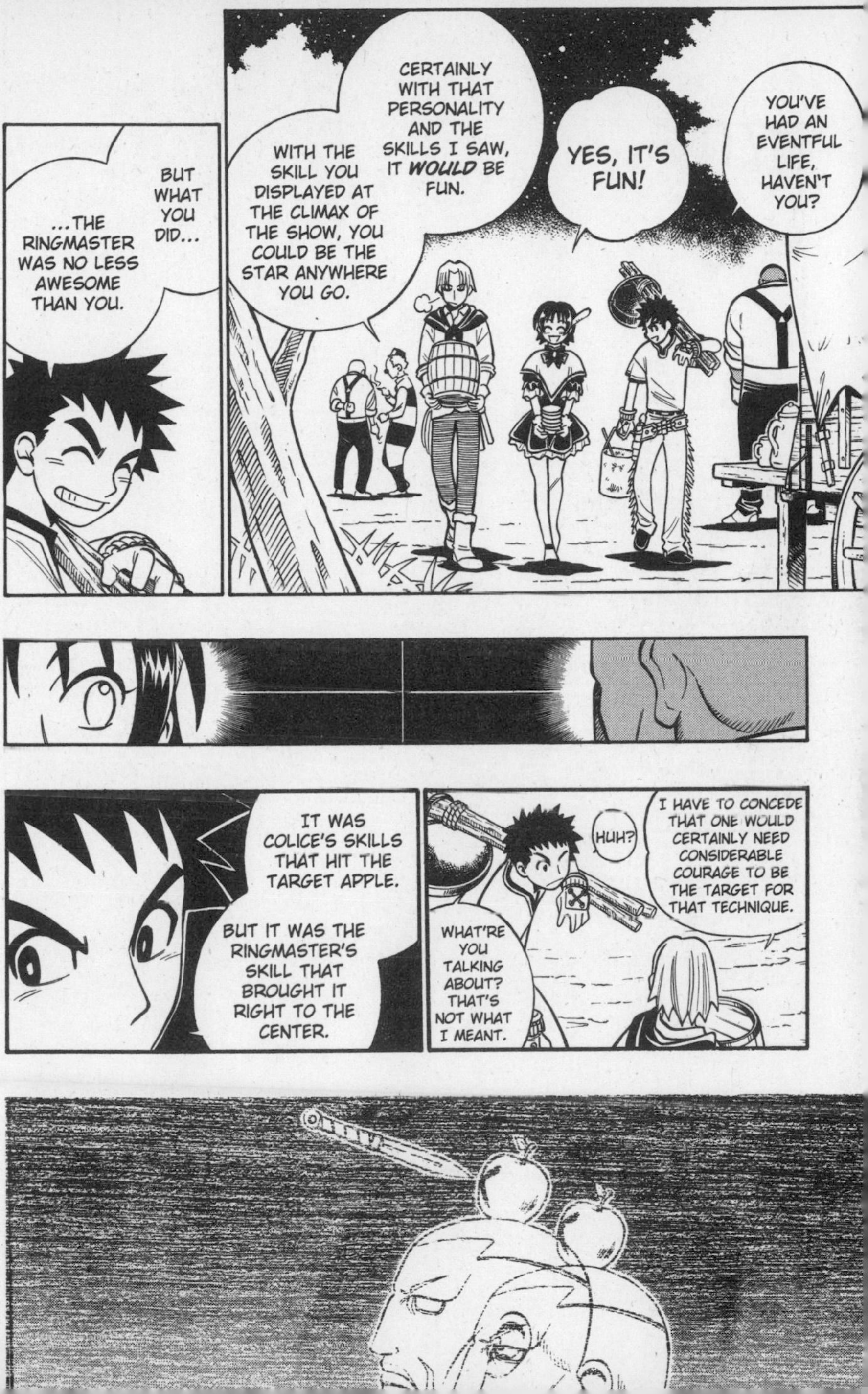
YOU'VE HAD AN EVENTFUL LIFE, HAVEN'T YOU?
YES, IT'S FUN!
CERTAINLY WITH THAT PERSONALITY AND THE SKILLS I SAW, IT *WOULD* BE FUN.
WITH THE SKILL YOU DISPLAYED AT THE CLIMAX OF THE SHOW, YOU COULD BE THE STAR ANYWHERE YOU GO.
BUT WHAT YOU DID...
...THE RINGMASTER WAS NO LESS AWESOME THAN YOU.
I HAVE TO CONCEDE THAT ONE WOULD CERTAINLY NEED CONSIDERABLE COURAGE TO BE THE TARGET FOR THAT TECHNIQUE.
HUH?
WHAT'RE YOU TALKING ABOUT? THAT'S NOT WHAT I MEANT.
IT WAS COLICE'S SKILLS THAT HIT THE TARGET APPLE.
BUT IT WAS THE RINGMASTER'S SKILL THAT BROUGHT IT RIGHT TO THE CENTER.

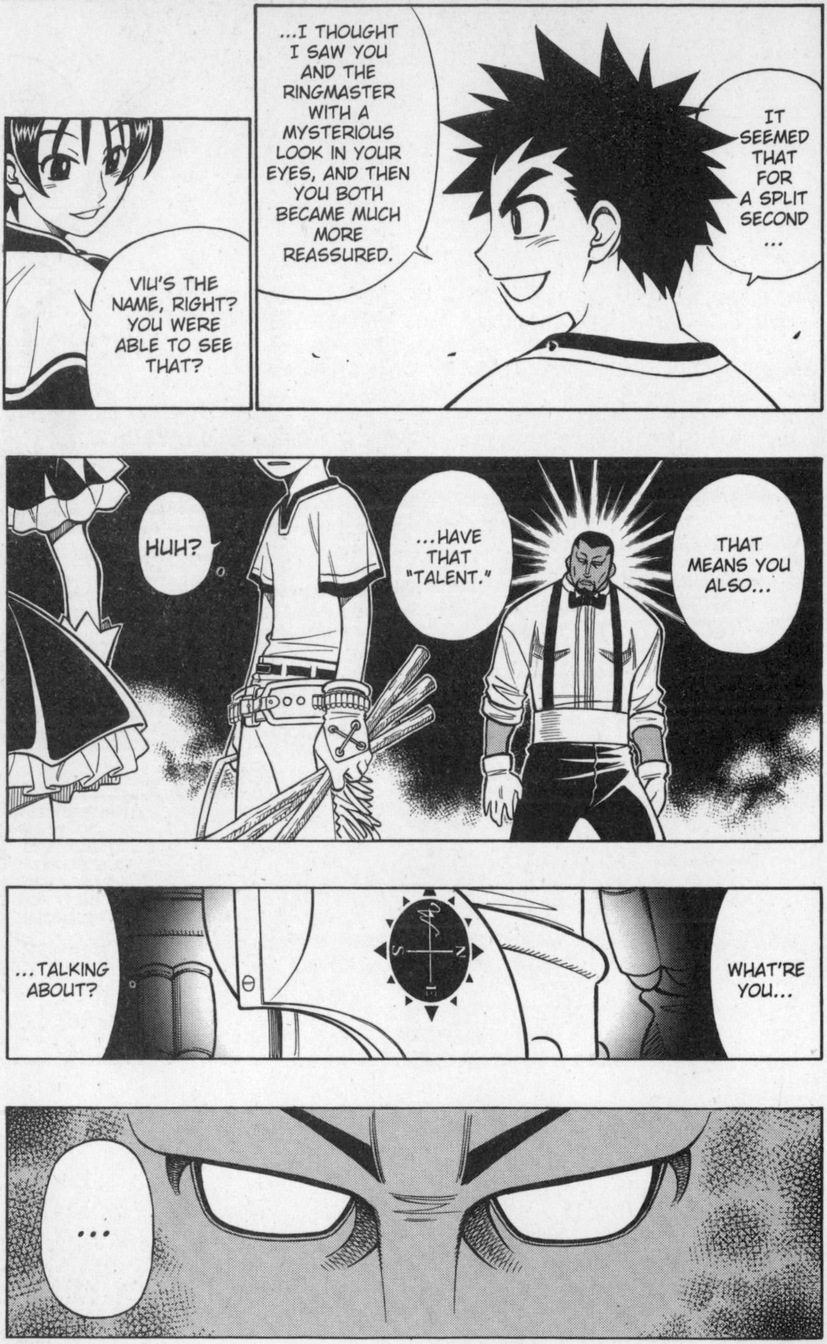
IT SEEMED THAT FOR A SPLIT SECOND...
...I THOUGHT I SAW YOU AND THE RINGMASTER WITH A MYSTERIOUS LOOK IN YOUR EYES, AND THEN YOU BOTH BECAME MUCH MORE REASSURED.
VIU'S THE NAME, RIGHT? YOU WERE ABLE TO SEE THAT?
THAT MEANS YOU ALSO...
...HAVE THAT "TALENT."
HUH?
WHAT'RE YOU...
...TALKING ABOUT?
...

CONCEPT: WITH COLICE, THE HEROINE OF THIS VOLUME, APPEARING QUITE
LATE, CISSY WAS INTRODUCED AS A SUBSTITUTE HEROINE. I MADE HER VERY
CONVENTIONAL IN ORDER FOR HER TO BEAR TWO ROLES: THAT OF LITTLE VIU'S
GUARDIAN AND AN AVERAGE PERSON WITH COMMON SENSE.

AT FIRST, SHE WAS NOT A TEACHER, BUT AT THE SUGGESTION OF MY EDITOR,
WHO WANTED TO INSERT A SCHOOL SCENE IF POSSIBLE, SHE BECAME A
TEACHER. IN THE END, I ONLY INSERTED THAT PARTICULAR SCENE AT THE START
OF NUMBER 2. HMMM...

# CHARACTER FILE #03

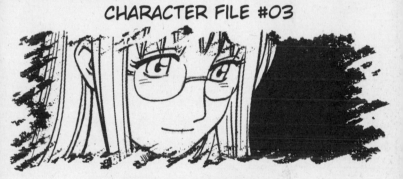

# CISSY BANNES

IMAGE SOURCE: THERE WAS ABSOLUTELY NONE FOR CISSY. THERE WAS NO TIME,
SO I COULDN'T THINK IT THROUGH THOROUGHLY.

DESIGN: I DID THIS PRACTICALLY OFF THE TOP OF MY HEAD BECAUSE I HAD NO
TIME. I DREW HER AS A VERY CONVENTIONAL ANGLO-SAXON WOMAN. GIVEN THAT,
THOUGH, IT'S A DESIGN I SORT OF LIKE.

ON A SIDE NOTE, I PUT GLASSES ON HER TO MATCH THE FACT SHE WAS A
TEACHER, BUT I NEVER CONSIDERED HER A "GLASSES GIRL."

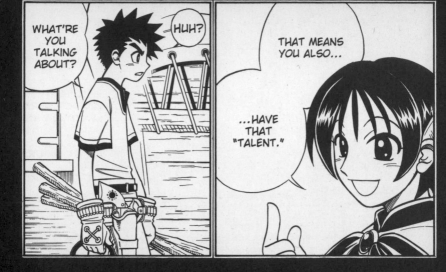

# CHAPTER 12: SIGN TO THE WEST

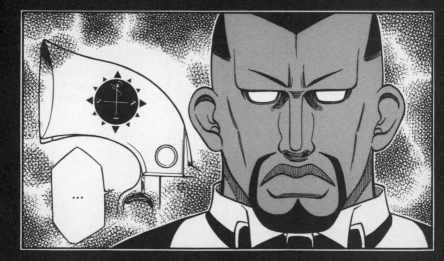

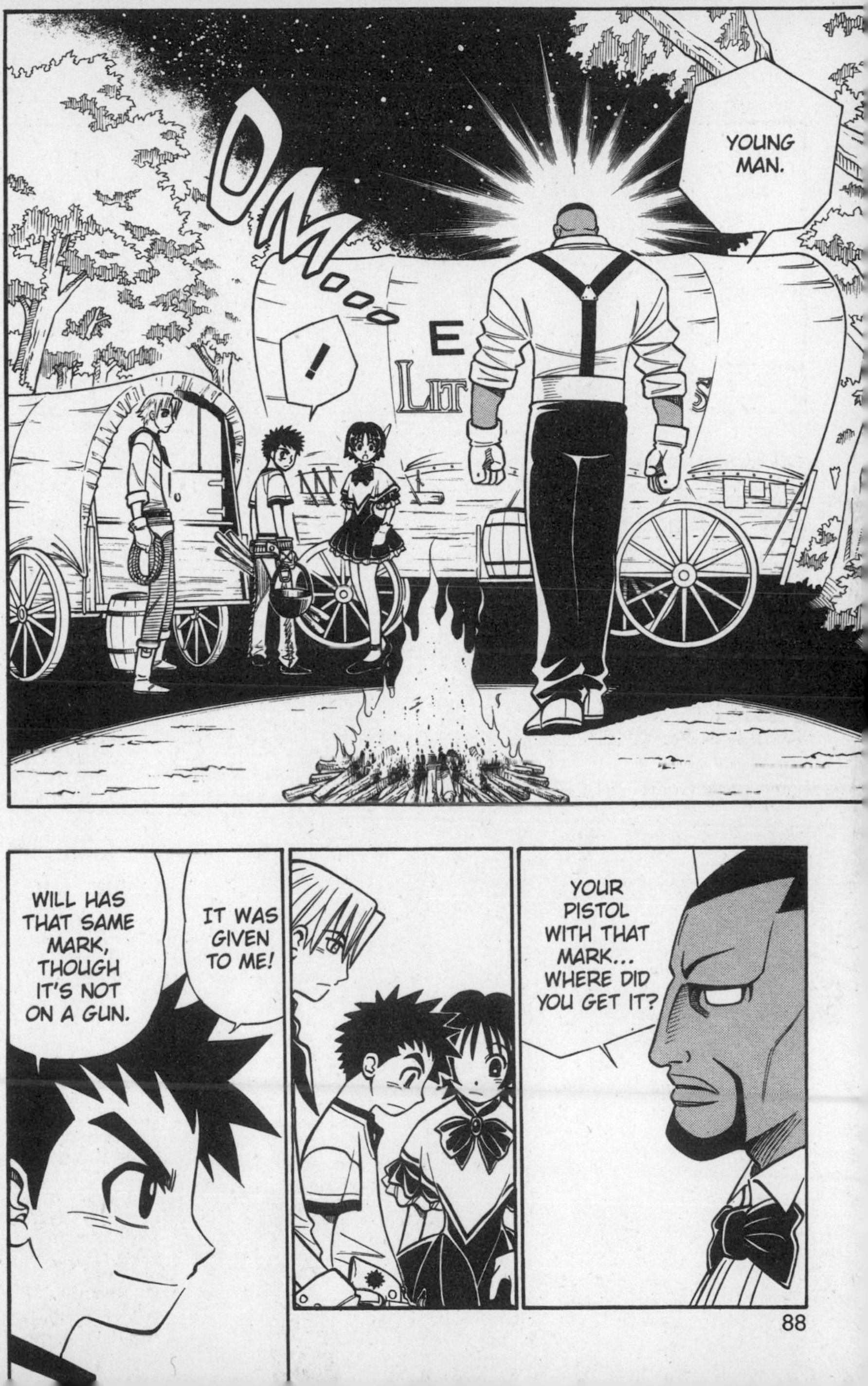

YOUNG MAN.
!
YOUR PISTOL WITH THAT MARK... WHERE DID YOU GET IT?
IT WAS GIVEN TO ME!
WILL HAS THAT SAME MARK, THOUGH IT'S NOT ON A GUN.

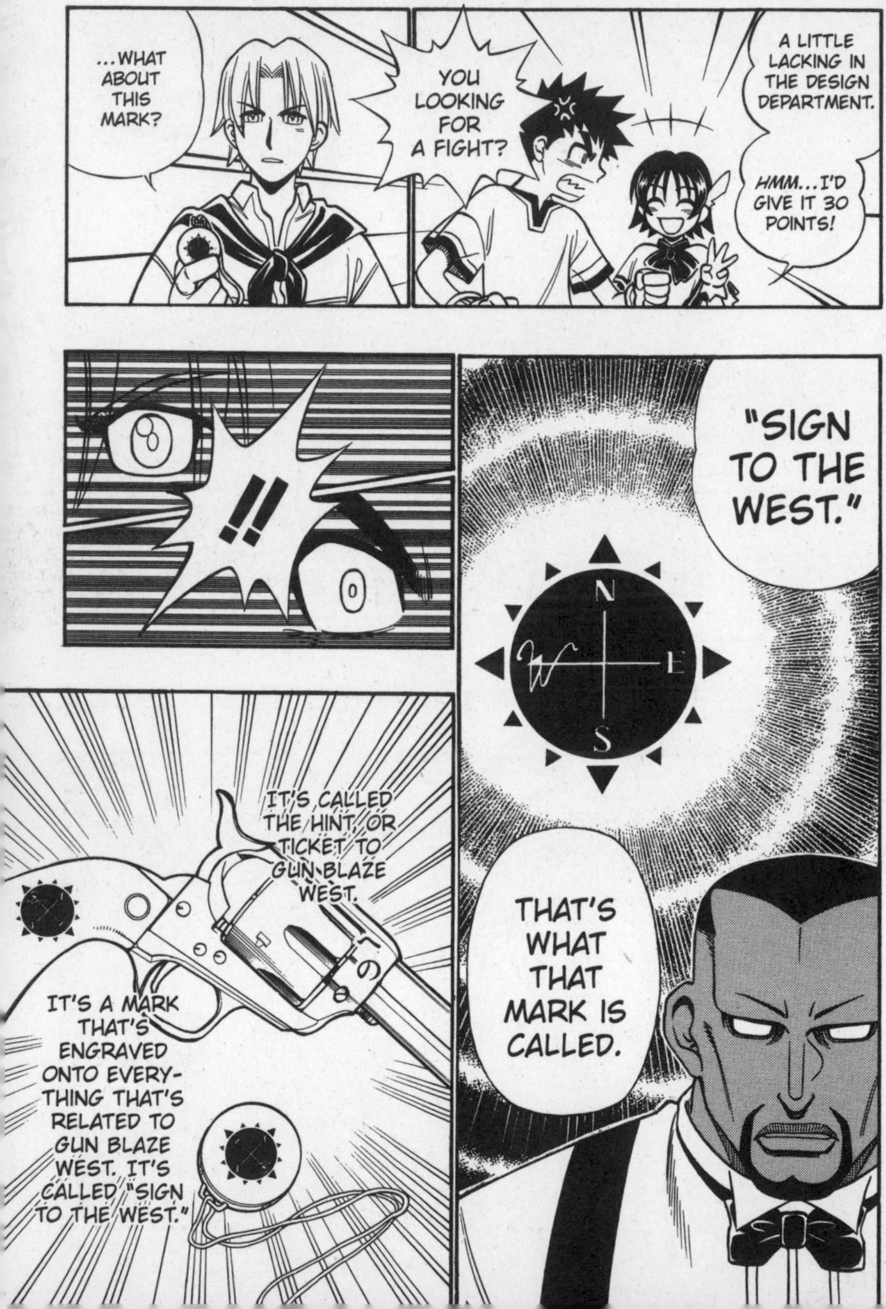
A LITTLE LACKING IN THE DESIGN DEPARTMENT.
HMM...I'D GIVE IT 30 POINTS!
YOU LOOKING FOR A FIGHT?
...WHAT ABOUT THIS MARK?
"SIGN TO THE WEST."
THAT'S WHAT THAT MARK IS CALLED.
!!
IT'S CALLED THE HINT, OR TICKET TO GUN BLAZE WEST.
IT'S A MARK THAT'S ENGRAVED ONTO EVERY-THING THAT'S RELATED TO GUN BLAZE WEST. IT'S CALLED "SIGN TO THE WEST."

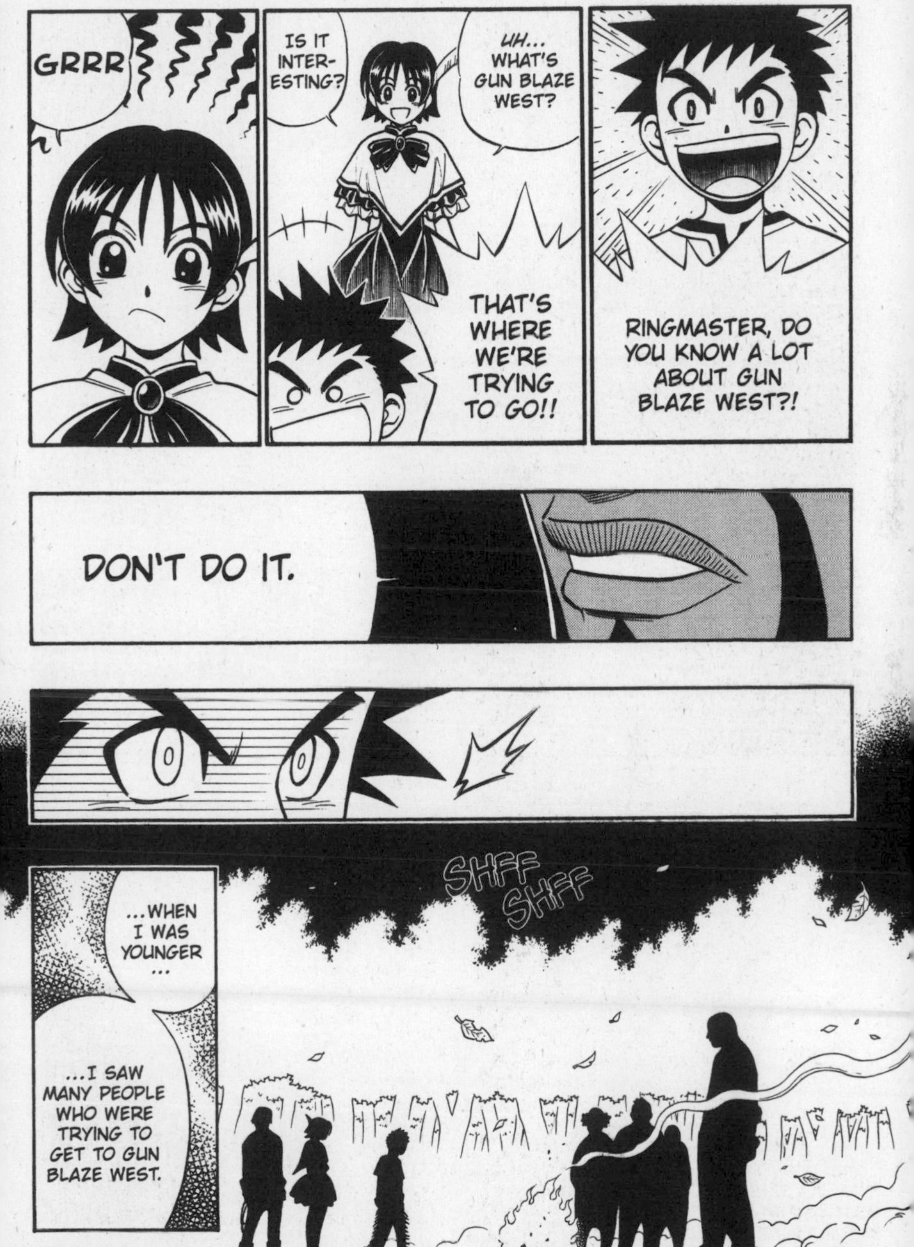
RINGMASTER, DO YOU KNOW A LOT ABOUT GUN BLAZE WEST?!
UH... WHAT'S GUN BLAZE WEST?
IS IT INTERESTING?
THAT'S WHERE WE'RE TRYING TO GO!!
GRRR
DON'T DO IT.
SHFF SHFF
...WHEN I WAS YOUNGER...
...I SAW MANY PEOPLE WHO WERE TRYING TO GET TO GUN BLAZE WEST.

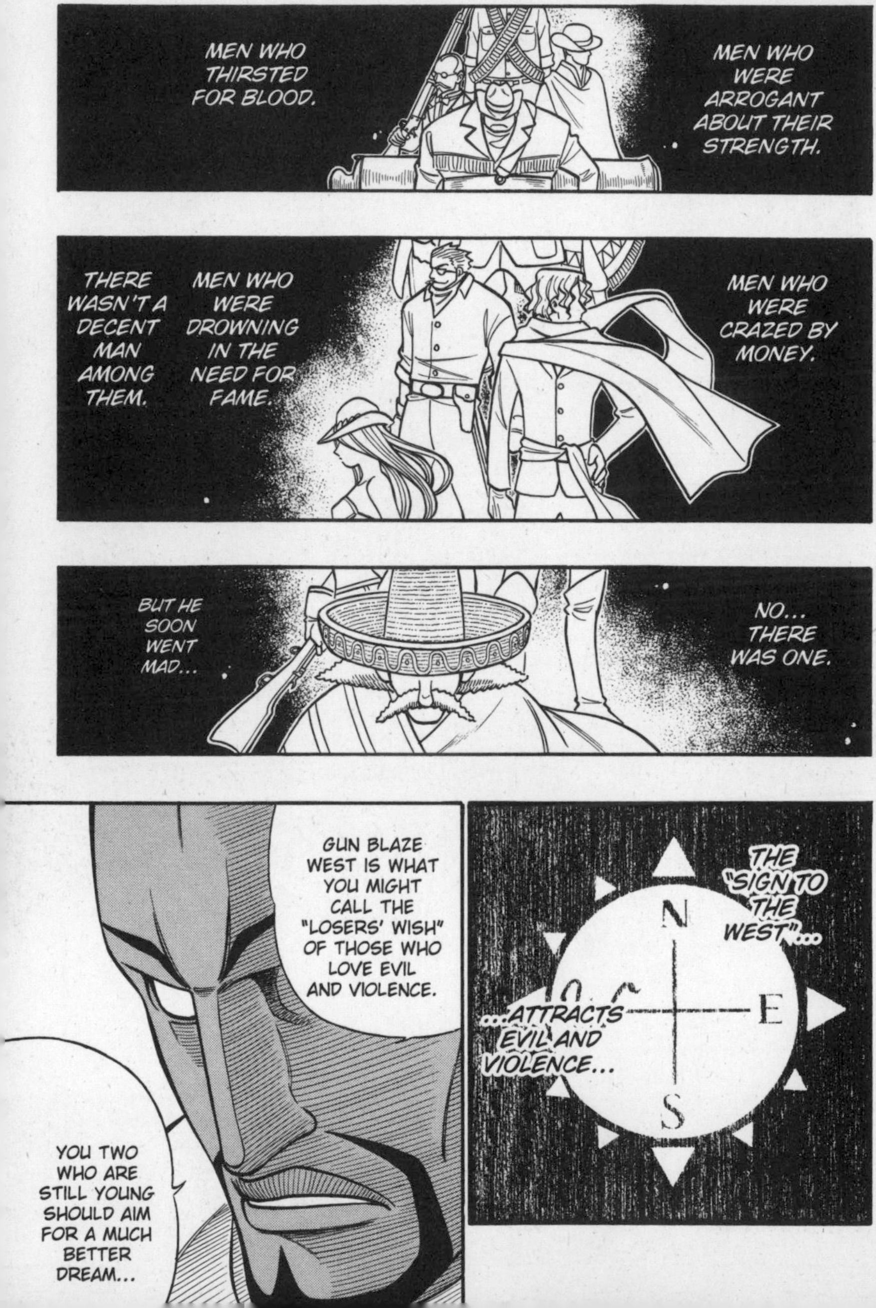
MEN WHO WERE ARROGANT ABOUT THEIR STRENGTH.
MEN WHO THIRSTED FOR BLOOD.
MEN WHO WERE CRAZED BY MONEY.
MEN WHO WERE DROWNING IN THE NEED FOR FAME.
THERE WASN'T A DECENT MAN AMONG THEM.
NO... THERE WAS ONE.
BUT HE SOON WENT MAD...
THE "SIGN TO THE WEST"...
...ATTRACTS EVIL AND VIOLENCE...
N
E
S
GUN BLAZE WEST IS WHAT YOU MIGHT CALL THE "LOSERS' WISH" OF THOSE WHO LOVE EVIL AND VIOLENCE.
YOU TWO WHO ARE STILL YOUNG SHOULD AIM FOR A MUCH BETTER DREAM...

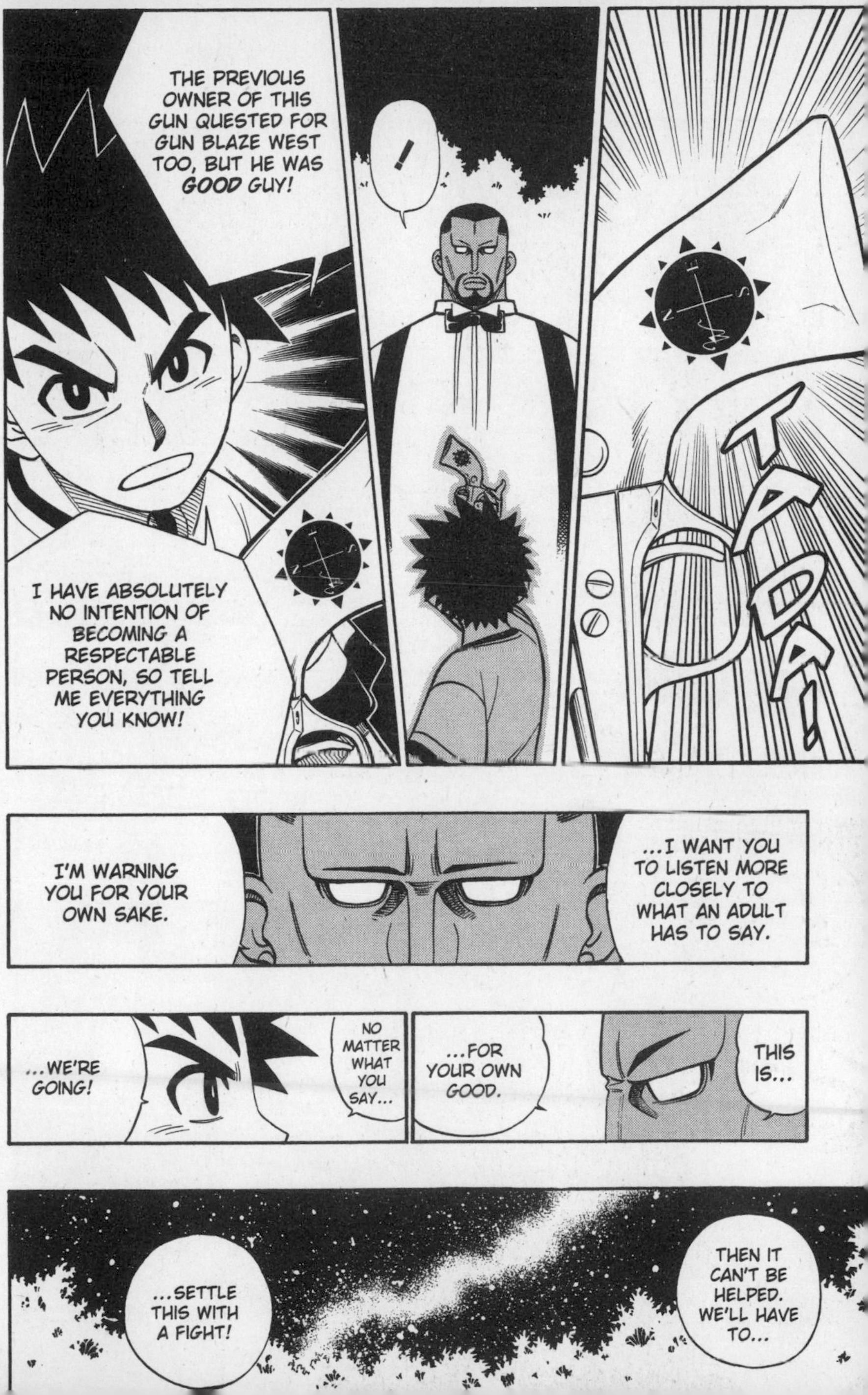
TA-DA!
!
THE PREVIOUS OWNER OF THIS GUN QUESTED FOR GUN BLAZE WEST TOO, BUT HE WAS GOOD GUY!
I HAVE ABSOLUTELY NO INTENTION OF BECOMING A RESPECTABLE PERSON, SO TELL ME EVERYTHING YOU KNOW!
...I WANT YOU TO LISTEN MORE CLOSELY TO WHAT AN ADULT HAS TO SAY.
I'M WARNING YOU FOR YOUR OWN SAKE.
THIS IS...
...FOR YOUR OWN GOOD.
NO MATTER WHAT YOU SAY...
...WE'RE GOING!
THEN IT CAN'T BE HELPED. WE'LL HAVE TO...
...SETTLE THIS WITH A FIGHT!

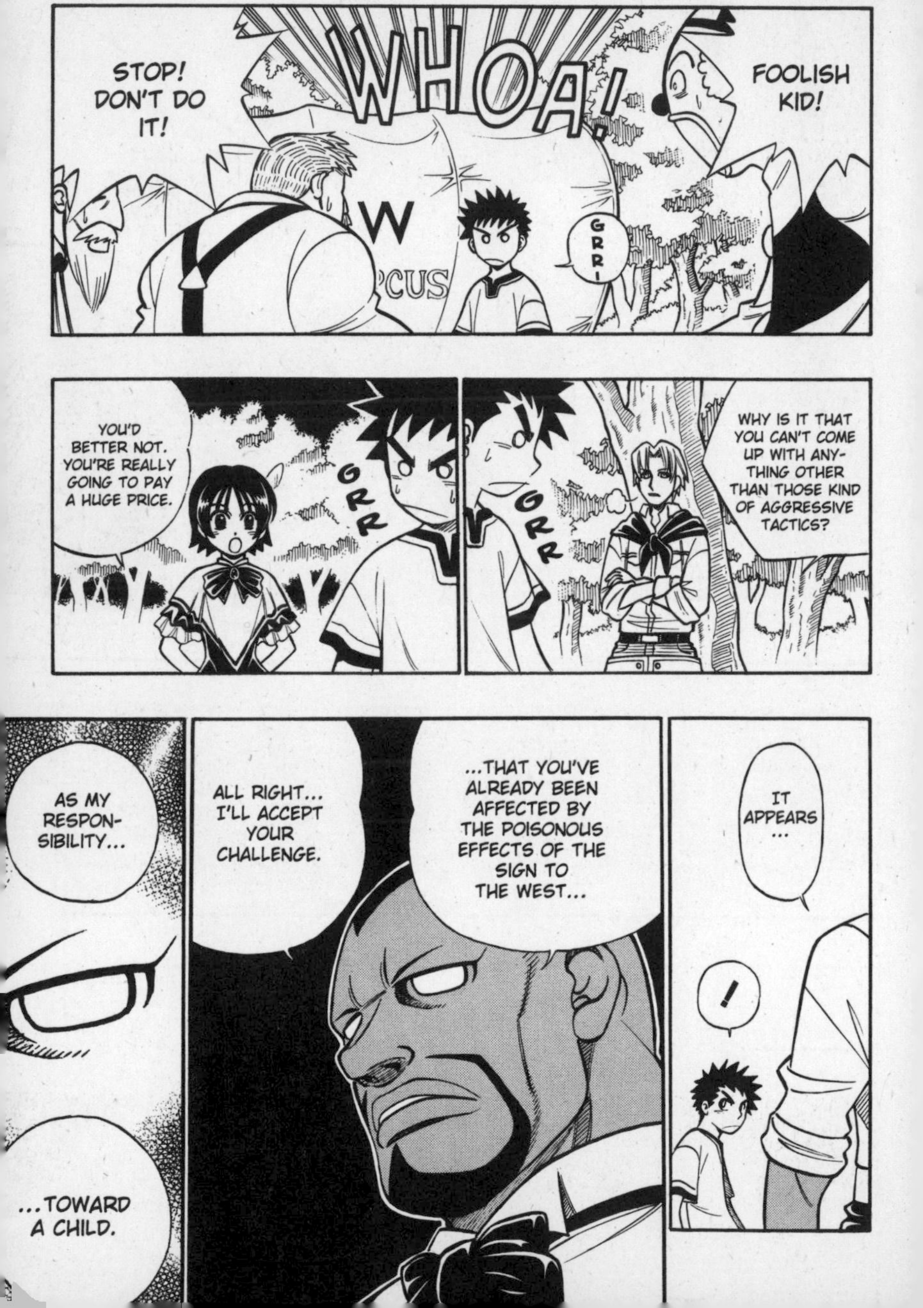
FOOLISH KID!
WHOA!
STOP! DON'T DO IT!
GRR!
W
PCUS
WHY IS IT THAT YOU CAN'T COME UP WITH ANY-THING OTHER THAN THOSE KIND OF AGGRESSIVE TACTICS?
GRR
GRR
YOU'D BETTER NOT. YOU'RE REALLY GOING TO PAY A HUGE PRICE.
IT APPEARS ...
!
...THAT YOU'VE ALREADY BEEN AFFECTED BY THE POISONOUS EFFECTS OF THE SIGN TO THE WEST...
ALL RIGHT... I'LL ACCEPT YOUR CHALLENGE.
AS MY RESPON-SIBILITY...
...TOWARD A CHILD.

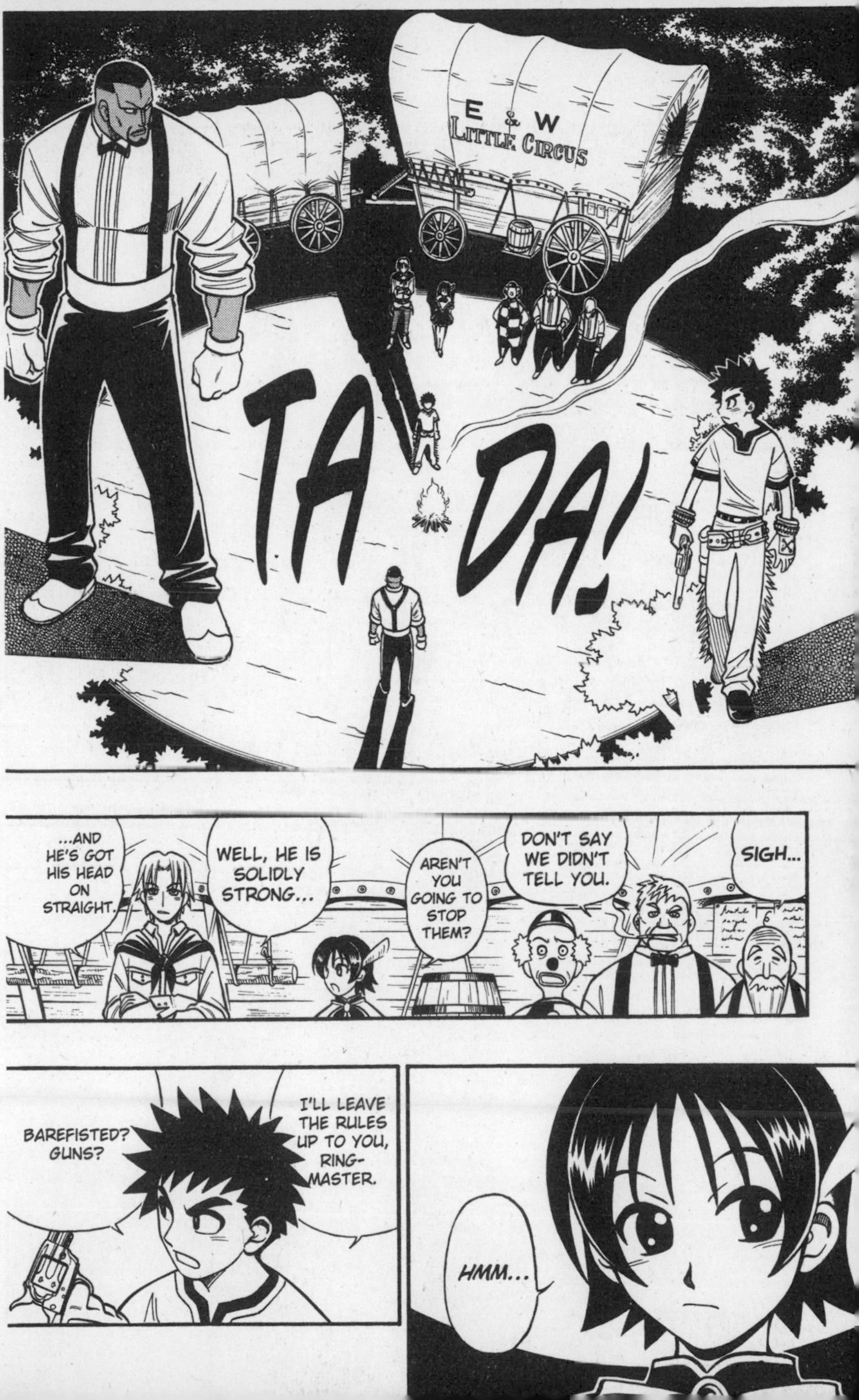
E & W
LITTLE CIRCUS
TA DA!
SIGH...
DON'T SAY WE DIDN'T TELL YOU.
AREN'T YOU GOING TO STOP THEM?
WELL, HE IS SOLIDLY STRONG...
...AND HE'S GOT HIS HEAD ON STRAIGHT.
HMM...
I'LL LEAVE THE RULES UP TO YOU, RING-MASTER.
BAREFISTED? GUNS?

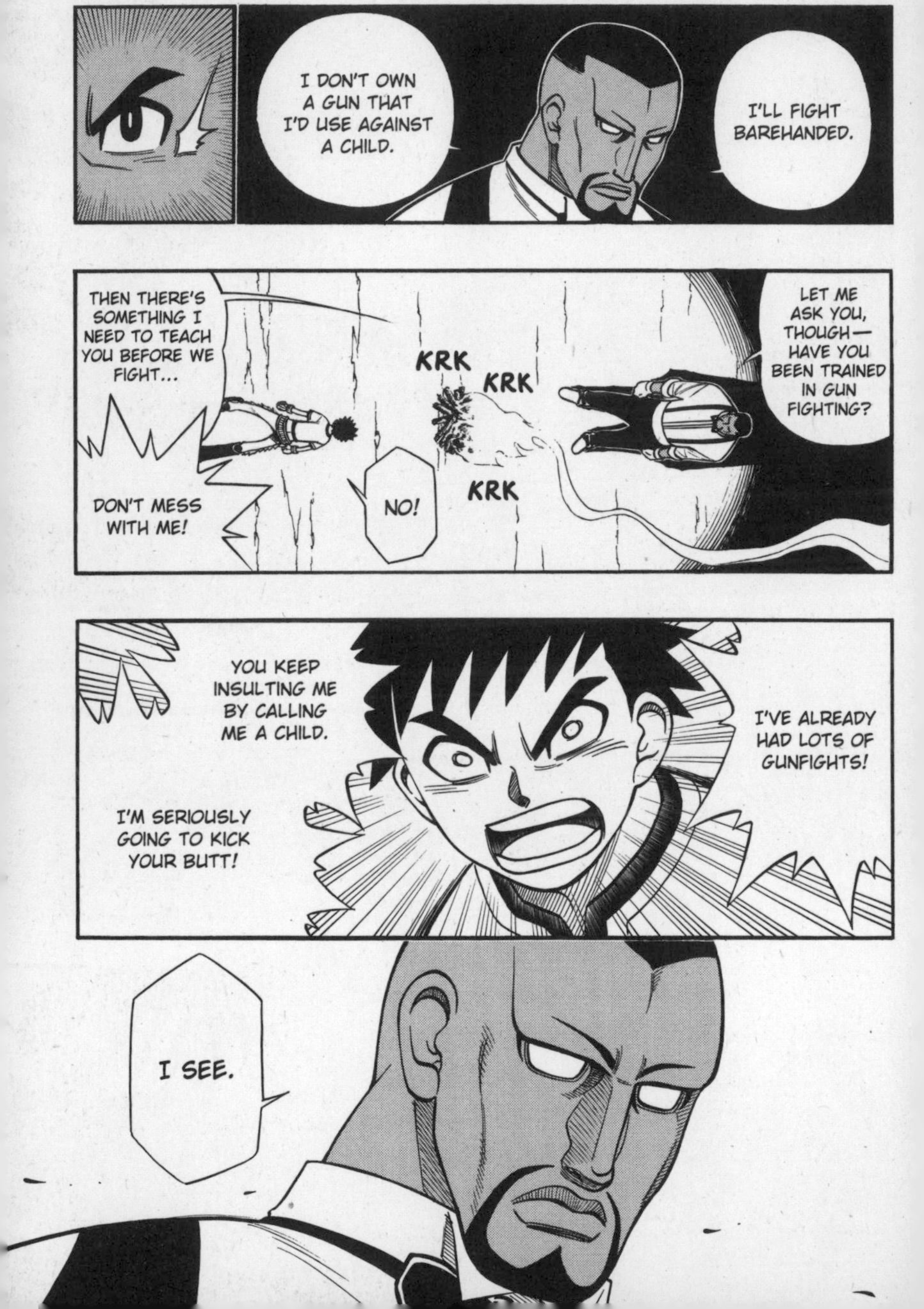
I DON'T OWN A GUN THAT I'D USE AGAINST A CHILD.
I'LL FIGHT BAREHANDED.
LET ME ASK YOU, THOUGH—HAVE YOU BEEN TRAINED IN GUN FIGHTING?
NO!
KRK
KRK
KRK
THEN THERE'S SOMETHING I NEED TO TEACH YOU BEFORE WE FIGHT...
DON'T MESS WITH ME!
I'VE ALREADY HAD LOTS OF GUNFIGHTS!
YOU KEEP INSULTING ME BY CALLING ME A CHILD.
I'M SERIOUSLY GOING TO KICK YOUR BUTT!
I SEE.

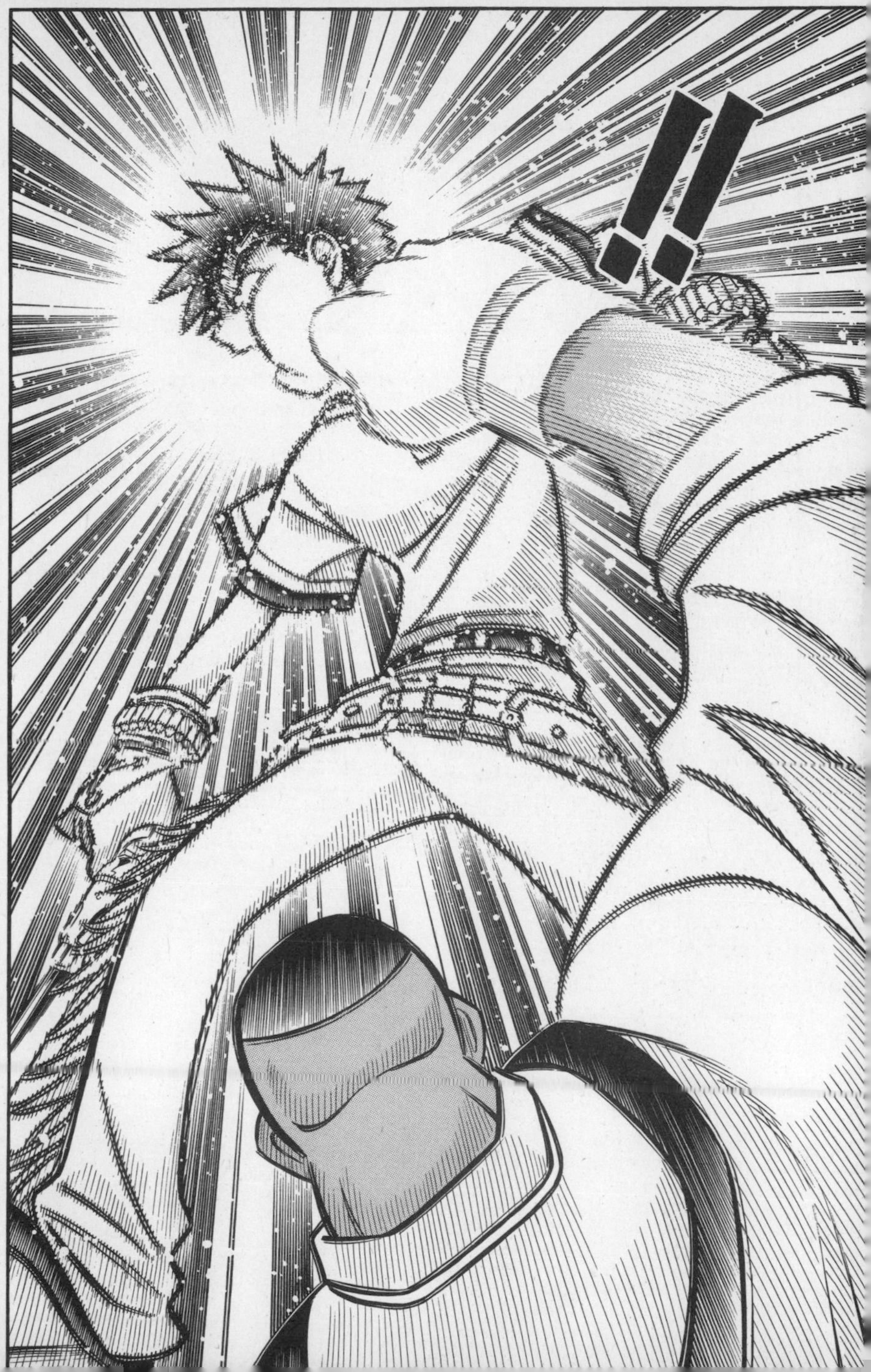
!!

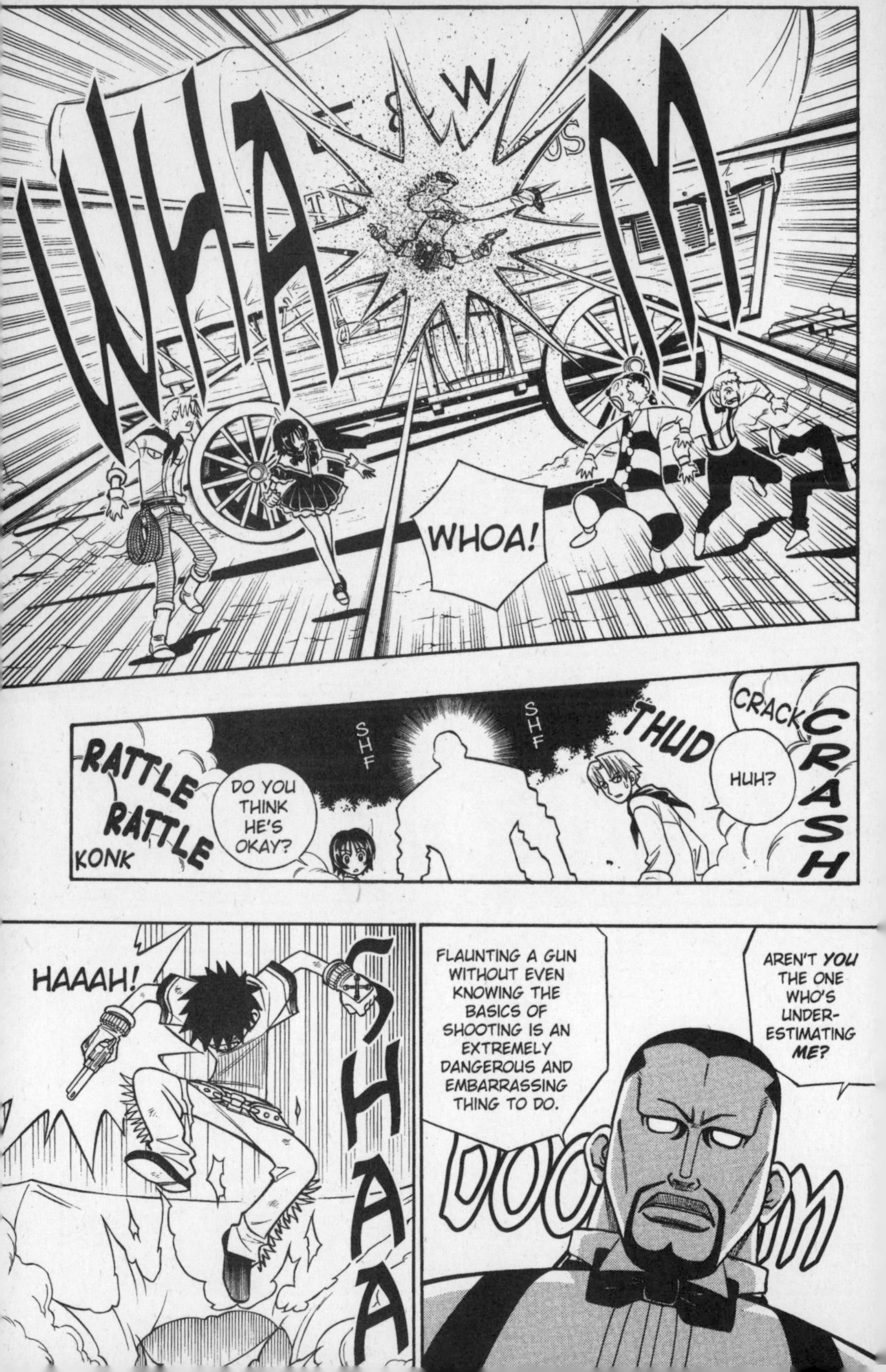
WHAM
WHOA!
CRACK
CRASH
HUH?
THUD
SHF
SHF
DO YOU THINK HE'S OKAY?
RATTLE RATTLE
KONK
AREN'T *YOU* THE ONE WHO'S UNDER-ESTIMATING *ME?*
FLAUNTING A GUN WITHOUT EVEN KNOWING THE BASICS OF SHOOTING IS AN EXTREMELY DANGEROUS AND EMBARRASSING THING TO DO.
DOOOM
HAAAH!
SHAAA

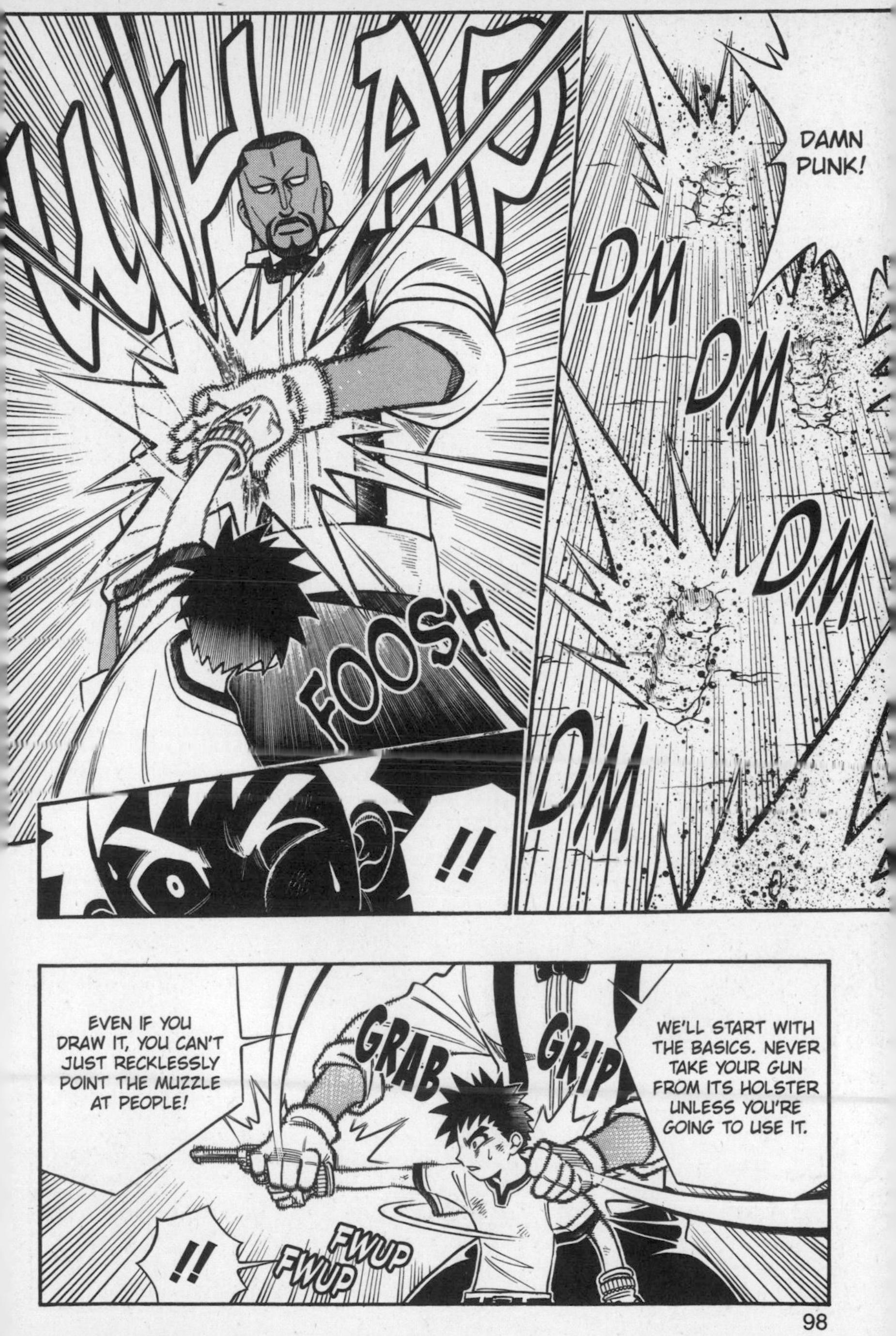
DAMN PUNK!
DM
DM
DM
DM
WHAP
FOOSH
!!
WE'LL START WITH THE BASICS. NEVER TAKE YOUR GUN FROM ITS HOLSTER UNLESS YOU'RE GOING TO USE IT.
GRIP
GRAB
EVEN IF YOU DRAW IT, YOU CAN'T JUST RECKLESSLY POINT THE MUZZLE AT PEOPLE!
FWUP
FWUP
!!

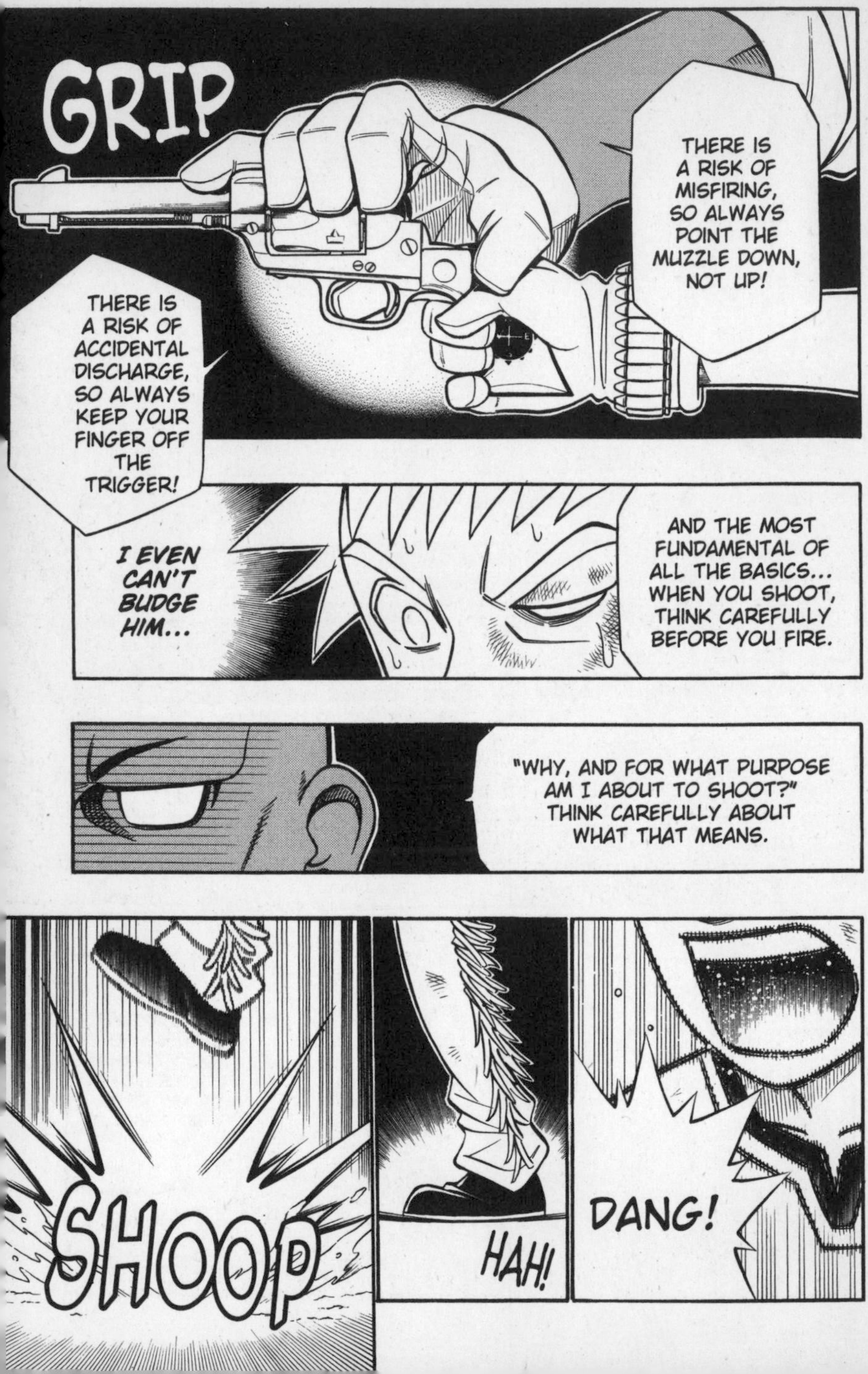
THERE IS A RISK OF MISFIRING, SO ALWAYS POINT THE MUZZLE DOWN, NOT UP!
GRIP
THERE IS A RISK OF ACCIDENTAL DISCHARGE, SO ALWAYS KEEP YOUR FINGER OFF THE TRIGGER!
AND THE MOST FUNDAMENTAL OF ALL THE BASICS... WHEN YOU SHOOT, THINK CAREFULLY BEFORE YOU FIRE.
I EVEN CAN'T BUDGE HIM...
"WHY, AND FOR WHAT PURPOSE AM I ABOUT TO SHOOT?" THINK CAREFULLY ABOUT WHAT THAT MEANS.
DANG!
HAH!
SHOOP

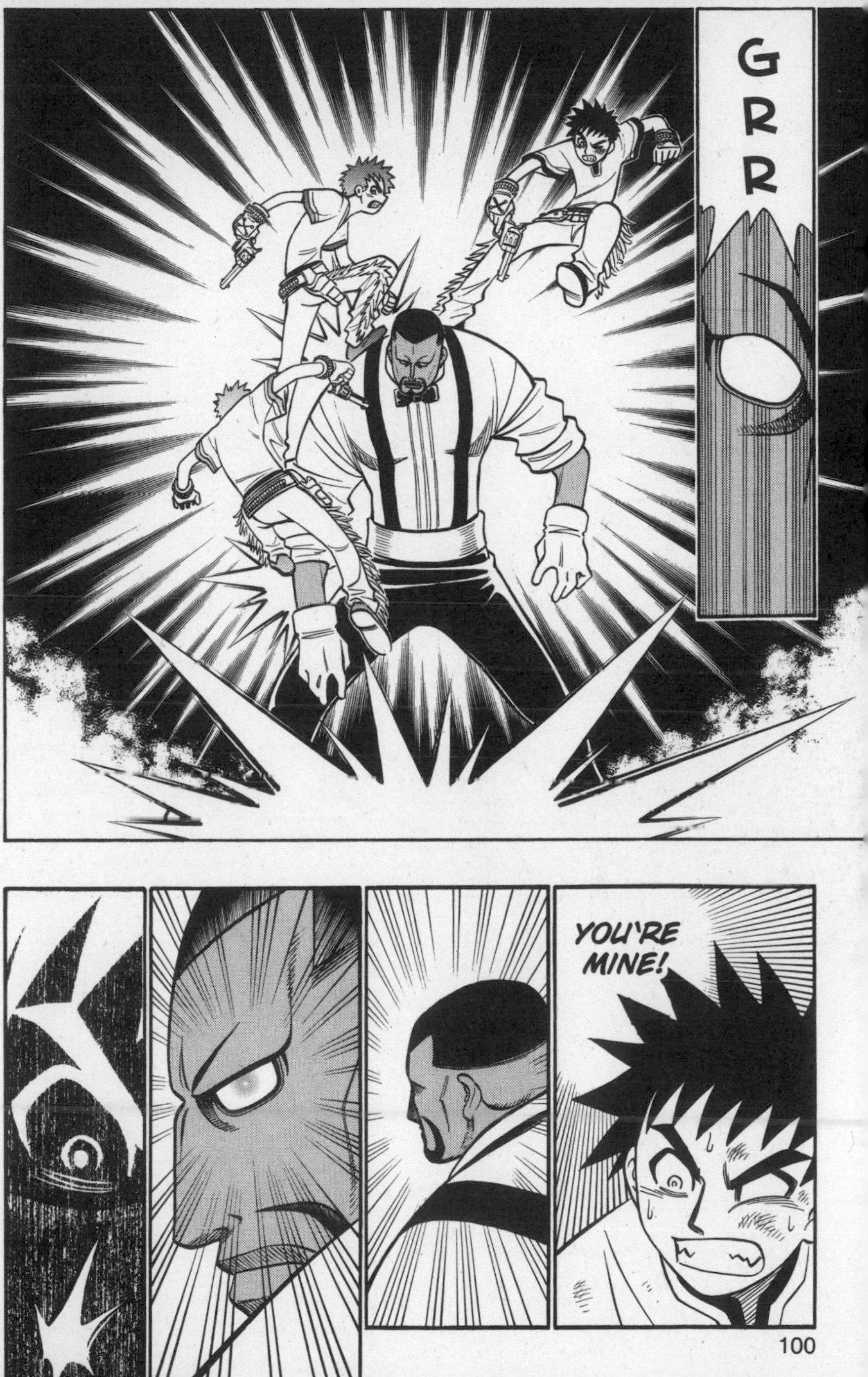
GRR
YOU'RE MINE!

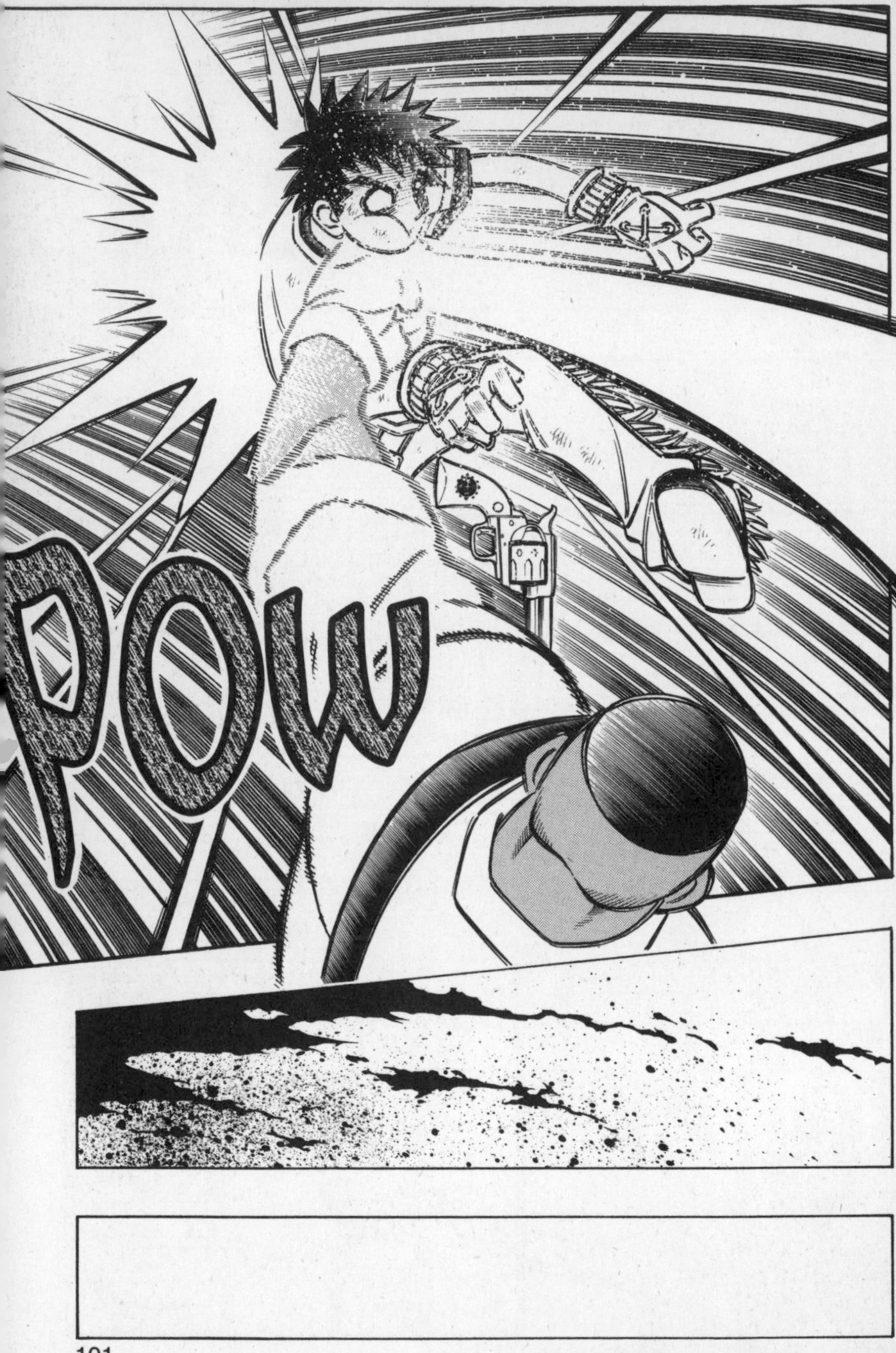
POW

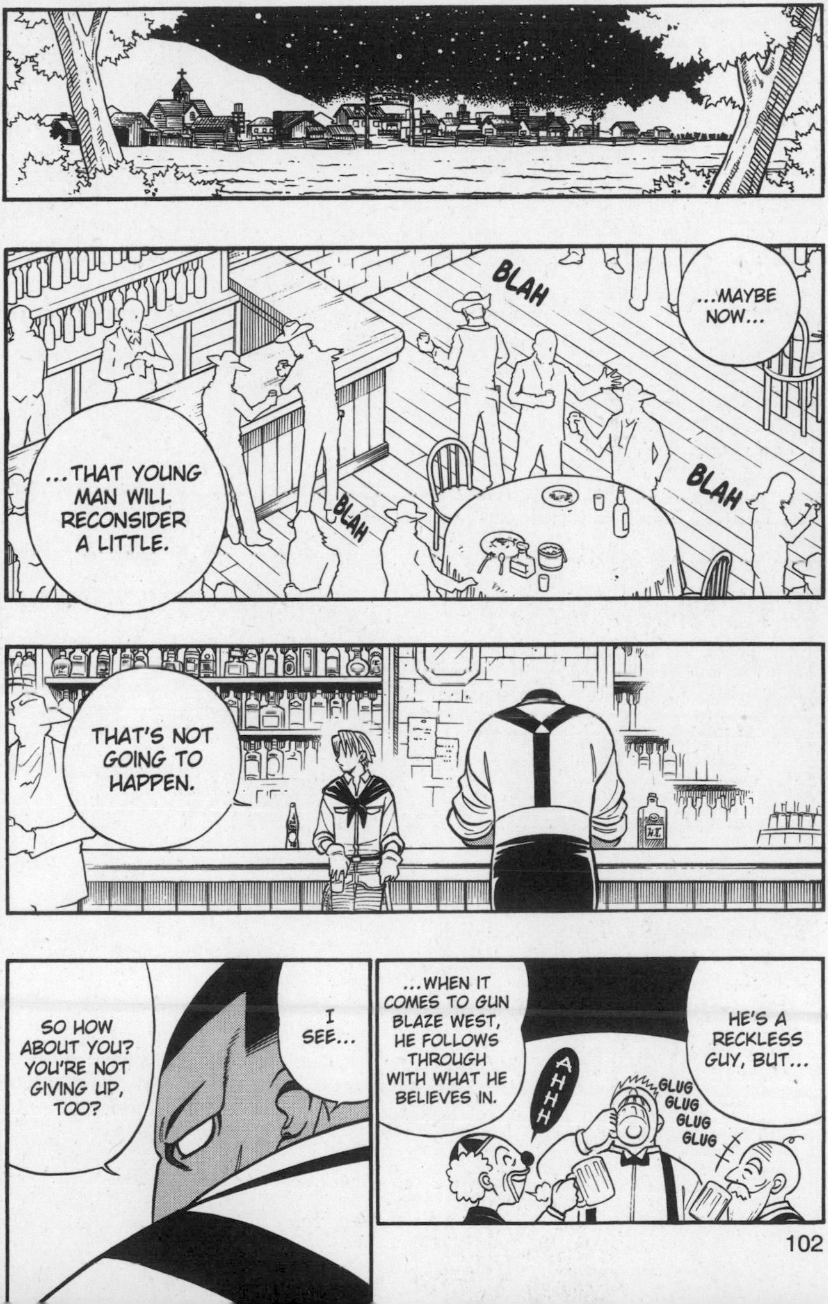
...MAYBE NOW...
BLAH
BLAH
BLAH
...THAT YOUNG MAN WILL RECONSIDER A LITTLE.
THAT'S NOT GOING TO HAPPEN.
HE'S A RECKLESS GUY, BUT...
GLUG GLUG GLUG GLUG
AHHH
...WHEN IT COMES TO GUN BLAZE WEST, HE FOLLOWS THROUGH WITH WHAT HE BELIEVES IN.
I SEE...
SO HOW ABOUT YOU? YOU'RE NOT GIVING UP, TOO?

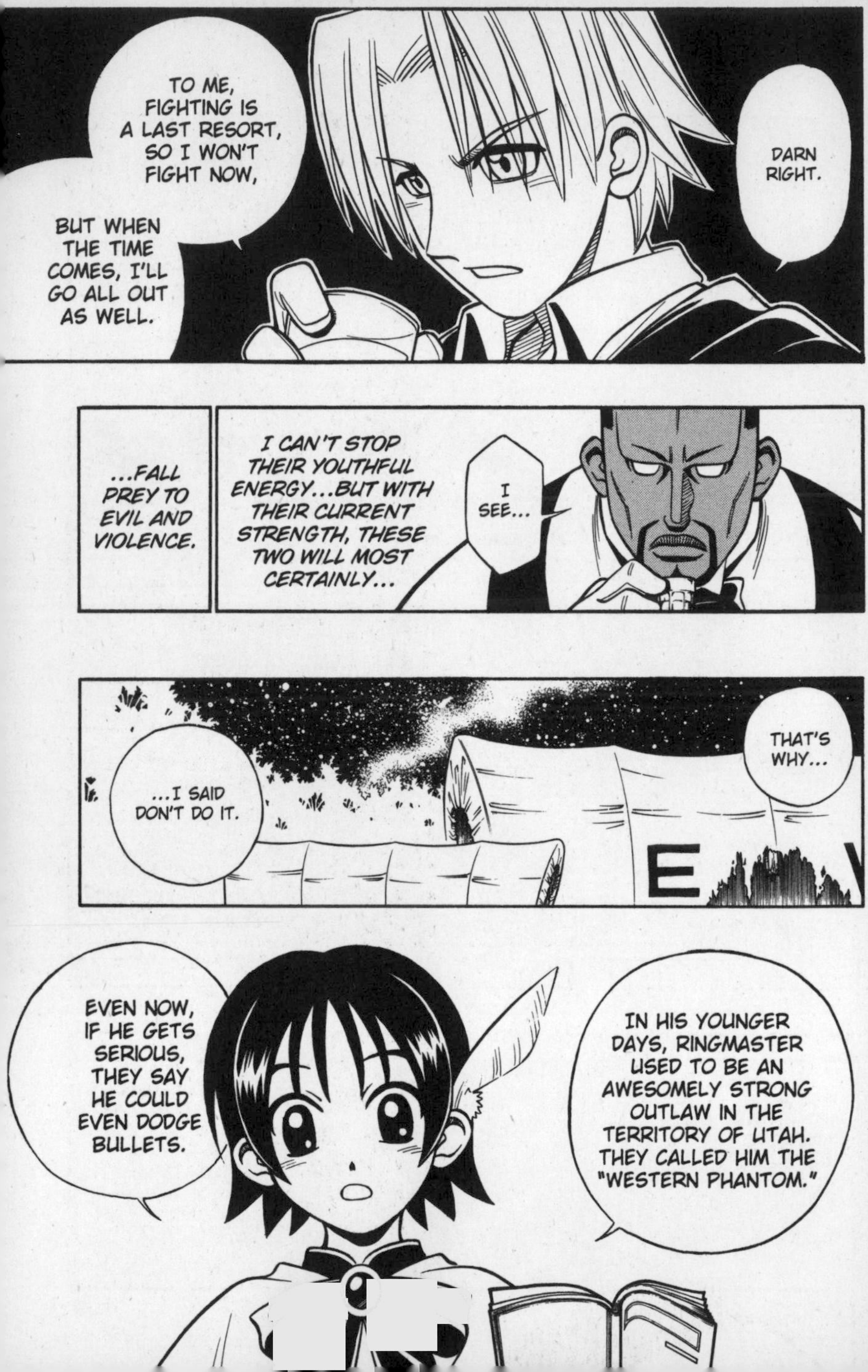

TO ME, FIGHTING IS A LAST RESORT, SO I WON'T FIGHT NOW,
BUT WHEN THE TIME COMES, I'LL GO ALL OUT AS WELL.
DARN RIGHT.
I SEE...
I CAN'T STOP THEIR YOUTHFUL ENERGY...BUT WITH THEIR CURRENT STRENGTH, THESE TWO WILL MOST CERTAINLY...
...FALL PREY TO EVIL AND VIOLENCE.
THAT'S WHY...
...I SAID DON'T DO IT.
IN HIS YOUNGER DAYS, RINGMASTER USED TO BE AN AWESOMELY STRONG OUTLAW IN THE TERRITORY OF UTAH. THEY CALLED HIM THE "WESTERN PHANTOM."
EVEN NOW, IF HE GETS SERIOUS, THEY SAY HE COULD EVEN DODGE BULLETS.

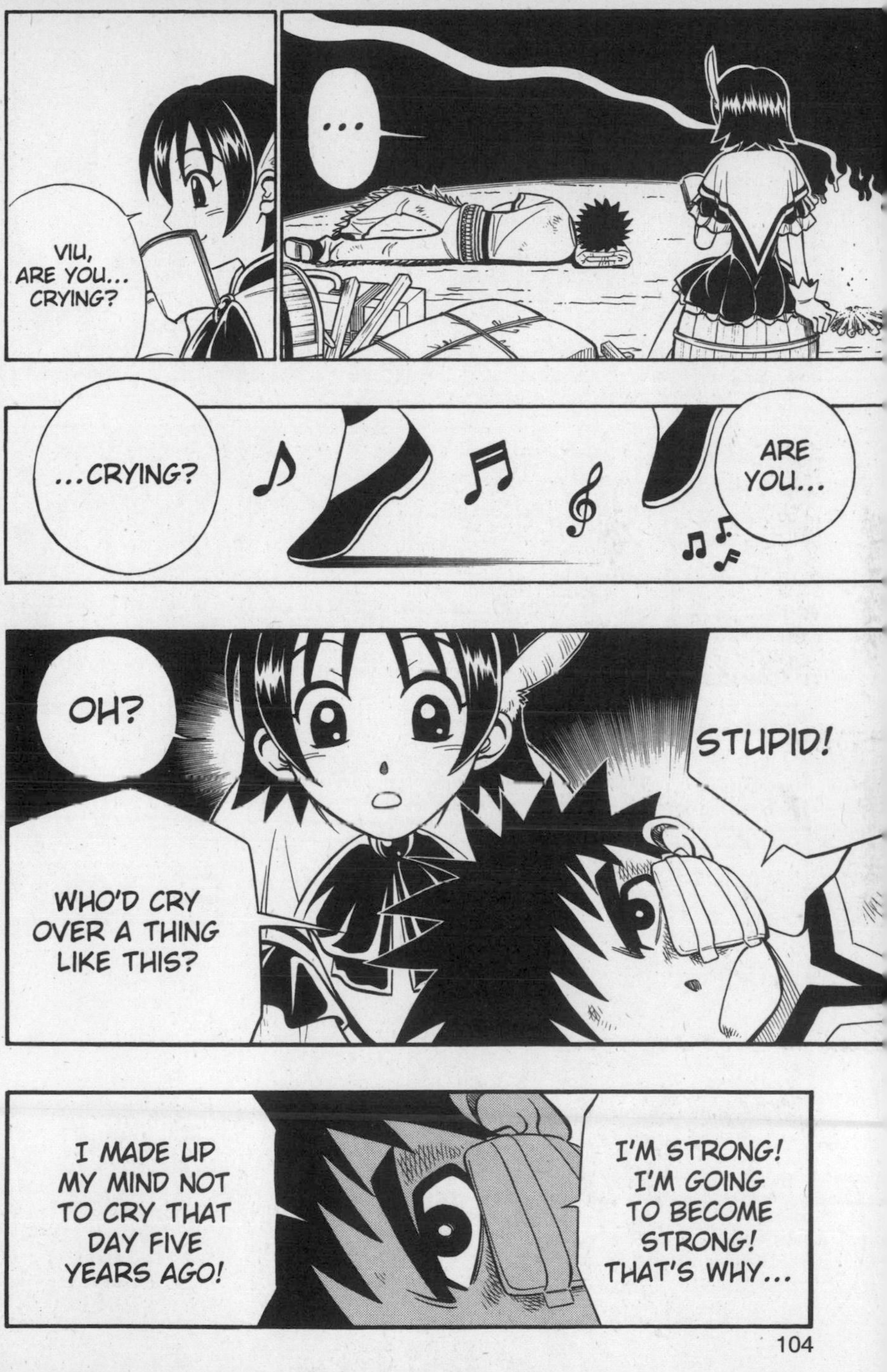
...
VIU, ARE YOU... CRYING?
ARE YOU...
...CRYING?
STUPID!
OH?
WHO'D CRY OVER A THING LIKE THIS?
I'M STRONG! I'M GOING TO BECOME STRONG! THAT'S WHY...
I MADE UP MY MIND NOT TO CRY THAT DAY FIVE YEARS AGO!

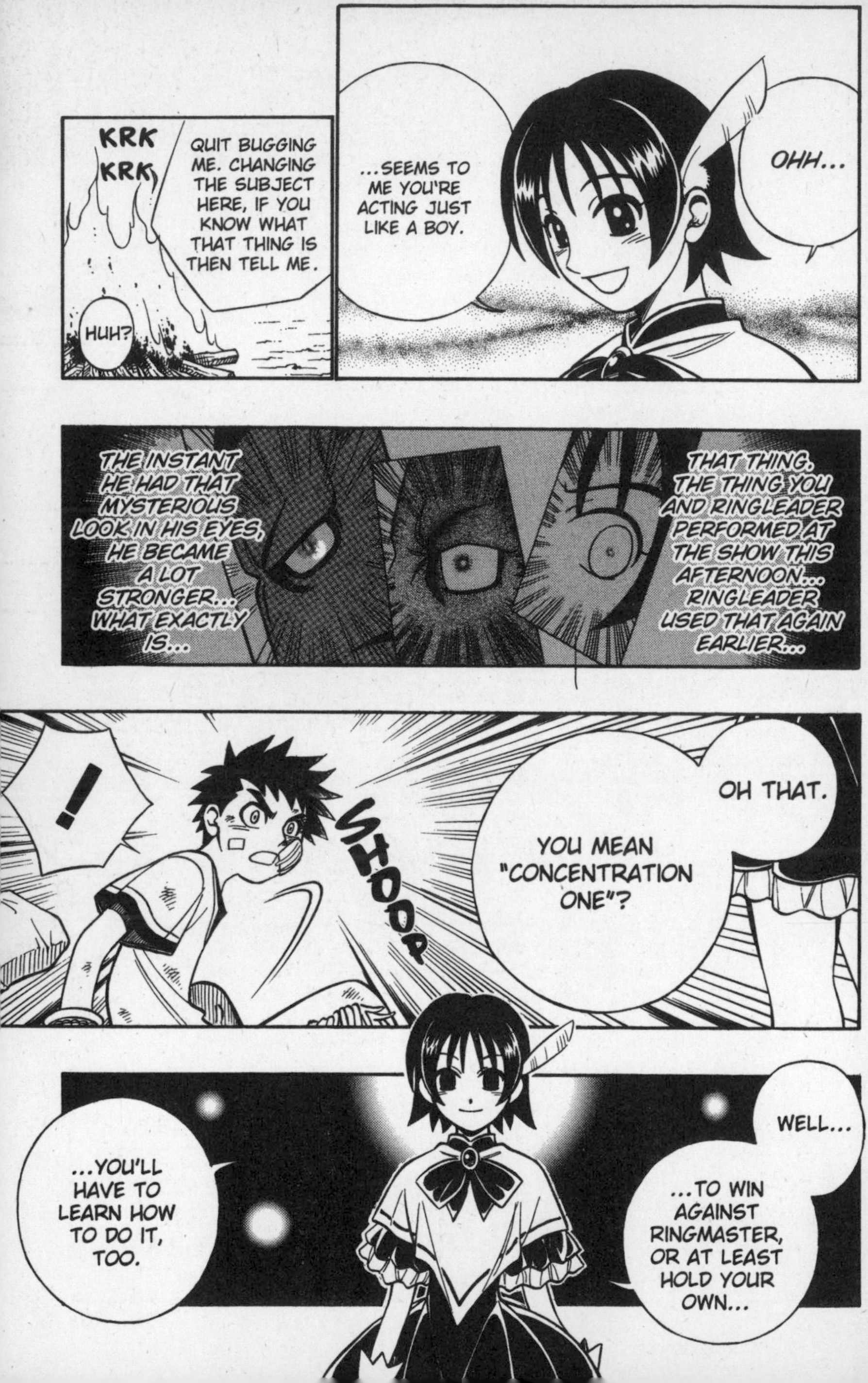
OHH...
...SEEMS TO ME YOU'RE ACTING JUST LIKE A BOY.
QUIT BUGGING ME. CHANGING THE SUBJECT HERE, IF YOU KNOW WHAT THAT THING IS THEN TELL ME.
KRK KRK
HUH?
THAT THING. THE THING YOU AND RINGLEADER PERFORMED AT THE SHOW THIS AFTERNOON... RINGLEADER USED THAT AGAIN EARLIER...
THE INSTANT HE HAD THAT MYSTERIOUS LOOK IN HIS EYES, HE BECAME A LOT STRONGER... WHAT EXACTLY IS...
OH THAT.
YOU MEAN "CONCENTRATION ONE"?
SHOOOP
!
WELL...
...TO WIN AGAINST RINGMASTER, OR AT LEAST HOLD YOUR OWN...
...YOU'LL HAVE TO LEARN HOW TO DO IT, TOO.

CONCEPT: HE'S A CHARACTER I CONSIDER A CONVENTIONAL "EVIL OUTLAW."

AT THE START, I GAVE A LOT OF THOUGHT TO "HOW BEST DO I ACCUSTOM READERS IN A SIMPLE WAY TO UNDERSTAND THE WORLD OF A WESTERN, SOMETHING THAT THEY ARE NOT TOO FAMILIAR WITH?" DOING THAT, HOWEVER, APPEARED TO HAVE LED TO SHACKLING BOTH THE CHARACTERS AND STORY AND PREVENTED THEM FROM REALLY DEVELOPING. WHEN I THINK ABOUT IT NOW, I FEEL VERY SORRY FOR THIS CHARACTER. I SHOULD HAVE SPICED HIM UP MUCH MORE.

IMAGE SOURCE: HE IS THE IMAGE, AS-IS, OF A TYPICAL "EVIL OUTLAW."

## CHARACTER FILE #04

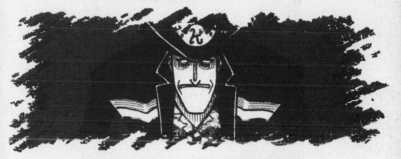

# WILLIAM KENBROWN

DESIGN: I MADE A VERY SIMPLISTIC DECISION THAT AN "EVIL OUTLAW" NEEDED A BLACK TEN-GALLON HAT AND BLACK SUIT. HIS PECULIAR JUTTING JAW AND LONG, SLENDER ARMS AND LEGS WERE A PRODUCT OF MY UNCHANGING PENCHANT FOR "WANTING TO DRAW SOMETHING WEIRD!!" I LIKE IT A LOT.

ON A SIDE NOTE, KENBROWN HAS A JUNIOR. THERE WAS A STORY PROPOSAL FOR HIM TO LATER BECOME VIU'S SELF-PROCLAIMED RIVAL. I WAS THINKING OF JUNIOR BECOMING AN ENJOYABLE AND STRONGLY UNIQUE GANG CHARACTER. I WISH I COULD HAVE DRAWN HIM...

# CHAPTER 13: SHOOTING TRAINING

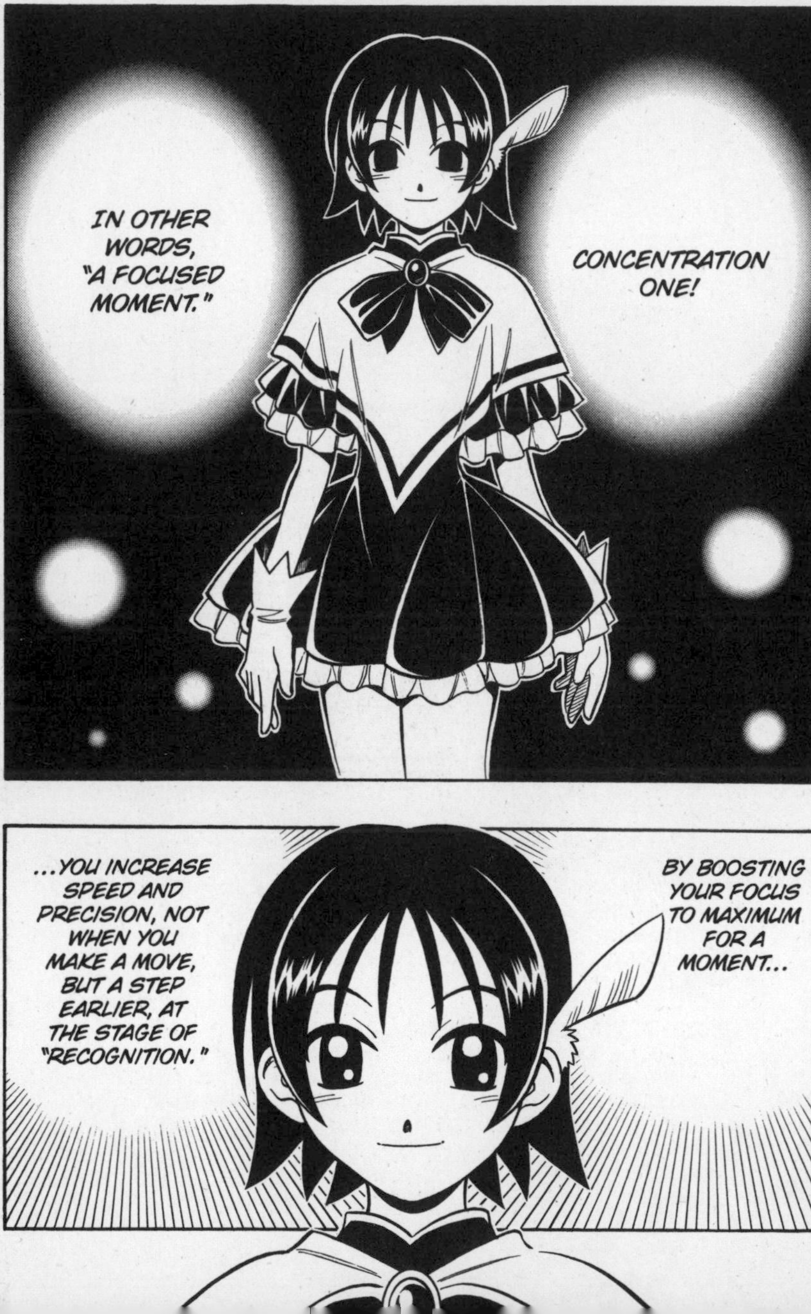
CONCENTRATION ONE!
IN OTHER WORDS, "A FOCUSED MOMENT."
BY BOOSTING YOUR FOCUS TO MAXIMUM FOR A MOMENT...
...YOU INCREASE SPEED AND PRECISION, NOT WHEN YOU MAKE A MOVE, BUT A STEP EARLIER, AT THE STAGE OF "RECOGNITION."

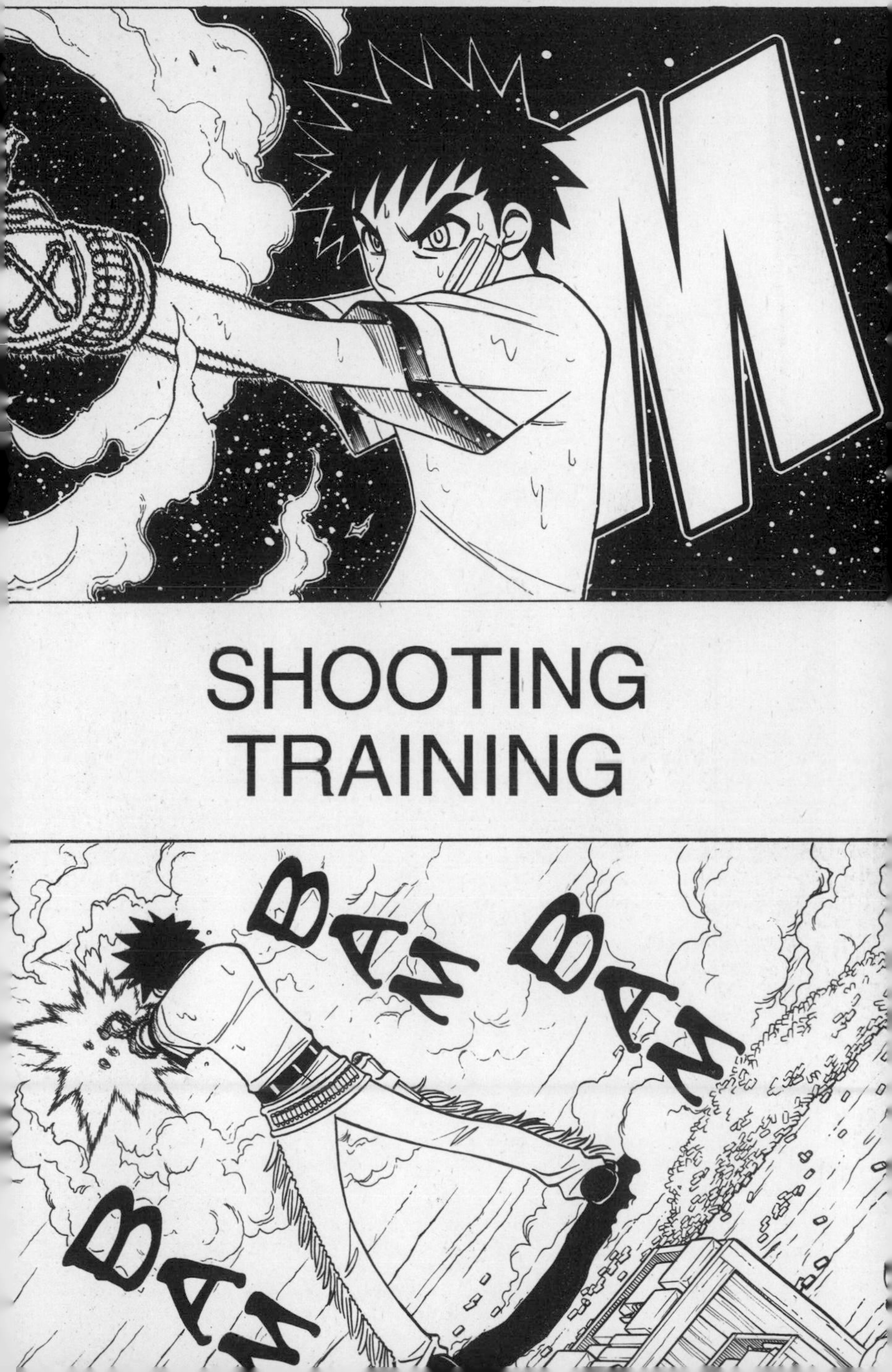
M
SHOOTING TRAINING
BAM
BAM
BAM

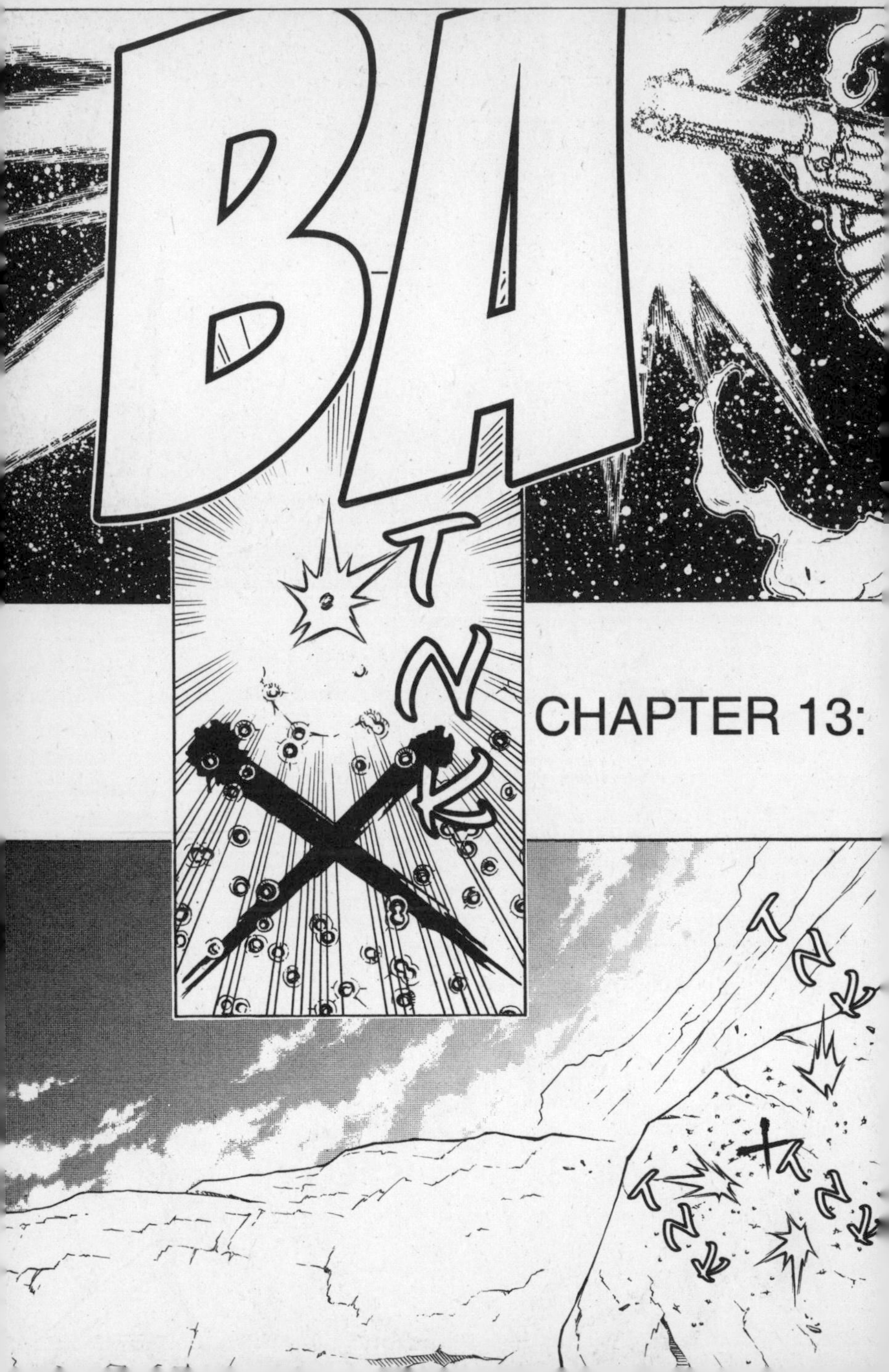
BA
TNK
TNK
TNK
TNK

# CHAPTER 13:

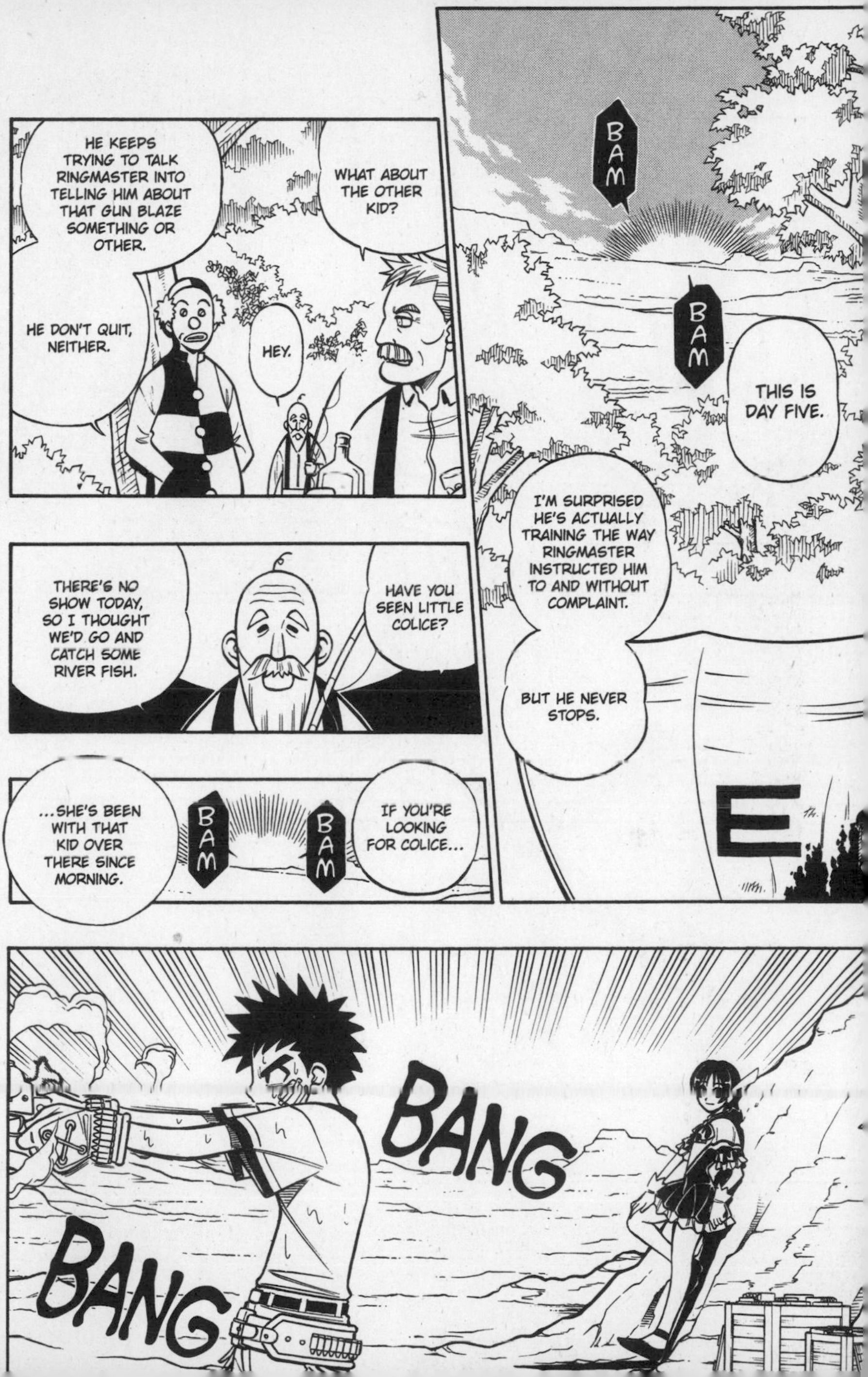
BAM
BAM
THIS IS DAY FIVE.
I'M SURPRISED HE'S ACTUALLY TRAINING THE WAY RINGMASTER INSTRUCTED HIM TO AND WITHOUT COMPLAINT.
BUT HE NEVER STOPS.
WHAT ABOUT THE OTHER KID?
HE KEEPS TRYING TO TALK RINGMASTER INTO TELLING HIM ABOUT THAT GUN BLAZE SOMETHING OR OTHER.
HEY.
HE DON'T QUIT, NEITHER.
HAVE YOU SEEN LITTLE COLICE?
THERE'S NO SHOW TODAY, SO I THOUGHT WE'D GO AND CATCH SOME RIVER FISH.
IF YOU'RE LOOKING FOR COLICE...
BAM
BAM
...SHE'S BEEN WITH THAT KID OVER THERE SINCE MORNING.
BANG
BANG

READ THIS WAY

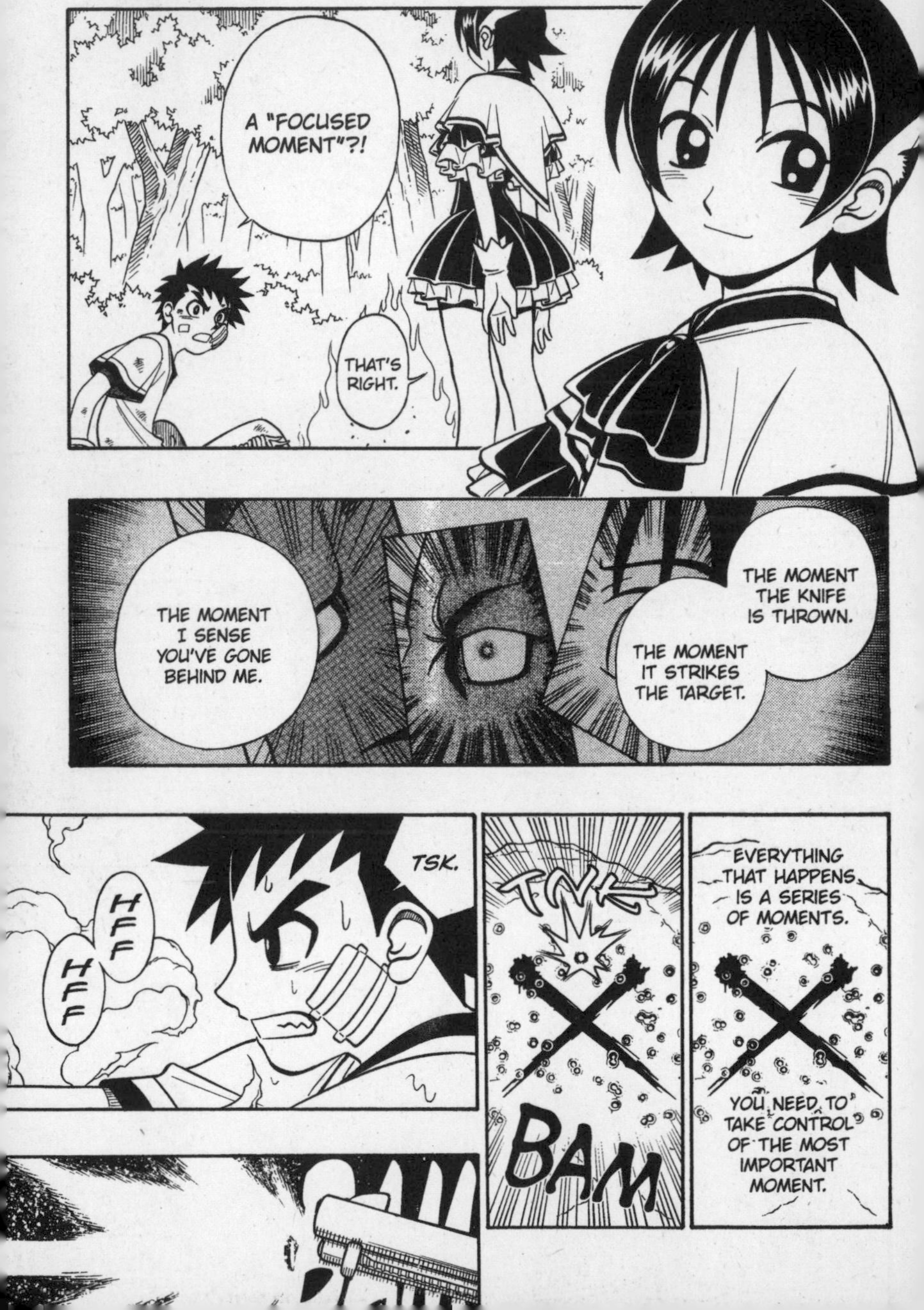
A "FOCUSED MOMENT"?!
THAT'S RIGHT.
THE MOMENT THE KNIFE IS THROWN.
THE MOMENT IT STRIKES THE TARGET.
THE MOMENT I SENSE YOU'VE GONE BEHIND ME.
EVERYTHING THAT HAPPENS IS A SERIES OF MOMENTS.
YOU NEED TO TAKE CONTROL OF THE MOST IMPORTANT MOMENT.
TNK
BAM
TSK.
HFF
HFF

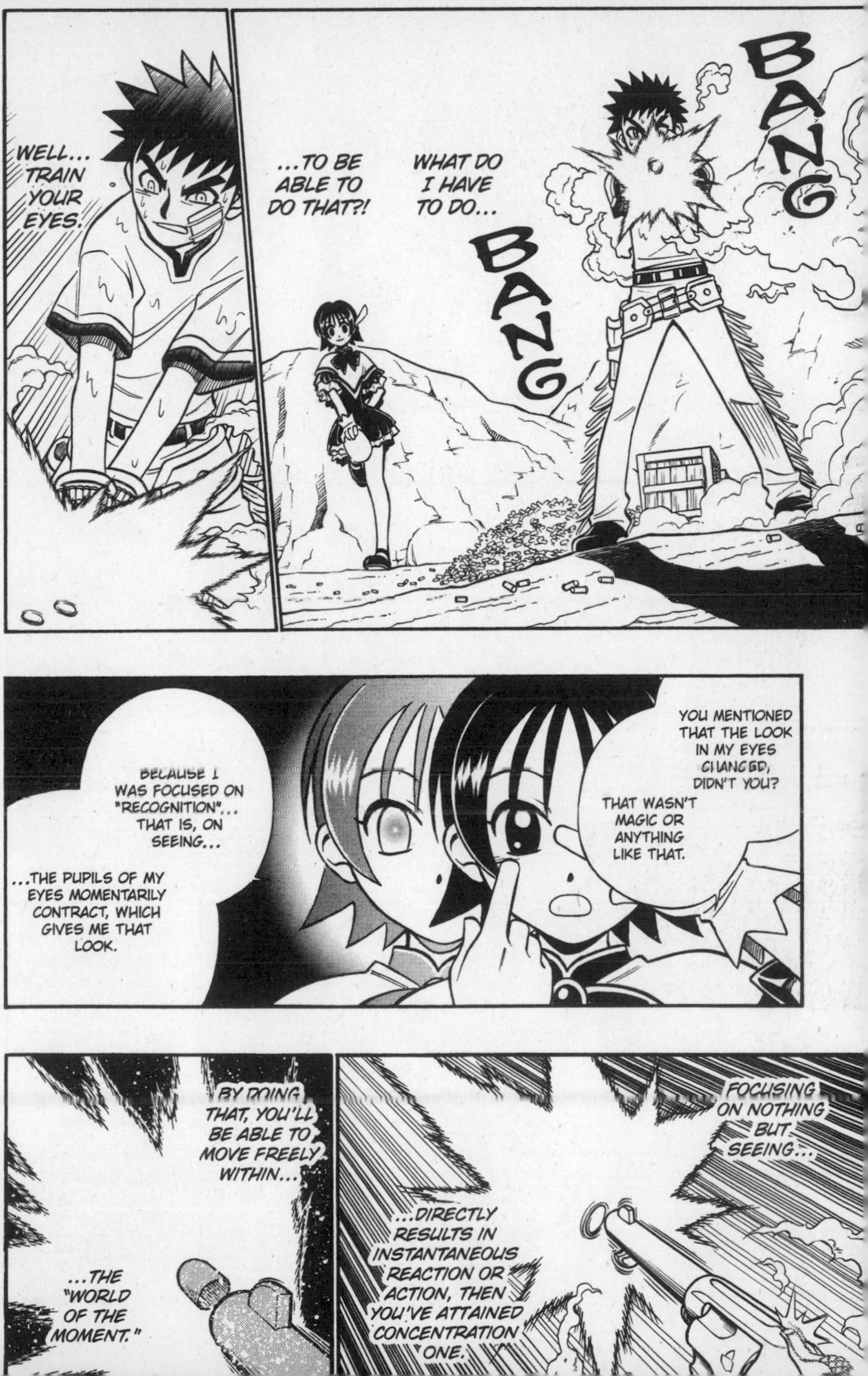
BANG
BANG
WHAT DO I HAVE TO DO...
...TO BE ABLE TO DO THAT?!
WELL... TRAIN YOUR EYES.
YOU MENTIONED THAT THE LOOK IN MY EYES CHANGED, DIDN'T YOU?
THAT WASN'T MAGIC OR ANYTHING LIKE THAT.
BECAUSE I WAS FOCUSED ON "RECOGNITION"... THAT IS, ON SEEING...
...THE PUPILS OF MY EYES MOMENTARILY CONTRACT, WHICH GIVES ME THAT LOOK.
FOCUSING ON NOTHING BUT SEEING...
...DIRECTLY RESULTS IN INSTANTANEOUS REACTION OR ACTION, THEN YOU'VE ATTAINED CONCENTRATION ONE.
BY DOING THAT, YOU'LL BE ABLE TO MOVE FREELY WITHIN...
...THE "WORLD OF THE MOMENT."

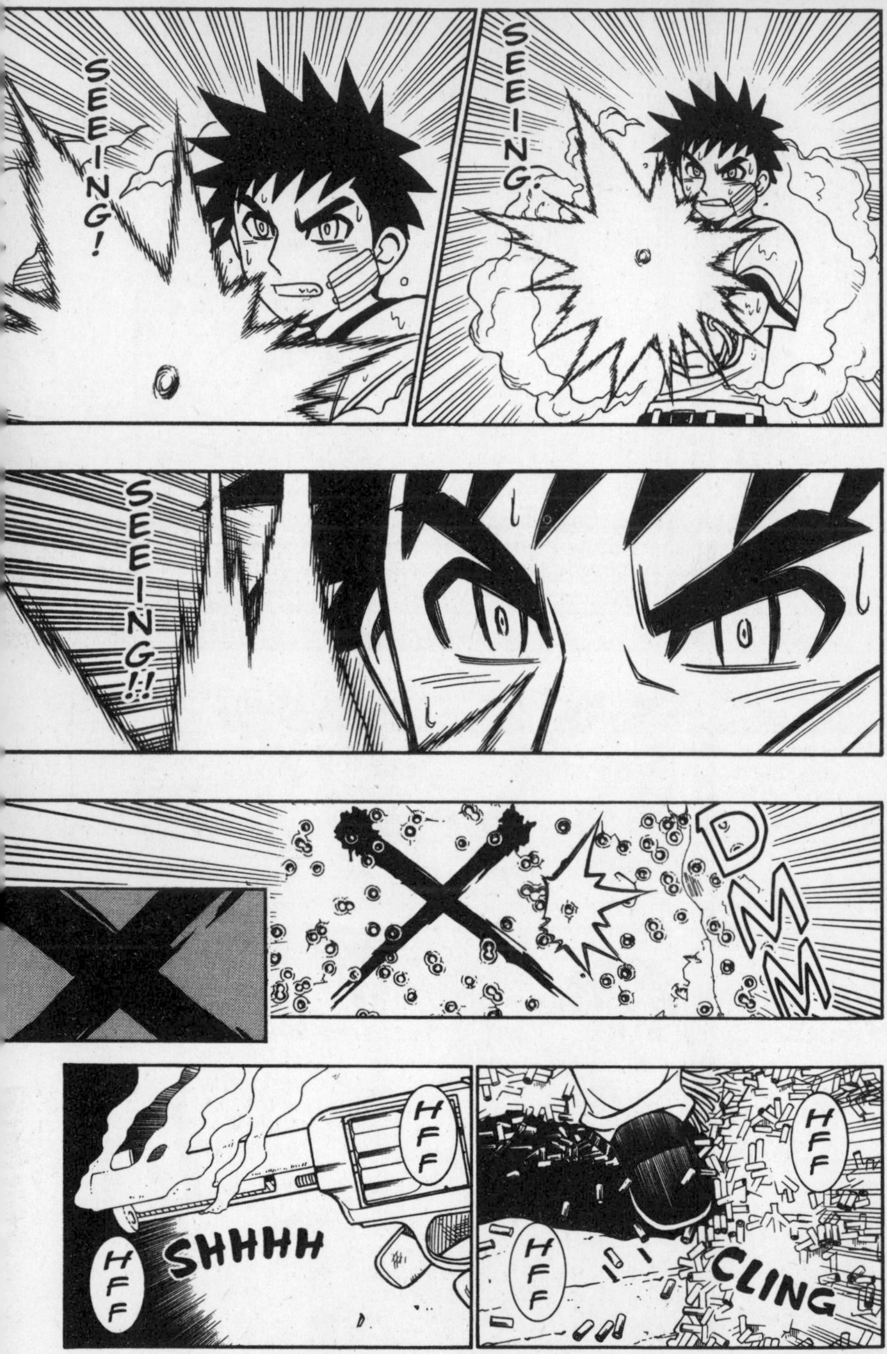
SEEING.
SEEING!
SEEING!!
DMMM
HFF
HFF
CLING
HFF
SHHHH
HFF

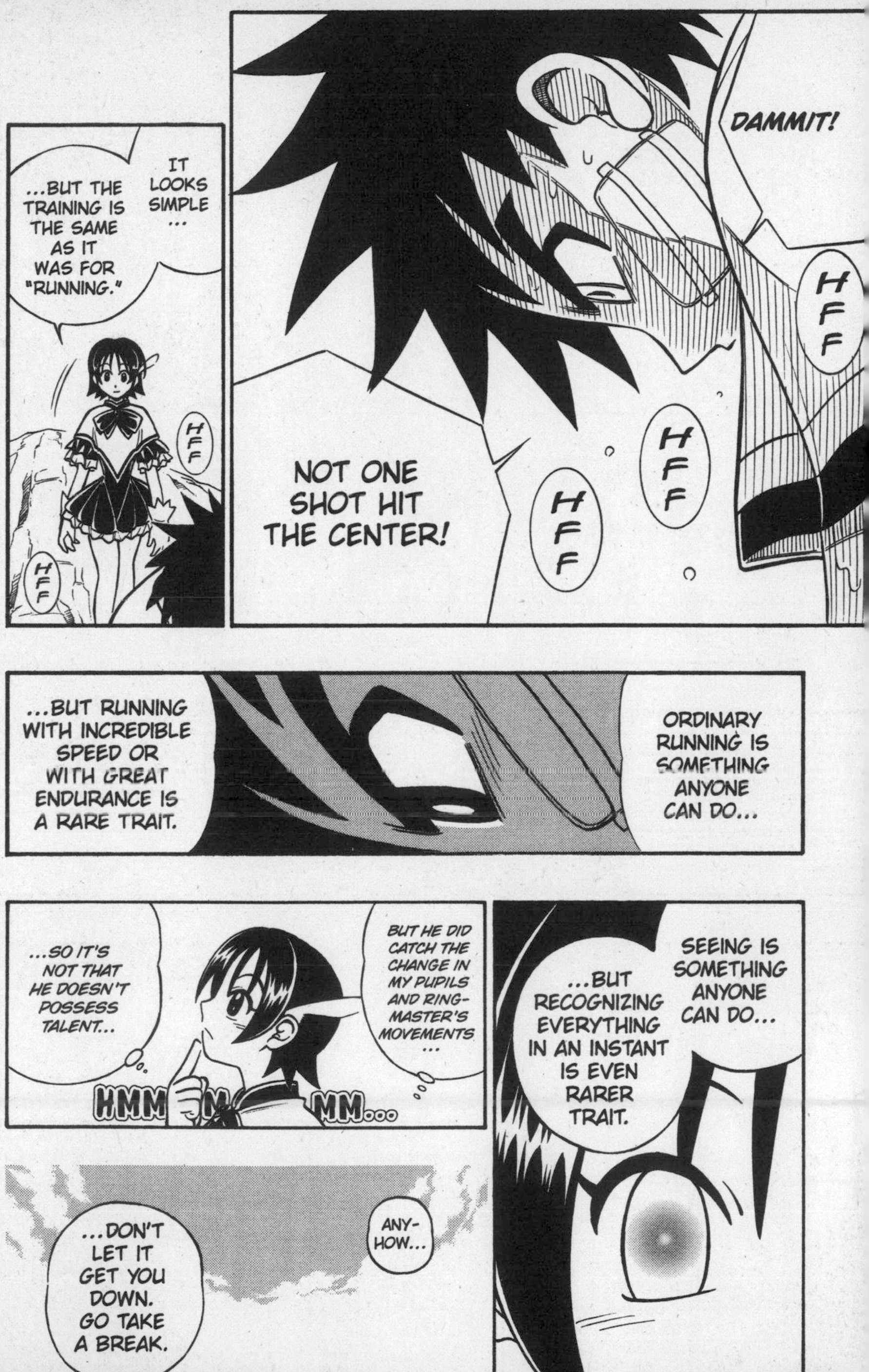
DAMMIT!
HFF
HFF
HFF
NOT ONE SHOT HIT THE CENTER!
IT LOOKS SIMPLE...
...BUT THE TRAINING IS THE SAME AS IT WAS FOR "RUNNING."
HFF
HFF
ORDINARY RUNNING IS SOMETHING ANYONE CAN DO...
...BUT RUNNING WITH INCREDIBLE SPEED OR WITH GREAT ENDURANCE IS A RARE TRAIT.
SEEING IS SOMETHING ANYONE CAN DO...
...BUT RECOGNIZING EVERYTHING IN AN INSTANT IS EVEN RARER TRAIT.
BUT HE DID CATCH THE CHANGE IN MY PUPILS AND RING-MASTER'S MOVEMENTS...
...SO IT'S NOT THAT HE DOESN'T POSSESS TALENT...
HMM M MM...
ANY-HOW...
...DON'T LET IT GET YOU DOWN. GO TAKE A BREAK.

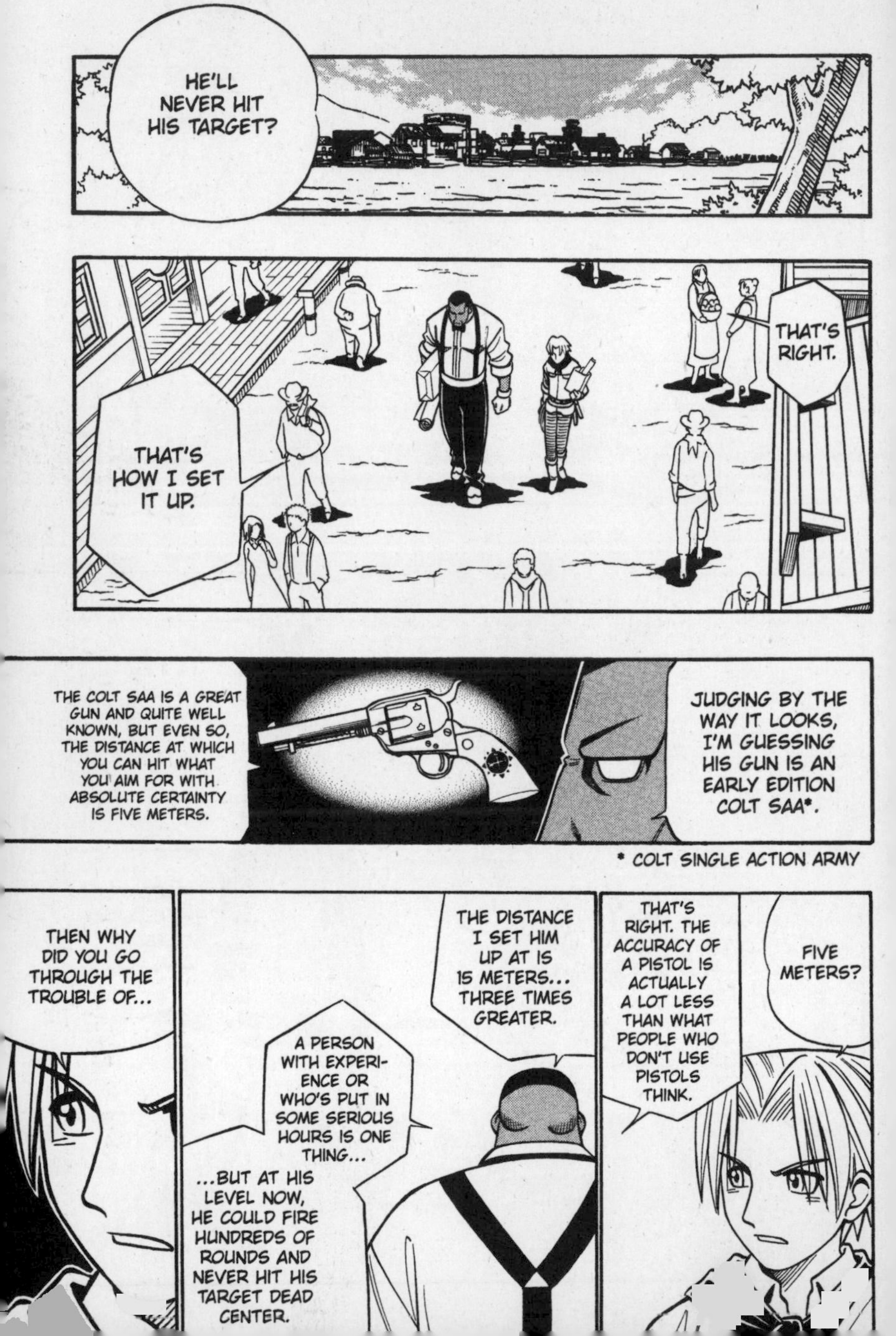
HE'LL NEVER HIT HIS TARGET?
THAT'S RIGHT.
THAT'S HOW I SET IT UP.
JUDGING BY THE WAY IT LOOKS, I'M GUESSING HIS GUN IS AN EARLY EDITION COLT SAA*.
THE COLT SAA IS A GREAT GUN AND QUITE WELL KNOWN, BUT EVEN SO, THE DISTANCE AT WHICH YOU CAN HIT WHAT YOU AIM FOR WITH ABSOLUTE CERTAINTY IS FIVE METERS.
* COLT SINGLE ACTION ARMY
FIVE METERS?
THAT'S RIGHT. THE ACCURACY OF A PISTOL IS ACTUALLY A LOT LESS THAN WHAT PEOPLE WHO DON'T USE PISTOLS THINK.
THE DISTANCE I SET HIM UP AT IS 15 METERS... THREE TIMES GREATER.
A PERSON WITH EXPERI-ENCE OR WHO'S PUT IN SOME SERIOUS HOURS IS ONE THING...
...BUT AT HIS LEVEL NOW, HE COULD FIRE HUNDREDS OF ROUNDS AND NEVER HIT HIS TARGET DEAD CENTER.
THEN WHY DID YOU GO THROUGH THE TROUBLE OF...

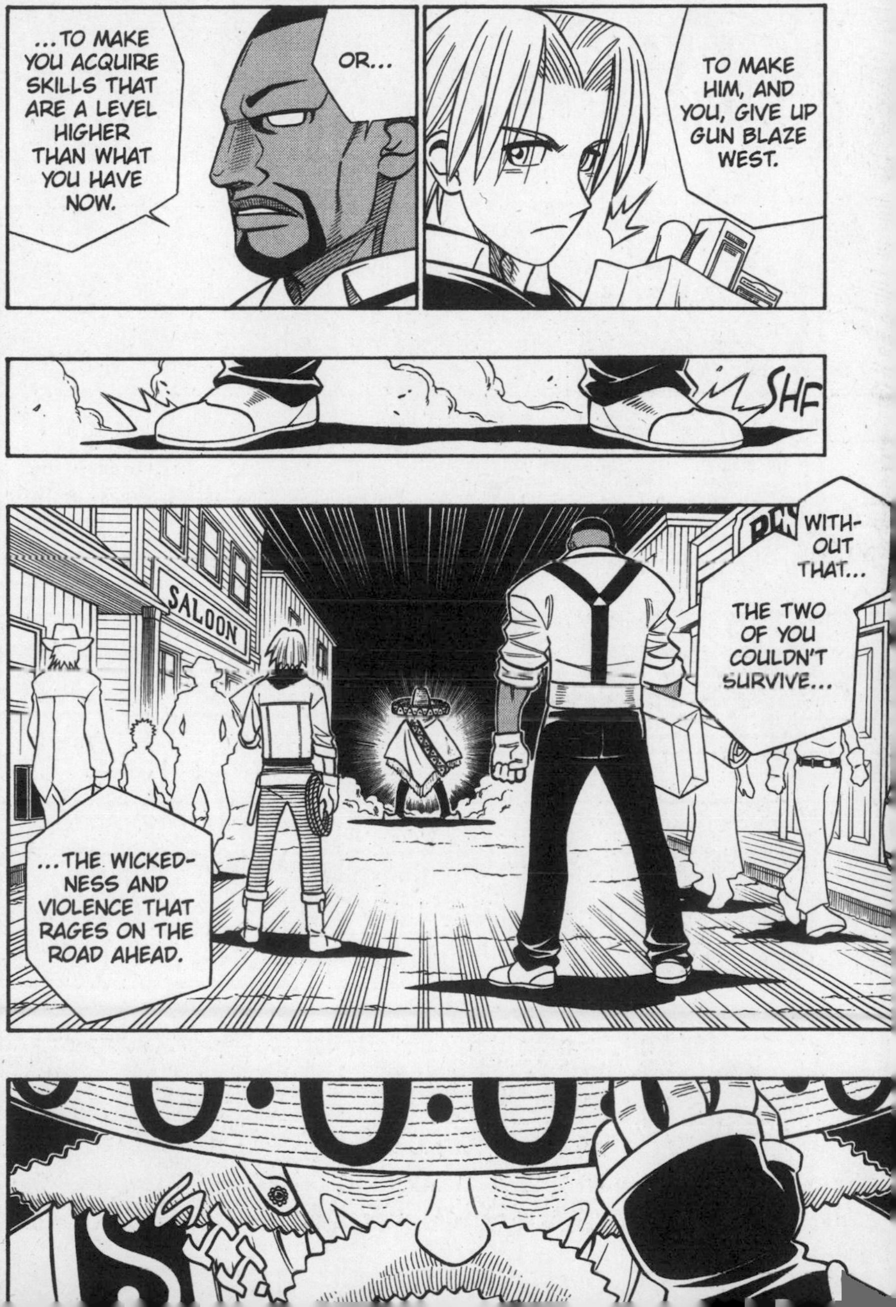
TO MAKE HIM, AND YOU, GIVE UP GUN BLAZE WEST.
OR...
...TO MAKE YOU ACQUIRE SKILLS THAT ARE A LEVEL HIGHER THAN WHAT YOU HAVE NOW.
SHF
WITH-OUT THAT...
THE TWO OF YOU COULDN'T SURVIVE...
SALOON
...THE WICKED-NESS AND VIOLENCE THAT RAGES ON THE ROAD AHEAD.

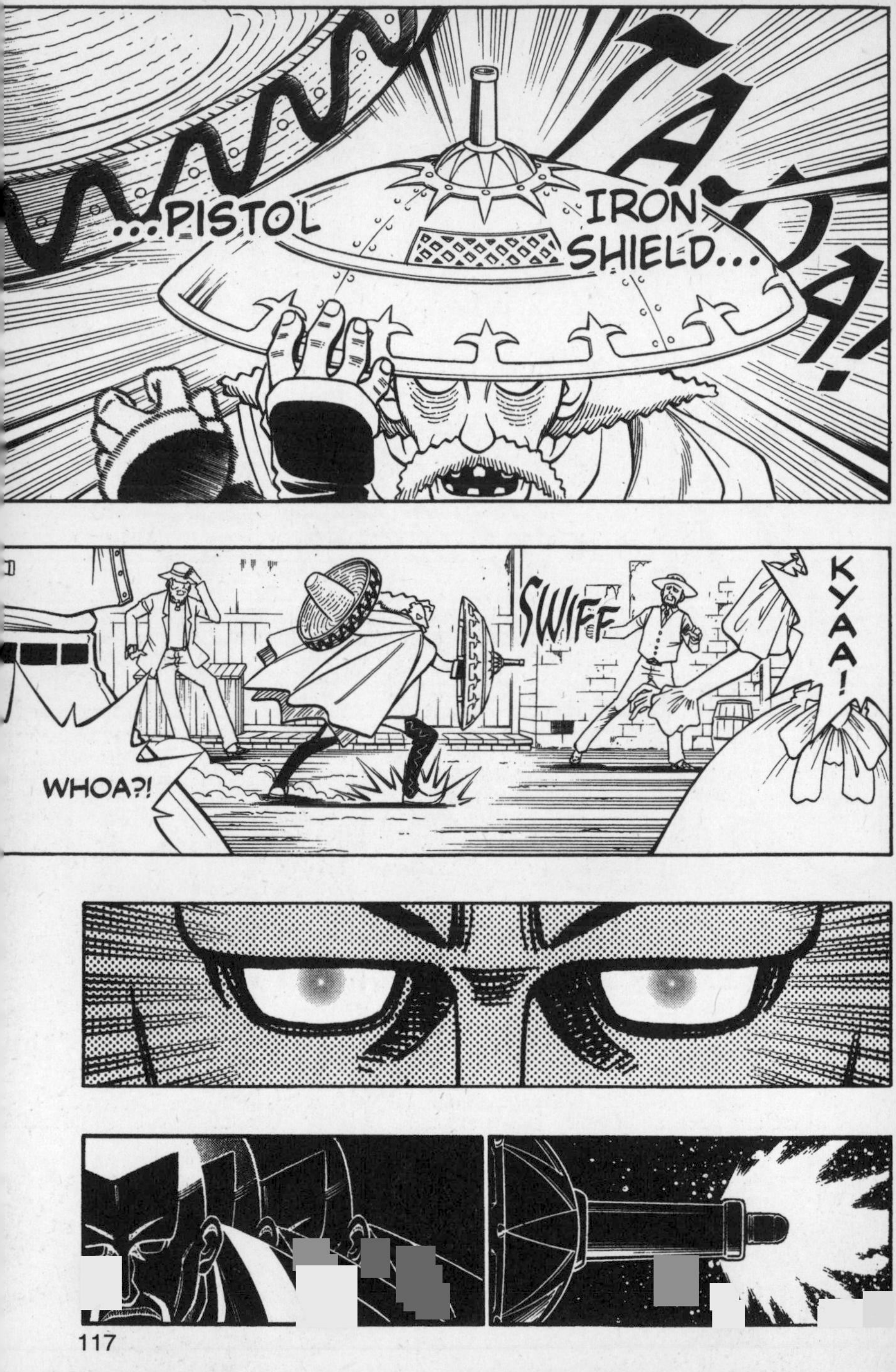
TADA!
IRON SHIELD...
...PISTOL
KYAA!
SWIFF
WHOA?!

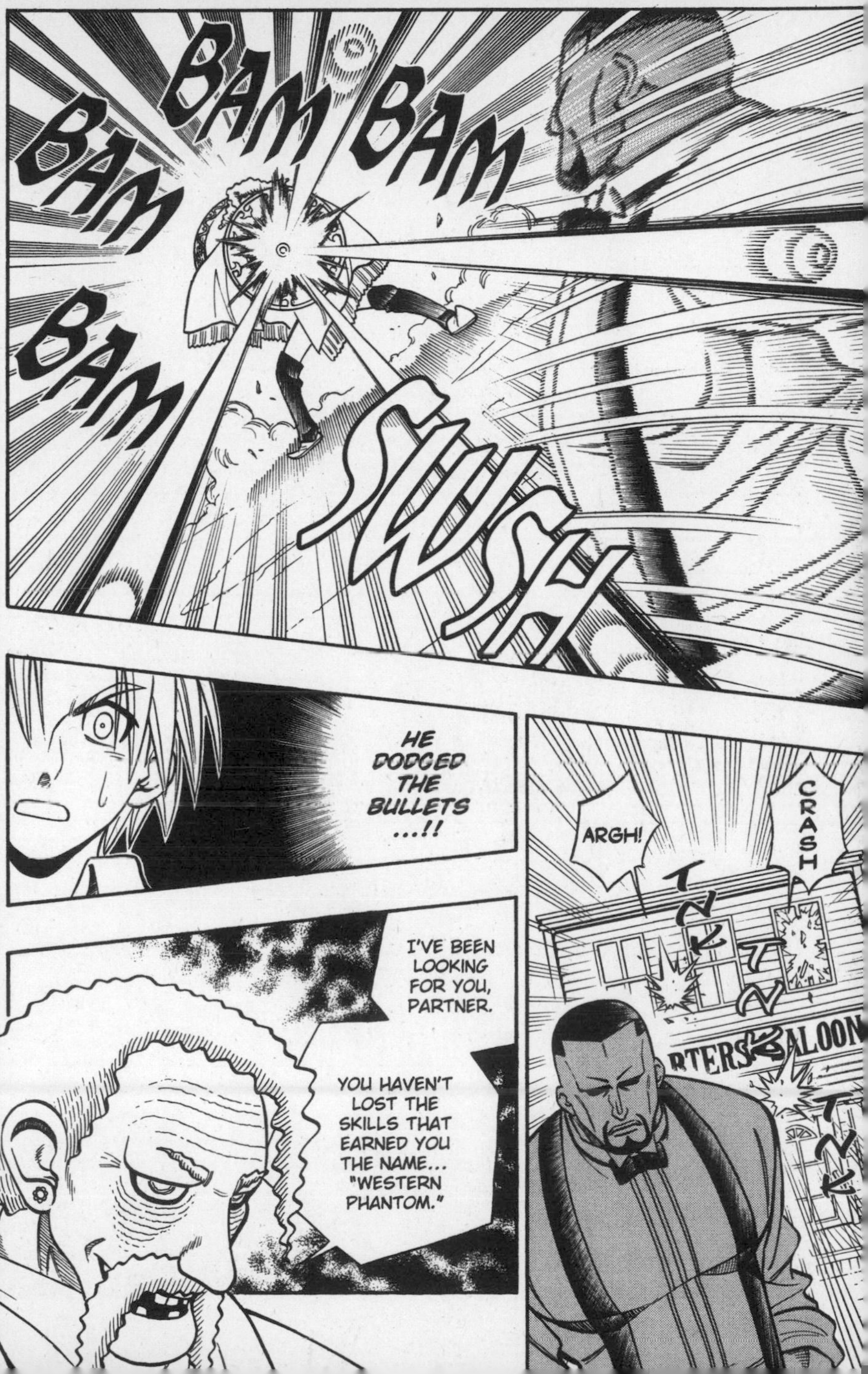
BAM BAM BAM BAM BAM
SWISH
ARGH!
CRASH
TINK
TINK
TINK
HE DODGED THE BULLETS ...!!
I'VE BEEN LOOKING FOR YOU, PARTNER.
YOU HAVEN'T LOST THE SKILLS THAT EARNED YOU THE NAME... "WESTERN PHANTOM."

READ THIS WAY

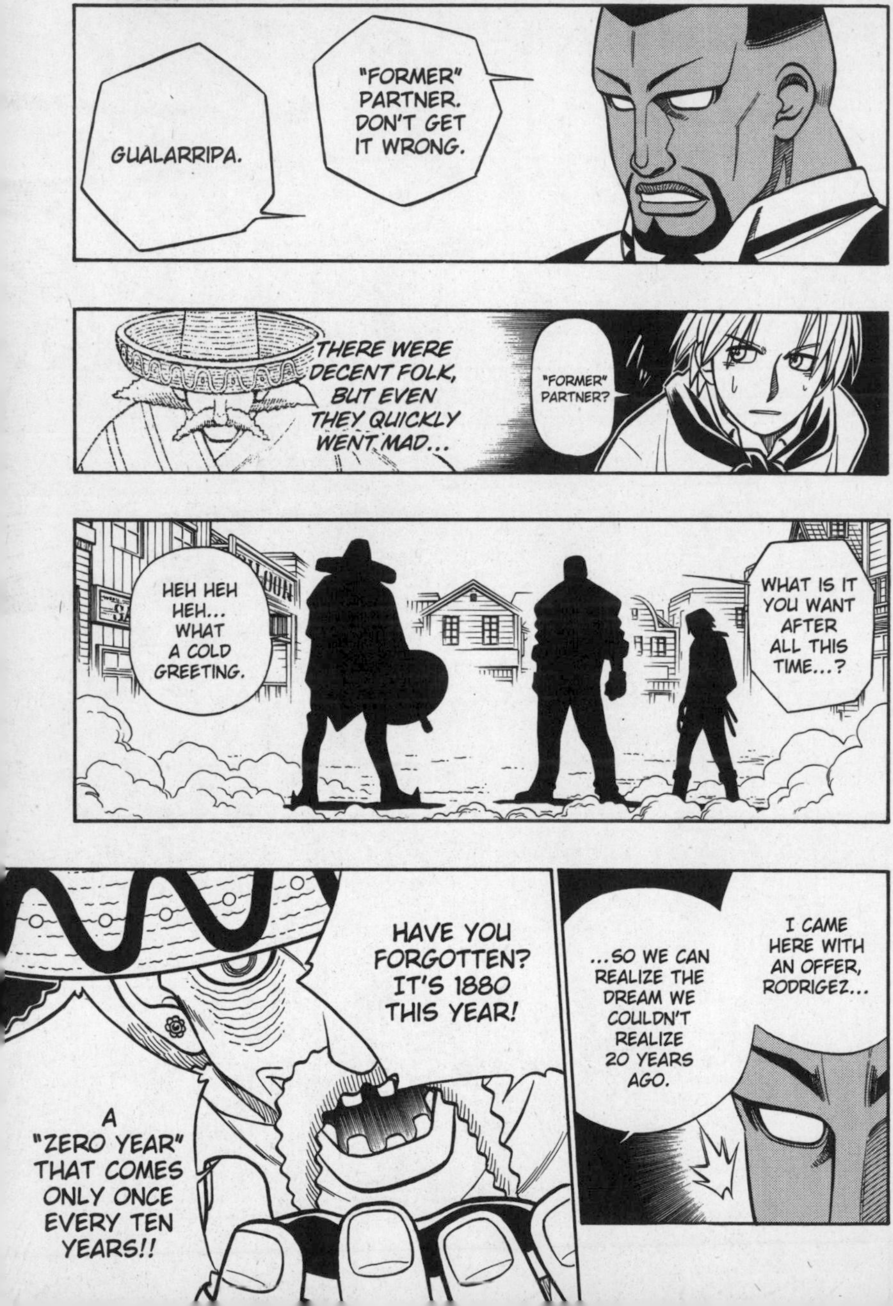
"FORMER" PARTNER. DON'T GET IT WRONG.
GUALARRIPA.
"FORMER" PARTNER?
THERE WERE DECENT FOLK, BUT EVEN THEY QUICKLY WENT MAD...
WHAT IS IT YOU WANT AFTER ALL THIS TIME...?
HEH HEH HEH... WHAT A COLD GREETING.
I CAME HERE WITH AN OFFER, RODRIGEZ...
...SO WE CAN REALIZE THE DREAM WE COULDN'T REALIZE 20 YEARS AGO.
HAVE YOU FORGOTTEN? IT'S 1880 THIS YEAR!
A "ZERO YEAR" THAT COMES ONLY ONCE EVERY TEN YEARS!!

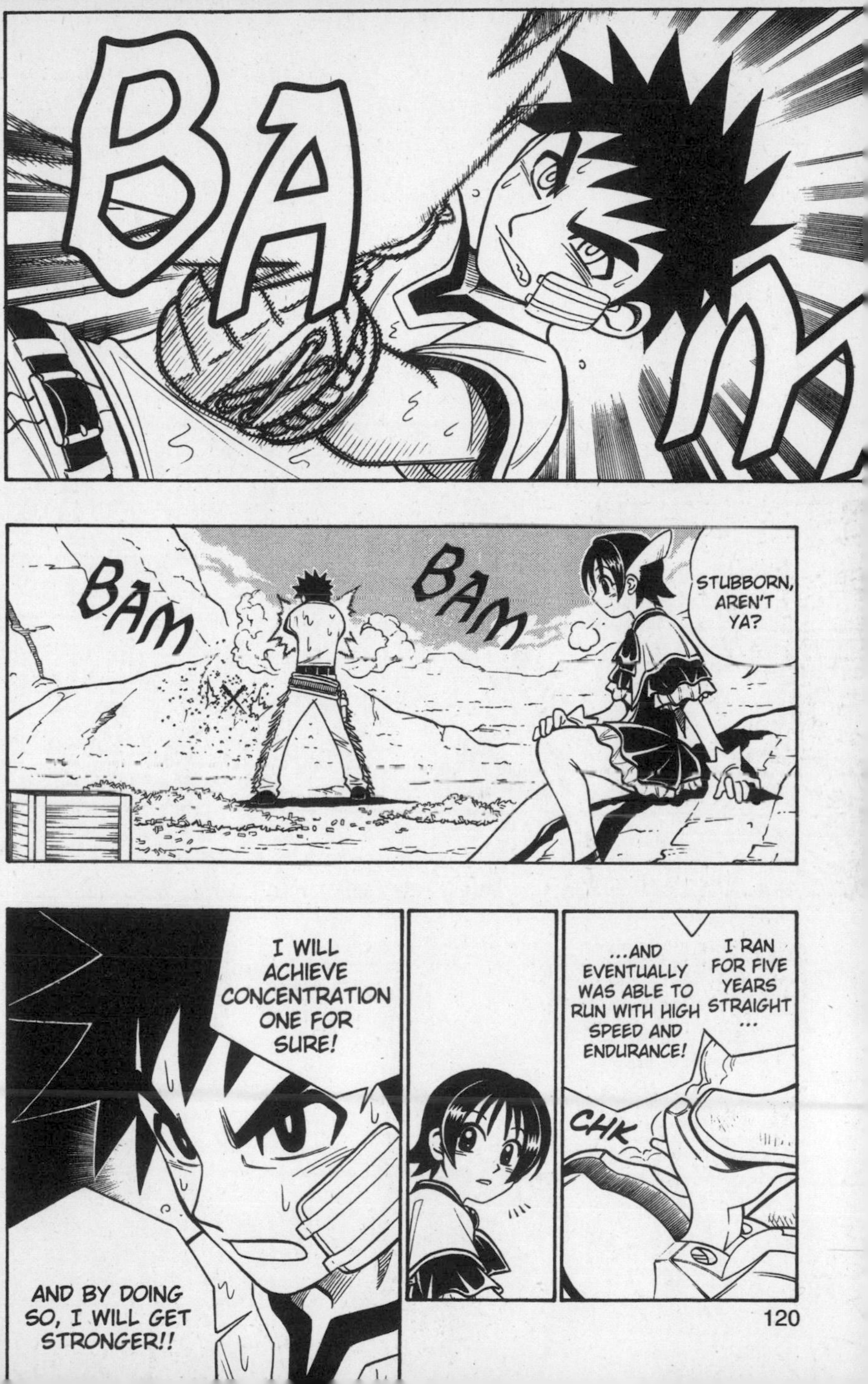
BA
STUBBORN, AREN'T YA?
BAM
BAM
I RAN FOR FIVE YEARS STRAIGHT...
...AND EVENTUALLY WAS ABLE TO RUN WITH HIGH SPEED AND ENDURANCE!
CHK
I WILL ACHIEVE CONCENTRATION ONE FOR SURE!
AND BY DOING SO, I WILL GET STRONGER!!

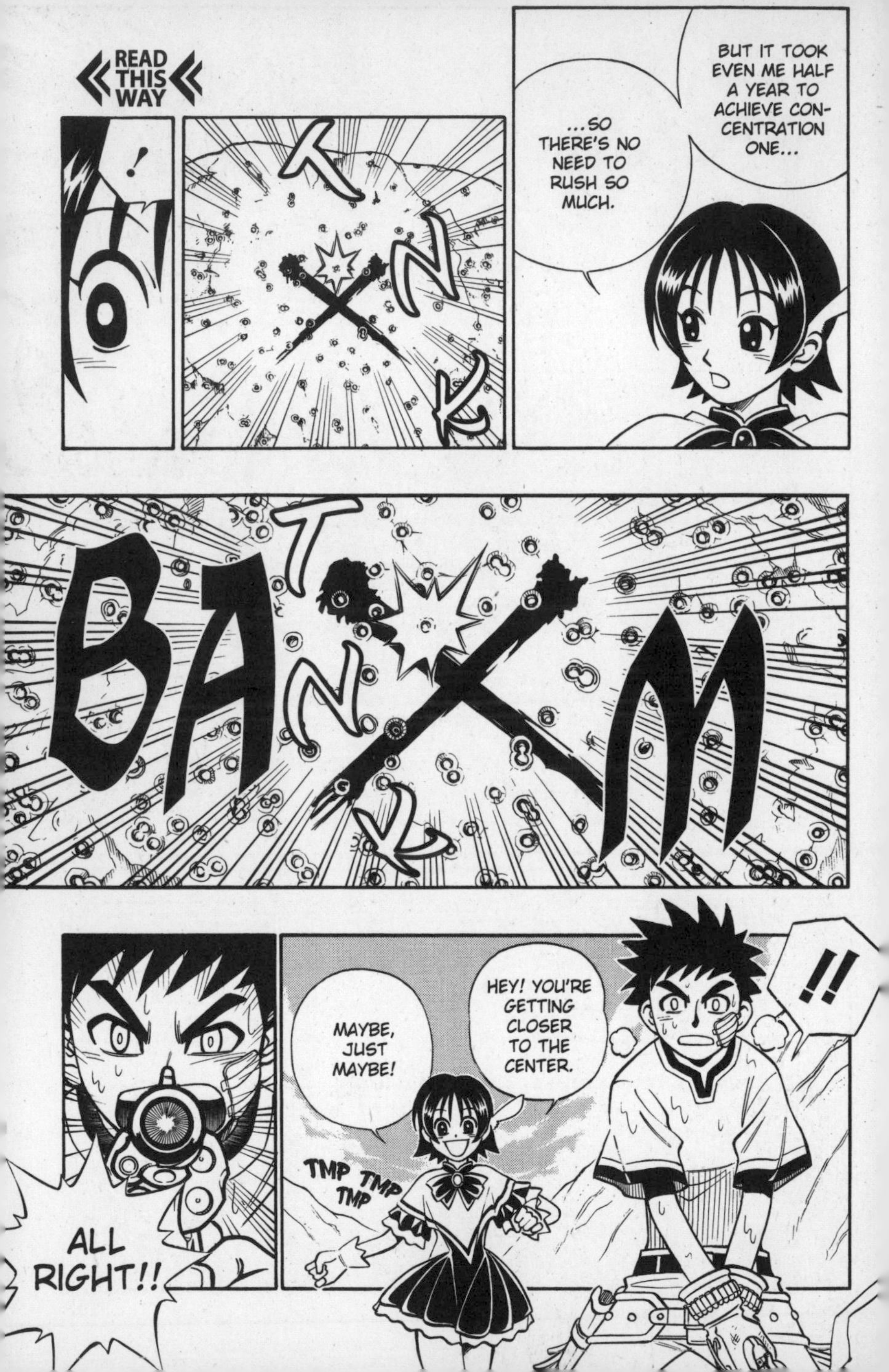READ THIS WAY
BUT IT TOOK EVEN ME HALF A YEAR TO ACHIEVE CONCENTRATION ONE...
...SO THERE'S NO NEED TO RUSH SO MUCH.
KNK
!
BAM
TNK
!!
HEY! YOU'RE GETTING CLOSER TO THE CENTER.
MAYBE, JUST MAYBE!
TMP TMP TMP
ALL RIGHT!!

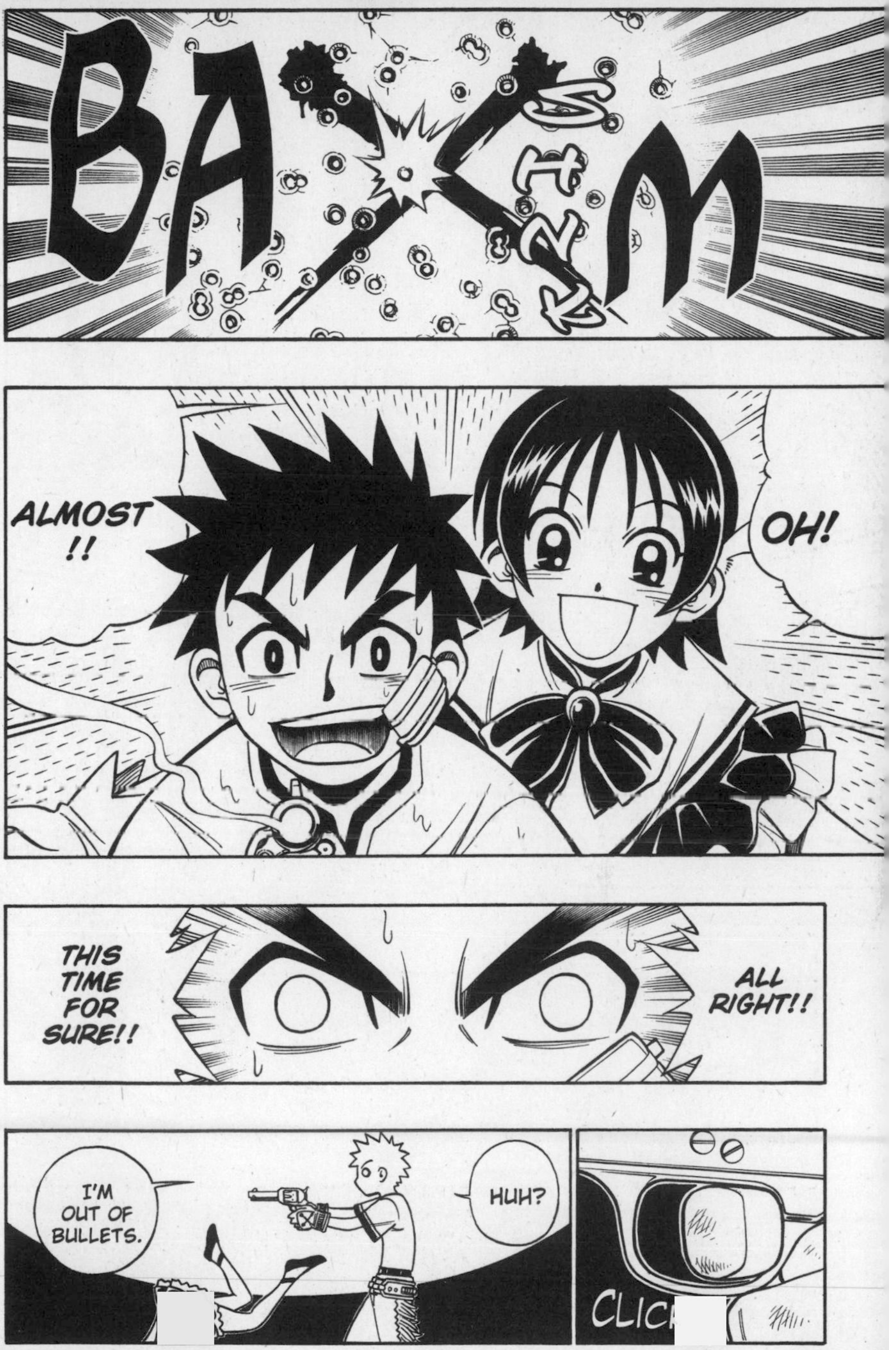

BAM
OH!
ALMOST !!
ALL RIGHT!!
THIS TIME FOR SURE!!
CLIC
HUH?
I'M OUT OF BULLETS.

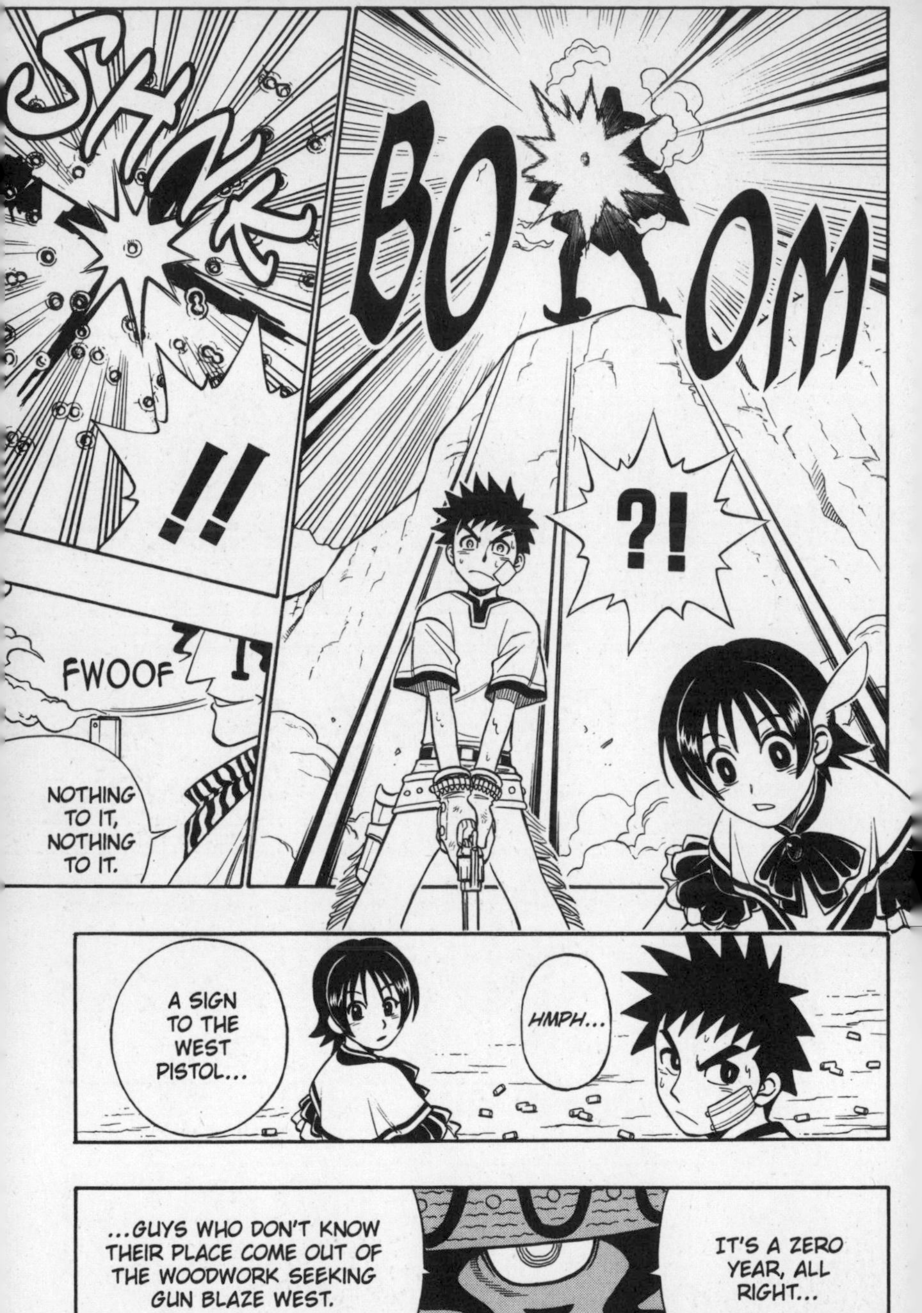
BOOM
?!
SHINK
!!
FWOOF
NOTHING TO IT, NOTHING TO IT.
HMPH...
A SIGN TO THE WEST PISTOL...
IT'S A ZERO YEAR, ALL RIGHT...
...GUYS WHO DON'T KNOW THEIR PLACE COME OUT OF THE WOODWORK SEEKING GUN BLAZE WEST.

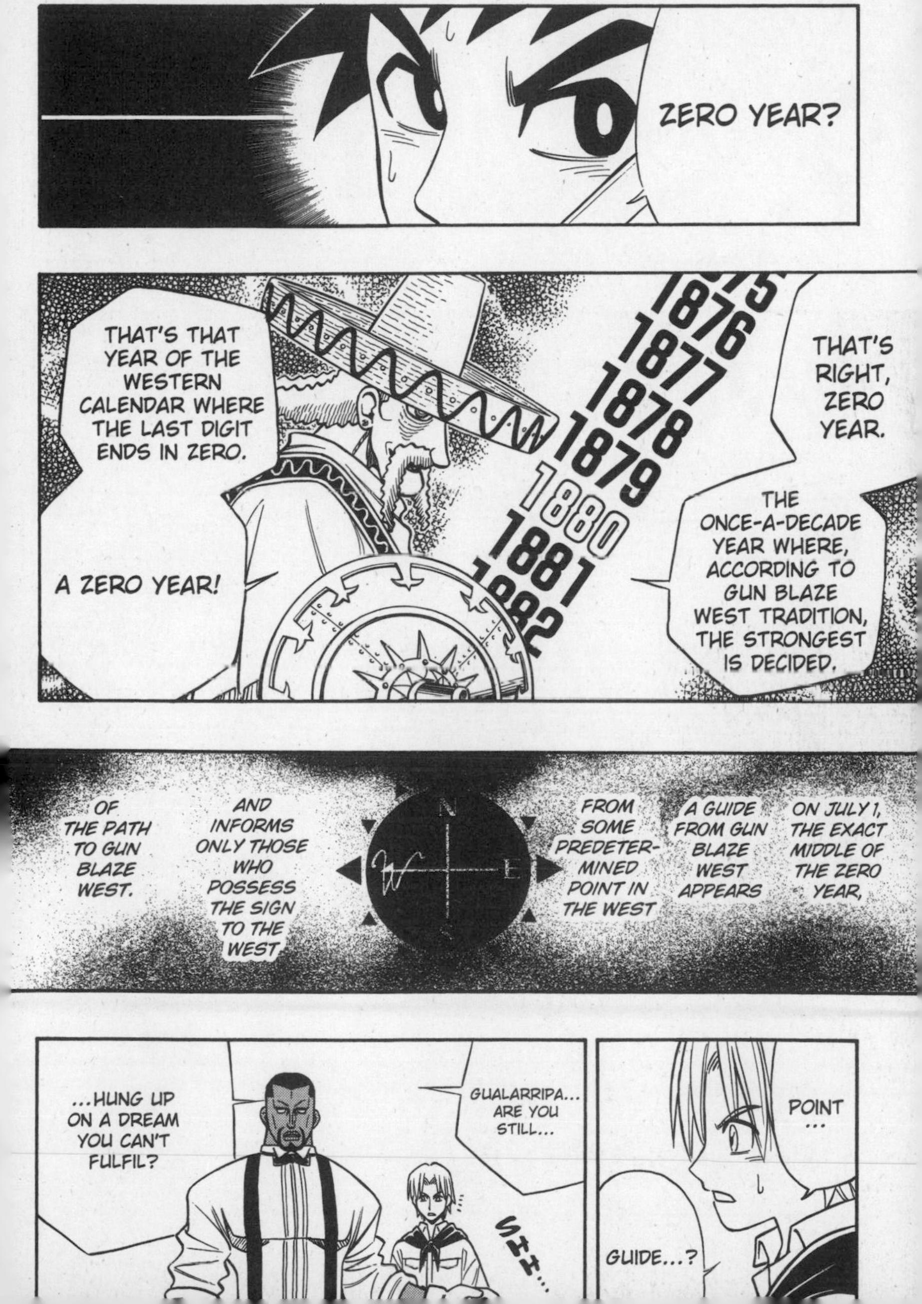
ZERO YEAR?
THAT'S RIGHT, ZERO YEAR.
THE ONCE-A-DECADE YEAR WHERE, ACCORDING TO GUN BLAZE WEST TRADITION, THE STRONGEST IS DECIDED.
1876
1877
1878
1879
1880
1881
THAT'S THAT YEAR OF THE WESTERN CALENDAR WHERE THE LAST DIGIT ENDS IN ZERO.
A ZERO YEAR!
ON JULY 1, THE EXACT MIDDLE OF THE ZERO YEAR,
A GUIDE FROM GUN BLAZE WEST APPEARS
FROM SOME PREDETER-MINED POINT IN THE WEST
N
E
W
AND INFORMS ONLY THOSE WHO POSSESS THE SIGN TO THE WEST
OF THE PATH TO GUN BLAZE WEST.
POINT...
GUIDE...?
GUALARRIPA... ARE YOU STILL...
...HUNG UP ON A DREAM YOU CAN'T FULFIL?
SHH...

READ THIS WAY

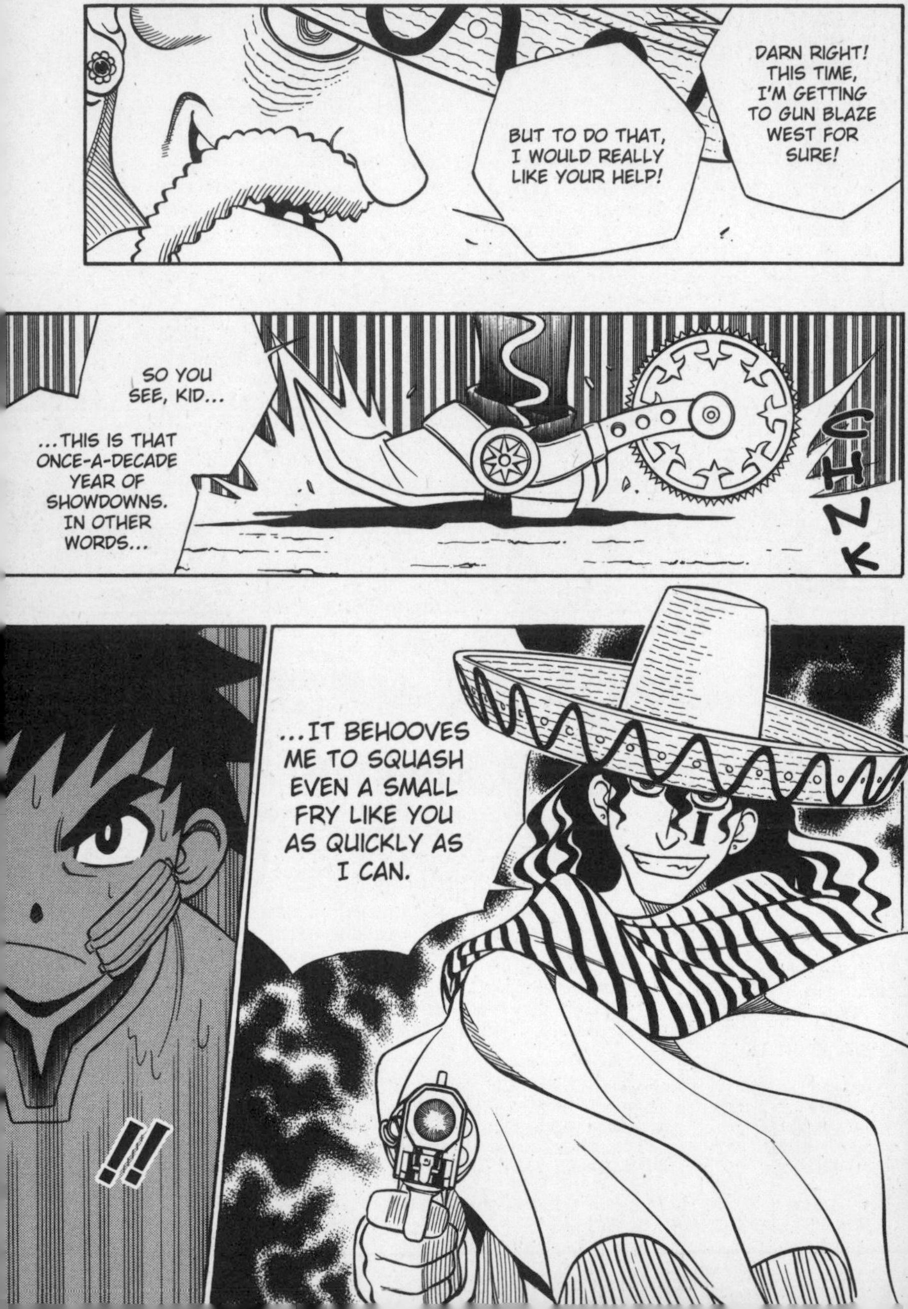
DARN RIGHT! THIS TIME, I'M GETTING TO GUN BLAZE WEST FOR SURE!
BUT TO DO THAT, I WOULD REALLY LIKE YOUR HELP!
CHINK
SO YOU SEE, KID...
...THIS IS THAT ONCE-A-DECADE YEAR OF SHOWDOWNS. IN OTHER WORDS...
...IT BEHOOVES ME TO SQUASH EVEN A SMALL FRY LIKE YOU AS QUICKLY AS I CAN.
!!

CONCEPT: SINCE VIU AND CORICE ARE CHARACTERS WITH SOME TRAITS ONE WOULD NOT NORMALLY EXPECT, I CONCEIVED OF WILL AS A CHARACTER THAT WOULD FOLLOW THEM BOTH. IN OTHER WORDS, HE IS THE INTELLECTUAL CHARACTER OF THE THREE TYPES--INTELLECTUAL, EMOTIONAL, AND VOLITIONAL--OF CHARACTERS. (JUST FYI, VIU IS THE VOLITIONAL AND COLICE IS THE ALL-AROUND CHARACTER WHO POSSESSES ALL THE TRAITS.)

UNLIKE VIU WHO HAD AN INFATUATION WITH STRENGTH OR COLICE WITH HER CURIOSITY, MY INITIAL CONCEPT OF WILL WAS AN INTELLECTUAL WITH A MORE ACADEMIC APPROACH TO SEEKING GUN BLAZE WEST BUT WHO, WHEN THE TIME CAME, BATTLED BY COMBINING KNOWLEDGE WITH COURAGE TO CREATE WISDOM. I THOUGHT THIS WAS TOO CONSERVATIVE, HOWEVER, SO I HURRIEDLY ADDED ON THE BOUNCER ELEMENT. IN HINDSIGHT, HOWEVER, I THINK THAT THIS NEUTRALIZED HIS STRONGEST CHARACTERISTIC, THAT OF BEING AN INTELLECTUAL, MAKING HIS CHARACTER WEAKER. I REGRET THAT.

SINCE VIU, COLICE AND WILL BEGAN MAKING THEIR MOVE ONLY AFTER THE THREE OF THEM GOT TOGETHER, WILL SERVED WELL AS THE VOICE OF REASON. I'D LIKE TO TRY ONCE AGAIN SOMETIME AT DOING AN INTELLECTUAL-TYPE CHARACTER.

# CHARACTER FILE #05

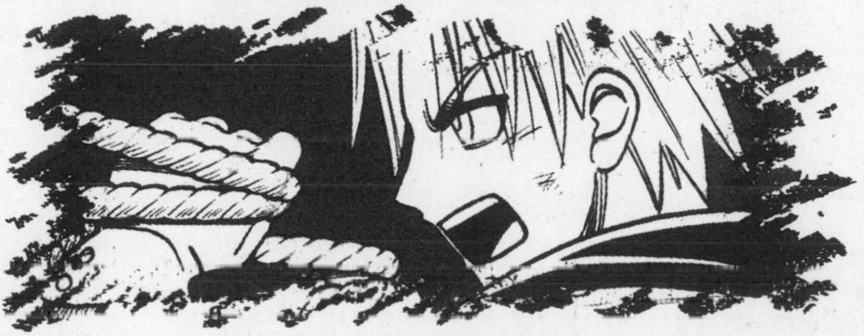

# WILL JOHNSTON

IMAGE SOURCE: MY IMAGE SOURCE FOR WILL WAS THE ECCENTRIC YOUNG QUENTIN WHO WAS TREATED LIKE AN OUTCAST BY THE REST OF HIS SCHOOL IN THE MOVIE *OCTOBER SKY*. THOSE WHO HAVE SEEN THE MOVIE MIGHT THINK, "WHAT? HE'S ENTIRELY DIFFERENT!" BUT IT WAS QUENTIN'S SINGLE-MINDED DILIGENCE IN HIS STUDIES DESPITE COMING FROM A POOR FAMILY THAT BECAME MY IMAGE SOURCE FOR WILL.

OCTOBER SKY IS AN UNSPECTACULAR FILM, BUT IT IS A GOOD MOVIE. I RECOMMEND IT WITH CONFIDENCE TO ANYONE WHO HAS EVEN ONCE DREAMED OF OUTER SPACE OR WHO IS A FAN OF *STAND BY ME*.

DESIGN: HERE AGAIN, SINCE VIU AND COLICE DO NOT LOOK LIKE WHAT ONE MIGHT NORMALLY EXPECT IN A WESTERN, I MADE WILL LOOK AS MUCH AS POSSIBLE LIKE A TYPICAL BOY IN A WESTERN.

ON ONE ASPECT, WILL'S HEIGHT, I WAS VERY PARTICULAR. IN MY PREVIOUS WORK, *RUROUNI KENSHIN*, I LOOKED FOR SOME WAY TO BLEND THE HEIGHTS OF THE CHARACTERS WHO ENDED UP AT OPPOSITE ENDS OF THE SCALE. (FOR EXAMPLE, IT WAS QUITE DIFFICULT TO HAVE AOSHI AND MISAO STAND NATURALLY NEXT TO EACH OTHER IN THE SAME PANEL.) AS A TEST, I TRIED THIS, THAT AND A LOT OF DIFFERENT THINGS. I HAD A BIT OF SUCCESS, I THINK.

ON A SIDE NOTE, THE IDEA FOR THE COMPASS IN WILL'S POSSESSION CAME FROM A GOOD NOVELIST FRIEND OF MINE. THANK YOU, MR. K.

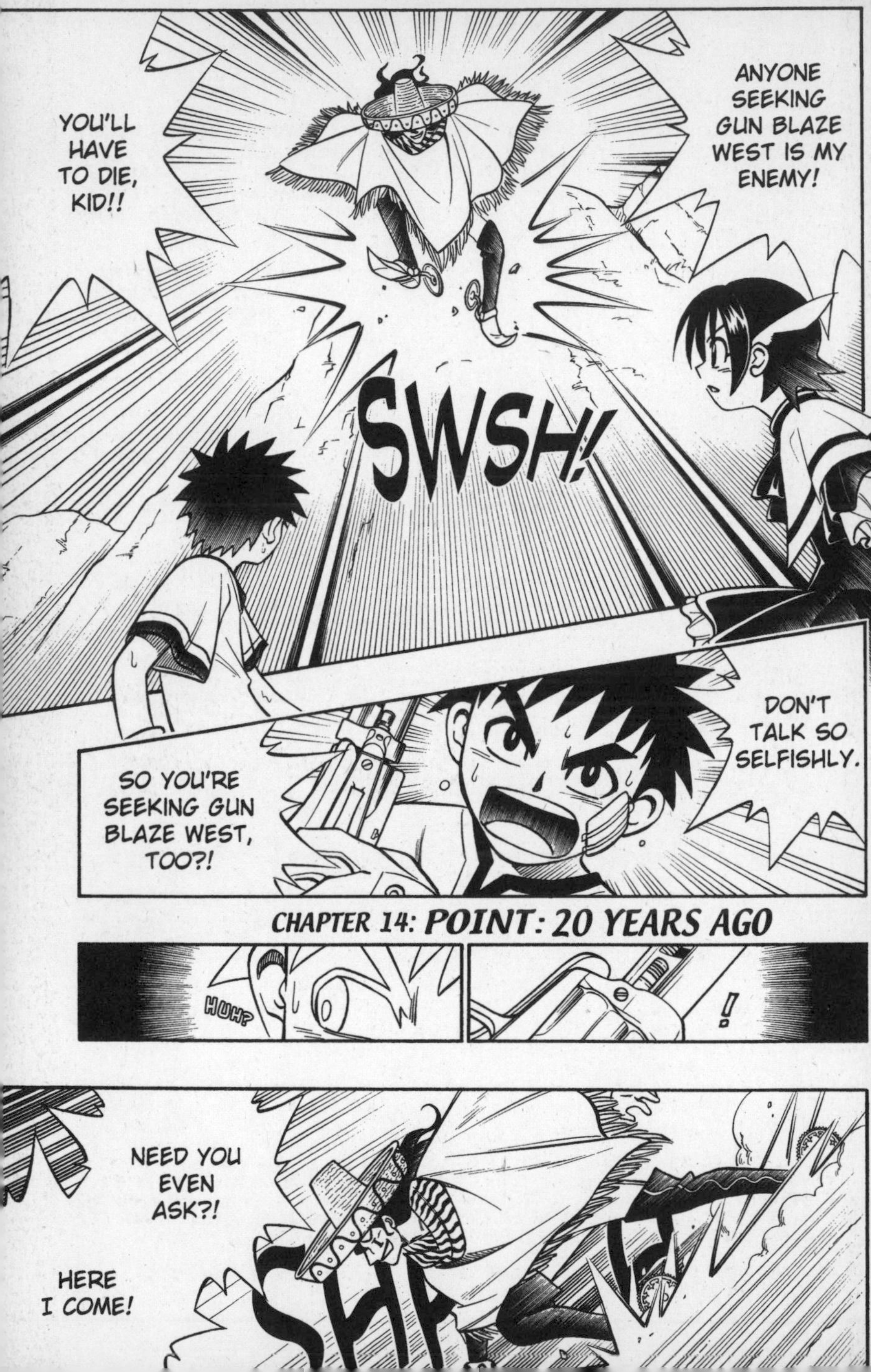
ANYONE SEEKING GUN BLAZE WEST IS MY ENEMY!
YOU'LL HAVE TO DIE, KID!!
SWSH!
DON'T TALK SO SELFISHLY.
SO YOU'RE SEEKING GUN BLAZE WEST, TOO?!
CHAPTER 14: POINT: 20 YEARS AGO
!
HUH?
NEED YOU EVEN ASK?!
HERE I COME!

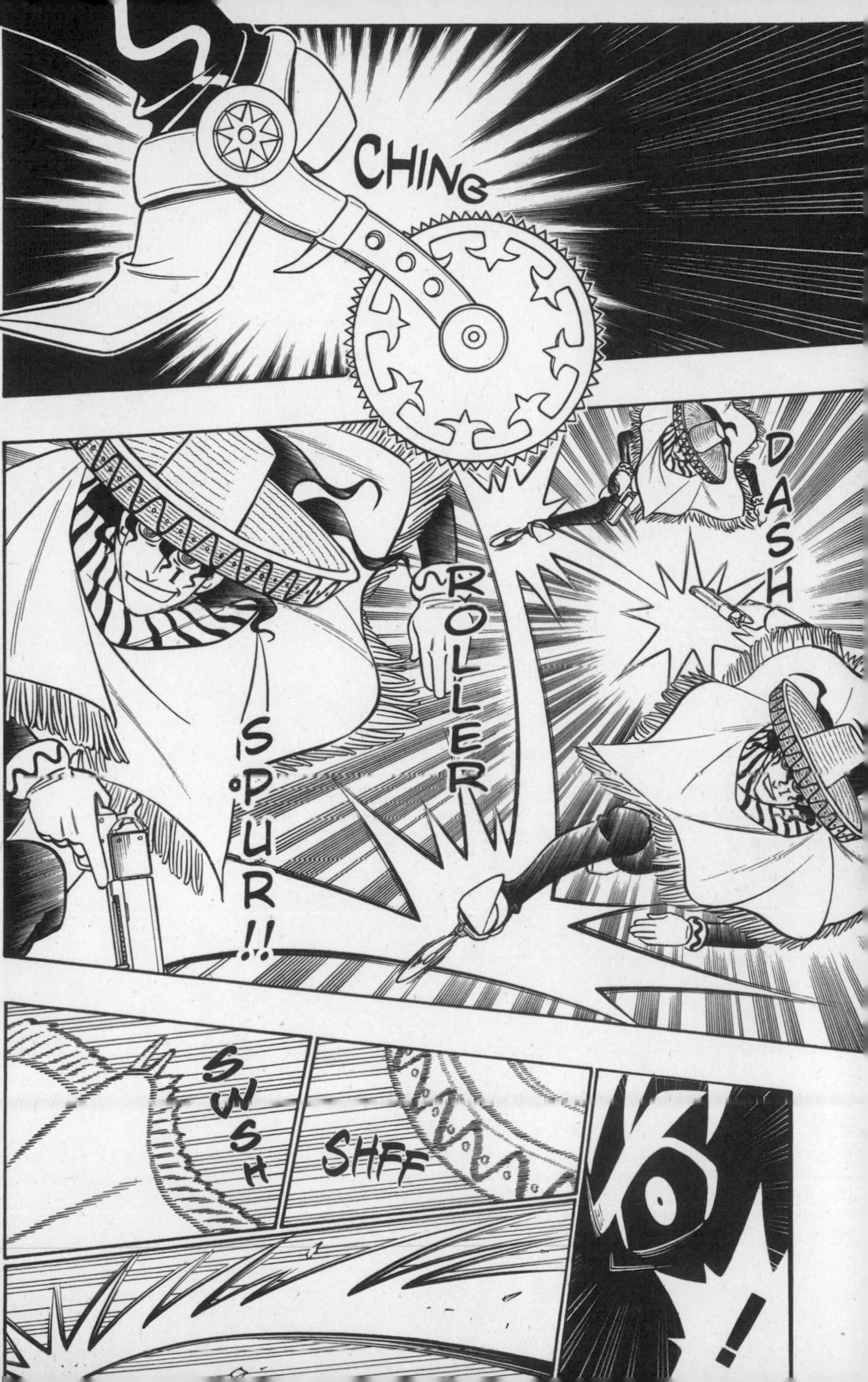
CHING
DASH
ROLLER
SPUR!!
!
SHFF
SWSH

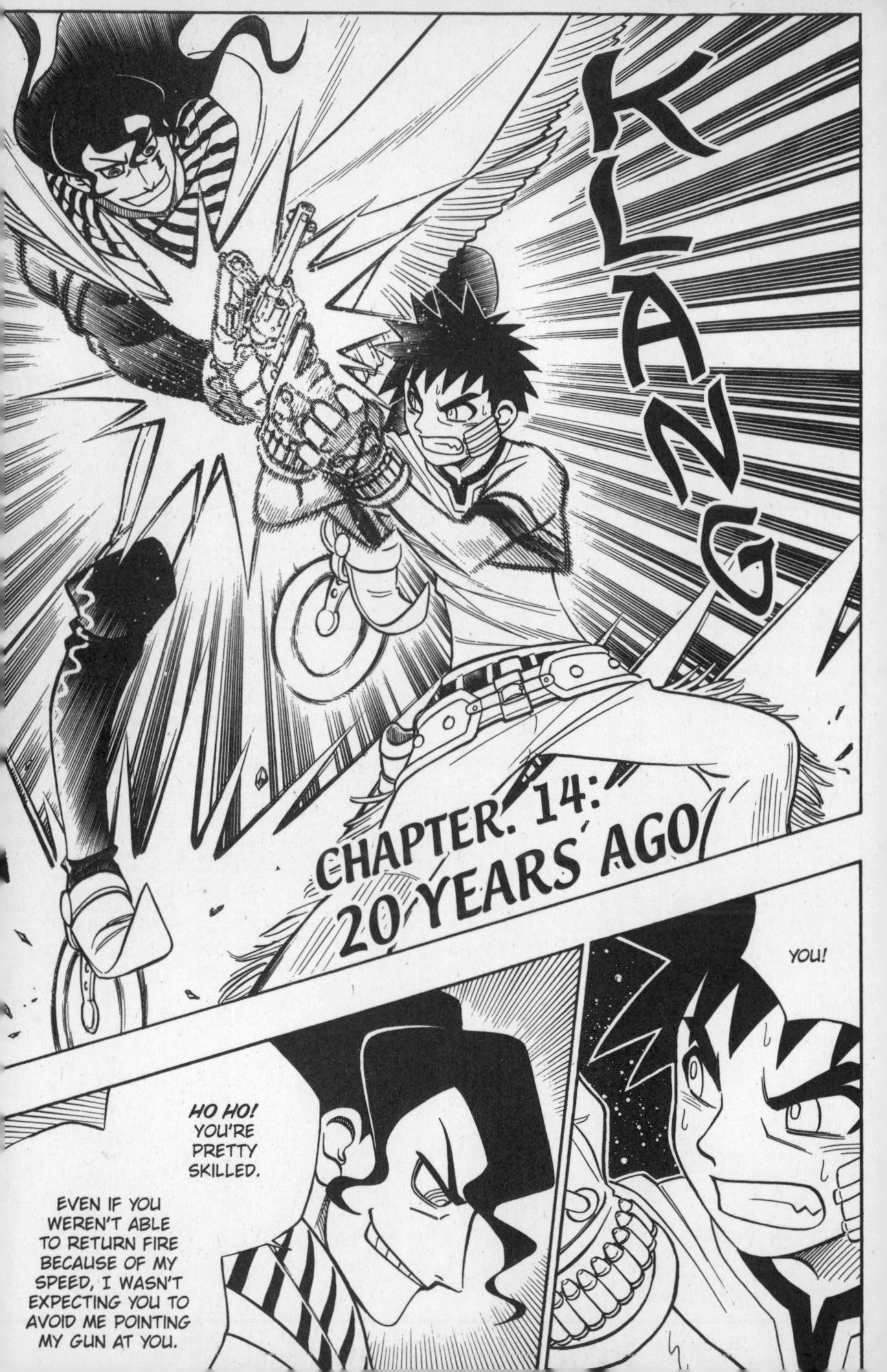
KLANG
CHAPTER. 14:
20 YEARS AGO
YOU!
HO HO! YOU'RE PRETTY SKILLED.
EVEN IF YOU WEREN'T ABLE TO RETURN FIRE BECAUSE OF MY SPEED, I WASN'T EXPECTING YOU TO AVOID ME POINTING MY GUN AT YOU.

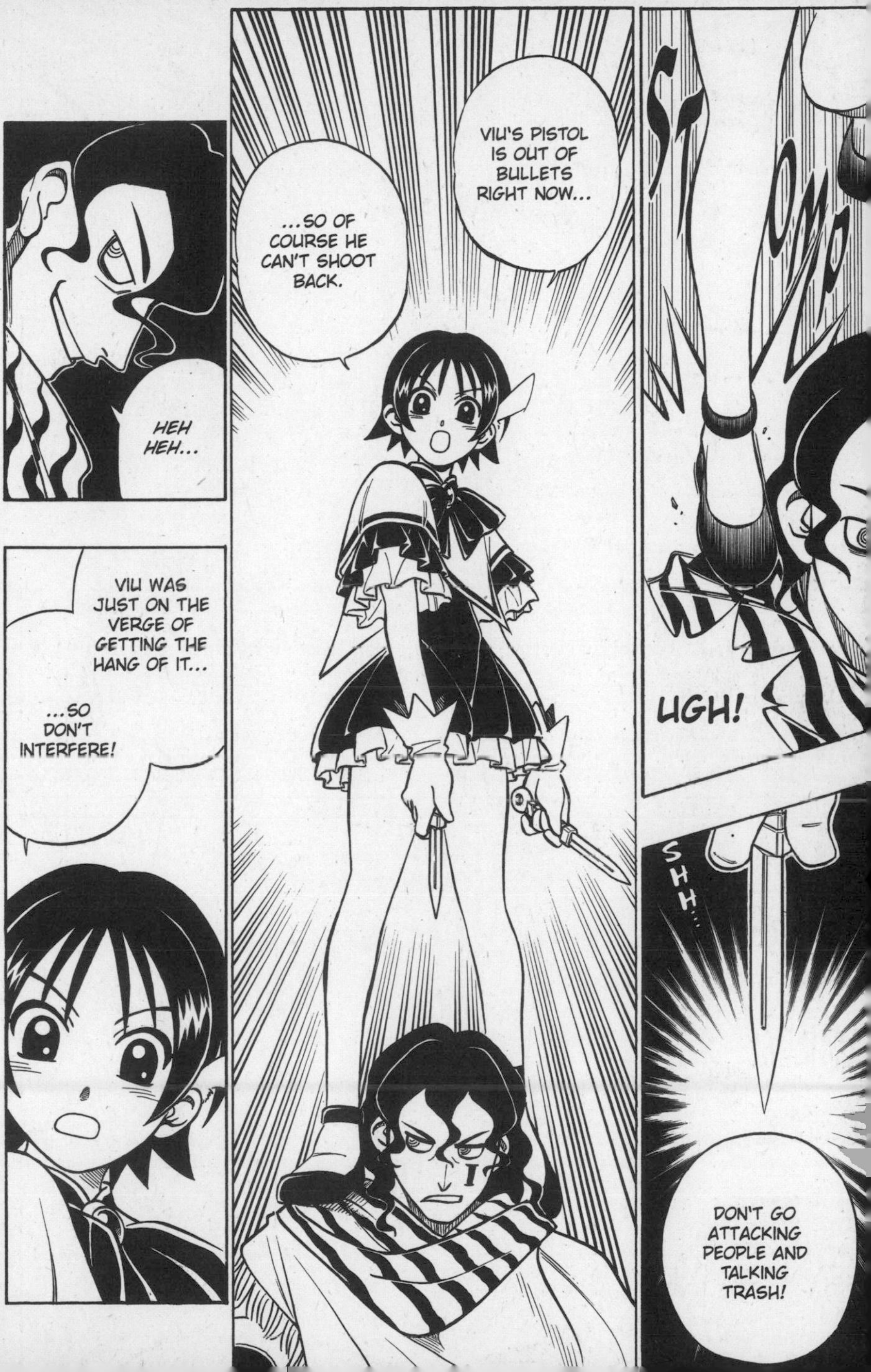
UGH!
SHH...
DON'T GO ATTACKING PEOPLE AND TALKING TRASH!
VIU'S PISTOL IS OUT OF BULLETS RIGHT NOW...
...SO OF COURSE HE CAN'T SHOOT BACK.
HEH HEH...
VIU WAS JUST ON THE VERGE OF GETTING THE HANG OF IT...
...SO DON'T INTERFERE!

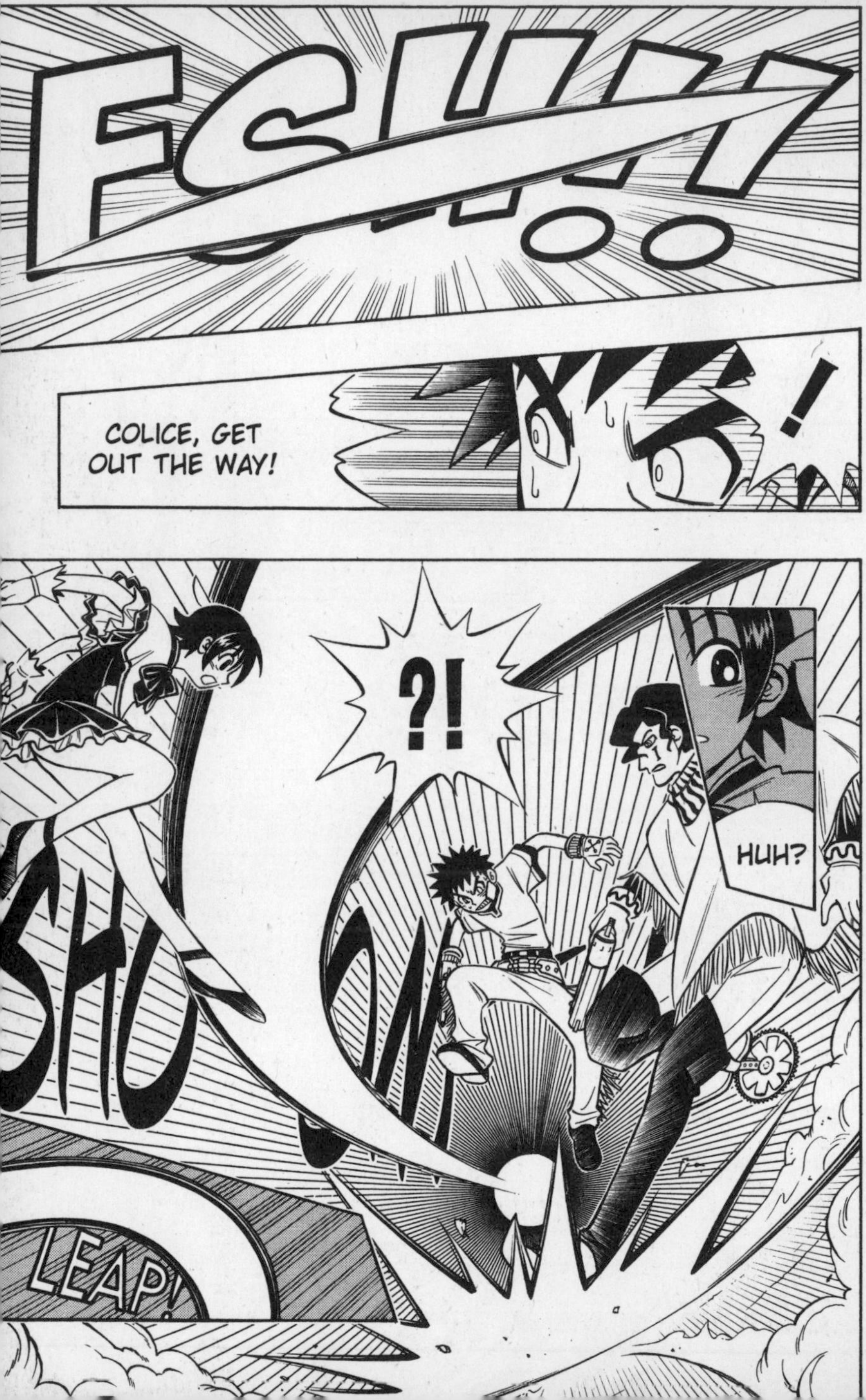

!
COLICE, GET OUT THE WAY!
HUH?
?!
LEAP!

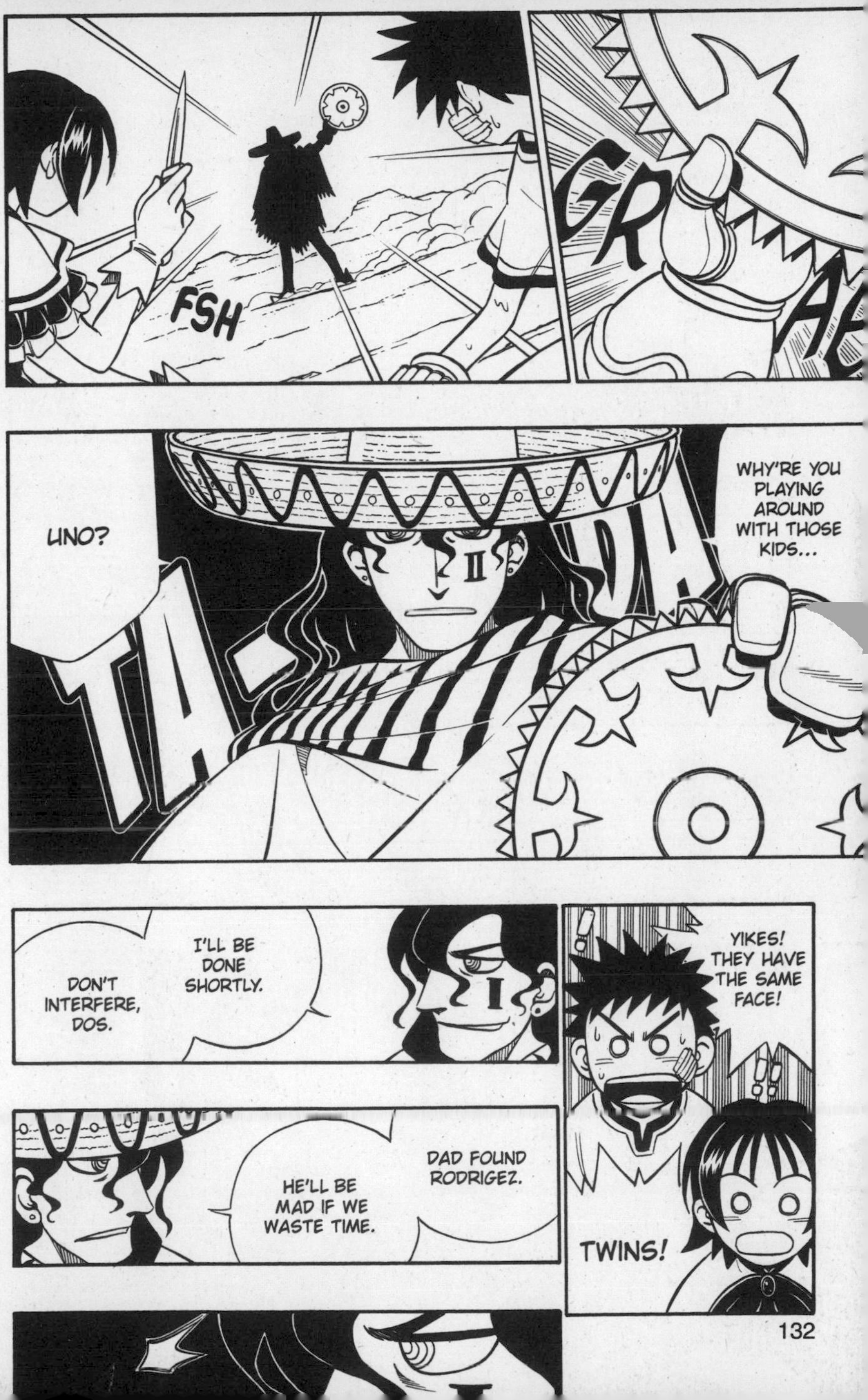
GR
FSH
WHY'RE YOU PLAYING AROUND WITH THOSE KIDS...
UNO?
YIKES! THEY HAVE THE SAME FACE!
TWINS!
I'LL BE DONE SHORTLY.
DON'T INTERFERE, DOS.
DAD FOUND RODRIGEZ.
HE'LL BE MAD IF WE WASTE TIME.

READ THIS WAY

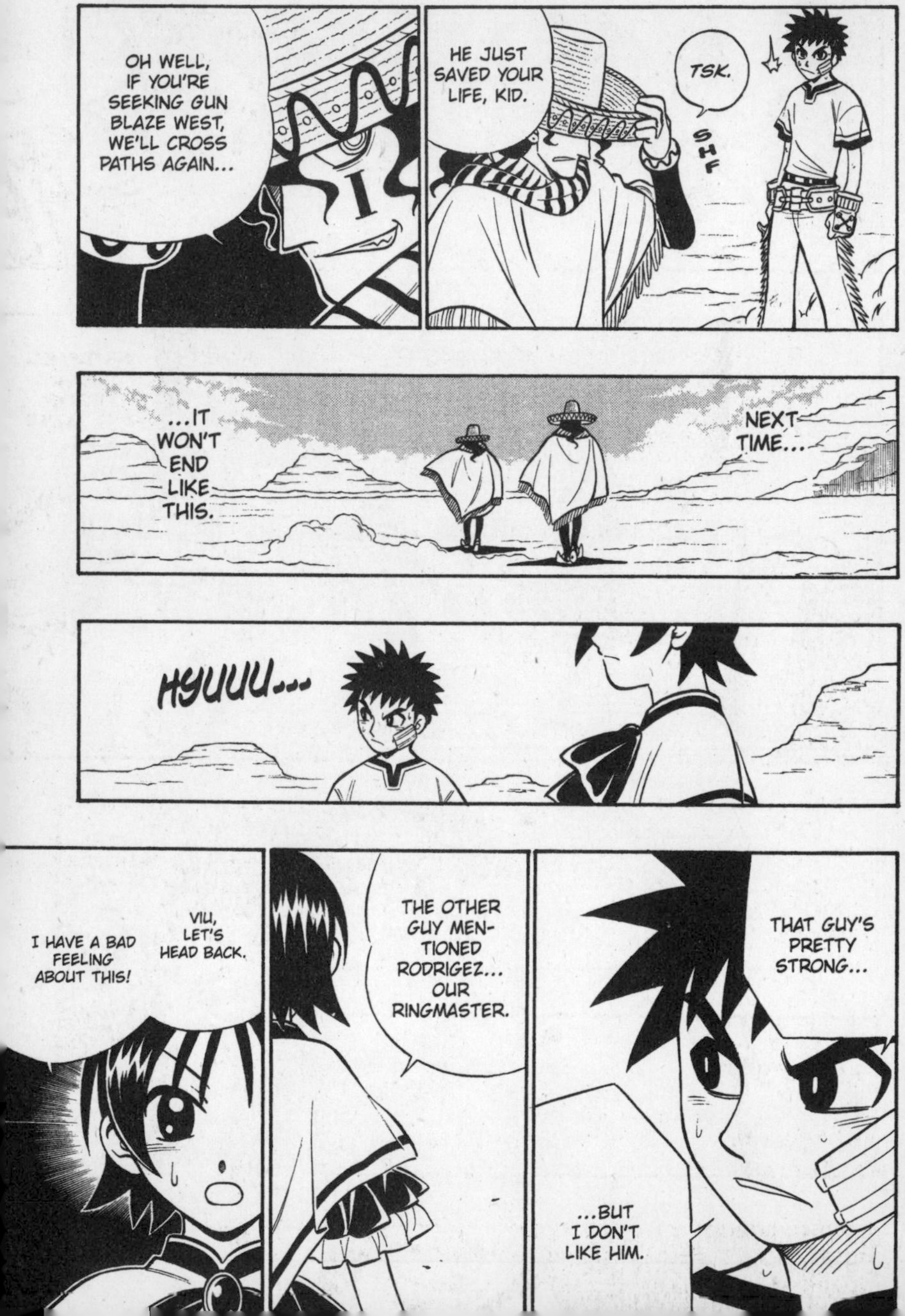

TSK.
SHF
HE JUST SAVED YOUR LIFE, KID.
OH WELL, IF YOU'RE SEEKING GUN BLAZE WEST, WE'LL CROSS PATHS AGAIN...
NEXT TIME...
...IT WON'T END LIKE THIS.
HYUUU...
THAT GUY'S PRETTY STRONG...
...BUT I DON'T LIKE HIM.
THE OTHER GUY MEN-TIONED RODRIGEZ... OUR RINGMASTER.
VIU, LET'S HEAD BACK.
I HAVE A BAD FEELING ABOUT THIS!

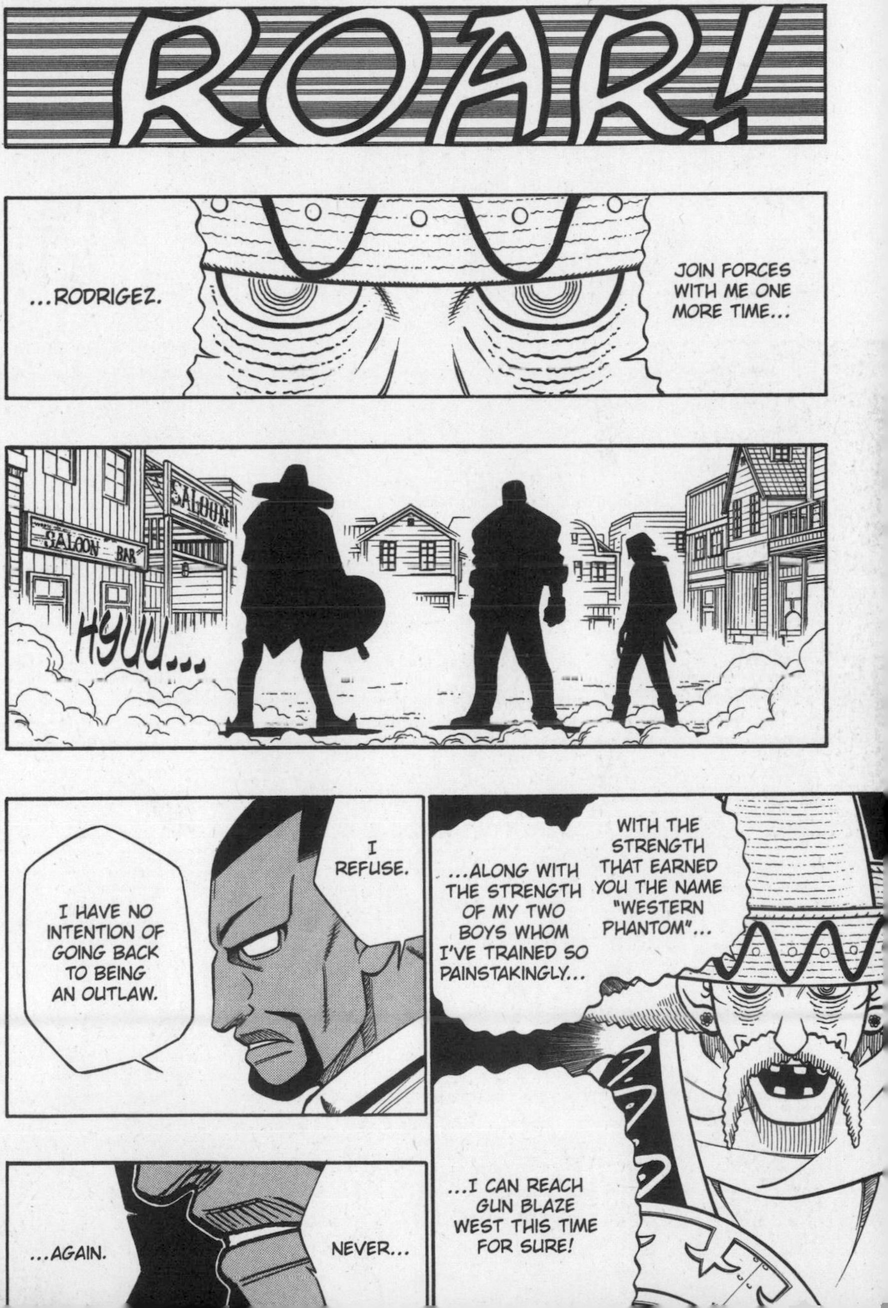
ROAR!
JOIN FORCES WITH ME ONE MORE TIME...
...RODRIGEZ.
SALOON
SALOON BAR
HYUU...
WITH THE STRENGTH THAT EARNED YOU THE NAME "WESTERN PHANTOM"...
...ALONG WITH THE STRENGTH OF MY TWO BOYS WHOM I'VE TRAINED SO PAINSTAKINGLY...
...I CAN REACH GUN BLAZE WEST THIS TIME FOR SURE!
I REFUSE.
I HAVE NO INTENTION OF GOING BACK TO BEING AN OUTLAW.
NEVER...
...AGAIN.

READ THIS WAY

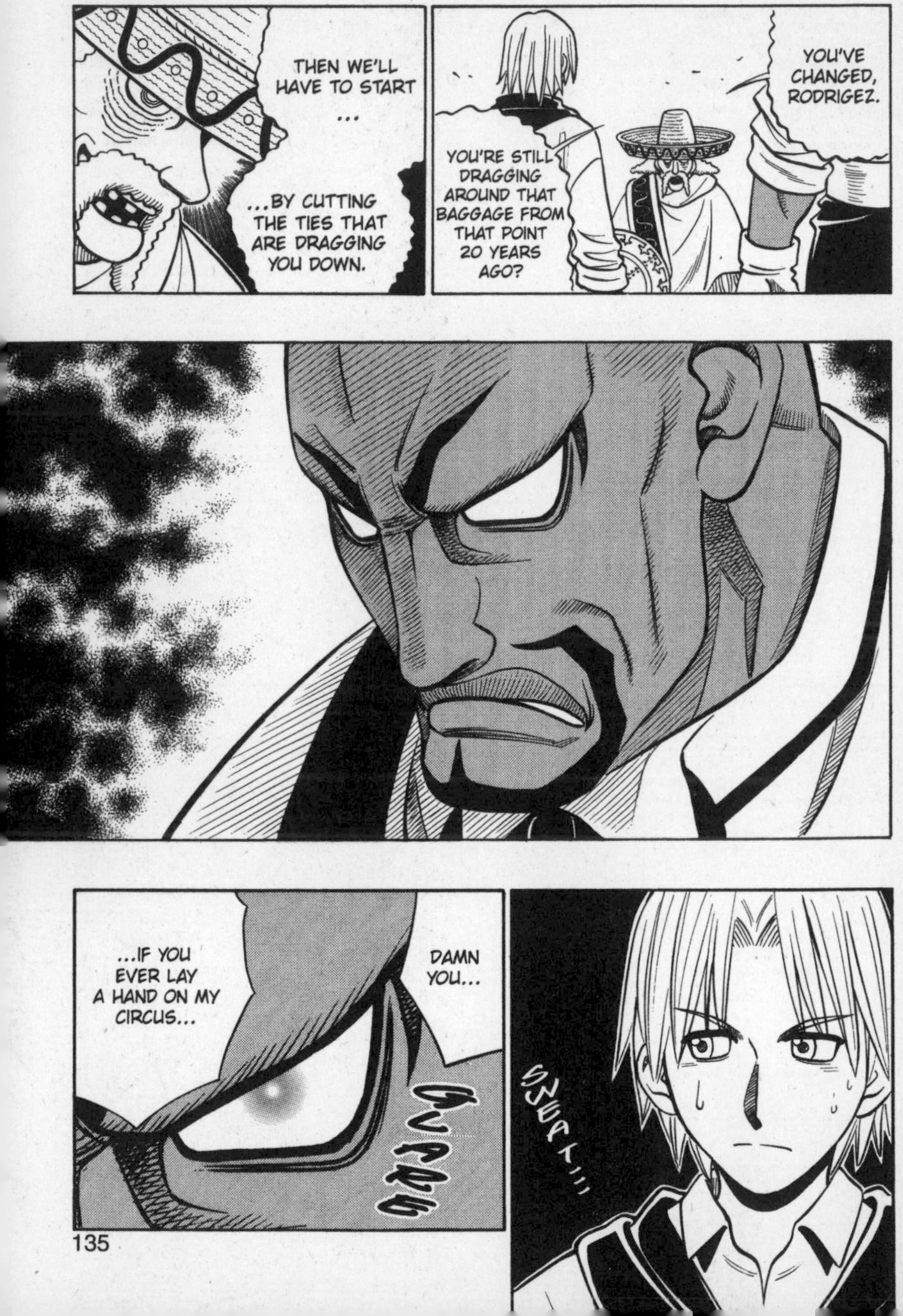

YOU'VE CHANGED, RODRIGEZ.
YOU'RE STILL DRAGGING AROUND THAT BAGGAGE FROM THAT POINT 20 YEARS AGO?
THEN WE'LL HAVE TO START ...
...BY CUTTING THE TIES THAT ARE DRAGGING YOU DOWN.
SWEAT...
DAMN YOU...
...IF YOU EVER LAY A HAND ON MY CIRCUS...
GLARE

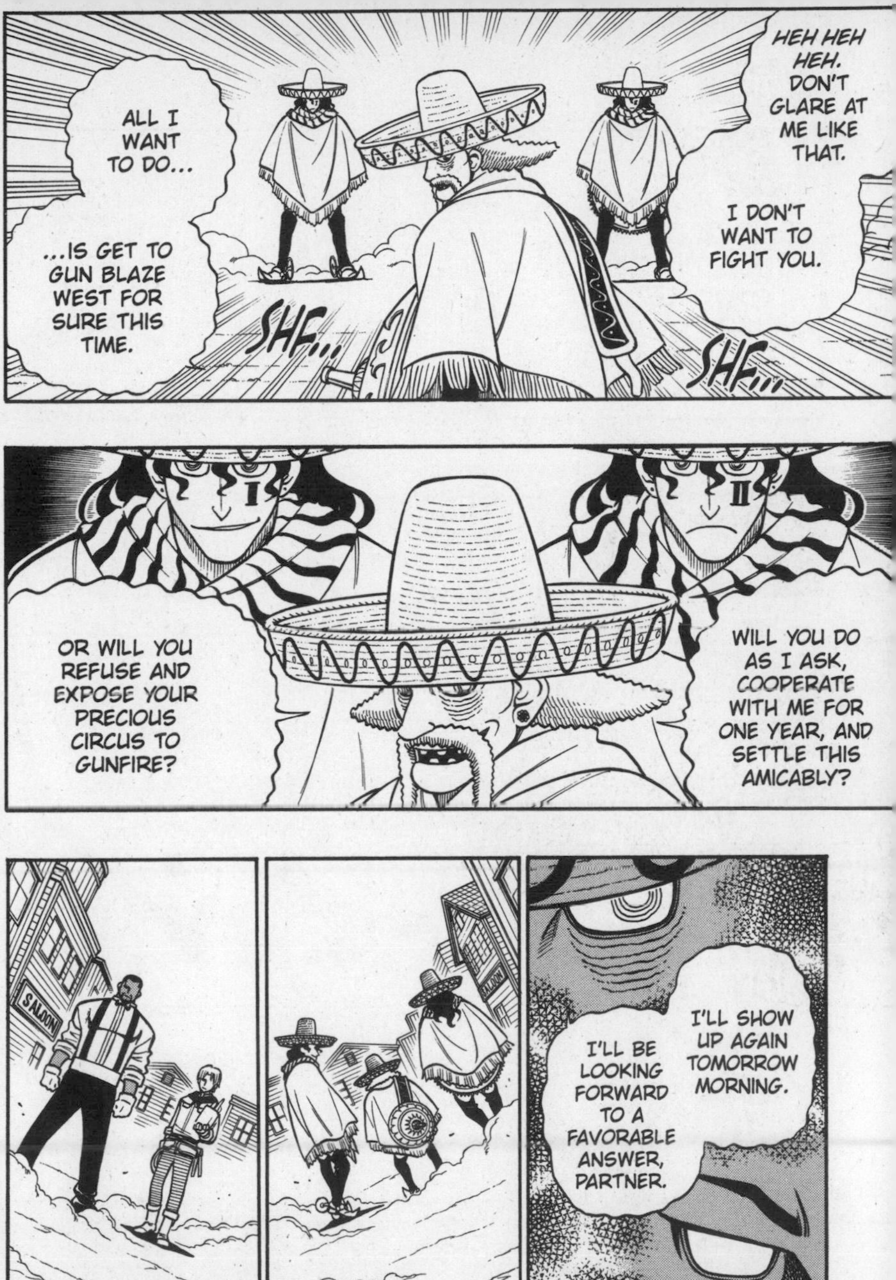
HEH HEH HEH. DON'T GLARE AT ME LIKE THAT.
I DON'T WANT TO FIGHT YOU.
SHF...
SHF...
ALL I WANT TO DO...
...IS GET TO GUN BLAZE WEST FOR SURE THIS TIME.
WILL YOU DO AS I ASK, COOPERATE WITH ME FOR ONE YEAR, AND SETTLE THIS AMICABLY?
OR WILL YOU REFUSE AND EXPOSE YOUR PRECIOUS CIRCUS TO GUNFIRE?
I'LL SHOW UP AGAIN TOMORROW MORNING.
I'LL BE LOOKING FORWARD TO A FAVORABLE ANSWER, PARTNER.
SALOON
SALOON

READ THIS WAY

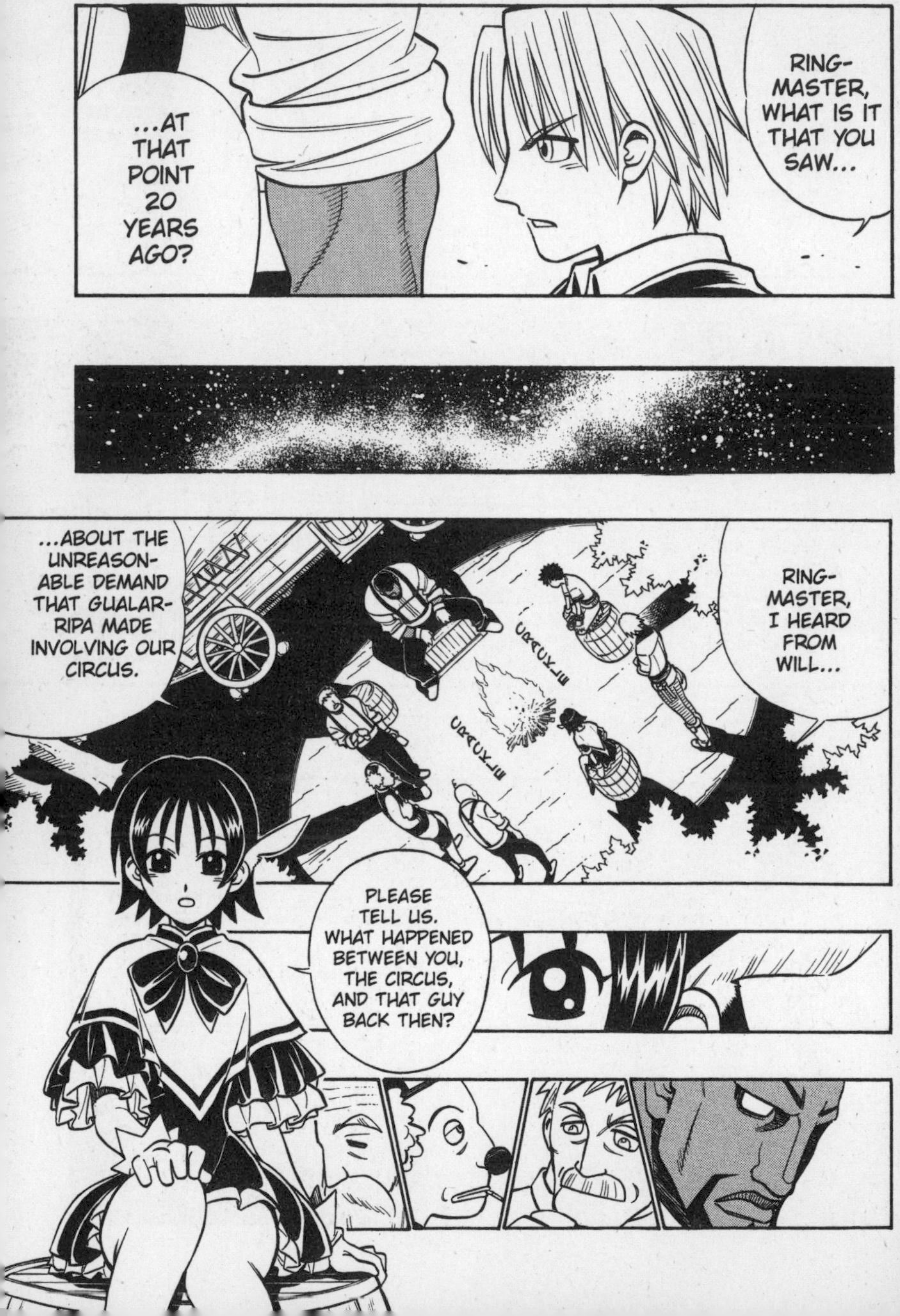
RING-MASTER, WHAT IS IT THAT YOU SAW...
...AT THAT POINT 20 YEARS AGO?
RING-MASTER, I HEARD FROM WILL...
...ABOUT THE UNREASONABLE DEMAND THAT GUALARRIPA MADE INVOLVING OUR CIRCUS.
PLEASE TELL US. WHAT HAPPENED BETWEEN YOU, THE CIRCUS, AND THAT GUY BACK THEN?

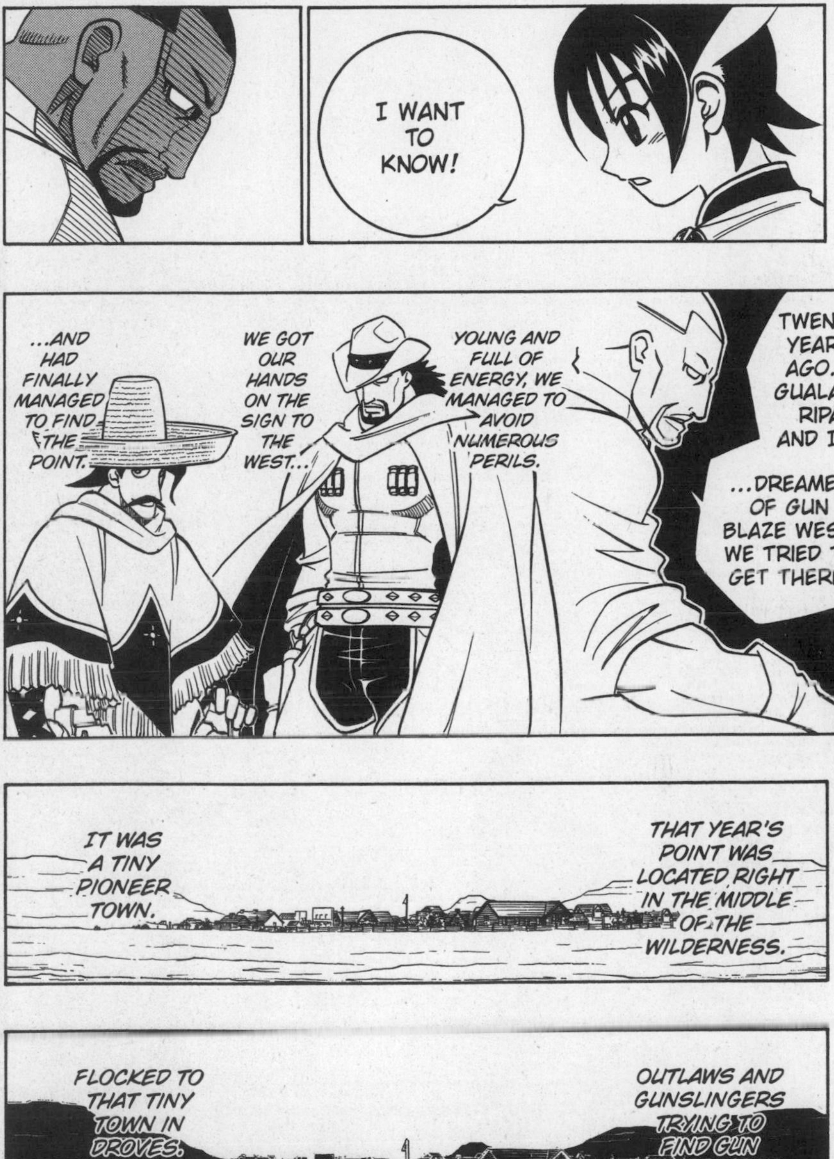
I WANT TO KNOW!
TWENTY YEARS AGO... GUALAR-RIPA AND I...
...DREAMED OF GUN BLAZE WEST. WE TRIED TO GET THERE.
YOUNG AND FULL OF ENERGY, WE MANAGED TO AVOID NUMEROUS PERILS.
WE GOT OUR HANDS ON THE SIGN TO THE WEST...
...AND HAD FINALLY MANAGED TO FIND THE POINT.
THAT YEAR'S POINT WAS LOCATED RIGHT IN THE MIDDLE OF THE WILDERNESS.
IT WAS A TINY PIONEER TOWN.
OUTLAWS AND GUNSLINGERS TRYING TO FIND GUN BLAZE WEST
FLOCKED TO THAT TINY TOWN IN DROVES.

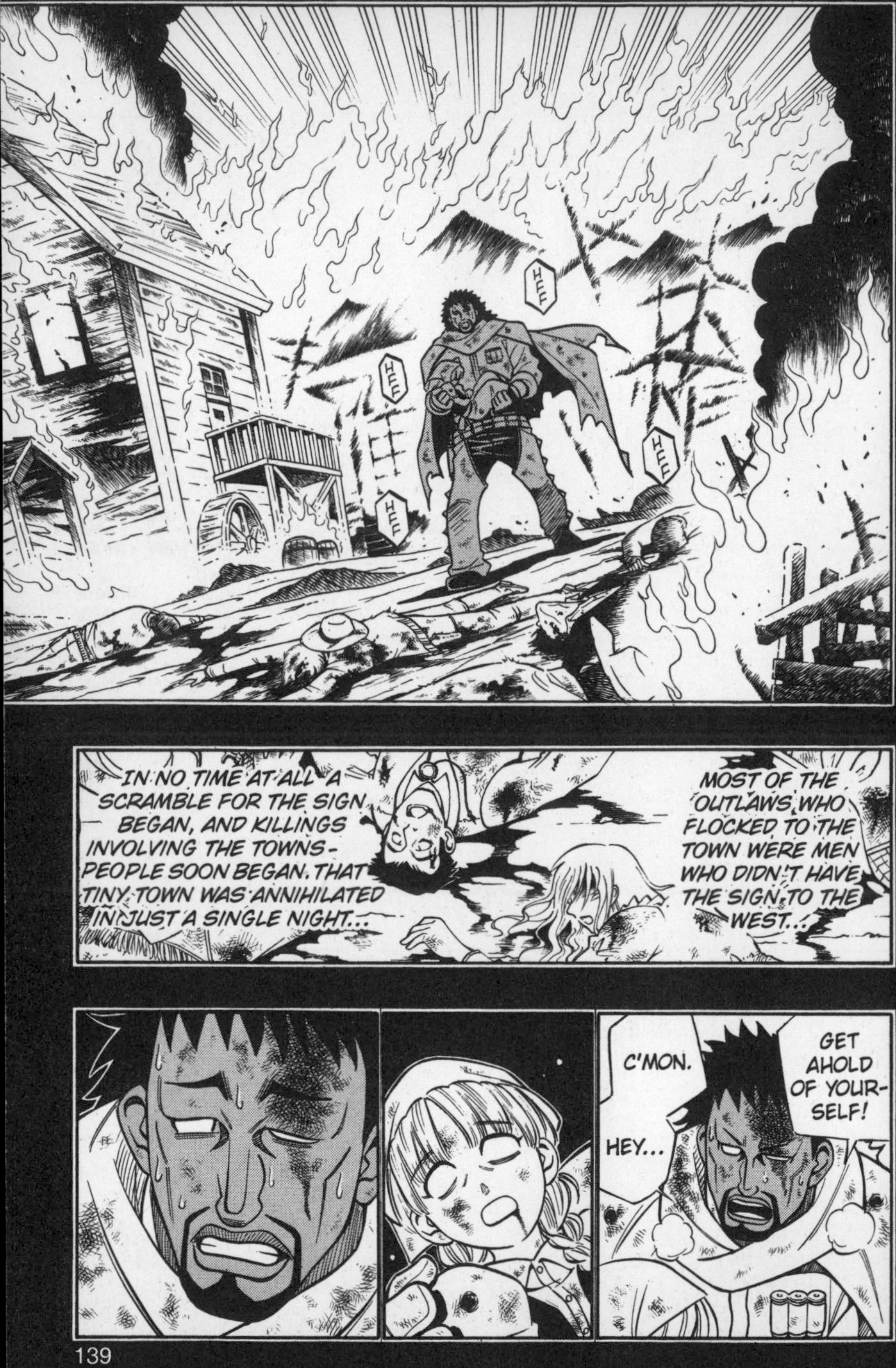
HEF
HEF
HEF
HEF
MOST OF THE OUTLAWS WHO FLOCKED TO THE TOWN WERE MEN WHO DIDN'T HAVE THE SIGN TO THE WEST...
IN NO TIME AT ALL A SCRAMBLE FOR THE SIGN BEGAN, AND KILLINGS INVOLVING THE TOWNS-PEOPLE SOON BEGAN. THAT TINY TOWN WAS ANNIHILATED IN JUST A SINGLE NIGHT...
GET AHOLD OF YOUR-SELF!
C'MON.
HEY...

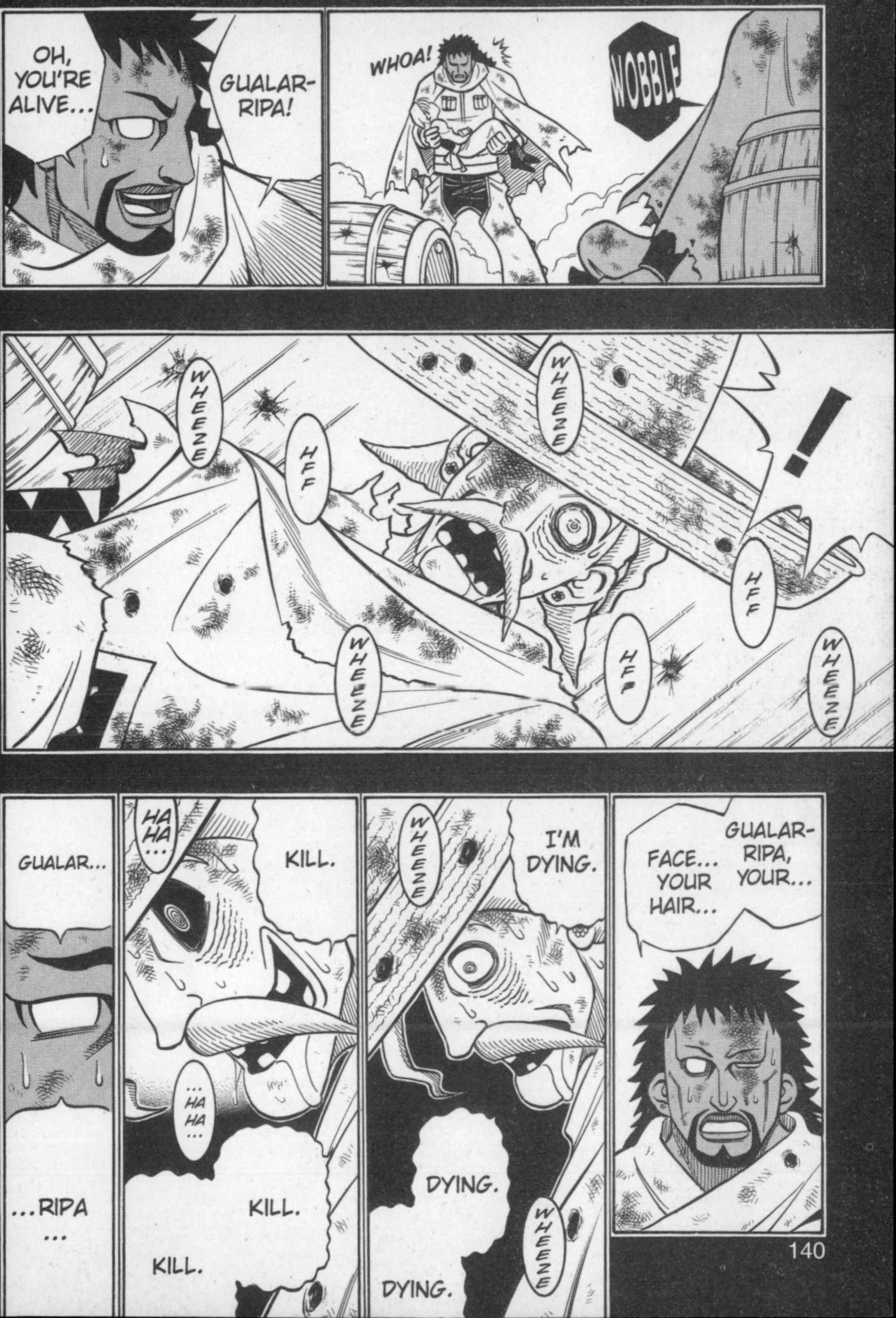
WHOA!
WOBBLE
OH, YOU'RE ALIVE...
GUALAR-RIPA!
!
WHEEZE
HFF
WHEEZE
HFF
WHEEZE
HFF
WHEEZE
WHEEZE
HFF
GUALAR-RIPA, YOUR...
FACE... YOUR HAIR...
I'M DYING.
WHEEZE
DYING.
WHEEZE
DYING.
KILL.
HA HA...
...HA HA...
KILL.
KILL.
GUALAR...
...RIPA ...

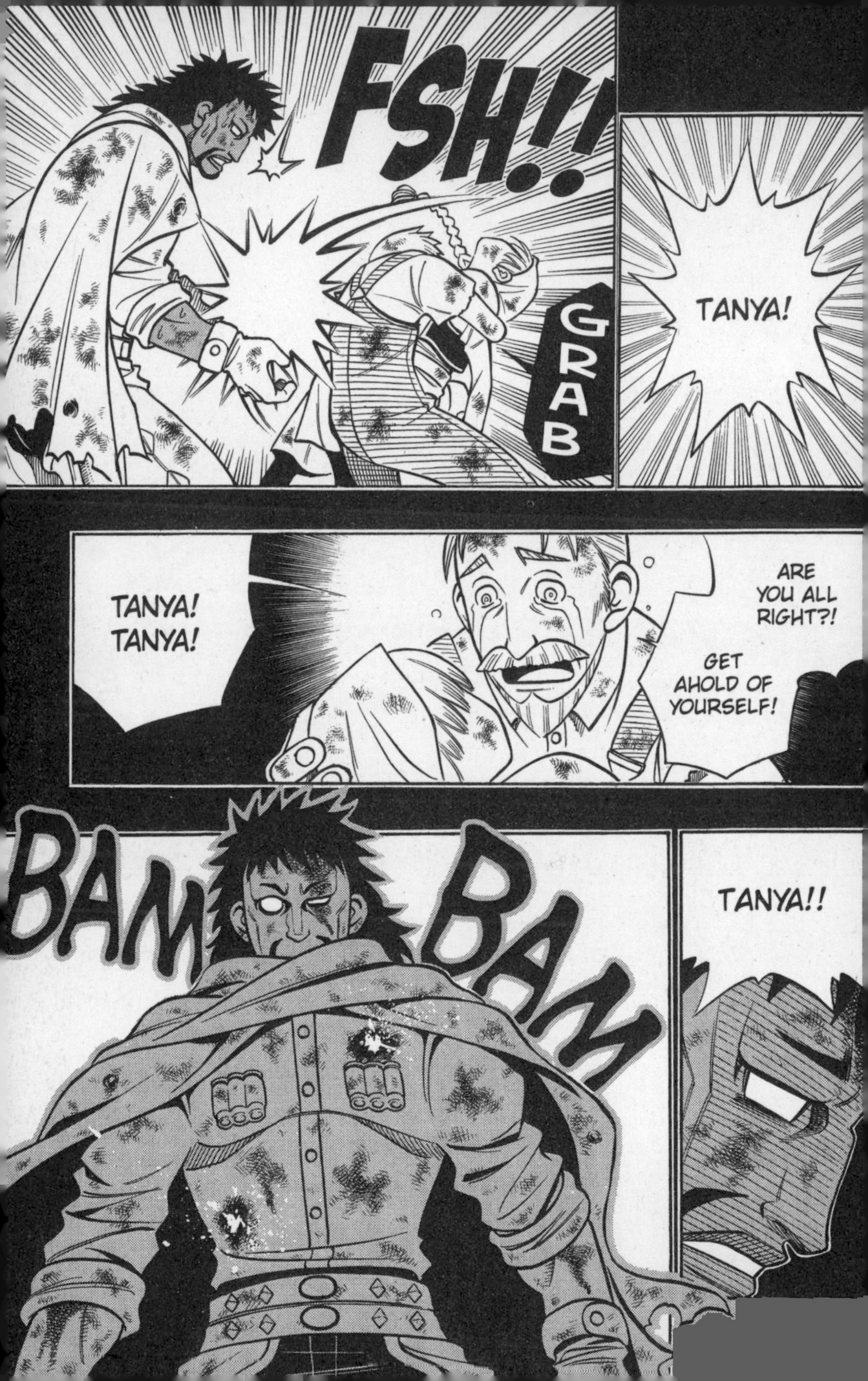
TANYA!
FSH!!
GRAB
ARE YOU ALL RIGHT?!
GET AHOLD OF YOURSELF!
TANYA! TANYA!
TANYA!!
BAM
BAM

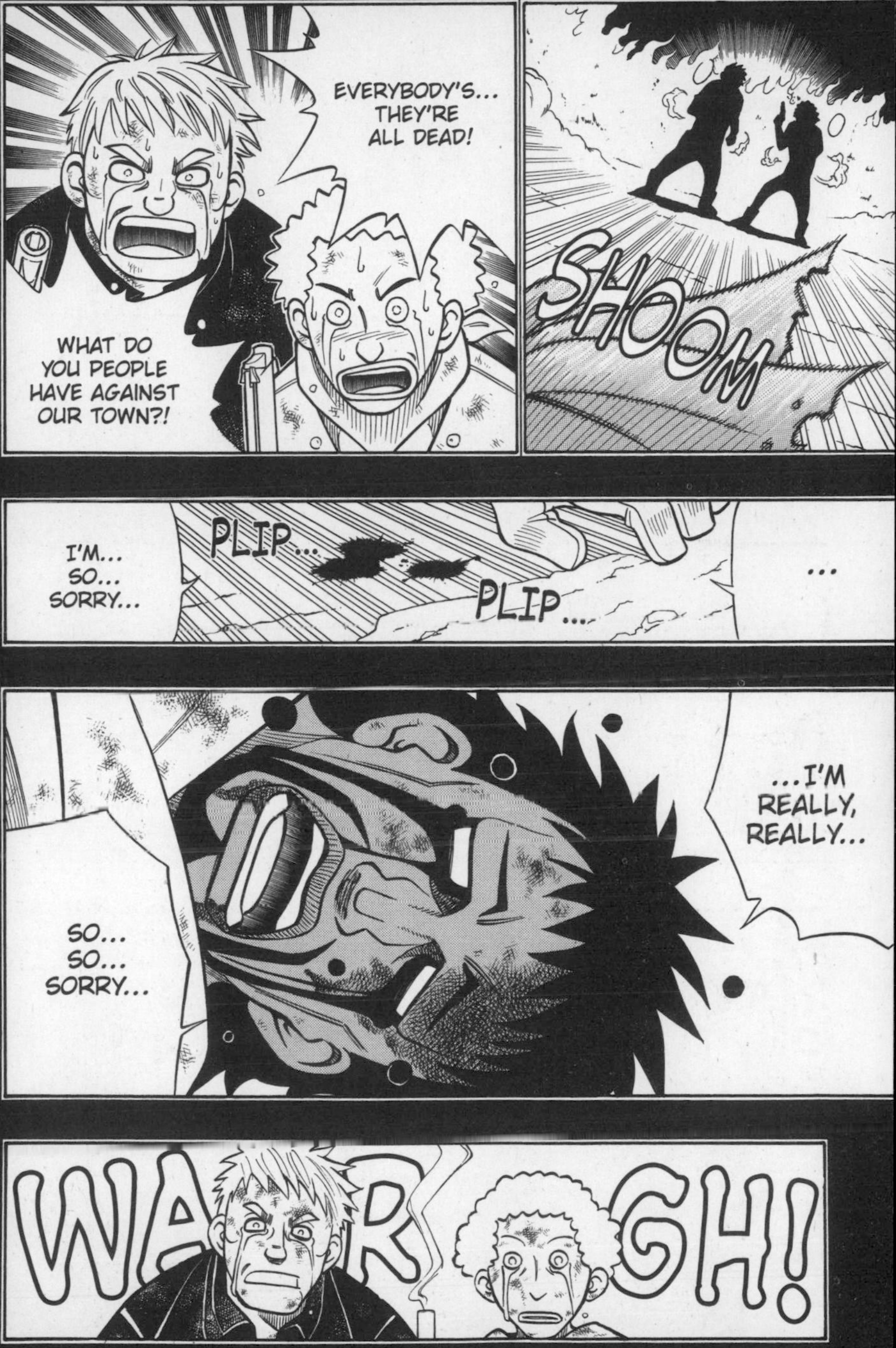
SHOOM
EVERYBODY'S... THEY'RE ALL DEAD!
WHAT DO YOU PEOPLE HAVE AGAINST OUR TOWN?!
...
PLIP...
PLIP...
I'M... SO... SORRY...
...I'M REALLY, REALLY...
SO... SO... SORRY...
WA R GH!

READ THIS WAY

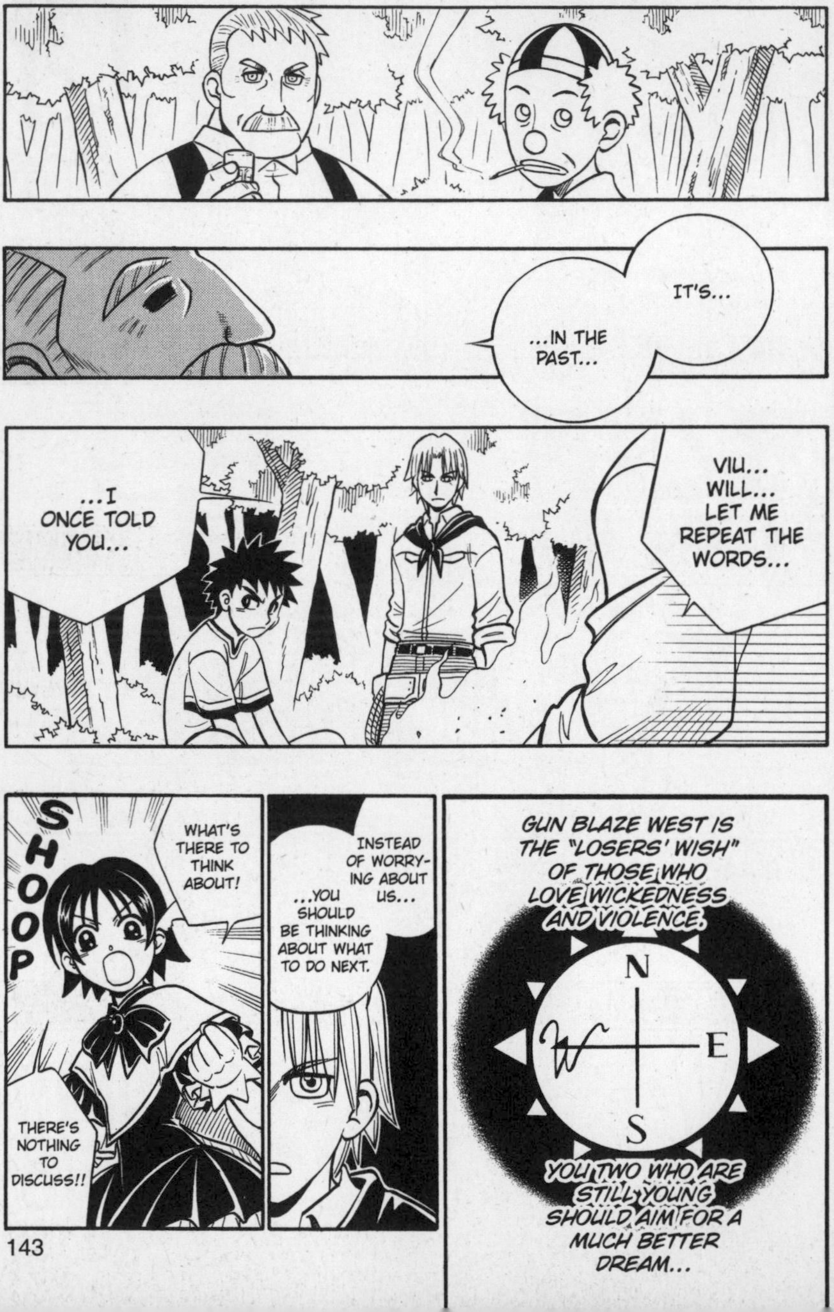
IT'S...
...IN THE PAST...
VIU... WILL... LET ME REPEAT THE WORDS...
...I ONCE TOLD YOU...
GUN BLAZE WEST IS THE "LOSERS' WISH" OF THOSE WHO LOVE WICKEDNESS AND VIOLENCE.
N
E
S
W
YOU TWO WHO ARE STILL YOUNG SHOULD AIM FOR A MUCH BETTER DREAM...
INSTEAD OF WORRYING ABOUT US...
...YOU SHOULD BE THINKING ABOUT WHAT TO DO NEXT.
WHAT'S THERE TO THINK ABOUT!
SHOOP
THERE'S NOTHING TO DISCUSS!!

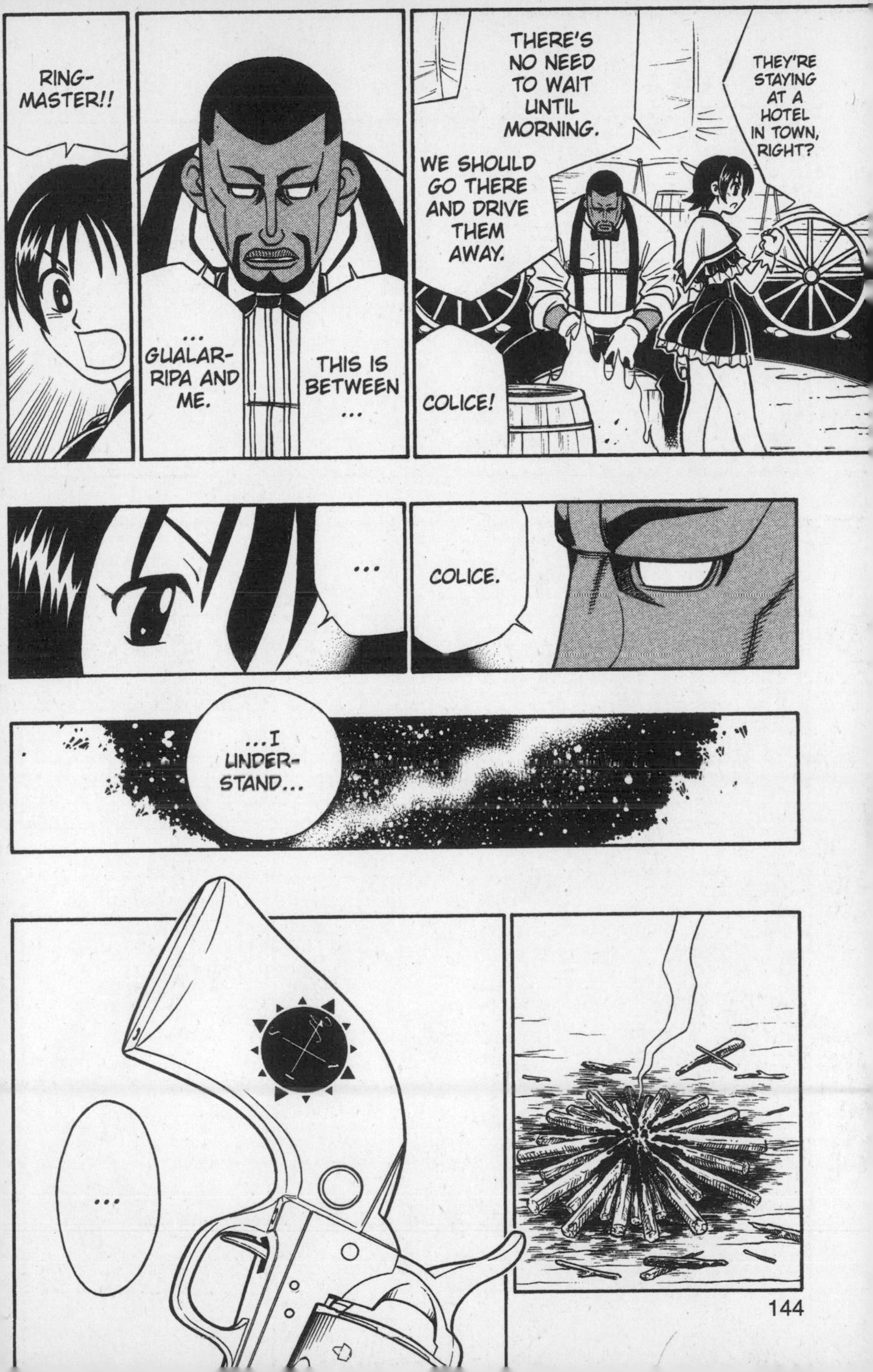
THEY'RE STAYING AT A HOTEL IN TOWN, RIGHT?
THERE'S NO NEED TO WAIT UNTIL MORNING.
WE SHOULD GO THERE AND DRIVE THEM AWAY.
COLICE!
THIS IS BETWEEN ...
... GUALAR-RIPA AND ME.
RING-MASTER!!
COLICE.
...
...I UNDER-STAND...
...

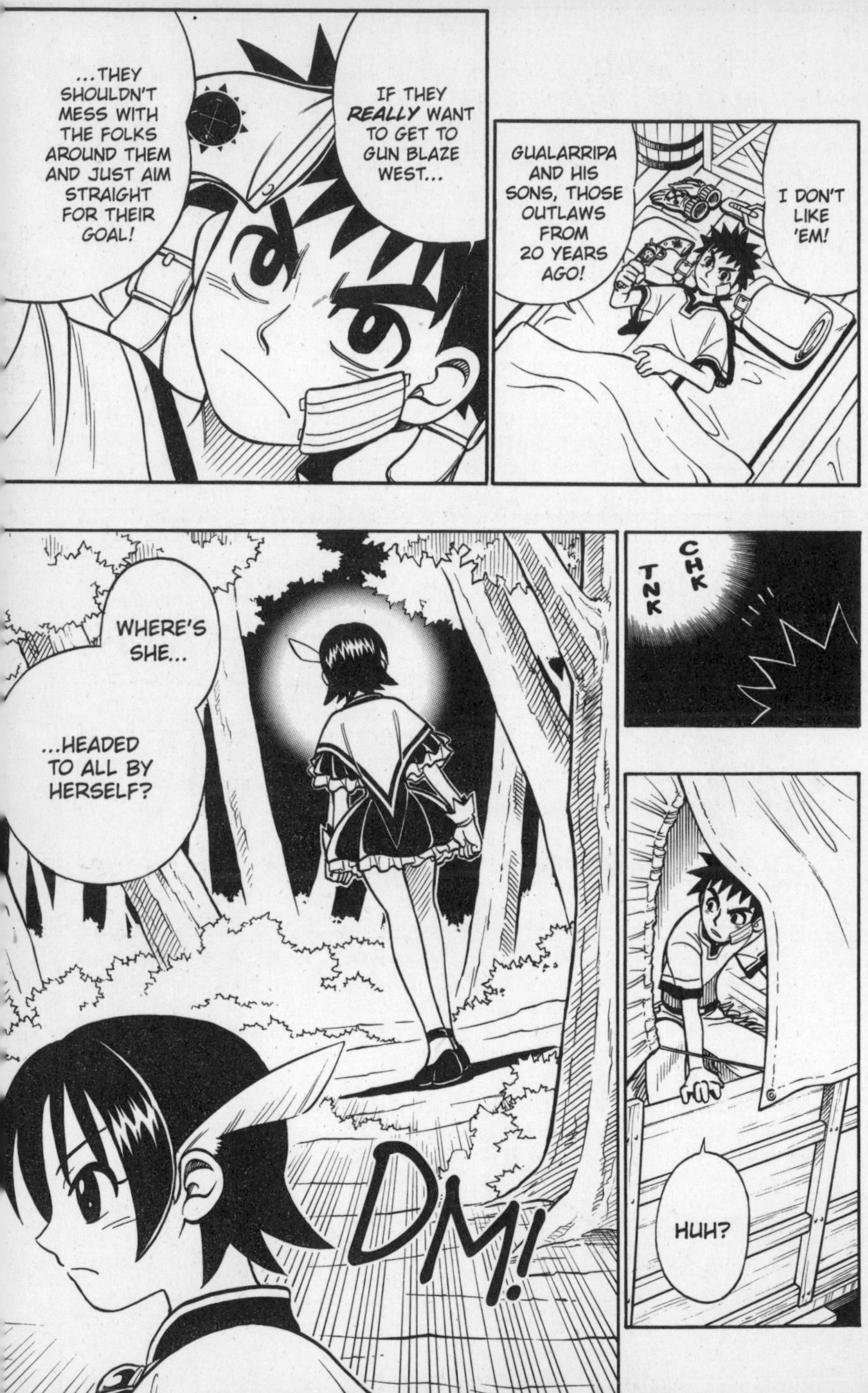
I DON'T LIKE 'EM!
GUALARRIPA AND HIS SONS, THOSE OUTLAWS FROM 20 YEARS AGO!
IF THEY REALLY WANT TO GET TO GUN BLAZE WEST...
...THEY SHOULDN'T MESS WITH THE FOLKS AROUND THEM AND JUST AIM STRAIGHT FOR THEIR GOAL!
CHK
TNK
HUH?
WHERE'S SHE...
...HEADED TO ALL BY HERSELF?
DM!

CONCEPT: WITH WILL'S CHARACTER ESTABLISHED, CAROL'S CHARACTER WAS COMPLETE, SO I DID NOT GIVE HER VERY DEEP THOUGHT.
THIS WAS DURING THE TIME WHEN I WAS IN THE WORST POSSIBLE CONDITION AND BOTH MY MIND AND BODY WERE IN SHAMBLES, SO I COULDN'T PUT TOO MUCH THOUGHT INTO HER.

IN THE BEGINNING, I THOUGHT OF WILL'S FAMILY AS BEING COMPRISED OF HIS PARENTS, A YOUNGER BROTHER AND TWO YOUNGER SISTERS, BUT WITH SO MANY PEOPLE, I DIDN'T THINK I COULD MAKE THE STORY COME TOGETHER WELL, SO I BOLDLY REDUCED IT TO JUST HIS FATHER AND YOUNGER SISTER. BUT REALLY, I ABSOLUTELY DIDN'T GIVE IT ANY FURTHER THOUGHT... READING OVER MY WORK, SHE WAS SO CONSIDERATE OF HER OLDER BROTHER, SO I SHOULD HAVE PUT MORE THOUGHT INTO HER...I HAVE NOTHING BUT REGRETS ABOUT THAT.

IMAGE SOURCE: SINCE I WAS IN THE CONDITION I DESCRIBED ABOVE, THERE WAS ABSOLUTELY NONE AT ALL. IF I HAD TO SAY SOMETHING, IT'D BE QUENTIN'S YOUNGER SISTER (AND YOUNGER BROTHER) FROM *OCTOBER SKY*.

## CHARACTER FILE #06

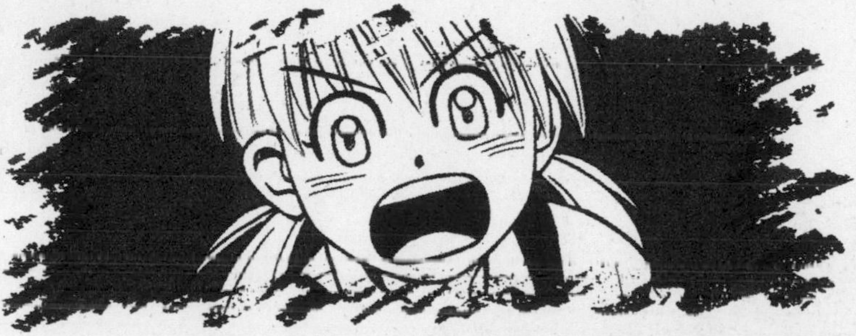

## CAROL JOHNSTON

DESIGN: AS I STATED ABOVE (*SNIP*). I TRIED MAKING HER IN THE IMAGE OF A TYPICAL COUNTRY GIRL WITH PIGTAILS. LOOKING AT HER CAREFULLY, YOU CAN SEE THE MARKS OF MY SEARCH FOR A NEW LOOK THAT IS DIFFERENT FROM THE YOUNG GIRL CHARACTERS I HAD ALREADY DONE. THEY ARE THE MARKS OF MY EFFORTS TO ACHIEVE SOMETHING EVEN WHEN MY MIND AND BODY WERE IN SHAMBLES. YES.

ON A SIDE NOTE, LOOKING CAREFULLY AT HER, CAROL'S CLOTHES ARE THE UNIFORM WORN BY THE WAITRESSES AT A COFFEE SHOP I ONCE FREQUENTED DURING MY YOUNGER DAYS, BUT WHICH HAS SINCE CLOSED DOWN. WHAT WAS I UNCONSCIOUSLY DRAWING?

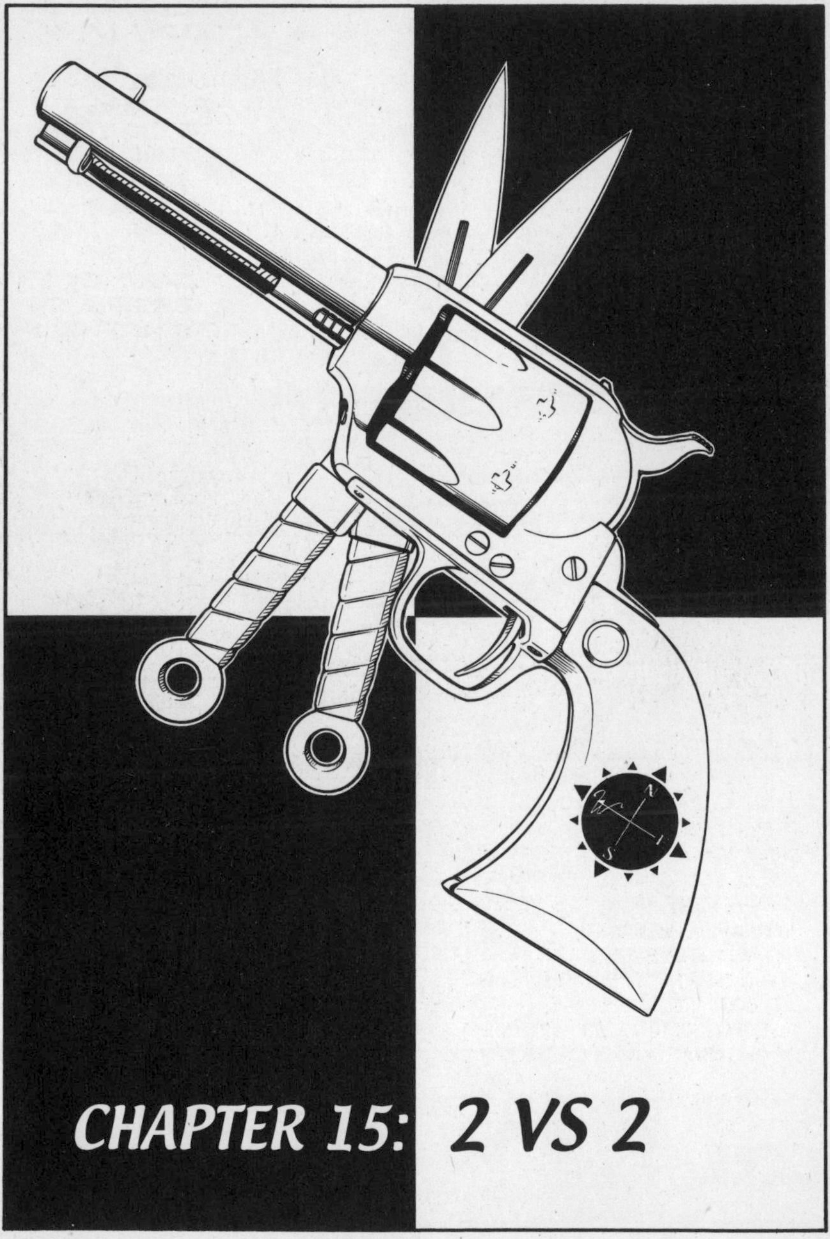

# CHAPTER 15: 2 VS 2

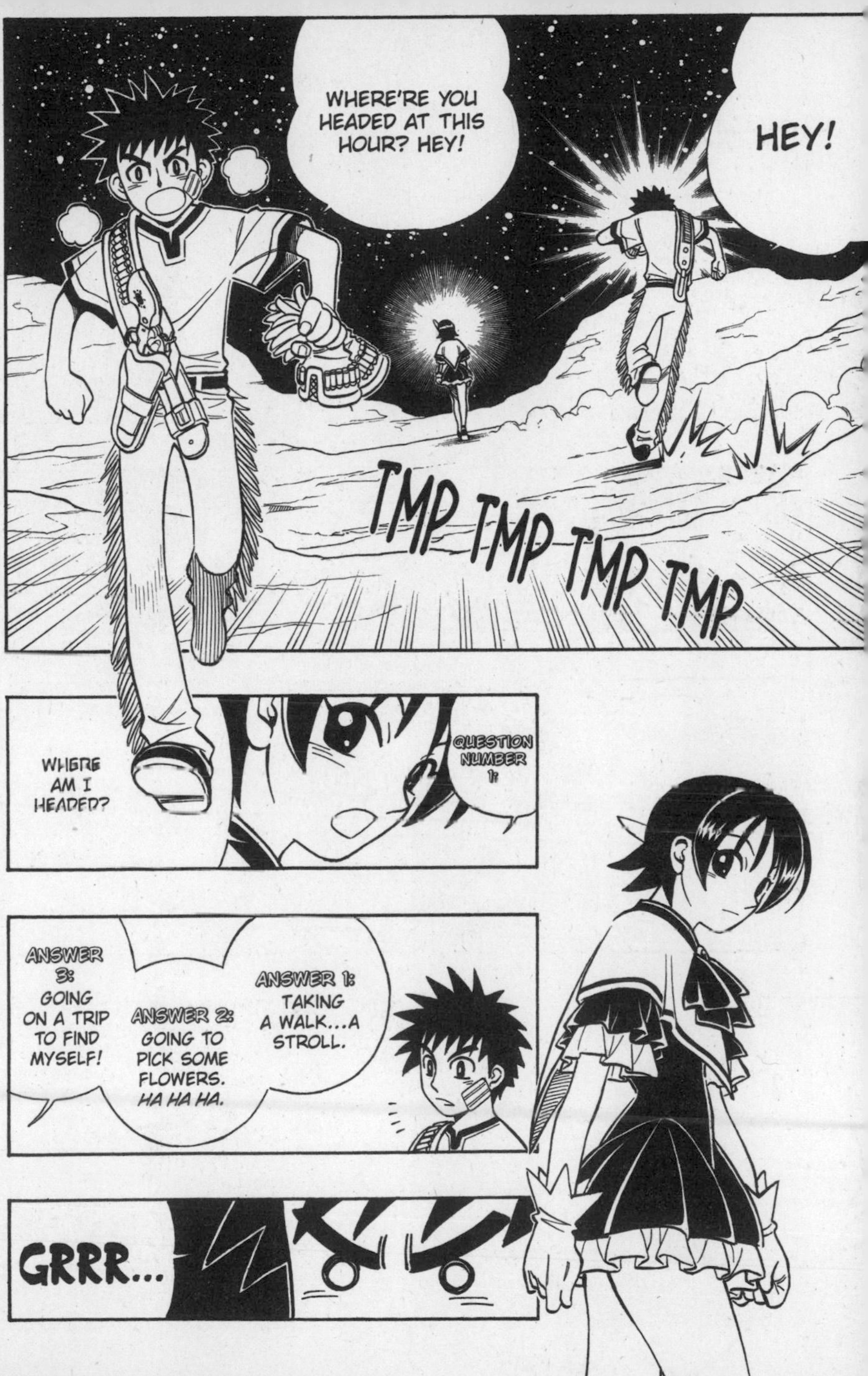
HEY!
WHERE'RE YOU HEADED AT THIS HOUR? HEY!
TMP TMP TMP TMP
QUESTION NUMBER 1:
WHERE AM I HEADED?
ANSWER 1: TAKING A WALK...A STROLL.
ANSWER 2: GOING TO PICK SOME FLOWERS. HA HA HA.
ANSWER 3: GOING ON A TRIP TO FIND MYSELF!
GRRR...

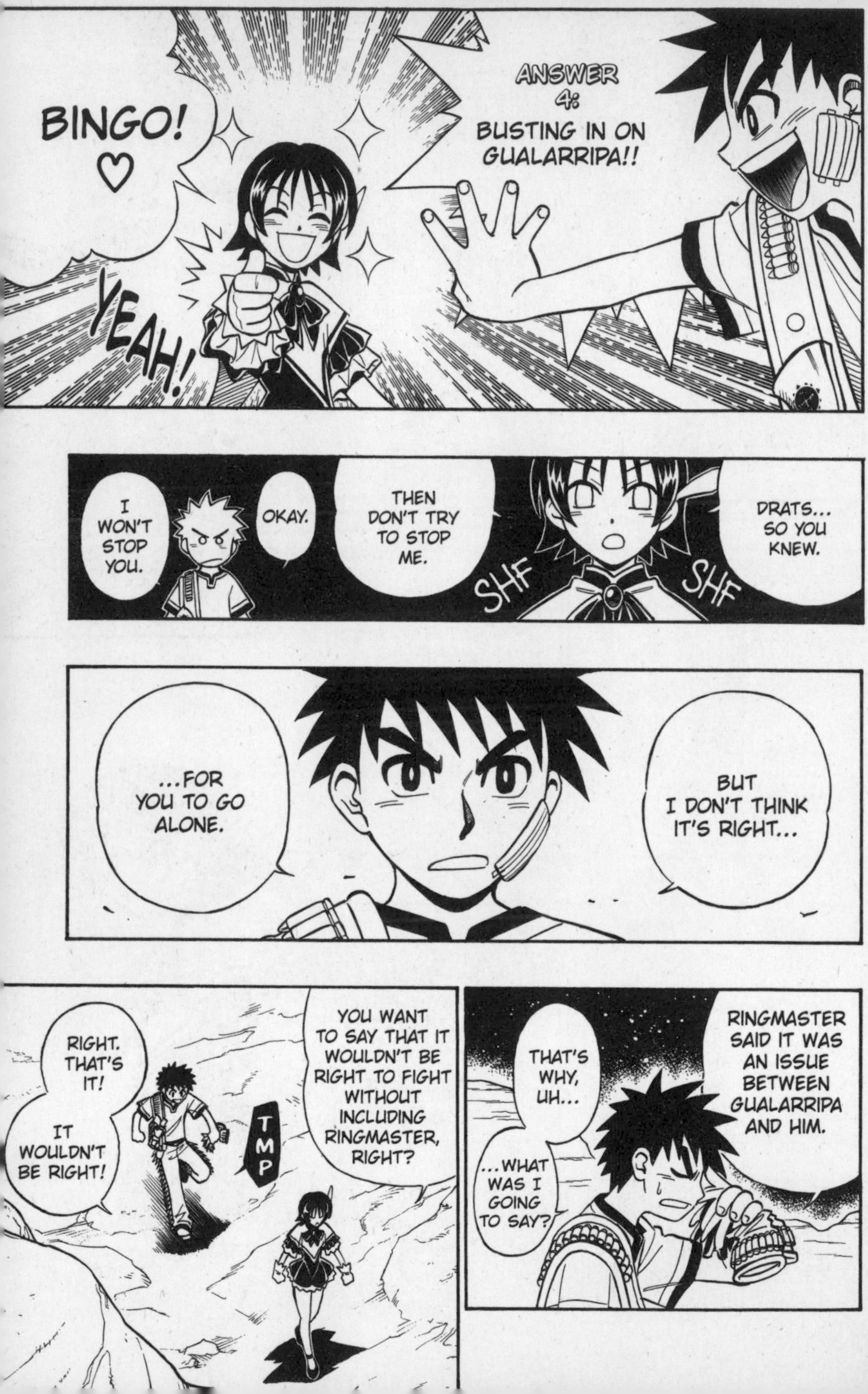
ANSWER 4: BUSTING IN ON GUALARRIPA!!
BINGO! ♡
YEAH!
DRATS... SO YOU KNEW.
SHF
SHF
THEN DON'T TRY TO STOP ME.
OKAY.
I WON'T STOP YOU.
BUT I DON'T THINK IT'S RIGHT...
...FOR YOU TO GO ALONE.
RINGMASTER SAID IT WAS AN ISSUE BETWEEN GUALARRIPA AND HIM.
THAT'S WHY, UH...
...WHAT WAS I GOING TO SAY?
YOU WANT TO SAY THAT IT WOULDN'T BE RIGHT TO FIGHT WITHOUT INCLUDING RINGMASTER, RIGHT?
TMP
RIGHT. THAT'S IT!
IT WOULDN'T BE RIGHT!

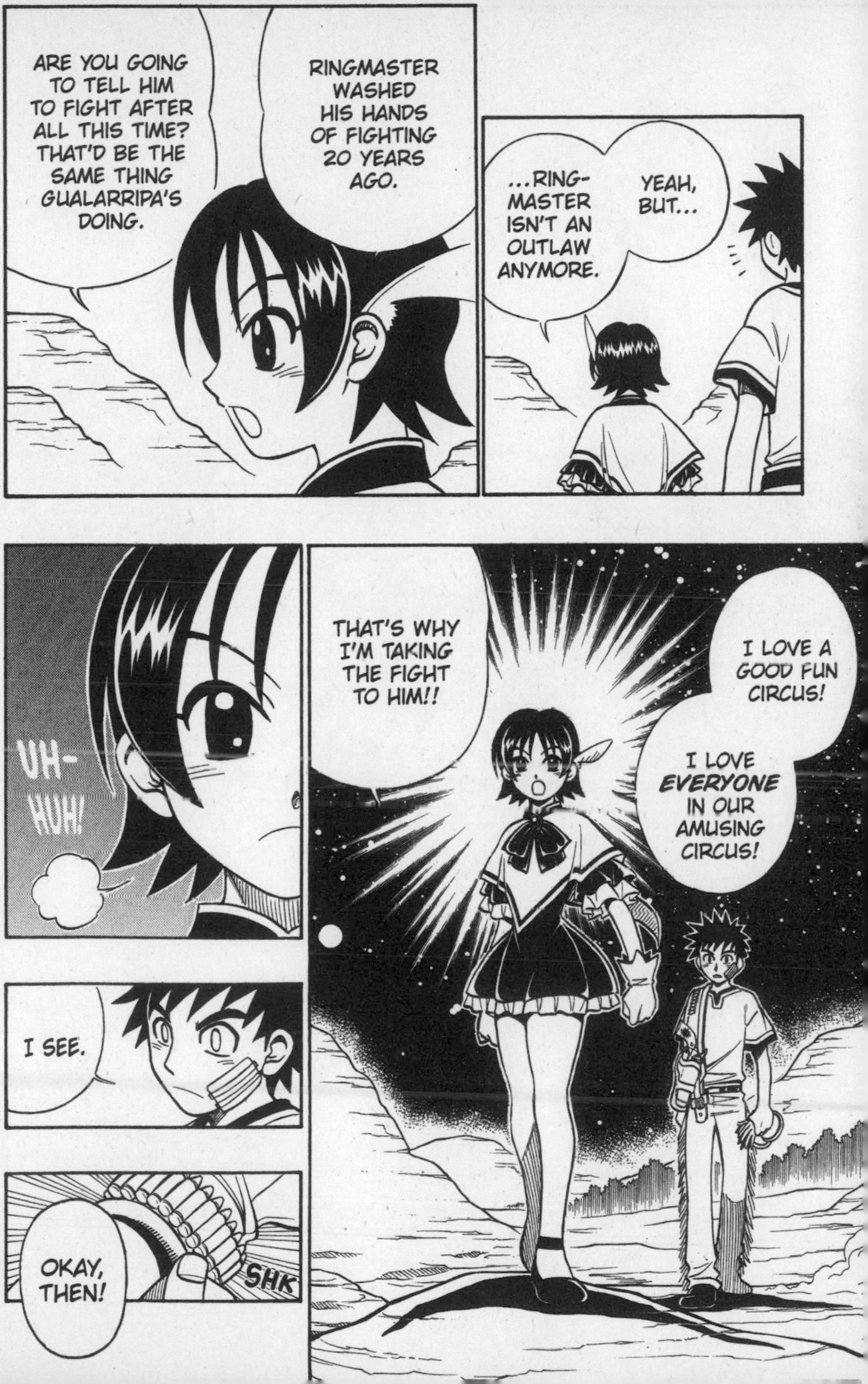
YEAH, BUT...
...RING-MASTER ISN'T AN OUTLAW ANYMORE.
RINGMASTER WASHED HIS HANDS OF FIGHTING 20 YEARS AGO.
ARE YOU GOING TO TELL HIM TO FIGHT AFTER ALL THIS TIME? THAT'D BE THE SAME THING GUALARRIPA'S DOING.
I LOVE A GOOD FUN CIRCUS!
I LOVE *EVERYONE* IN OUR AMUSING CIRCUS!
THAT'S WHY I'M TAKING THE FIGHT TO HIM!!
UH-HUH!
I SEE.
SHK
OKAY, THEN!

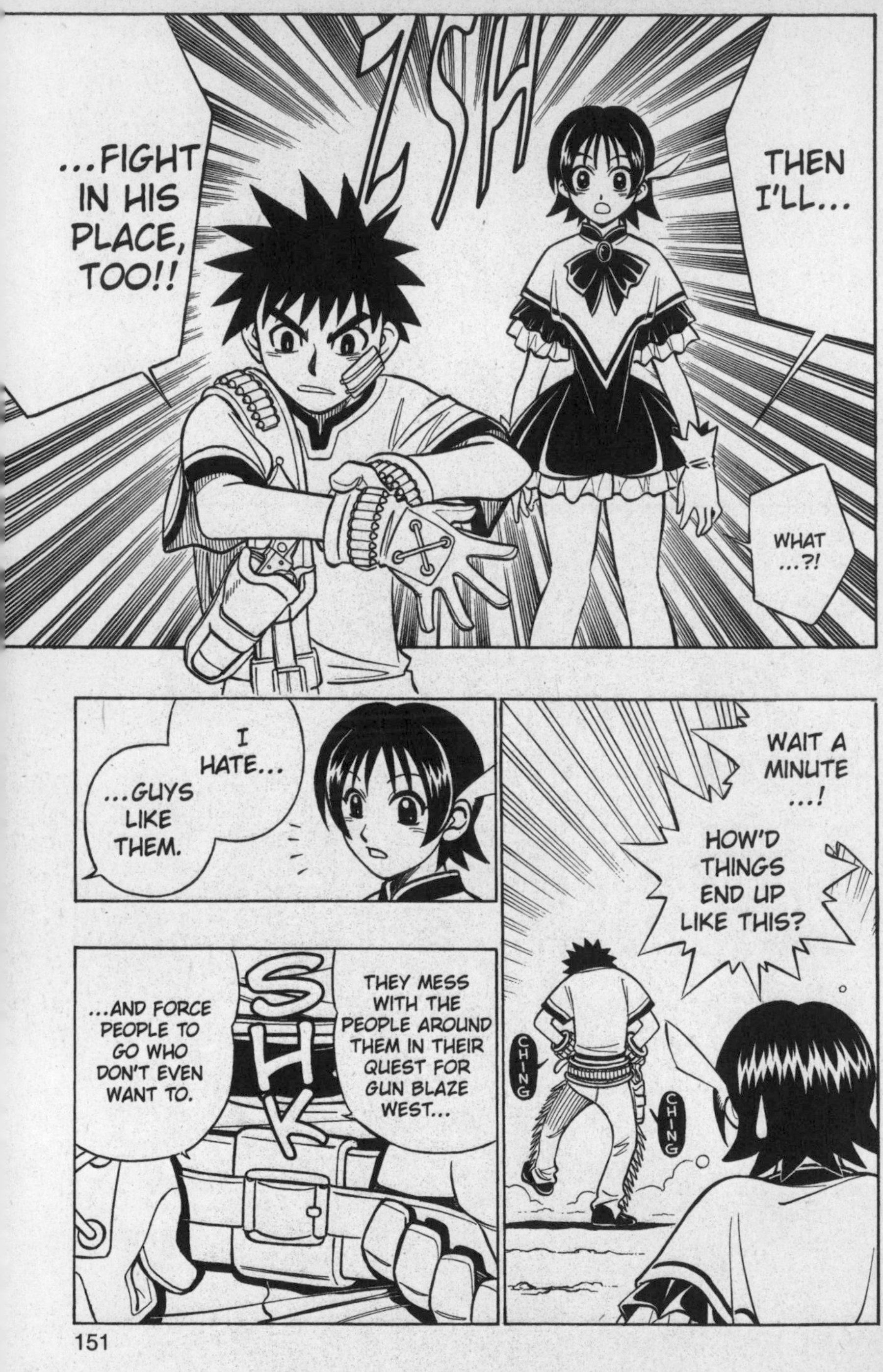
THEN I'LL...
ZSHA
...FIGHT IN HIS PLACE, TOO!!
WHAT ...?!
WAIT A MINUTE ...!
HOW'D THINGS END UP LIKE THIS?
CHING
CHING
I HATE...
...GUYS LIKE THEM.
THEY MESS WITH THE PEOPLE AROUND THEM IN THEIR QUEST FOR GUN BLAZE WEST...
SHK
...AND FORCE PEOPLE TO GO WHO DON'T EVEN WANT TO.

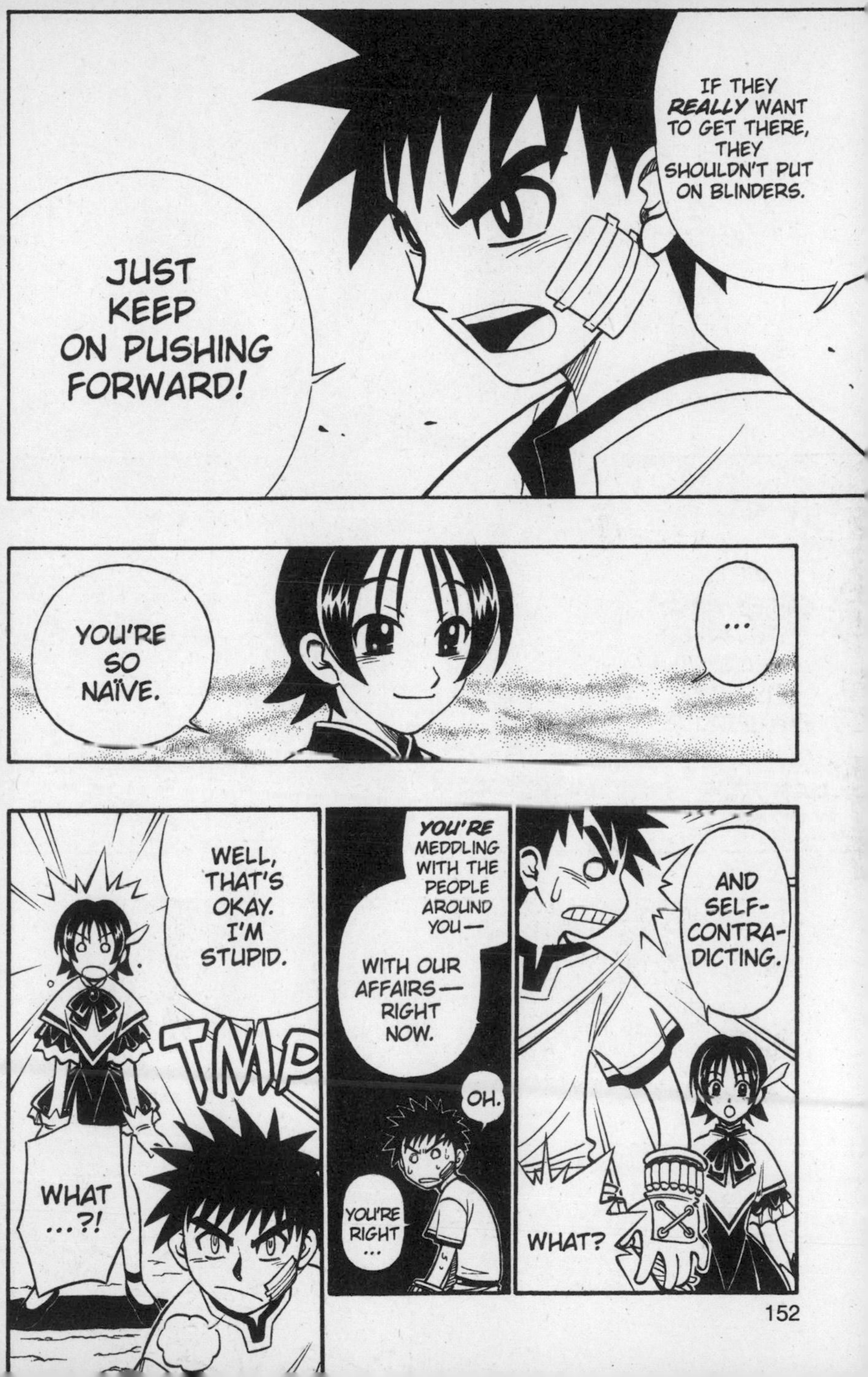
IF THEY *REALLY* WANT TO GET THERE, THEY SHOULDN'T PUT ON BLINDERS.
JUST KEEP ON PUSHING FORWARD!
...
YOU'RE SO NAÏVE.
AND SELF-CONTRA-DICTING.
WHAT?
*YOU'RE* MEDDLING WITH THE PEOPLE AROUND YOU—
WITH OUR AFFAIRS— RIGHT NOW.
OH.
YOU'RE RIGHT ...
WELL, THAT'S OKAY. I'M STUPID.
TMP
WHAT ...?!

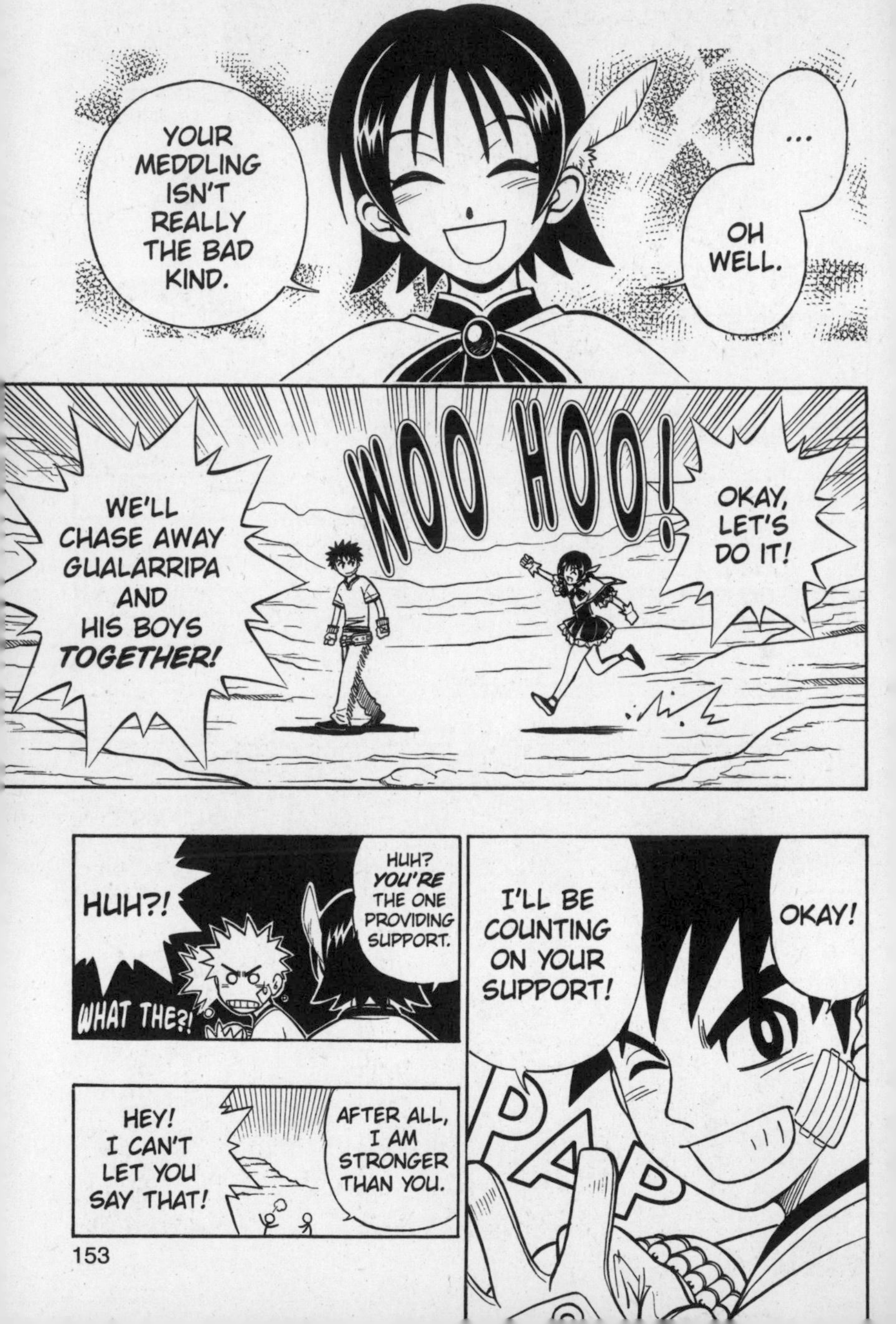
...
OH WELL.
YOUR MEDDLING ISN'T REALLY THE BAD KIND.
OKAY, LET'S DO IT!
WOO HOO!
WE'LL CHASE AWAY GUALARRIPA AND HIS BOYS *TOGETHER!*
OKAY!
I'LL BE COUNTING ON YOUR SUPPORT!
PAP
HUH? *YOU'RE* THE ONE PROVIDING SUPPORT.
HUH?!
WHAT THE?!
AFTER ALL, I AM STRONGER THAN YOU.
HEY! I CAN'T LET YOU SAY THAT!

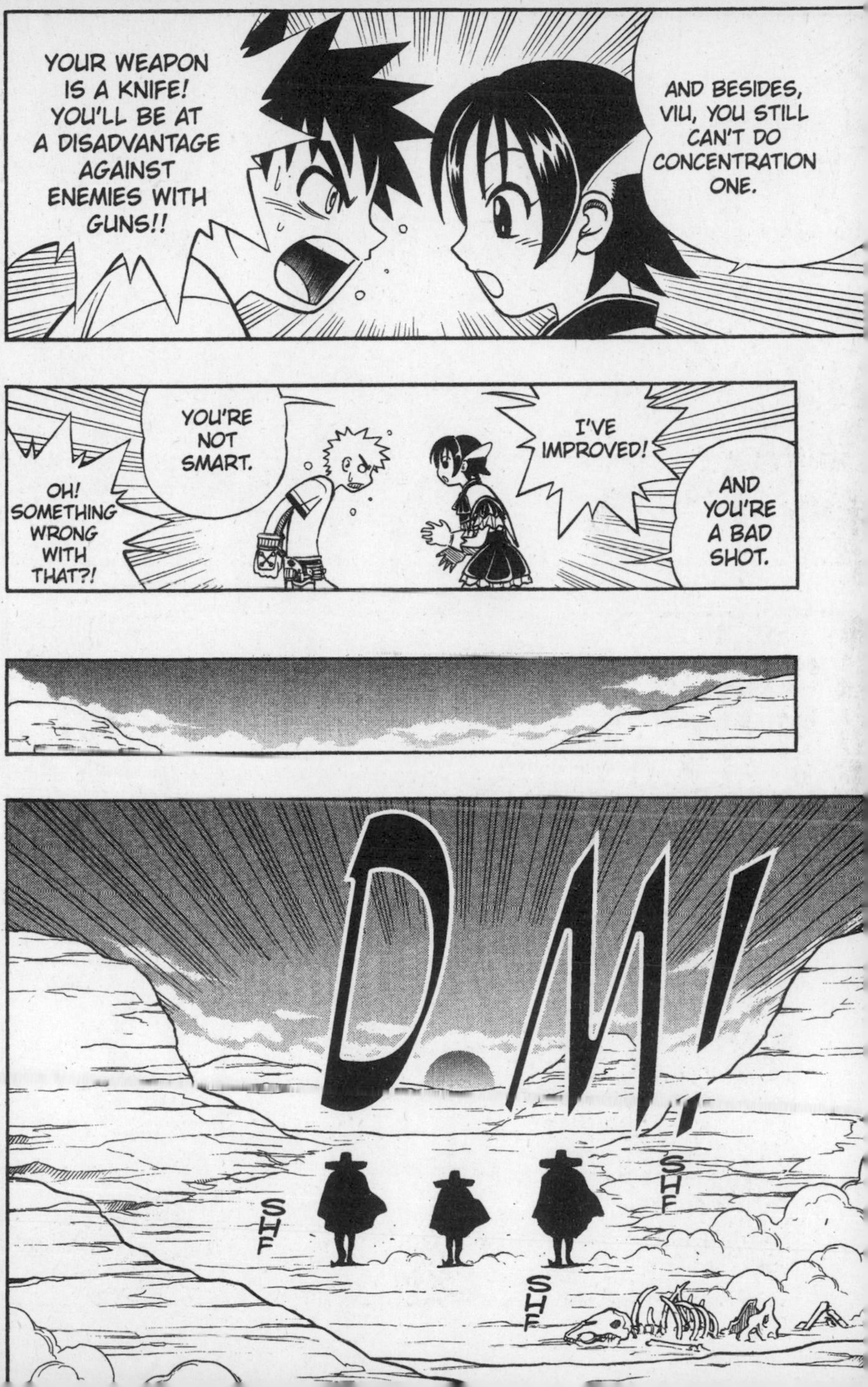
YOUR WEAPON IS A KNIFE! YOU'LL BE AT A DISADVANTAGE AGAINST ENEMIES WITH GUNS!!
AND BESIDES, VIU, YOU STILL CAN'T DO CONCENTRATION ONE.
YOU'RE NOT SMART.
OH! SOMETHING WRONG WITH THAT?!
I'VE IMPROVED!
AND YOU'RE A BAD SHOT.
DM!
SHF
SHF
SHF

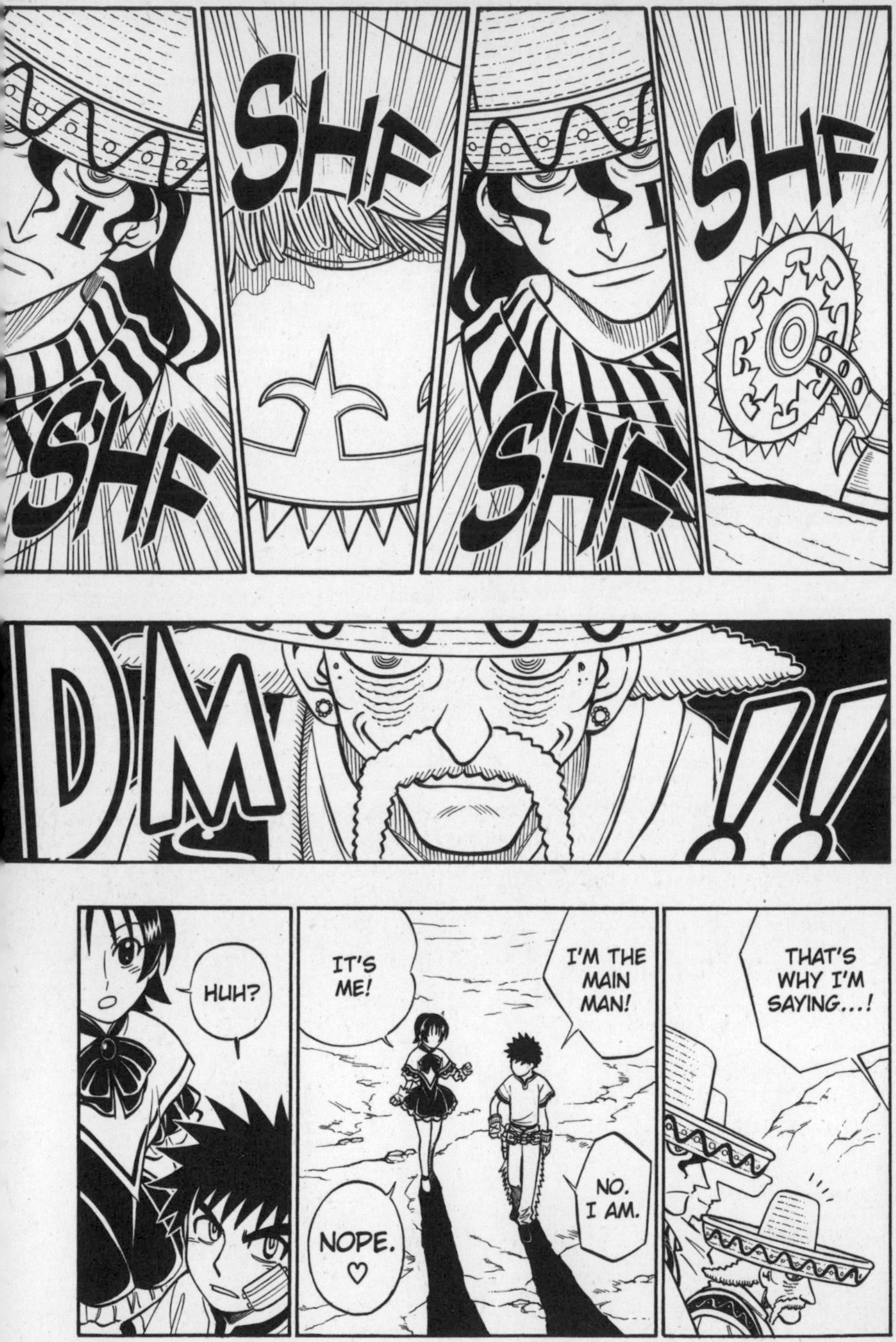
SHF
SHF
SHF
SHF
DM!!
THAT'S WHY I'M SAYING...!
I'M THE MAIN MAN!
IT'S ME!
NO. I AM.
NOPE. ♡
HUH?

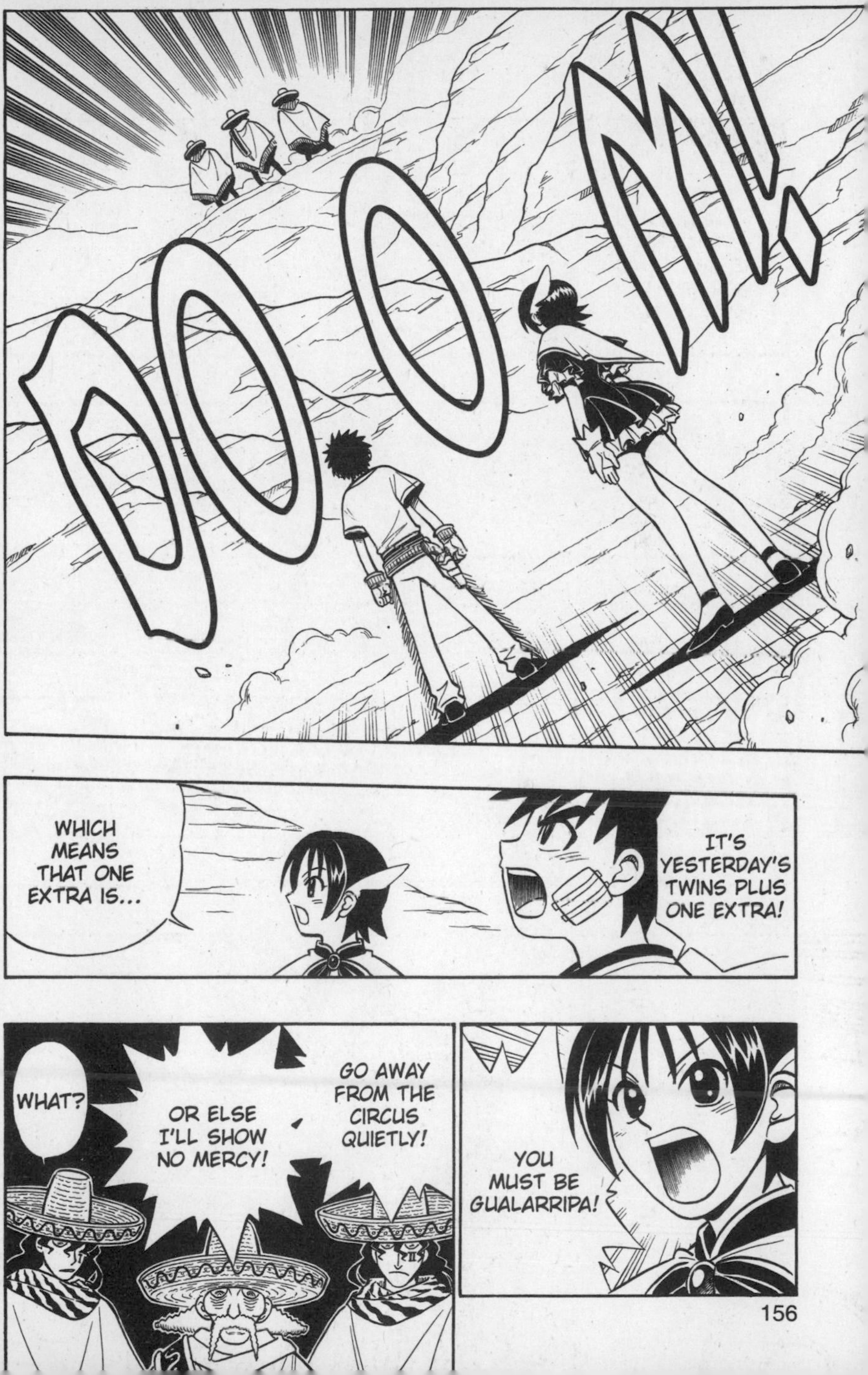
DOOM!!
IT'S YESTERDAY'S TWINS PLUS ONE EXTRA!
WHICH MEANS THAT ONE EXTRA IS...
YOU MUST BE GUALARRIPA!
GO AWAY FROM THE CIRCUS QUIETLY!
OR ELSE I'LL SHOW NO MERCY!
WHAT?

READ THIS WAY

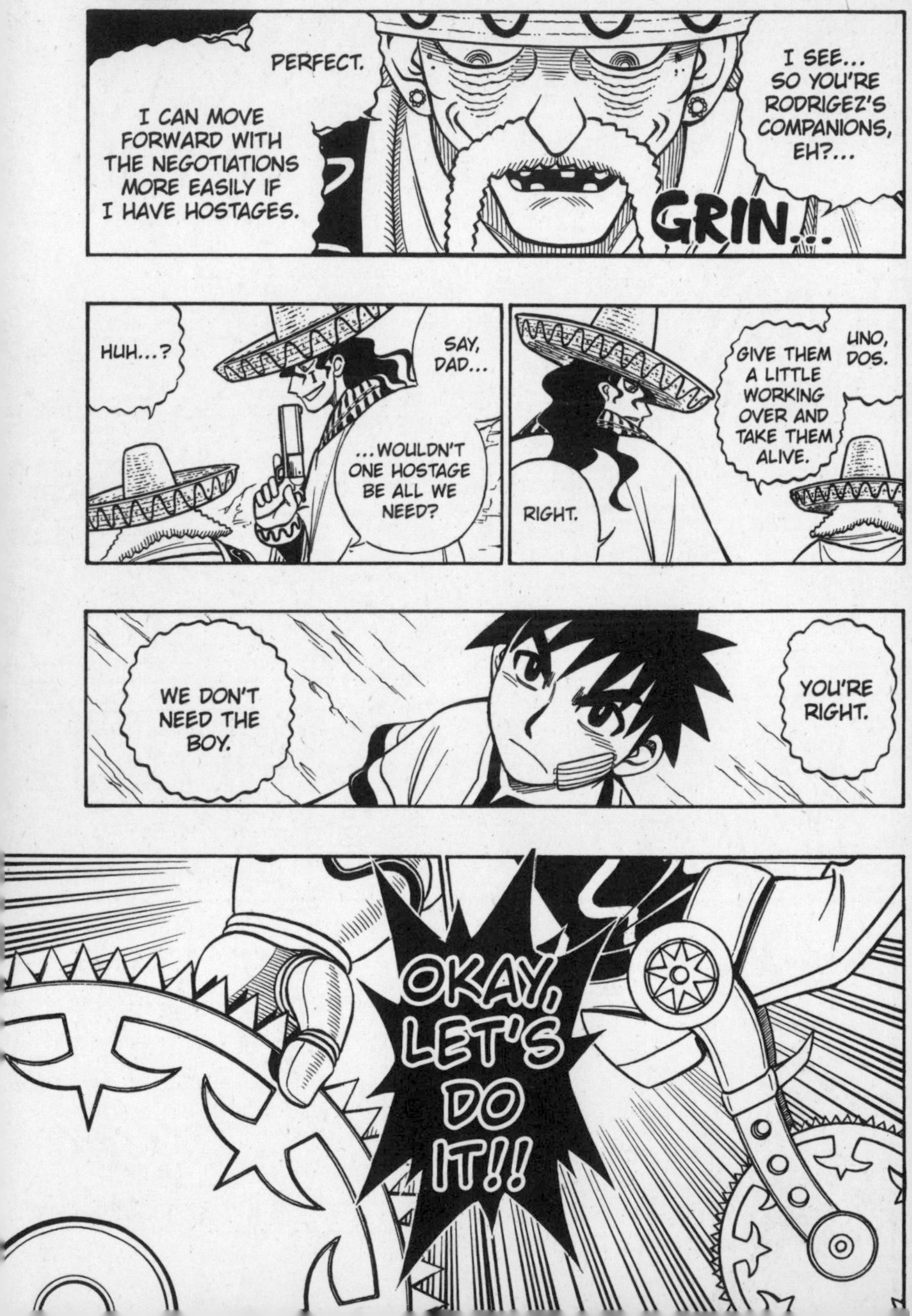
I SEE... SO YOU'RE RODRIGEZ'S COMPANIONS, EH?...
GRIN...
PERFECT.
I CAN MOVE FORWARD WITH THE NEGOTIATIONS MORE EASILY IF I HAVE HOSTAGES.
UNO, DOS.
GIVE THEM A LITTLE WORKING OVER AND TAKE THEM ALIVE.
RIGHT.
SAY, DAD...
...WOULDN'T ONE HOSTAGE BE ALL WE NEED?
HUH...?
YOU'RE RIGHT.
WE DON'T NEED THE BOY.
OKAY, LET'S DO IT!!

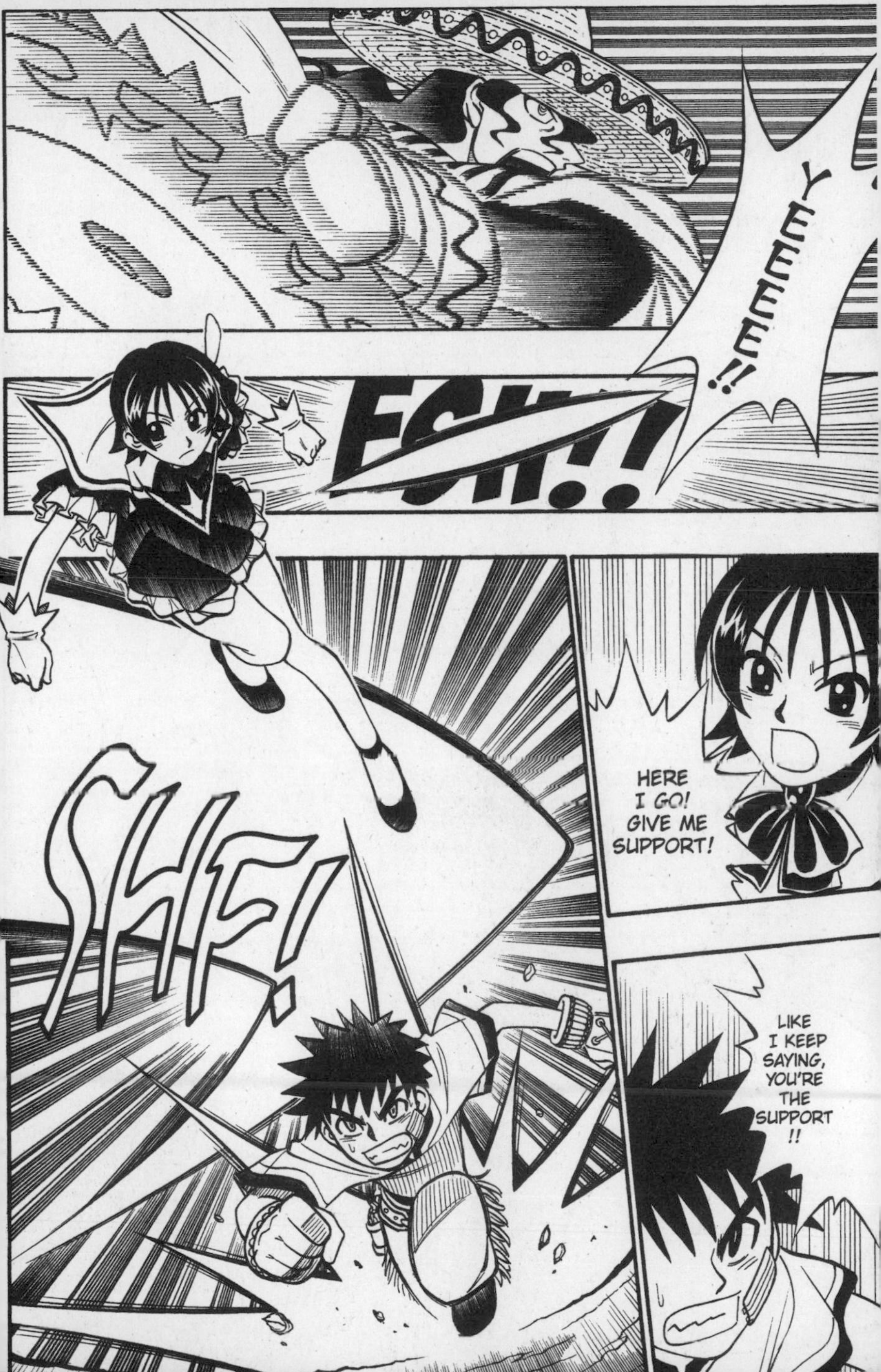
YEEEEE!!
ESH!!
HERE I GO! GIVE ME SUPPORT!
LIKE I KEEP SAYING, YOU'RE THE SUPPORT!!
SHF!

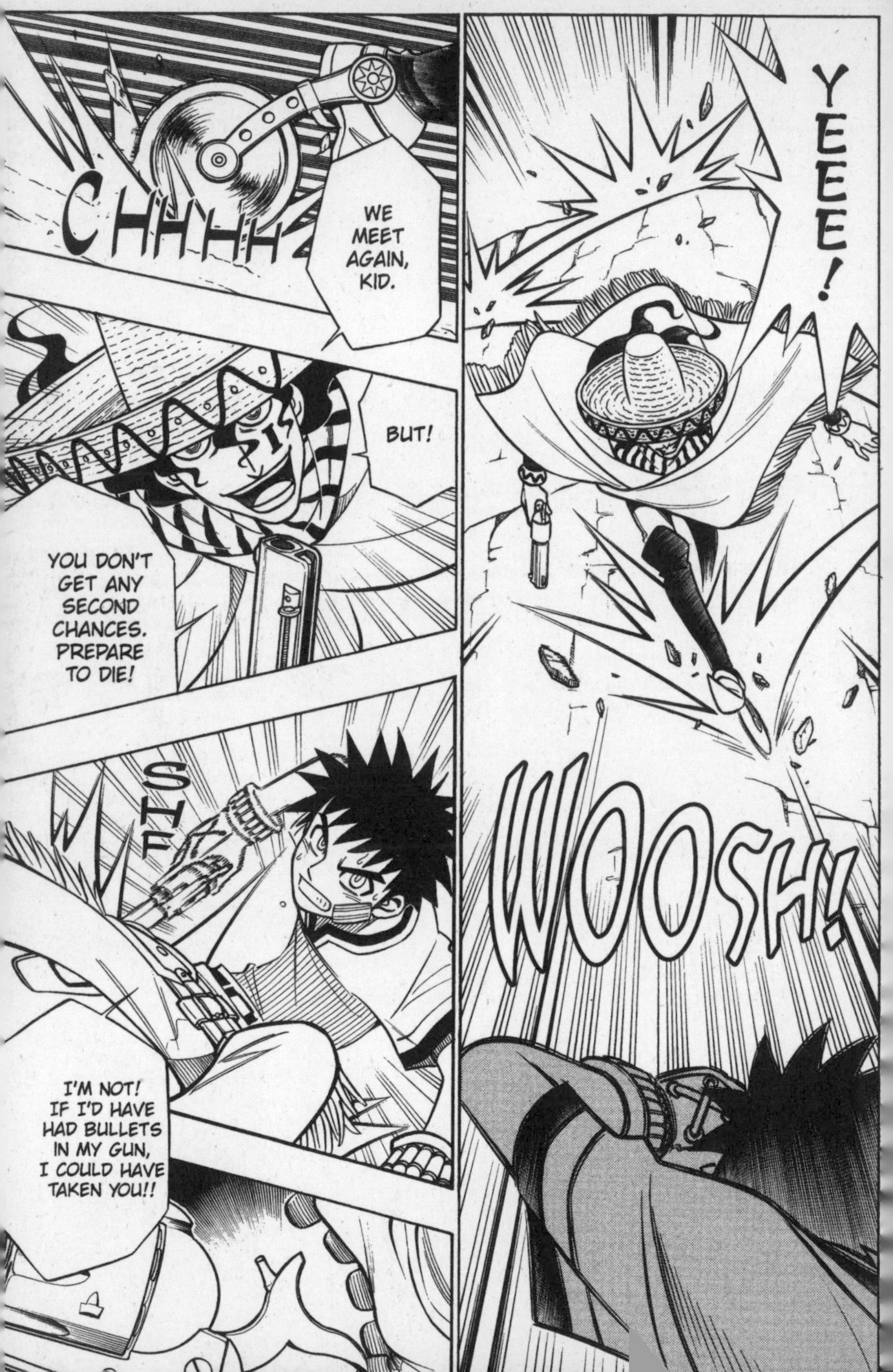
YEEE!
WOOSH!
CHHHH
WE MEET AGAIN, KID.
BUT!
YOU DON'T GET ANY SECOND CHANCES. PREPARE TO DIE!
SHF
I'M NOT! IF I'D HAVE HAD BULLETS IN MY GUN, I COULD HAVE TAKEN YOU!!

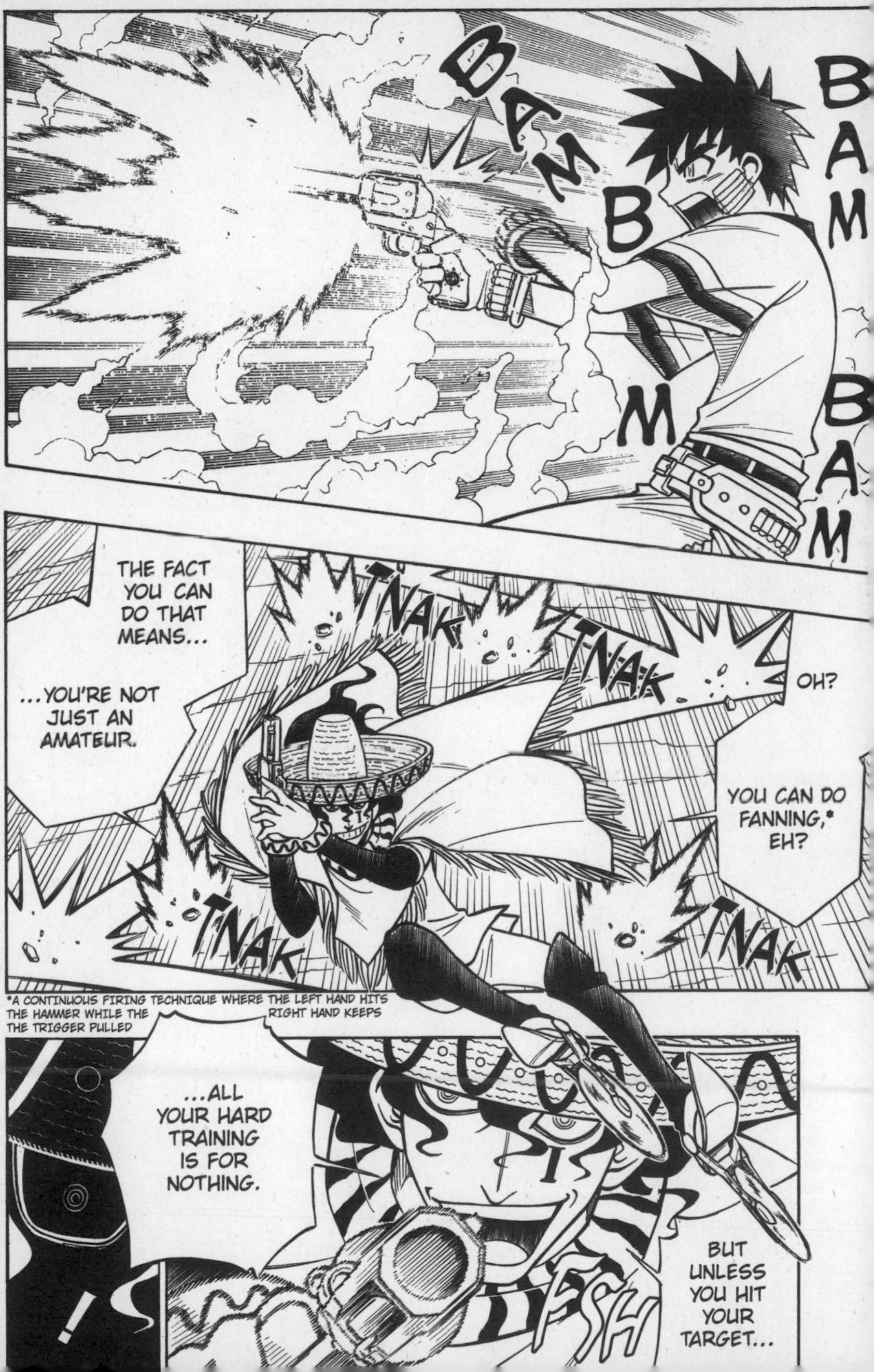
BAM BAM BAM
BAMM
OH?
YOU CAN DO FANNING,* EH?
TNAK
TNAK
TNAK
TNAK
THE FACT YOU CAN DO THAT MEANS...
...YOU'RE NOT JUST AN AMATEUR.
*A CONTINUOUS FIRING TECHNIQUE WHERE THE LEFT HAND HITS THE HAMMER WHILE THE RIGHT HAND KEEPS THE TRIGGER PULLED
BUT UNLESS YOU HIT YOUR TARGET...
FSH
...ALL YOUR HARD TRAINING IS FOR NOTHING.
!

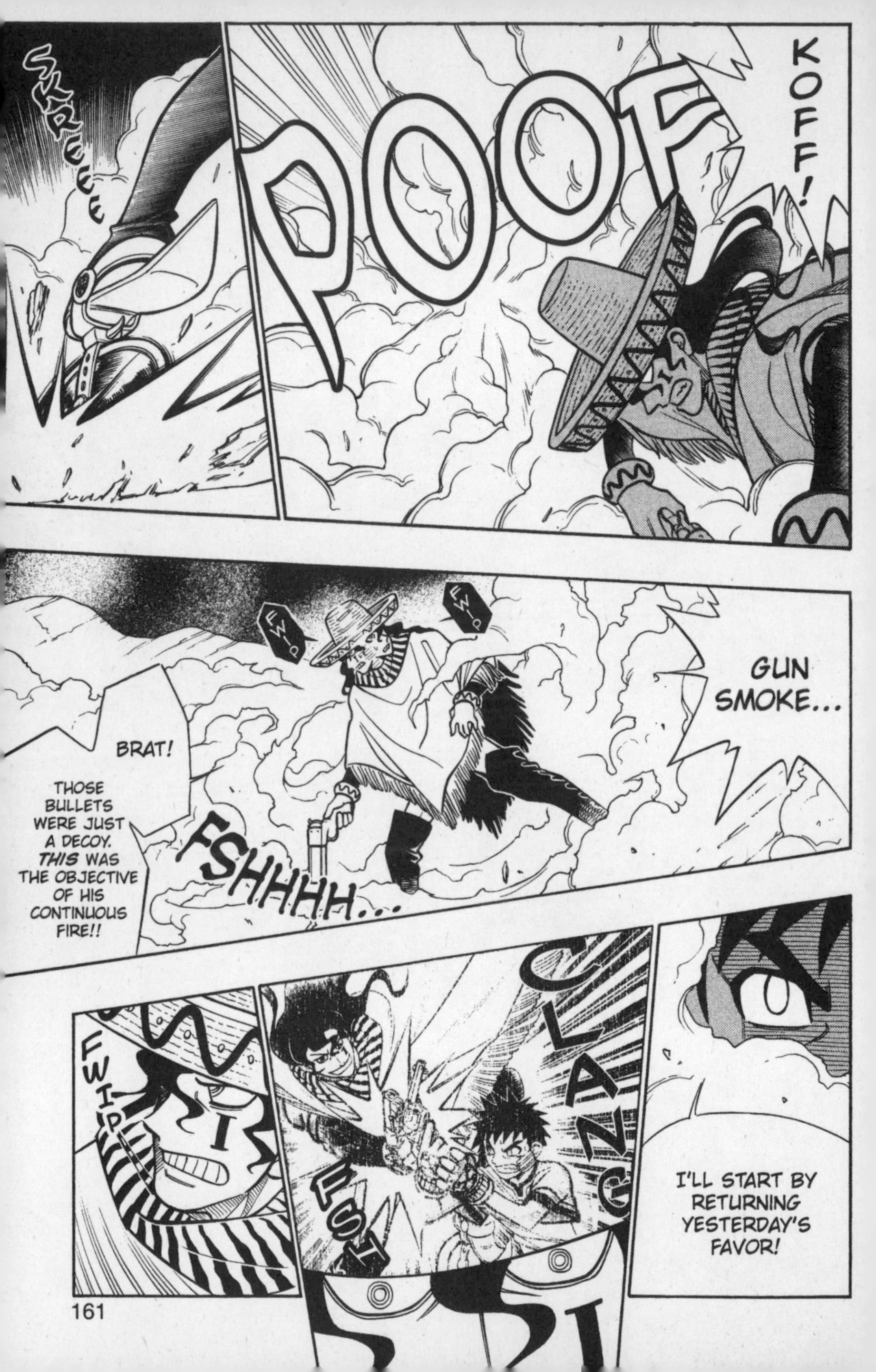
KOFF!
POOF
SKREEE
GUN SMOKE...
FWIP
FWIP
BRAT!
THOSE BULLETS WERE JUST A DECOY. *THIS* WAS THE OBJECTIVE OF HIS CONTINUOUS FIRE!!
FSHHHH...
I'LL START BY RETURNING YESTERDAY'S FAVOR!
CLANG
FST
FWIP

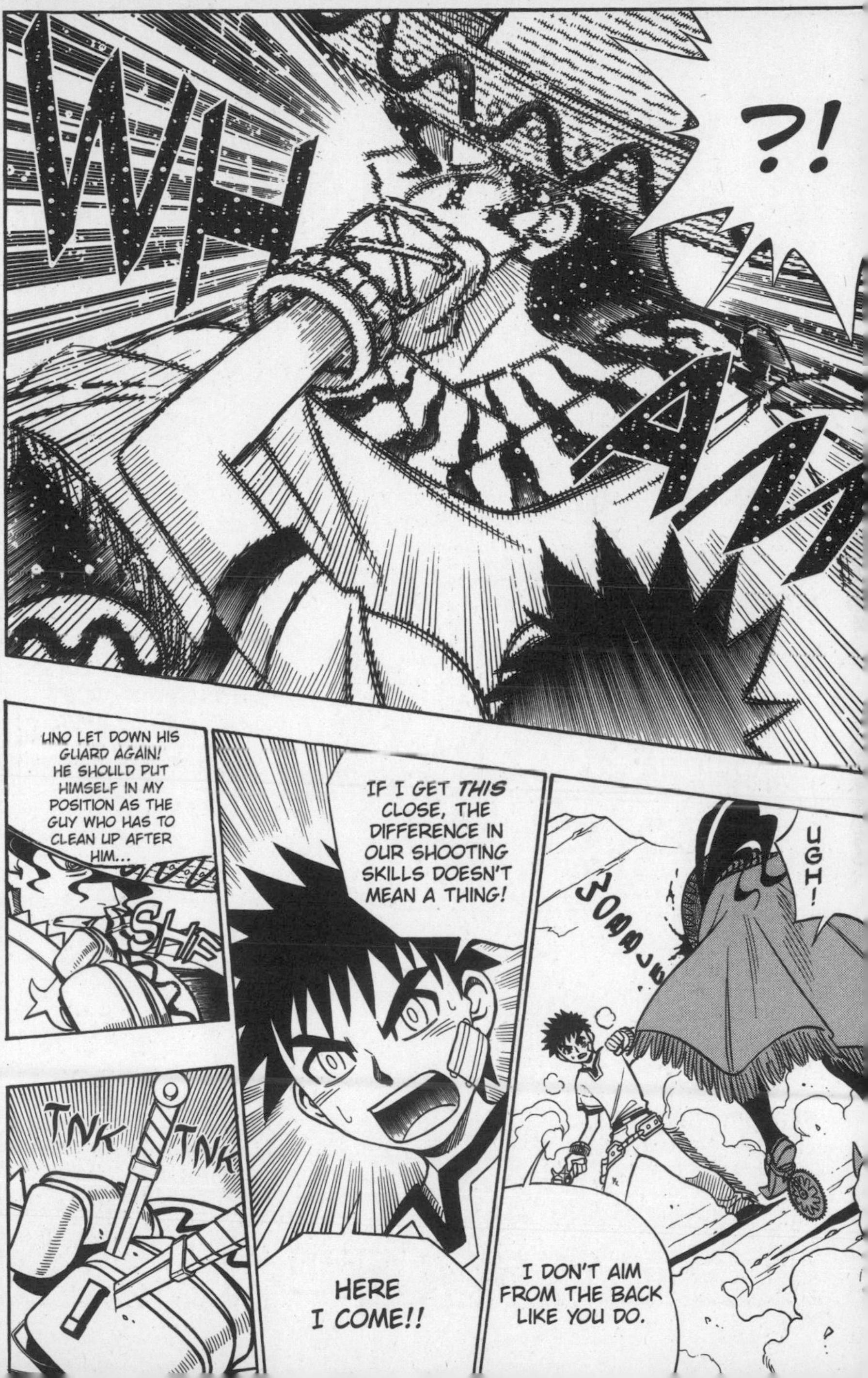
WHAM
?!
UGH!
I DON'T AIM FROM THE BACK LIKE YOU DO.
IF I GET *THIS* CLOSE, THE DIFFERENCE IN OUR SHOOTING SKILLS DOESN'T MEAN A THING!
HERE I COME!!
UNO LET DOWN HIS GUARD AGAIN! HE SHOULD PUT HIMSELF IN MY POSITION AS THE GUY WHO HAS TO CLEAN UP AFTER HIM...
SHF
TNK TNK

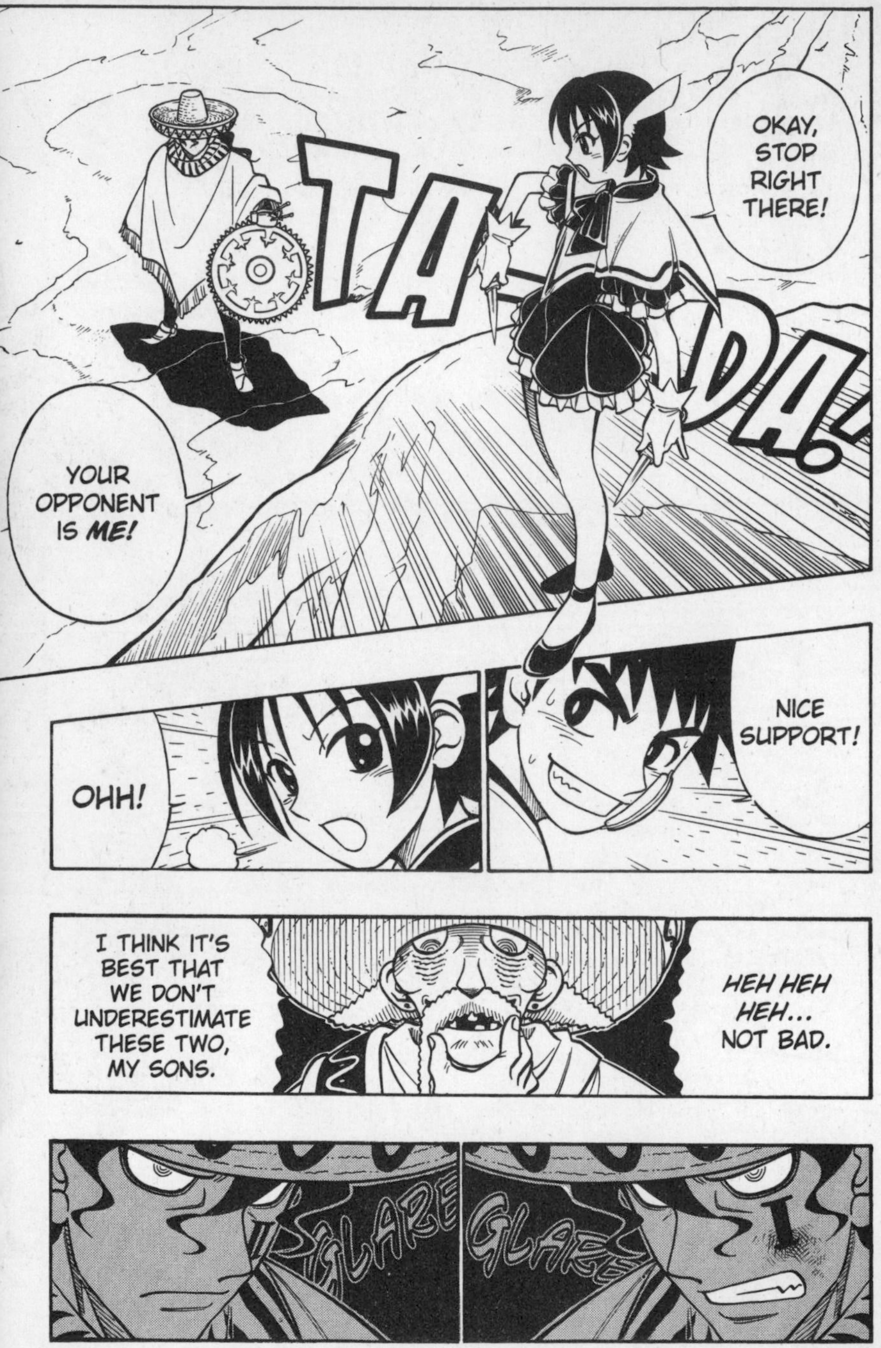
OKAY, STOP RIGHT THERE!
TA-DA!
YOUR OPPONENT IS *ME!*
NICE SUPPORT!
OHH!
*HEH HEH HEH...* NOT BAD.
I THINK IT'S BEST THAT WE DON'T UNDERESTIMATE THESE TWO, MY SONS.
GLARE
GLARE

CONCEPT: A CRAZY GUNMAN. FOR MY VILLAIN, I THOUGHT ABOUT WHAT MIGHT BE THE EASIEST TYPE TO DRAW—ONE THAT WOULD KEEP THE STORY MOVING CRISPLY WITHOUT CREATING A DETAILED BACK STORY—AND CAME UP WITH THE CONCEPT OF KEVIN.

KEVIN WAS ACTUALLY EASY TO DRAW, BUT HE WAS SO EASY TO DRAW THAT HE TURNED INTO QUITE A POOR CHARACTER WITH NOTHING BEHIND HIM.

I ATTEMPTED TO DEFINE HIM WITH THE SHOTGUN, BUT HE BECAME QUITE UNSPECTACULAR IN A MANNER THAT HAPPENS IN MANGA AIMED AT YOUNG MALES. IN ACTUALITY, A SHOTGUN HAS INCOMPARABLE DESTRUCTIVE POWER COMPARED TO A PISTOL, BUT AGAINST AN OPPONENT USING SUPERHUMAN ABILITIES ALL OVER THE PLACE, HE DIDN'T STAND A CHANCE.

## CHARACTER FILE #07

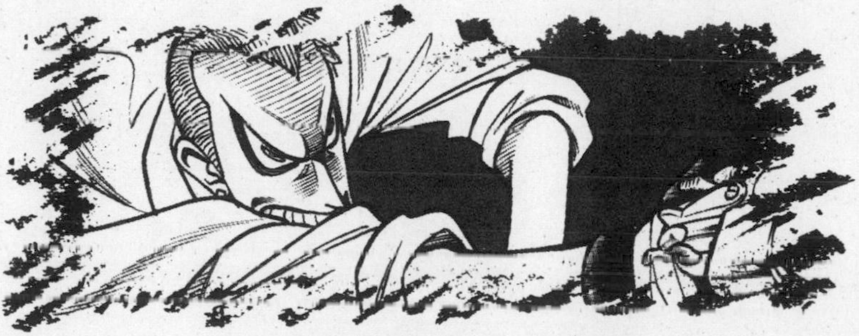

# "TARGET" KEVIN

IMAGE SOURCE: THE CONCEPT WAS OF A CRAZY VILLAIN, SO IN THE COURSE OF PLAYING A GAME OF ASSOCIATION WHERE WE ASKED, "SHOULD HIS UPPER BODY BE BARE?", "SHOULD HE WEAR A JACKET OVER HIS BARE UPPER BODY?" HE TURNED OUT LIKE THIS.

DESIGN: TO THE PROCESS I DESCRIBED ABOVE, I ADDED THE "DESIRE TO DRAW SOMETHING STRANGE" THAT'S A PART OF MY NATURE TO COME UP WITH KEVIN'S DESIGN. THE MAIN POINTS ARE HIS HUGE TRIANGULAR EYES AND ELONGATED PUPILS.

THE TRUTH IS, I SORT OF LIKE THIS DESIGN. I THINK "HE'D BE A DESIGN WE COULD USE AS AN IDIOSYNCRATIC MAIN CHARACTER." NO, MAYBE NOT.

ON A SIDE NOTE, THE BULL'S-EYE ON HIS CHEST WAS A "SHOOT ME IF YOU CAN" WAY OF SHOWING OFF KEVIN'S CRAZINESS, BUT AT THE SUGGESTION OF MY EDITOR, IT BECAME THE START OF THE IDEA FOR THE TARGET BATTLE.

# CHAPTER 16: VIOLENT ATTACK

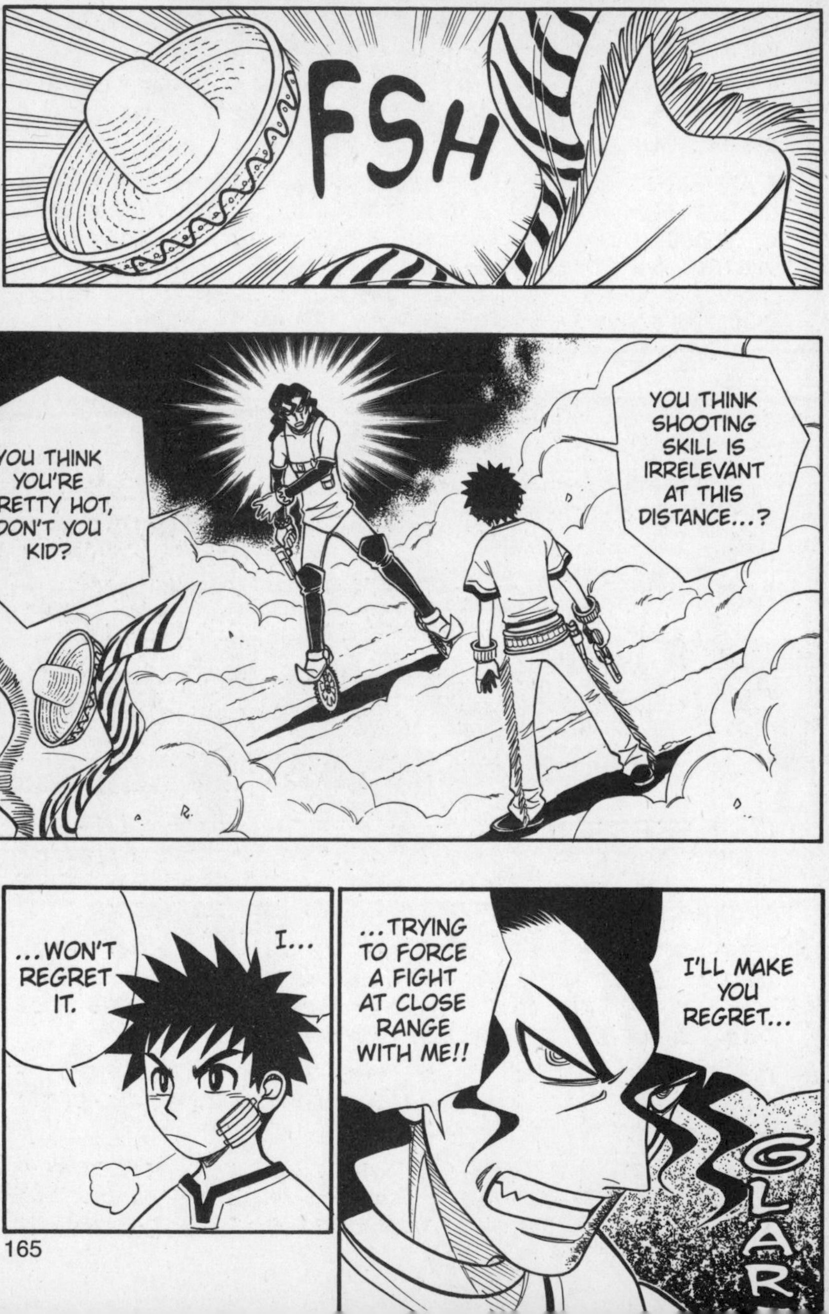
FSH
YOU THINK SHOOTING SKILL IS IRRELEVANT AT THIS DISTANCE...?
YOU THINK YOU'RE PRETTY HOT, DON'T YOU KID?
I'LL MAKE YOU REGRET...
...TRYING TO FORCE A FIGHT AT CLOSE RANGE WITH ME!!
GLAR
I...
...WON'T REGRET IT.

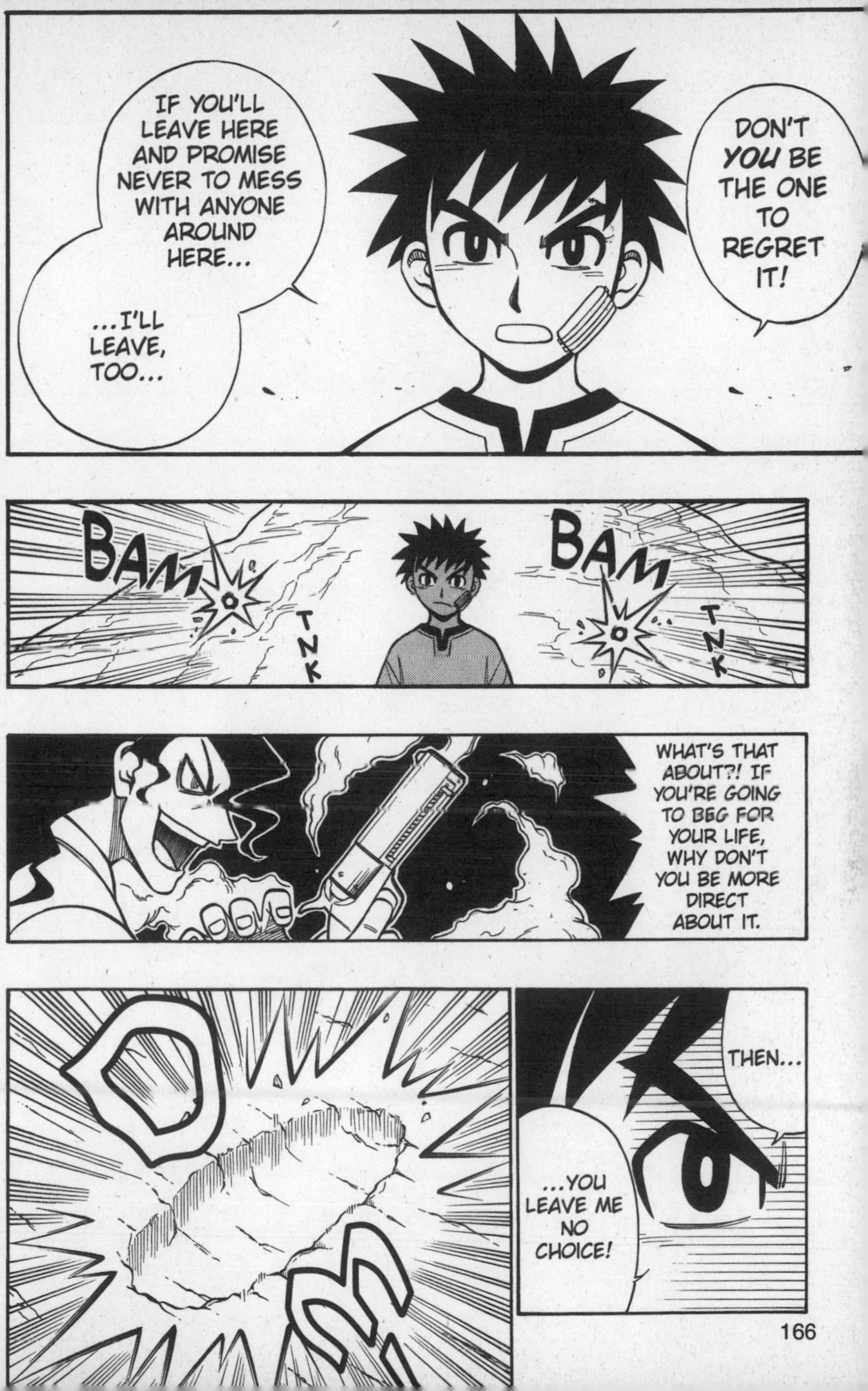
DON'T YOU BE THE ONE TO REGRET IT!
IF YOU'LL LEAVE HERE AND PROMISE NEVER TO MESS WITH ANYONE AROUND HERE...
...I'LL LEAVE, TOO...
BAM
TNK
BAM
TNK
WHAT'S THAT ABOUT?! IF YOU'RE GOING TO BEG FOR YOUR LIFE, WHY DON'T YOU BE MORE DIRECT ABOUT IT.
THEN...
...YOU LEAVE ME NO CHOICE!

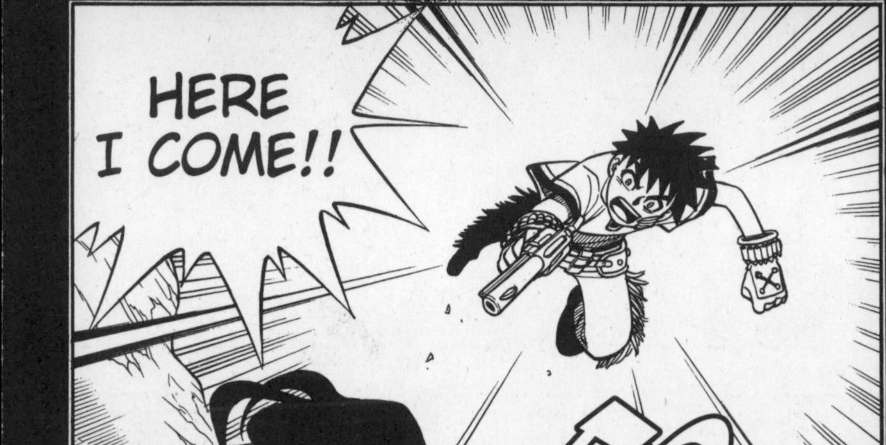
HERE I COME!!
FOOSH

## CHAPTER 16: VIOLENT ATTACK

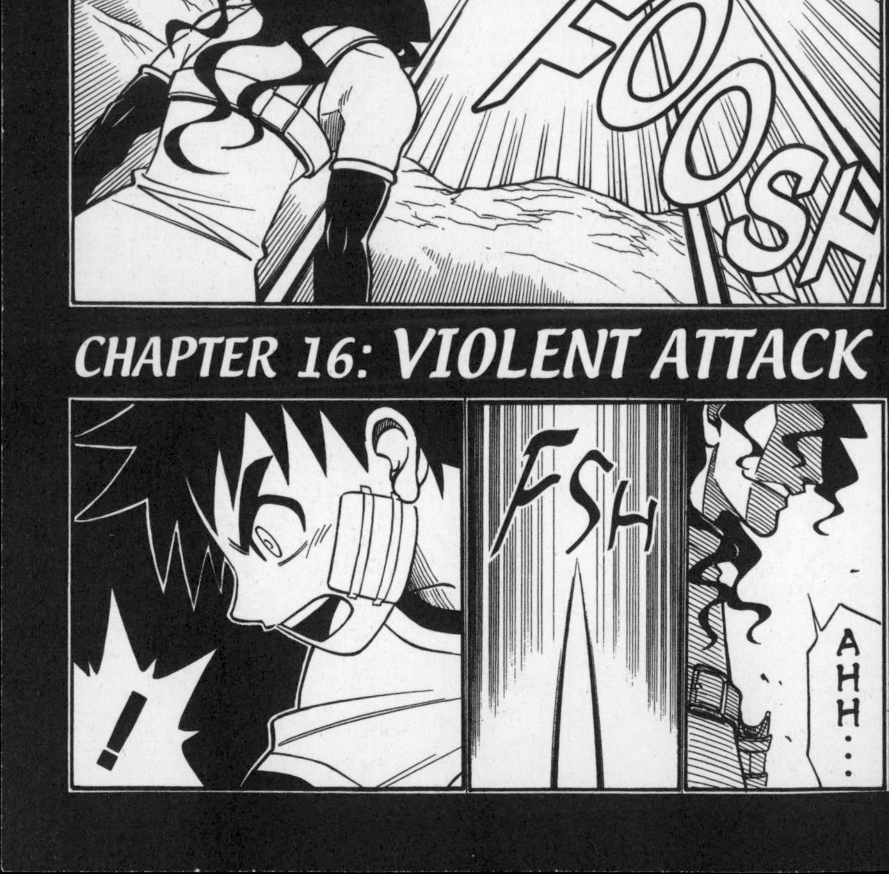
AHH...
FSH
!

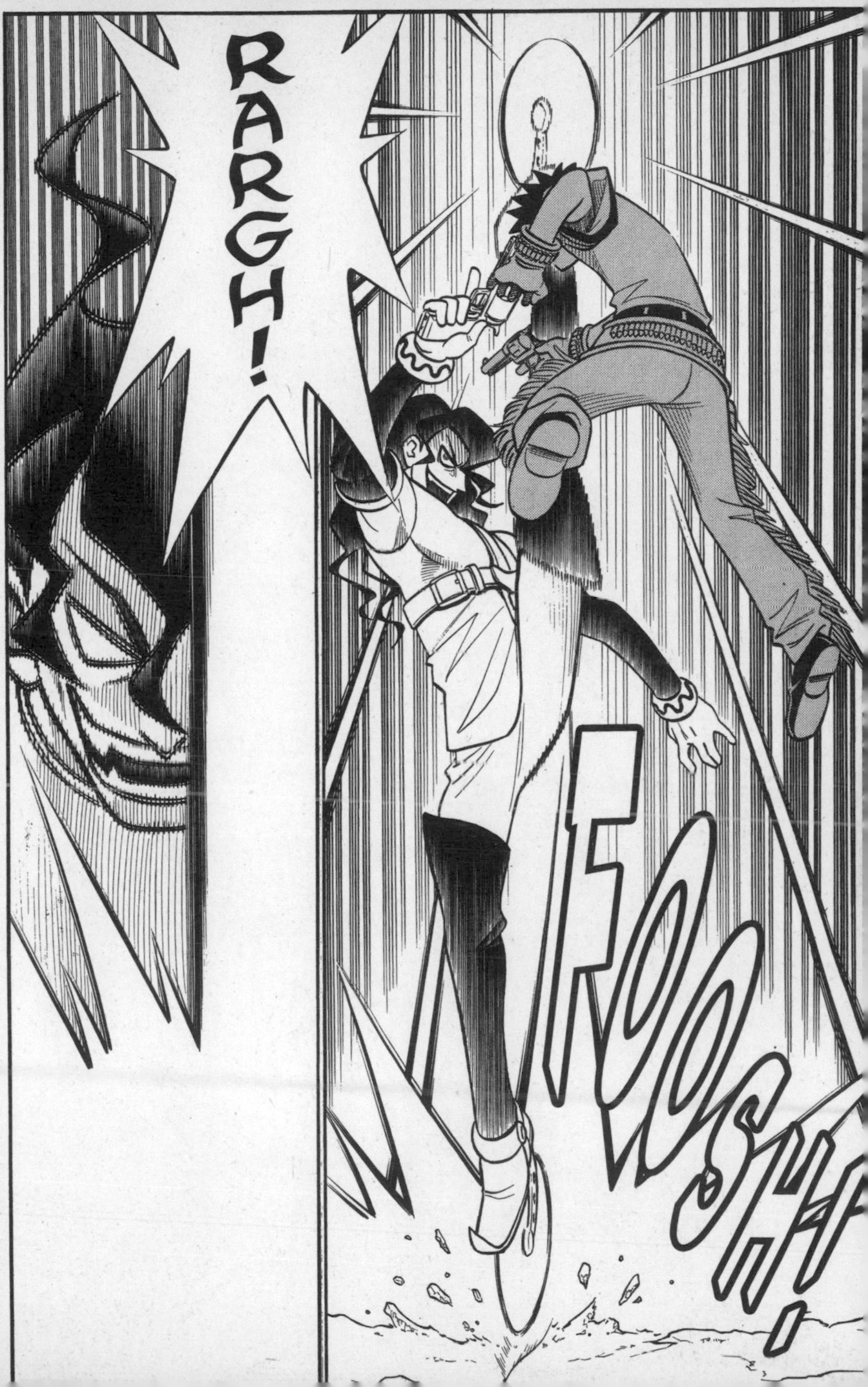
RARGH!
FOOSH!

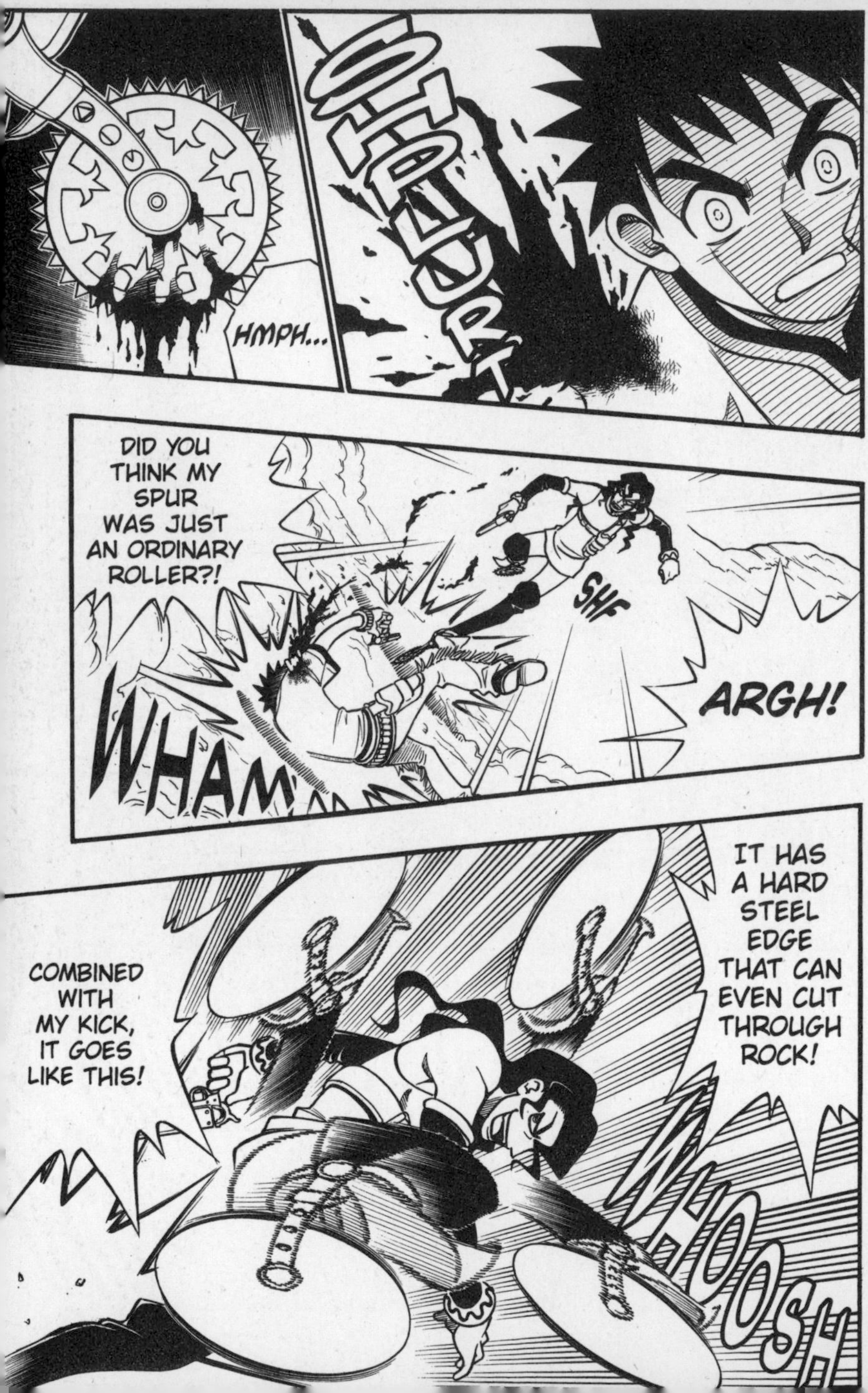
HMPH...
DID YOU THINK MY SPUR WAS JUST AN ORDINARY ROLLER?!
SHF
ARGH!
WHAM
IT HAS A HARD STEEL EDGE THAT CAN EVEN CUT THROUGH ROCK!
COMBINED WITH MY KICK, IT GOES LIKE THIS!
WHOOSH

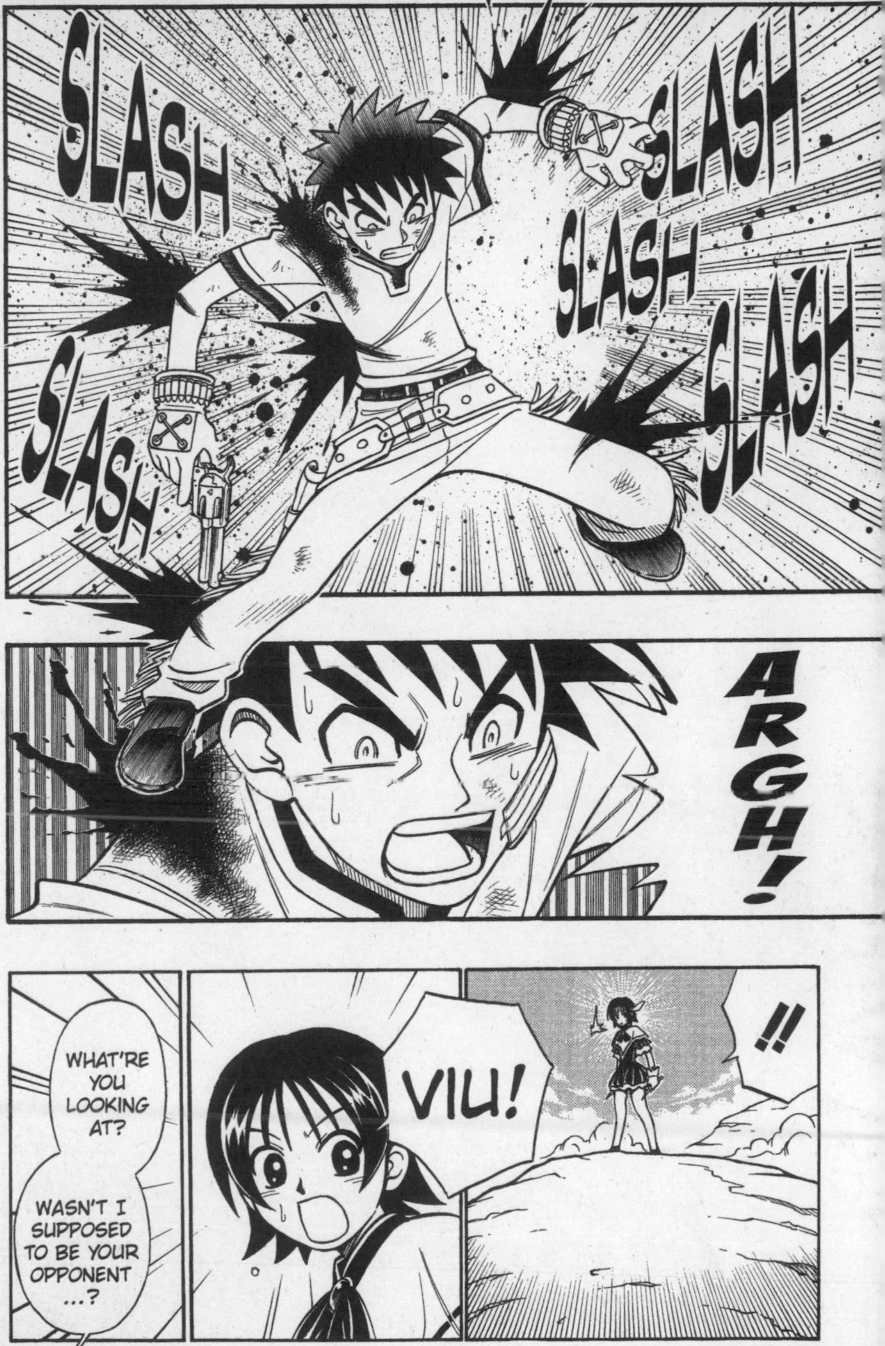
SLASH
SLASH
SLASH
SLASH
SLASH
ARGH!
!!
VIU!
WHAT'RE YOU LOOKING AT?
WASN'T I SUPPOSED TO BE YOUR OPPONENT ...?

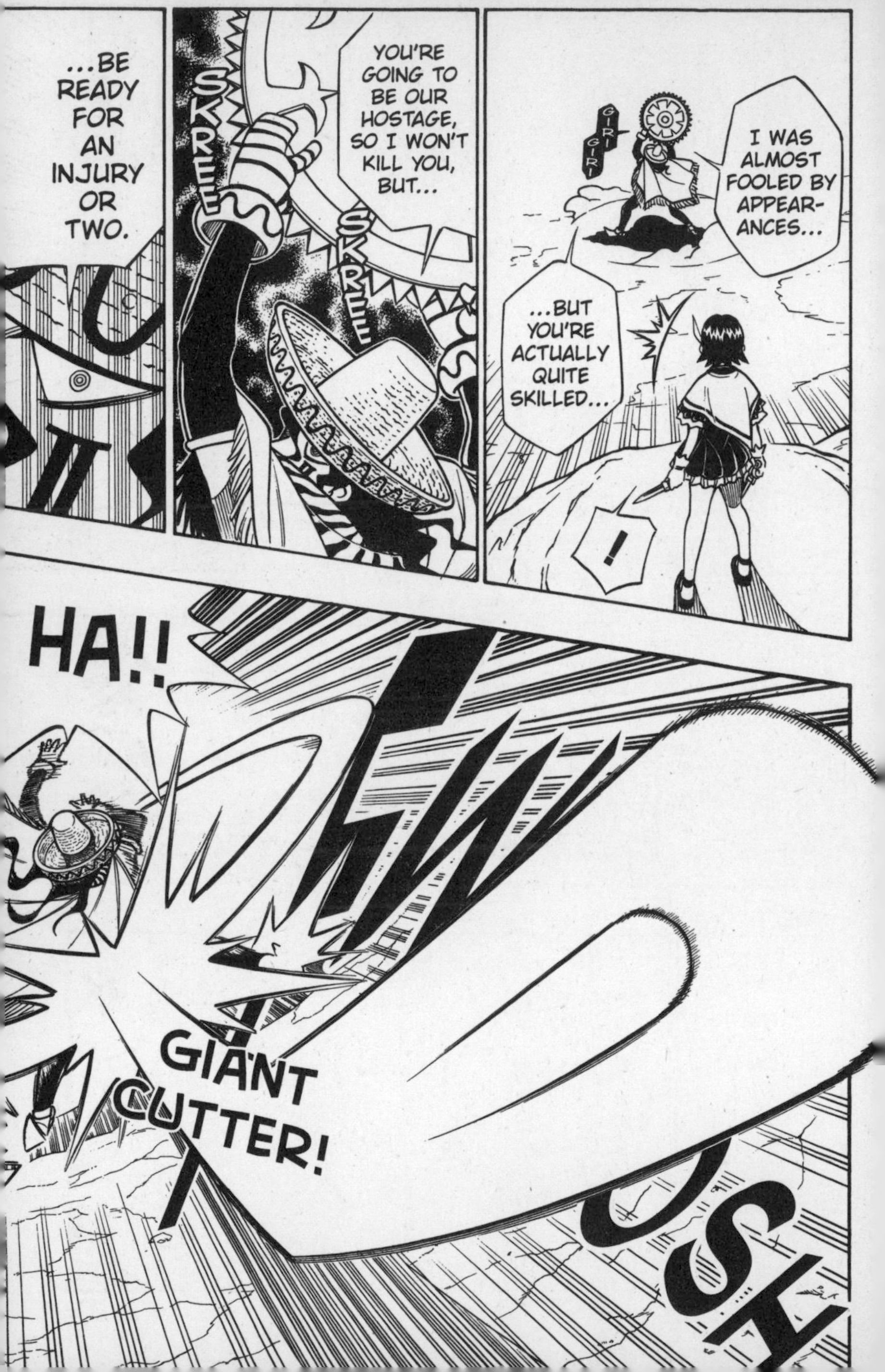
I WAS ALMOST FOOLED BY APPEARANCES...
GIRI GIRI
...BUT YOU'RE ACTUALLY QUITE SKILLED...
!
YOU'RE GOING TO BE OUR HOSTAGE, SO I WON'T KILL YOU, BUT...
SKREE
SKREE
...BE READY FOR AN INJURY OR TWO.
HA!!
GIANT CUTTER!

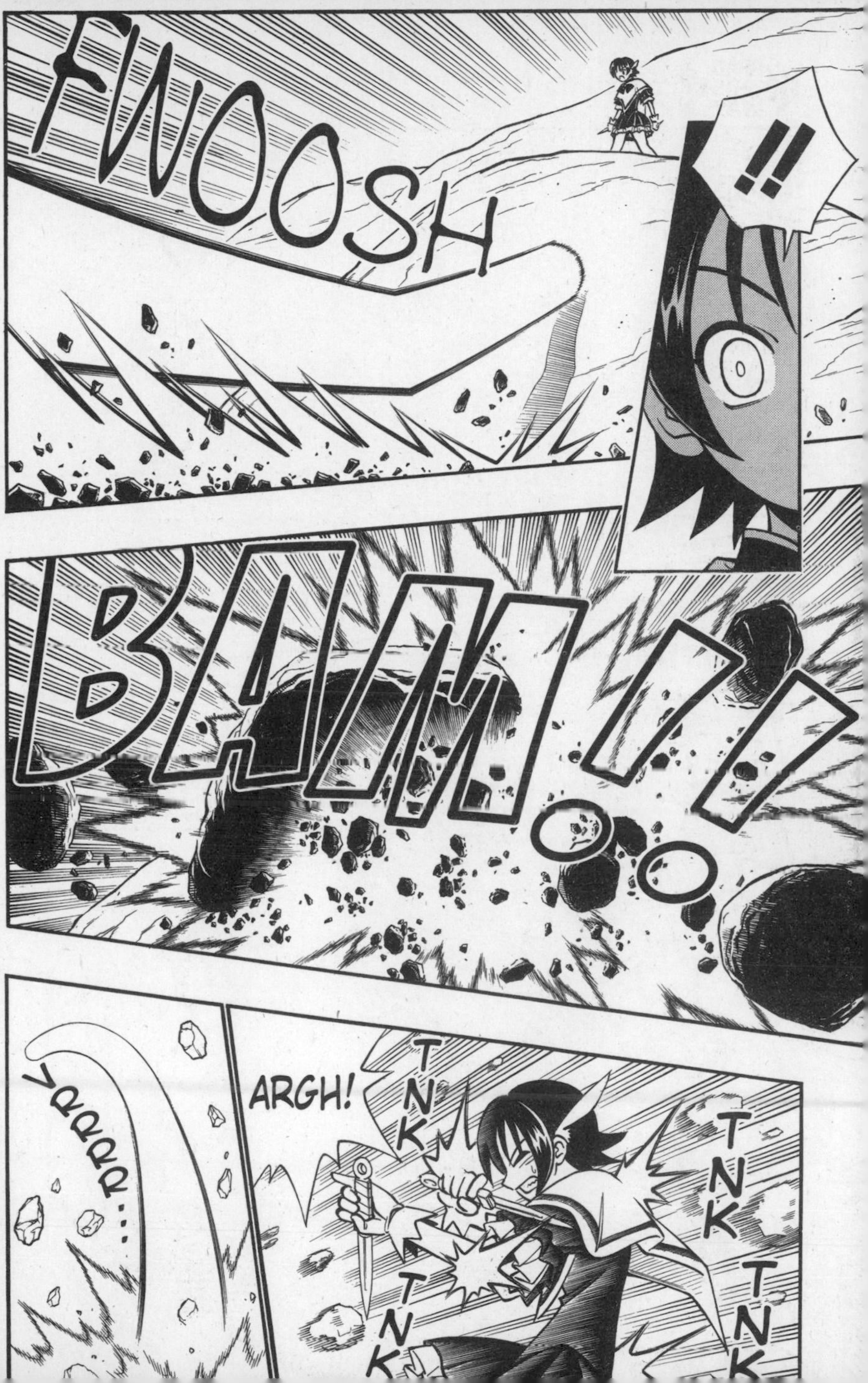
!!
FWOOSH
BAM!!
ARGH!
TNK
TNK
TNK
TNK
TNK
VRRRR...

READ THIS WAY

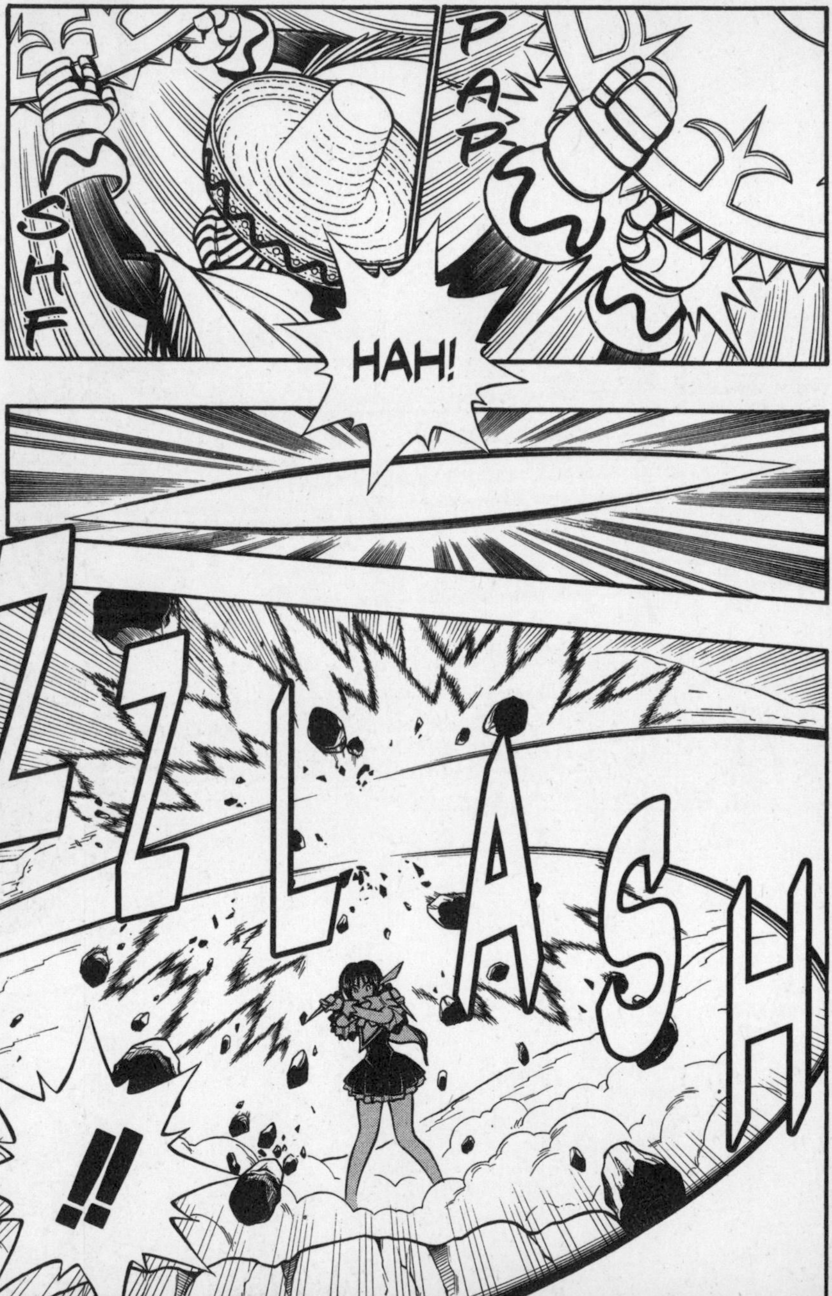
PAP PAP
SHF
HAH!
ZZLASH
!!

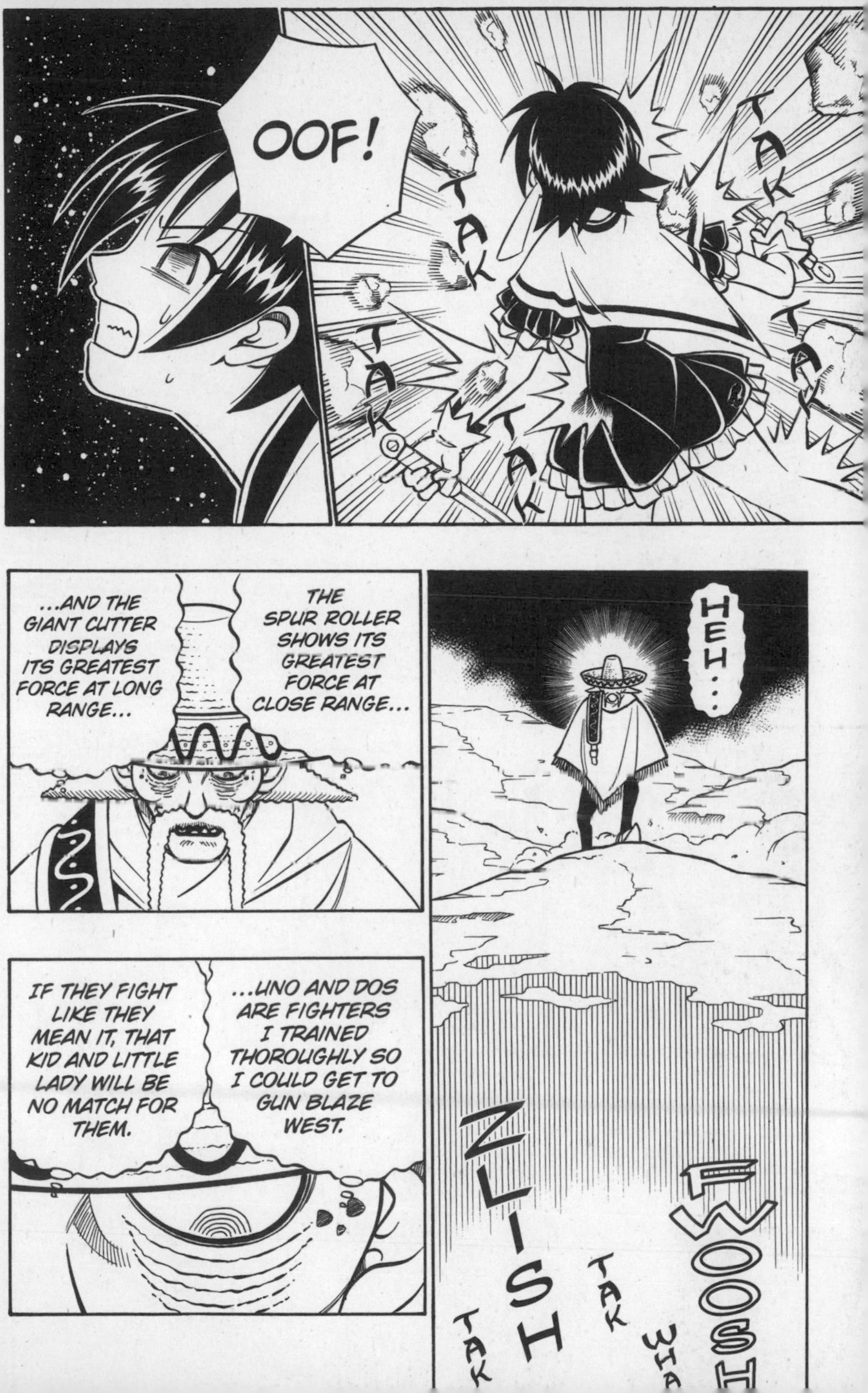
TAK
TAK
TAK
TAK
TAK
OOF!
HEH...
WOOSH
WHA
TAK
ZLISH
TAK
THE SPUR ROLLER SHOWS ITS GREATEST FORCE AT CLOSE RANGE...
...AND THE GIANT CUTTER DISPLAYS ITS GREATEST FORCE AT LONG RANGE...
...UNO AND DOS ARE FIGHTERS I TRAINED THOROUGHLY SO I COULD GET TO GUN BLAZE WEST.
IF THEY FIGHT LIKE THEY MEAN IT, THAT KID AND LITTLE LADY WILL BE NO MATCH FOR THEM.

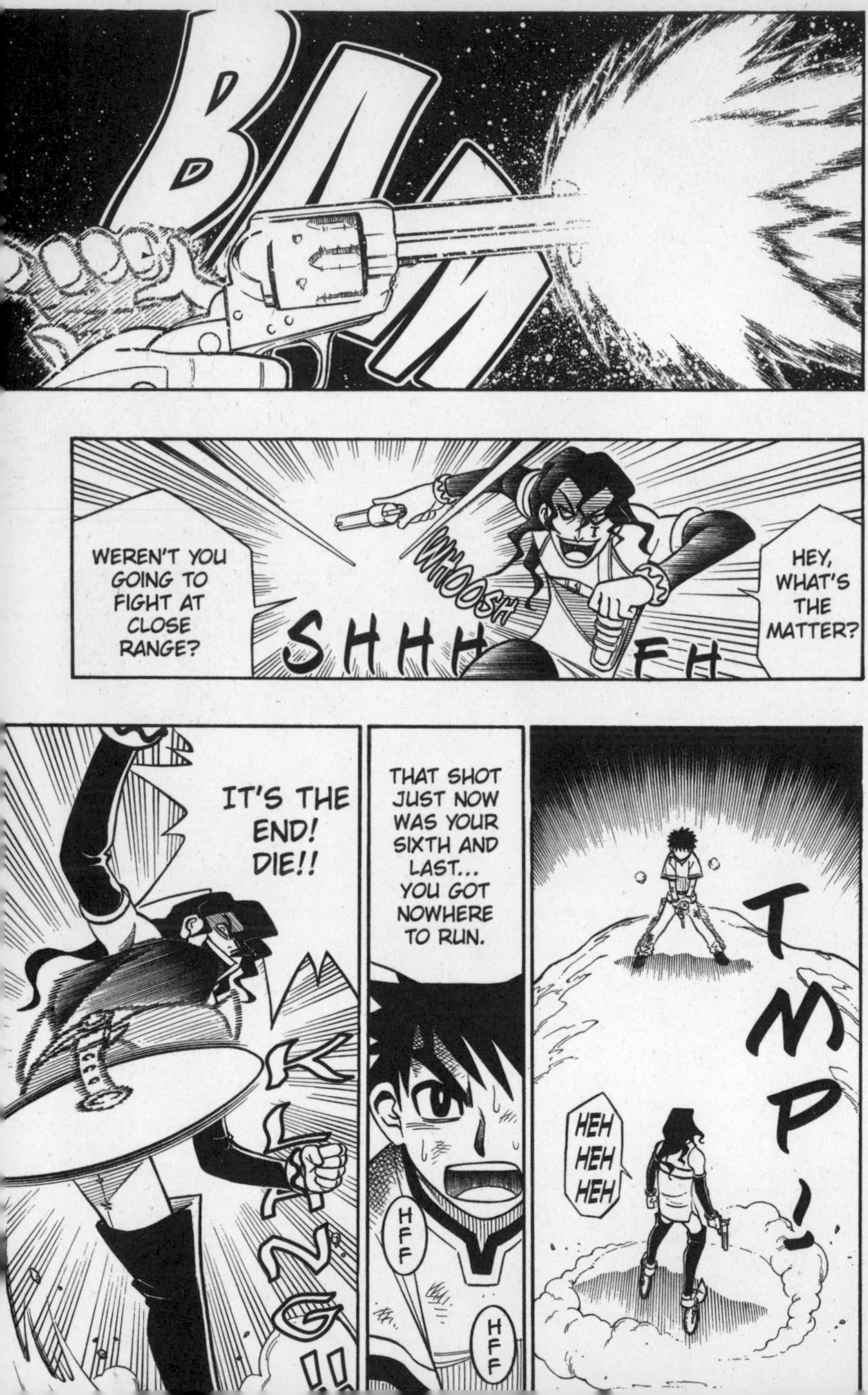
BLAM
HEY, WHAT'S THE MATTER?
WHOOSH
WEREN'T YOU GOING TO FIGHT AT CLOSE RANGE?
SHHH FH
TMP!
HEH HEH HEH
THAT SHOT JUST NOW WAS YOUR SIXTH AND LAST... YOU GOT NOWHERE TO RUN.
HFF
HFF
IT'S THE END! DIE!!
KLANG!!

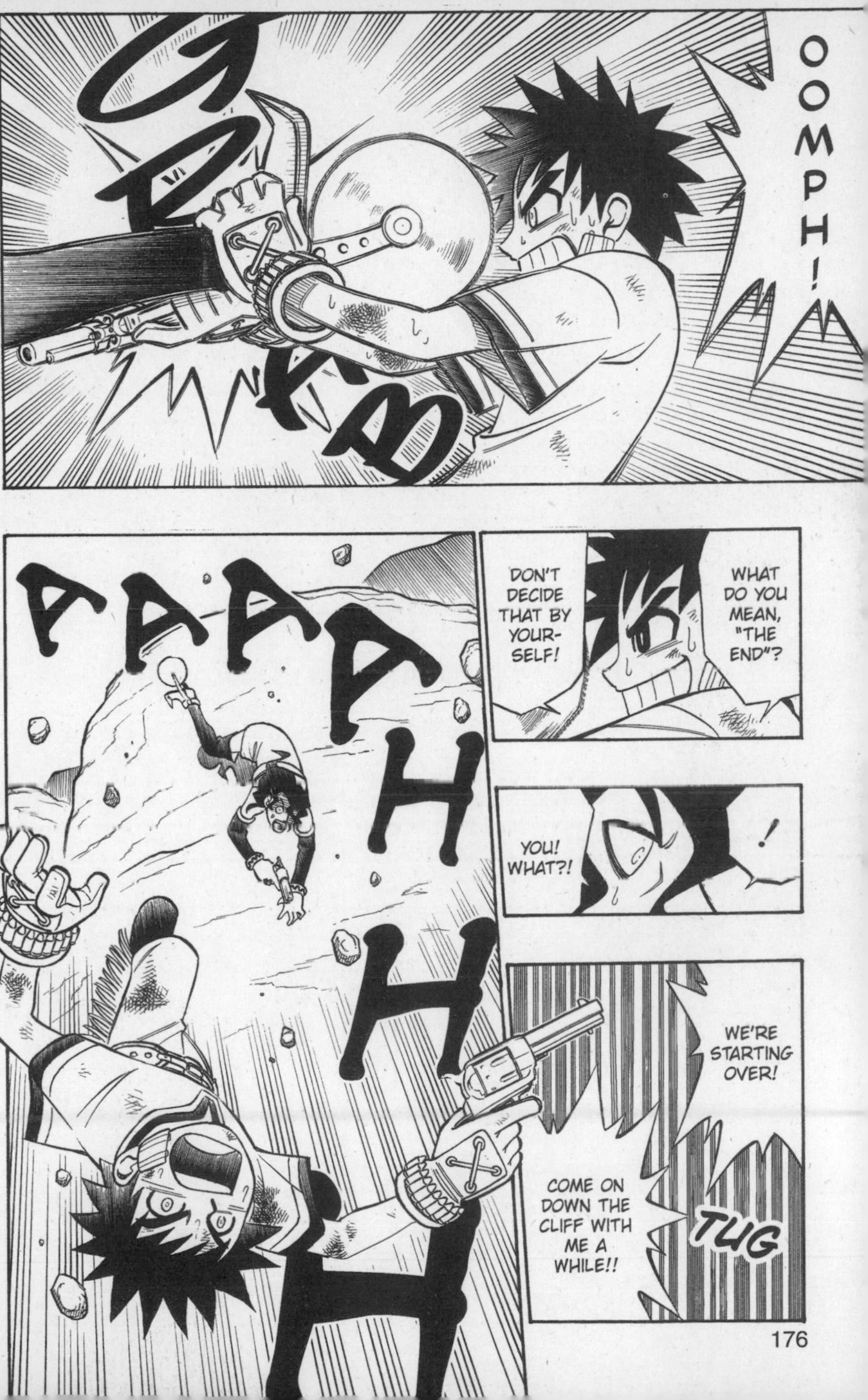
OOMPH!
WHAT DO YOU MEAN, "THE END"?
DON'T DECIDE THAT BY YOUR-SELF!
!
YOU! WHAT?!
WE'RE STARTING OVER!
TUG
COME ON DOWN THE CLIFF WITH ME A WHILE!!
AAAAHHH

READ THIS WAY

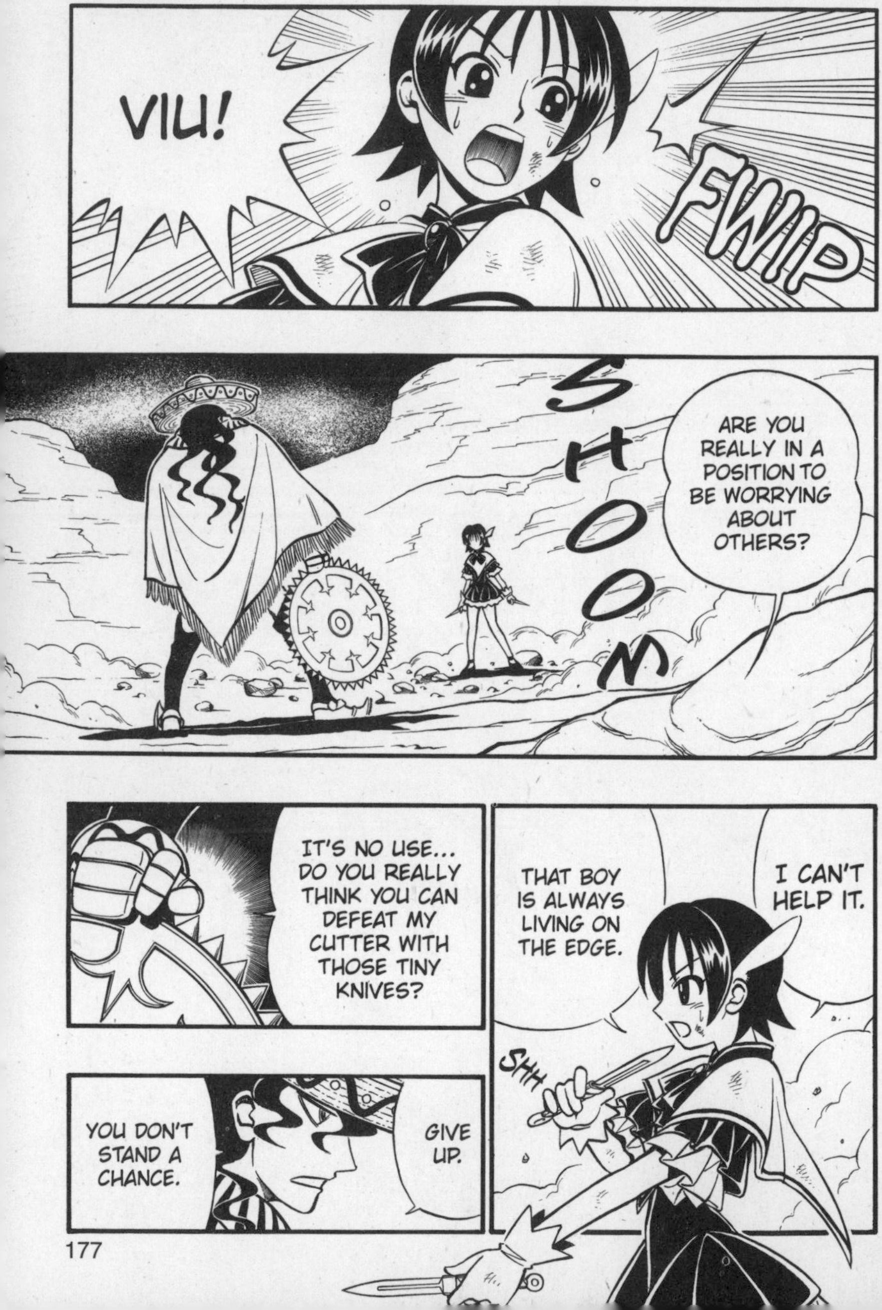
FWIP
VIU!
ARE YOU REALLY IN A POSITION TO BE WORRYING ABOUT OTHERS?
SHOOM
I CAN'T HELP IT.
THAT BOY IS ALWAYS LIVING ON THE EDGE.
SHH
IT'S NO USE... DO YOU REALLY THINK YOU CAN DEFEAT MY CUTTER WITH THOSE TINY KNIVES?
GIVE UP.
YOU DON'T STAND A CHANCE.

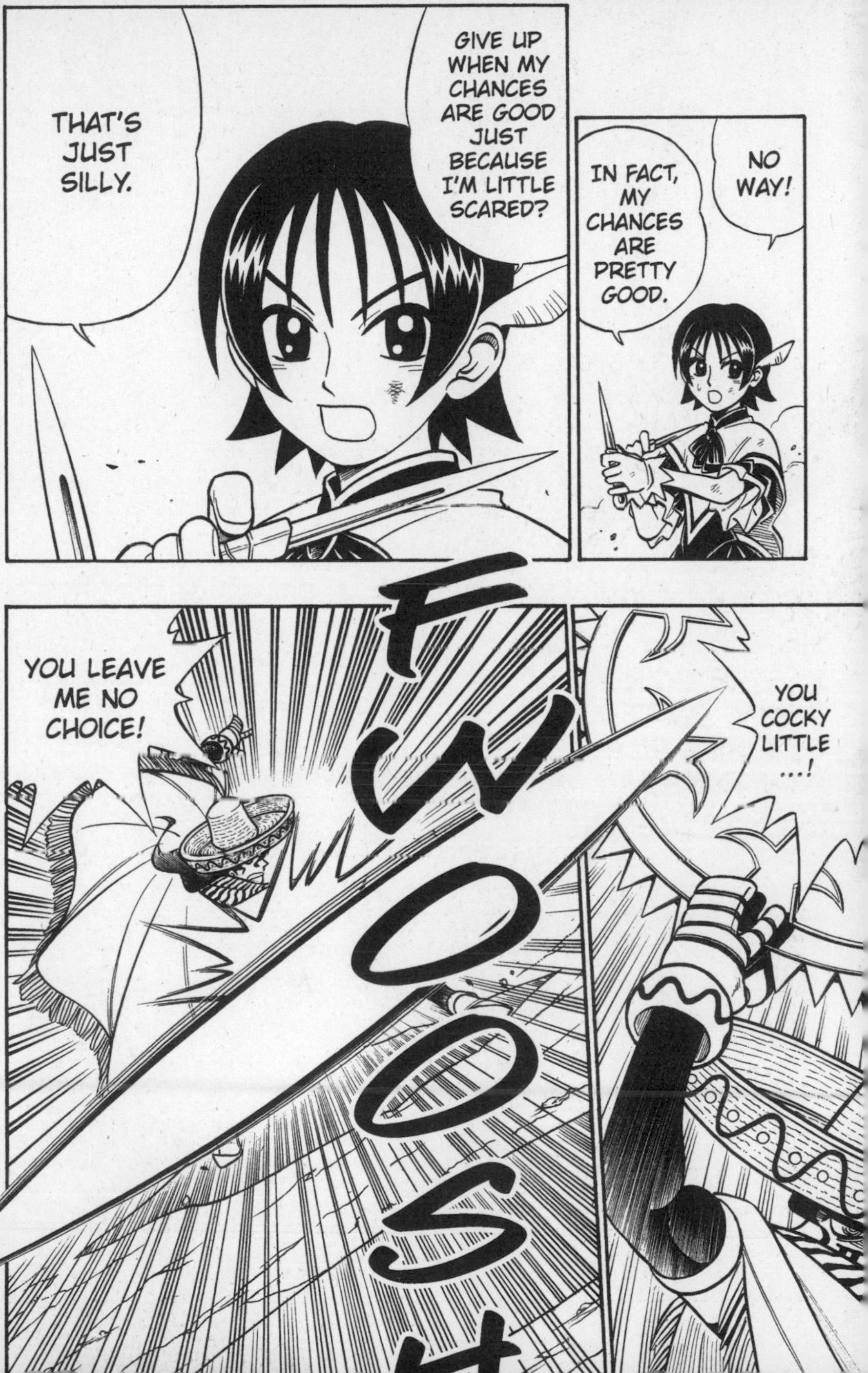
NO WAY!
IN FACT, MY CHANCES ARE PRETTY GOOD.
GIVE UP WHEN MY CHANCES ARE GOOD JUST BECAUSE I'M LITTLE SCARED?
THAT'S JUST SILLY.
YOU COCKY LITTLE ...!
YOU LEAVE ME NO CHOICE!

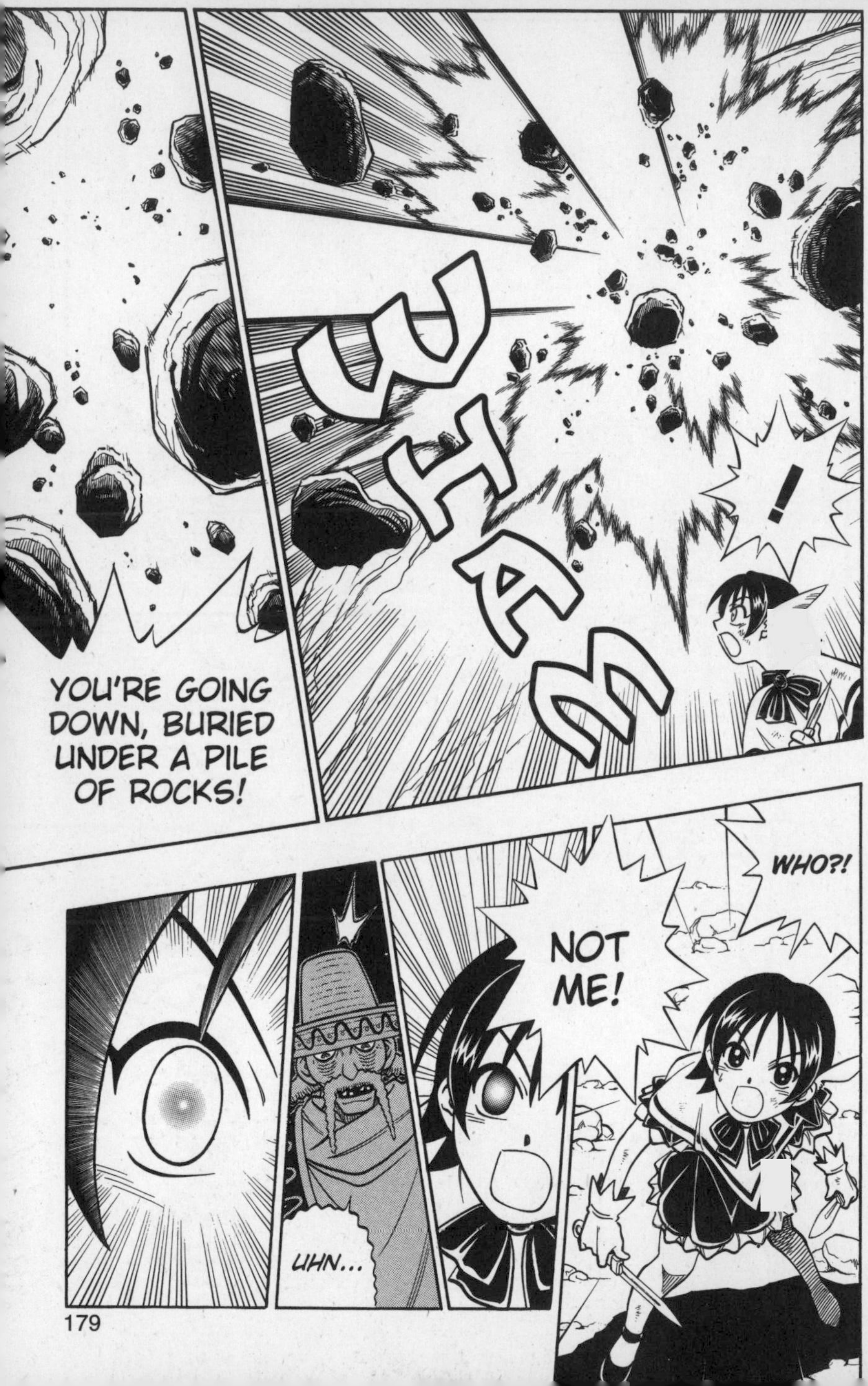
SLAM
!
YOU'RE GOING DOWN, BURIED UNDER A PILE OF ROCKS!
WHO?!
NOT ME!
UHN...

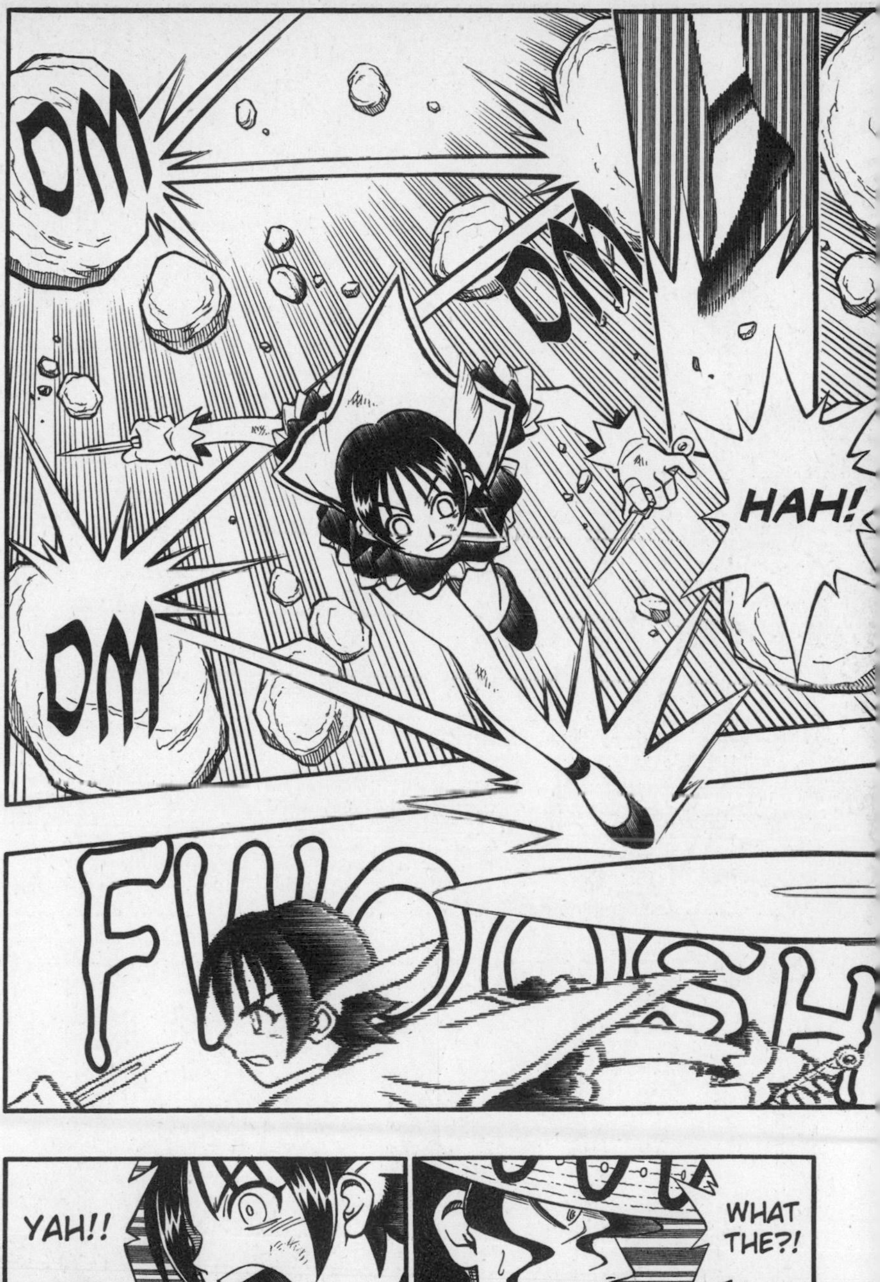
DM
DM
HAH!
DM
FWOOSH
WHAT THE?!
YAH!!

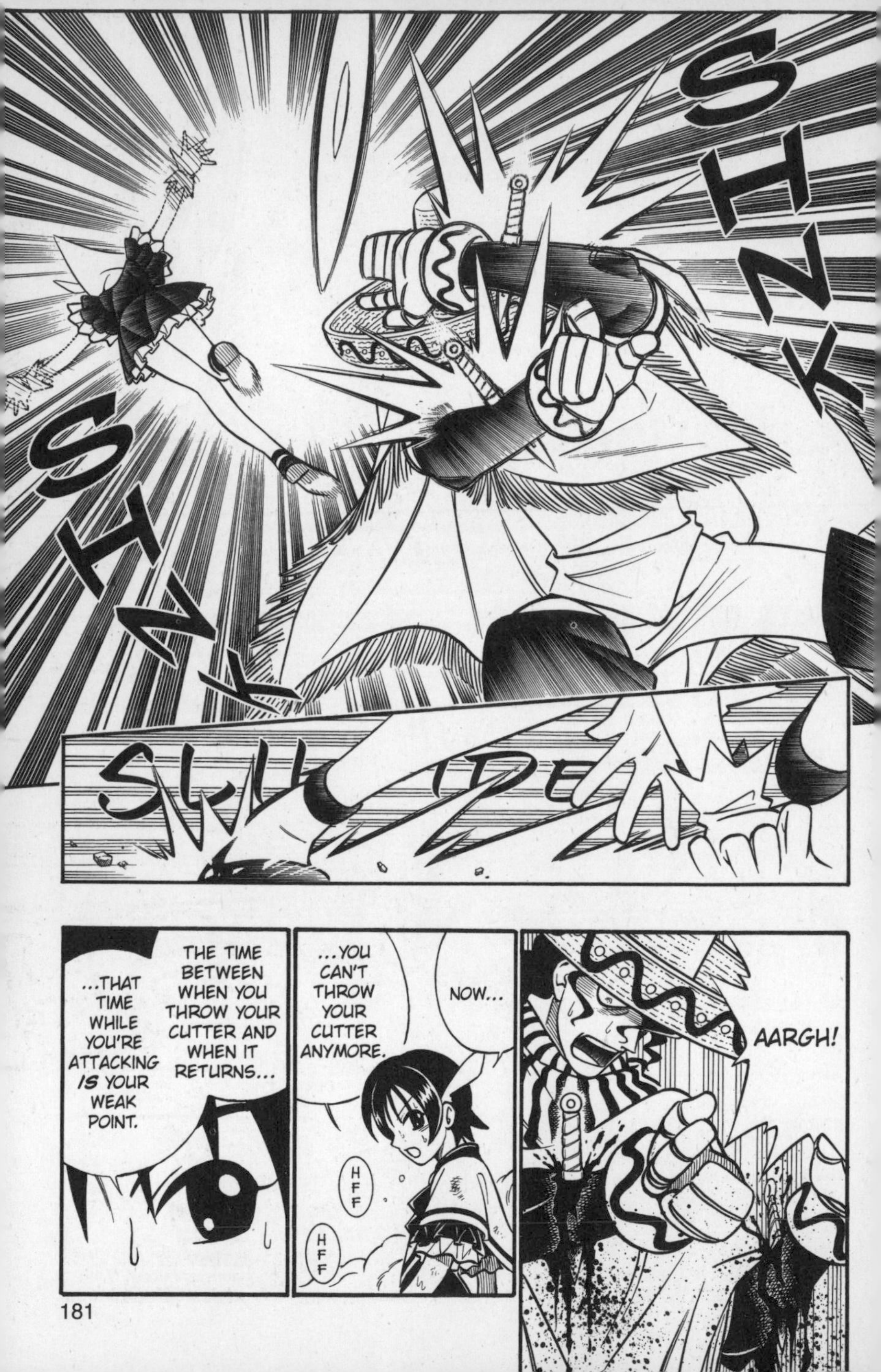
SHNK
SHNK
AARGH!
NOW...
...YOU CAN'T THROW YOUR CUTTER ANYMORE.
HFF
HFF
THE TIME BETWEEN WHEN YOU THROW YOUR CUTTER AND WHEN IT RETURNS...
...THAT TIME WHILE YOU'RE ATTACKING *IS* YOUR WEAK POINT.

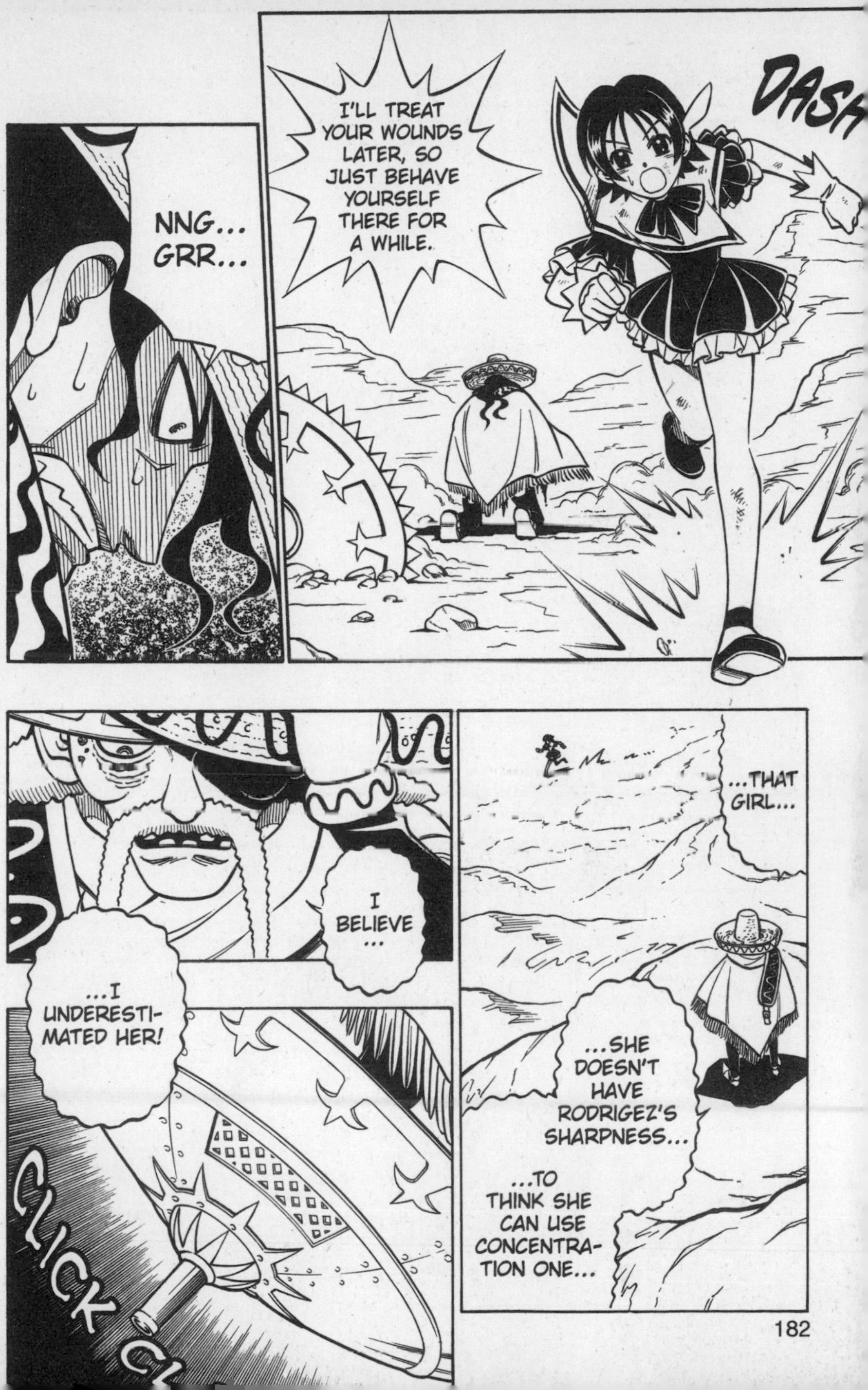
DASH
I'LL TREAT YOUR WOUNDS LATER, SO JUST BEHAVE YOURSELF THERE FOR A WHILE.
NNG... GRR...
...THAT GIRL...
...SHE DOESN'T HAVE RODRIGEZ'S SHARPNESS...
...TO THINK SHE CAN USE CONCENTRATION ONE...
I BELIEVE ...
...I UNDERESTIMATED HER!
CLICK CL

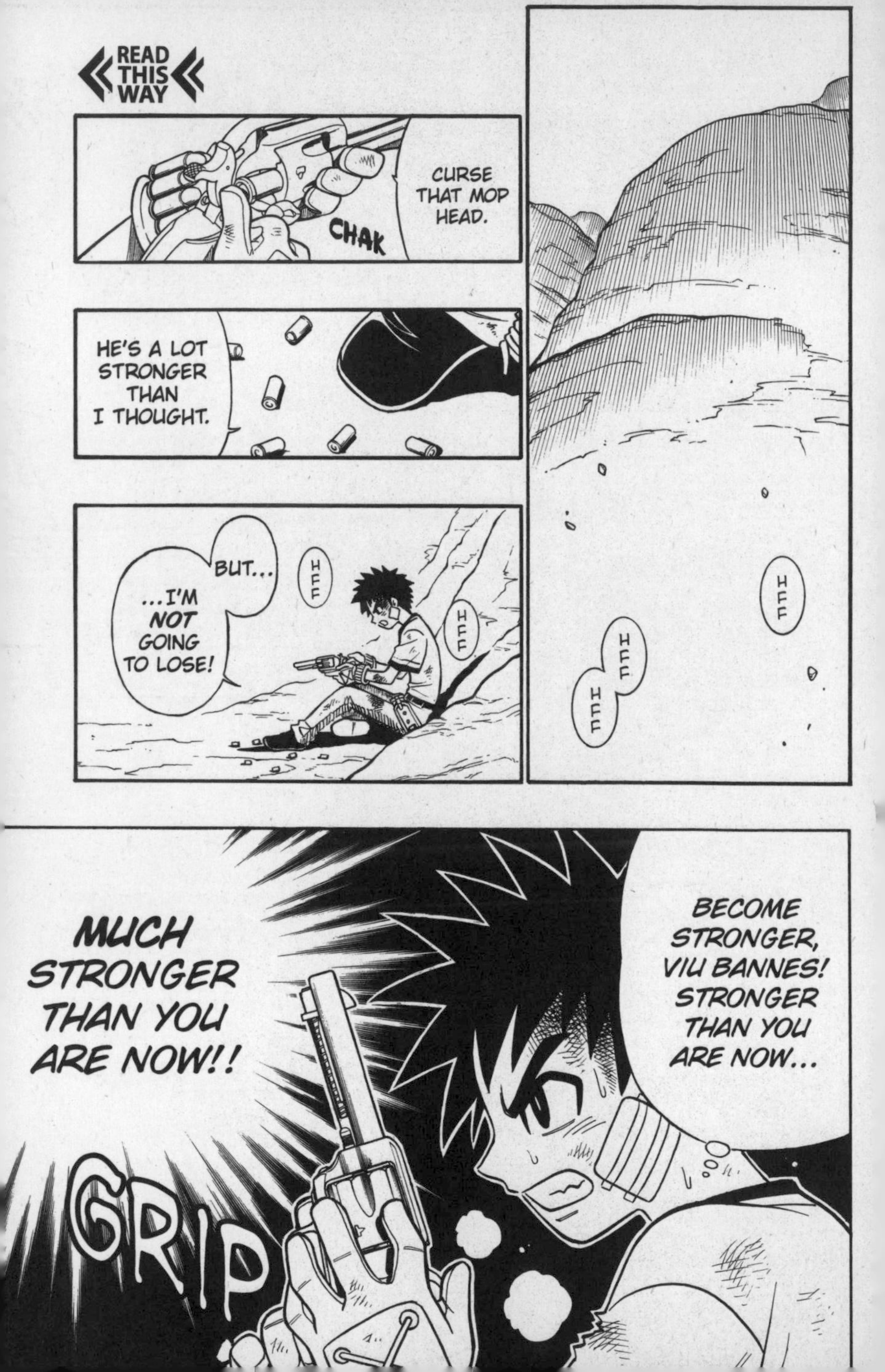
READ THIS WAY
HFF HFF
HFF HFF
CURSE THAT MOP HEAD.
CHAK
HE'S A LOT STRONGER THAN I THOUGHT.
BUT...
...I'M NOT GOING TO LOSE!
HFF
HFF
BECOME STRONGER, VIU BANNES! STRONGER THAN YOU ARE NOW...
MUCH STRONGER THAN YOU ARE NOW!!
GRIP

CONCEPT: COLICE IS MY "ABSOLUTE AND PERFECT BATTLE HEROINE" CREATED FROM REVIEWING MY PREVIOUS WORK, *RUROUNI KENSHIN*, AND MY OWN WISHES.

IT SEEMS ALMOST AS IF THE CHARACTERS ONLY BEGAN MOVING WHEN COLICE APPEARED AND THE THREE WERE TOGETHER. THAT'S HOW MUCH I LIKE THIS CHARACTER.

COLICE IS THE STRONGEST OF THE THREE, DOESN'T WORRY MUCH, AND HAS A STRAIGHTFORWARD PERSONALITY. SHE POSSESSES THE VITALITY TO LIVE BY HERSELF IN A FOREIGN LAND, AND REALLY HAS NO SHORTCOMINGS, WHICH IS WHAT CAUSES HER TO TAKE ACTION, BUT SHE WAS A CHARACTER WHO WAS DIFFICULT TO WORK INTO THE DRAMA OF THE STORY. (OH, PERHAPS THAT'S HER SHORTCOMING, MAYBE?)

COLICE IS AN OLDER SISTER TYPE OF CHARACTER WHO SOMETIMES ACTS SILLY WITH VIU, OR SOMETIMES DISCUSSES THINGS WITH WILL. SHE OPENLY REFLECTS THE WATSUKI INFATUATION WITH OLDER PEOPLE THAT GOES AGAINST THE TRENDS IN SOCIETY. HEROINES SHOULD, AFTER ALL, BE FILLED WITH MY OWN PERSONAL PREFERENCES!

NOT ONLY IS COLICE ONE OF THE FEW *GUN BLAZE WEST* CHARACTERS THAT I LIKE, SHE WAS RELATIVELY WELL DRAWN, AND I'D LIKE SOMEHOW TO REVIVE HER CHARACTER. ON AN UNRELATED NOTE, I'D LIKE TO TAKE ON THE CHALLENGE OF DOING A STORY BASED ON A BATTLE HEROINE ONE MORE TIME.

IMAGE SOURCE: NOTHING IN PARTICULAR. IF I HAD TO NAME SOMETHING, IT WAS A VERY SIMPLE THING THAT GOT ME STARTED: I LOOKED AT THE WORKS OF MY MANGA ARTIST FRIENDS, AND THOUGHT, "I'D LIKE TO DRAW SOMETHING LIKE THAT, TOO."

## CHARACTER FILE #08

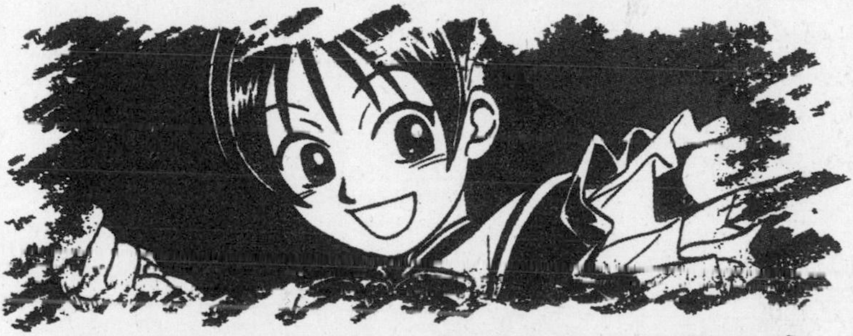

## COLICE SATOH (SATO KORISU)

DESIGN: I DESIGNED COLICE BY TRYING MANY DIFFERENT THINGS. SINCE I HAD A VERY TOUGH TIME DRAWING THE HAIR OF THE HEROINES IN MY PREVIOUS WORK, *RUROUNI KENSHIN*, I DECIDED AT THE START TO PART HER HAIR IN SECTIONS. LIKE WITH VIU, I WANTED TO SHOW HER EYEBROWS, SO I MADE HER HAIR IN FRONT HANG LOOSELY AND ADDED SOME NEEDED VOLUME AT THE SIDES. I DECIDED ON SEMI-LONG HAIR IN BACK WITH AN OUTWARD CURL TO BRING OUT A SENSE OF BUOYANCY. FOR HER EYES, I TRIED INCORPORATING THE CURRENT TREND, BUT I WAS DISAPPOINTED THAT IT SEEMED LIKE I DIDN'T PUT ENOUGH WORK INTO THEM. AS FOR HER COSTUME, AFTER READING *CARDCAPTOR SAKURA* BY CLAMP SENSEI, AND DESPITE THINKING IT WAS BEYOND MY ABILITIES, I THOUGHT, "GEE, I'D LIKE TO DRAW A FRILLY COSTUME LIKE THAT" AND DECIDED TO GIVE IT A TRY. I BASED THE COSTUME ON AN ORIGINAL DRESS A FASHION DESIGNER FRIEND PROUDLY SHOWED ME. ONE POINT THAT I MUST NOT FORGET TO MENTION IS COLICE'S THIGHS. I CAME TO THE SUDDEN REALIZATION OF THAT "EVERYONE WHO CAN DRAW YOUNG LADIES WELL, DRAWS THEM WITH LARGE THIGHS!" AND WORKED VERY HARD AT DRAWING HER THIGHS LARGE BY STUDYING STUDIO PHOTOS. (BUT I WONDER IF ANYONE EVEN NOTICED...?)

ALL THE SAME, DRAWING YOUNG LADIES IS FUN. I WANT TO APPLY MYSELF MUCH, MUCH MORE.

ON A SIDE NOTE, I HEARD A RUMOR THAT COLICE GREATLY RESEMBLES A CHARACTER THAT APPEARS IN THE ANIME *OJAMAJO DOREMI* (DOREMI, THE BOTHERSOME WITCH). "THAT COULDN'T BE!" I THOUGHT, AND TOOK A LOOK. ...THEY DO LOOK ALIKE. BUT SINCE WHEN DID THE NUMBER OF BOTHERSOME WITCHES INCREASE TO FIVE? THE LAST TIME I LOOKED, THERE WERE SUPPOSED TO BE ONLY THREE...

I WILL APPLY MYSELF MUCH, MUCH HARDER.

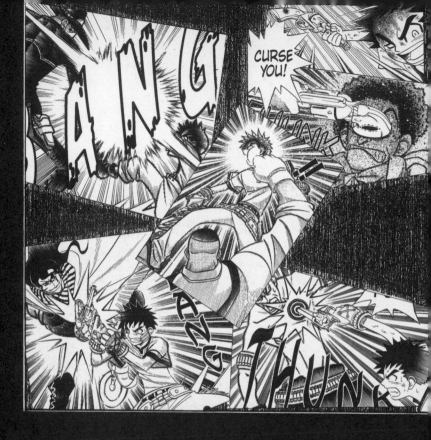

MUCH
STRONGER
THAN YOU
ARE NOW!!

BECOME
STRONGER,
VIU BANNES.
STRONGER THAN
YOU ARE NOW...

# CHAPTER 17 : 1 UP

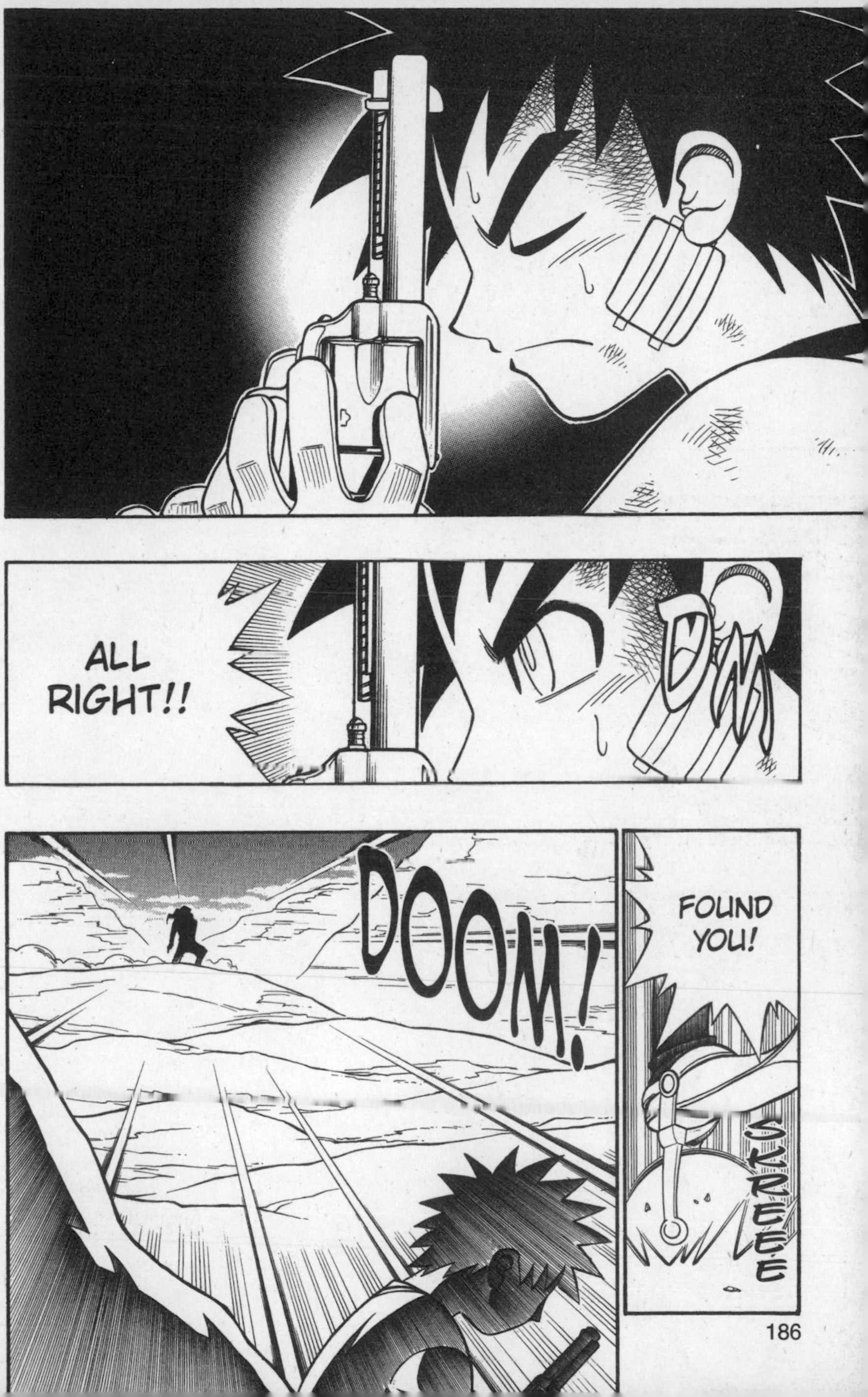
ALL RIGHT!!
FOUND YOU!
SKREEEE
DOOM!

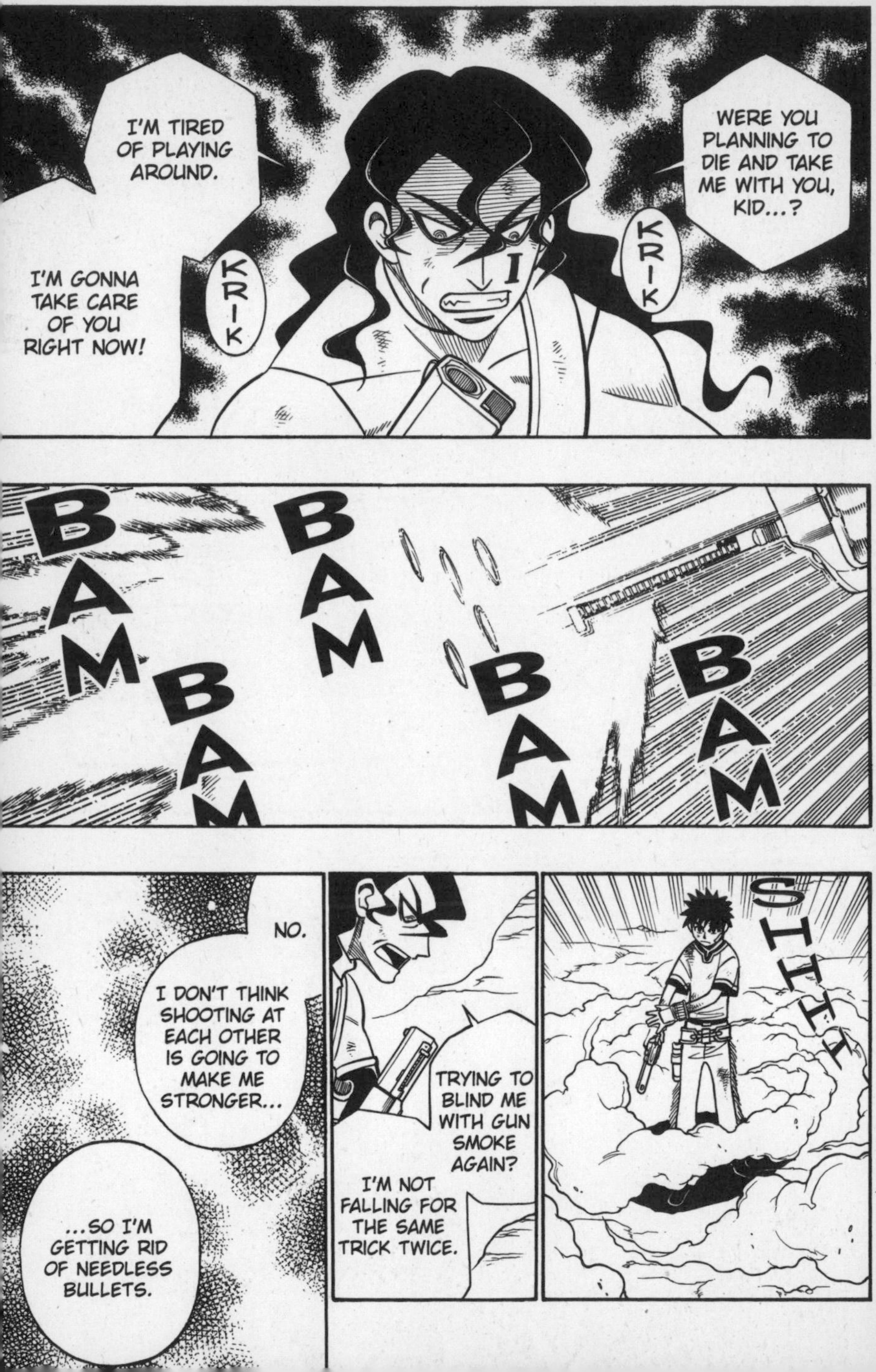
WERE YOU PLANNING TO DIE AND TAKE ME WITH YOU, KID...?
KRIK
I'M TIRED OF PLAYING AROUND.
KRIK
I'M GONNA TAKE CARE OF YOU RIGHT NOW!
BAM
BAM
BAM
BAM
BAM
SHHHH
TRYING TO BLIND ME WITH GUN SMOKE AGAIN?
I'M NOT FALLING FOR THE SAME TRICK TWICE.
NO.
I DON'T THINK SHOOTING AT EACH OTHER IS GOING TO MAKE ME STRONGER...
...SO I'M GETTING RID OF NEEDLESS BULLETS.

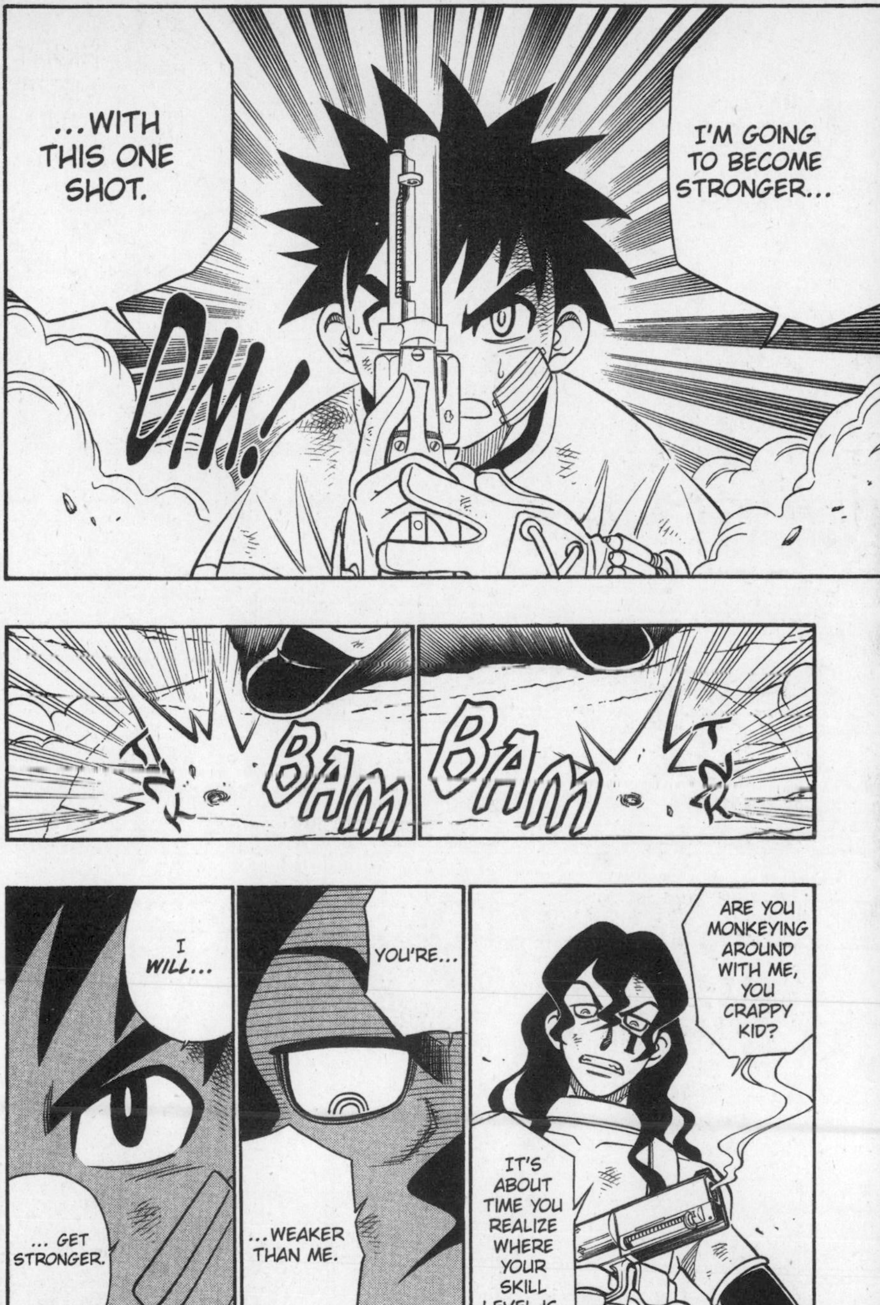
I'M GOING TO BECOME STRONGER...
...WITH THIS ONE SHOT.
DM!
BAM
TNK
BAM
TNK
ARE YOU MONKEYING AROUND WITH ME, YOU CRAPPY KID?
IT'S ABOUT TIME YOU REALIZE WHERE YOUR SKILL LEVEL IS.
YOU'RE...
...WEAKER THAN ME.
I WILL...
... GET STRONGER.

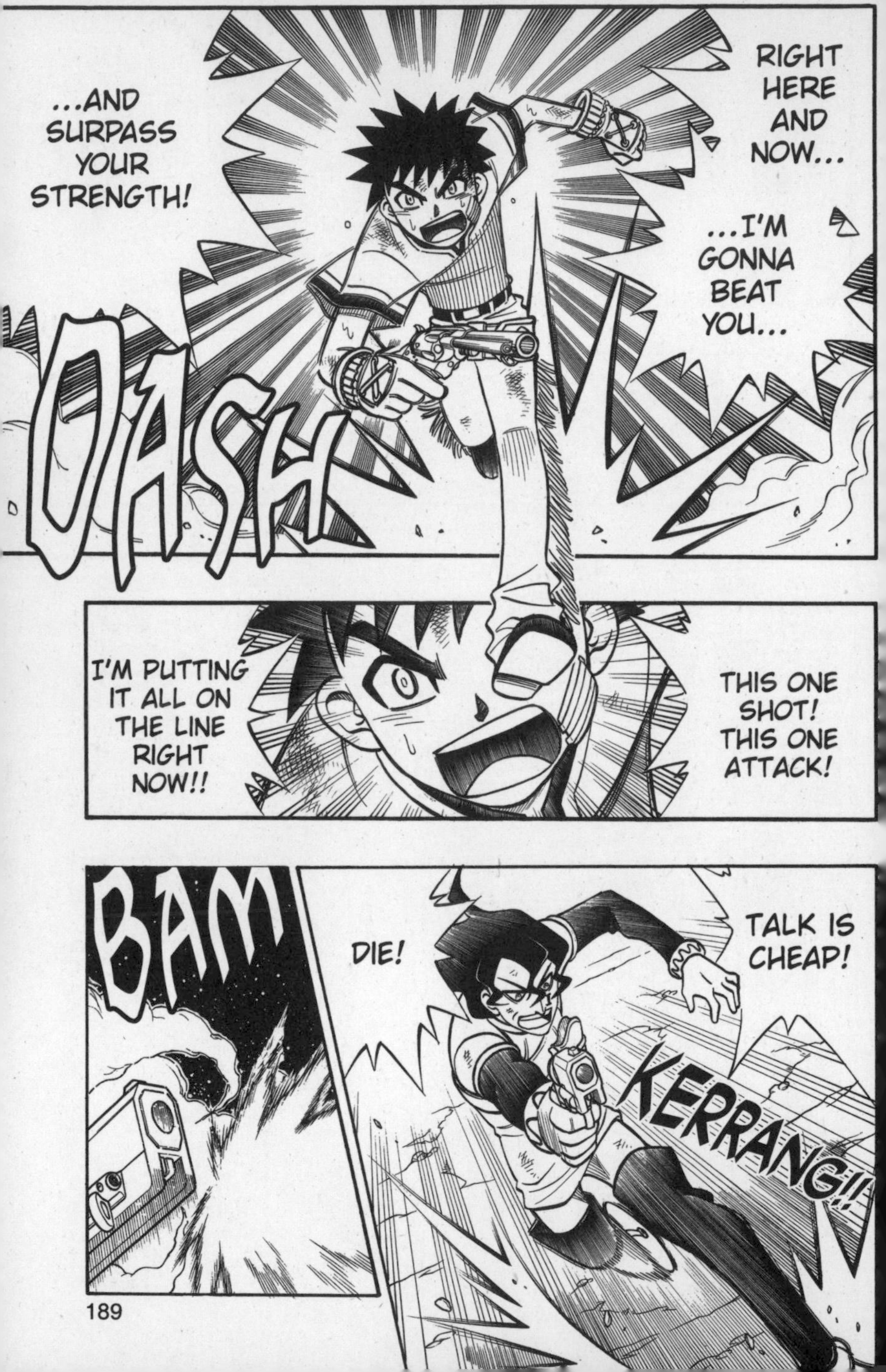
RIGHT HERE AND NOW...
...I'M GONNA BEAT YOU...
...AND SURPASS YOUR STRENGTH!
OASH
THIS ONE SHOT! THIS ONE ATTACK!
I'M PUTTING IT ALL ON THE LINE RIGHT NOW!!
TALK IS CHEAP!
DIE!
KERRANG!!
BAM

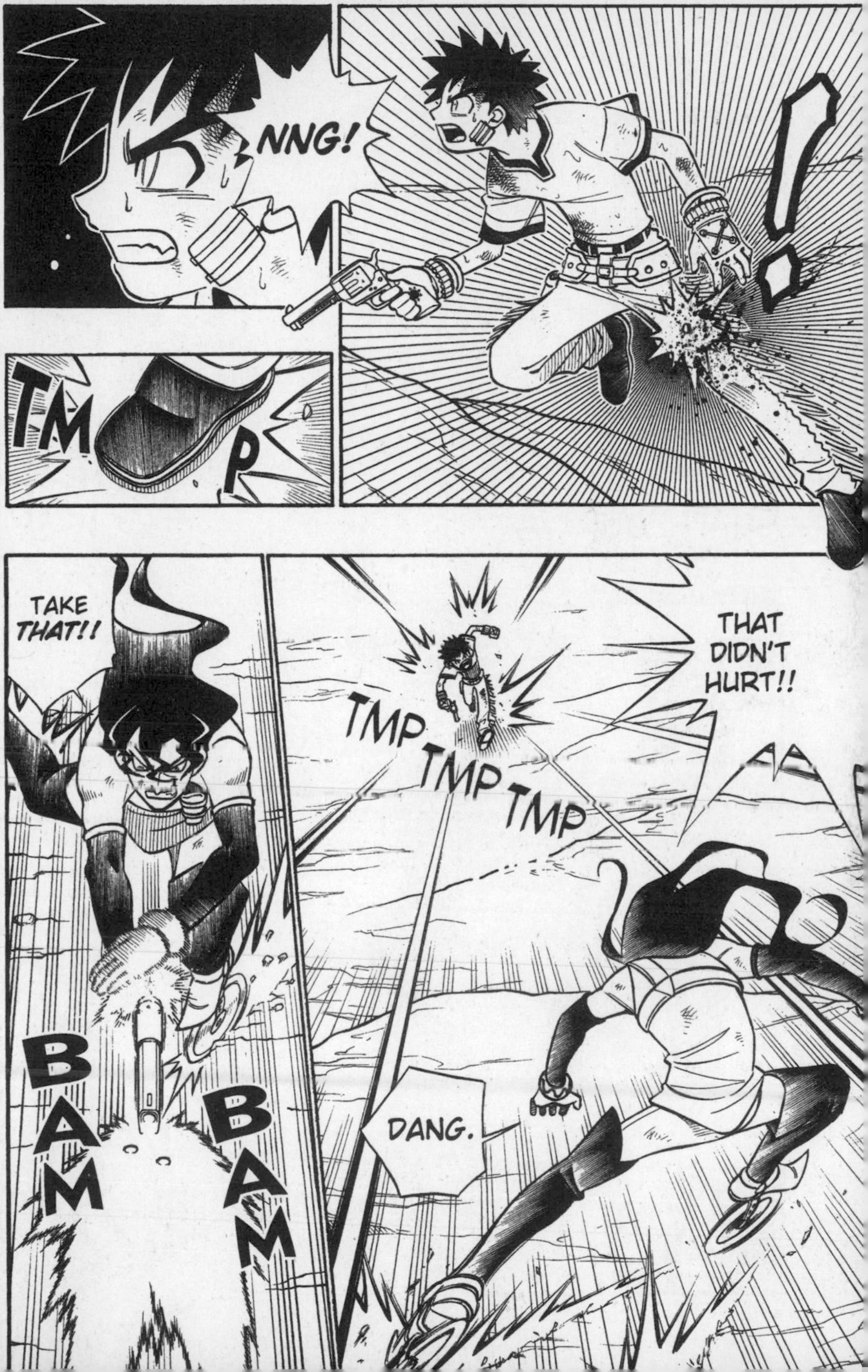
!
NNG!
TMP
THAT DIDN'T HURT!!
TMP TMP TMP
DANG.
TAKE THAT!!
BAM
BAM

READ THIS WAY

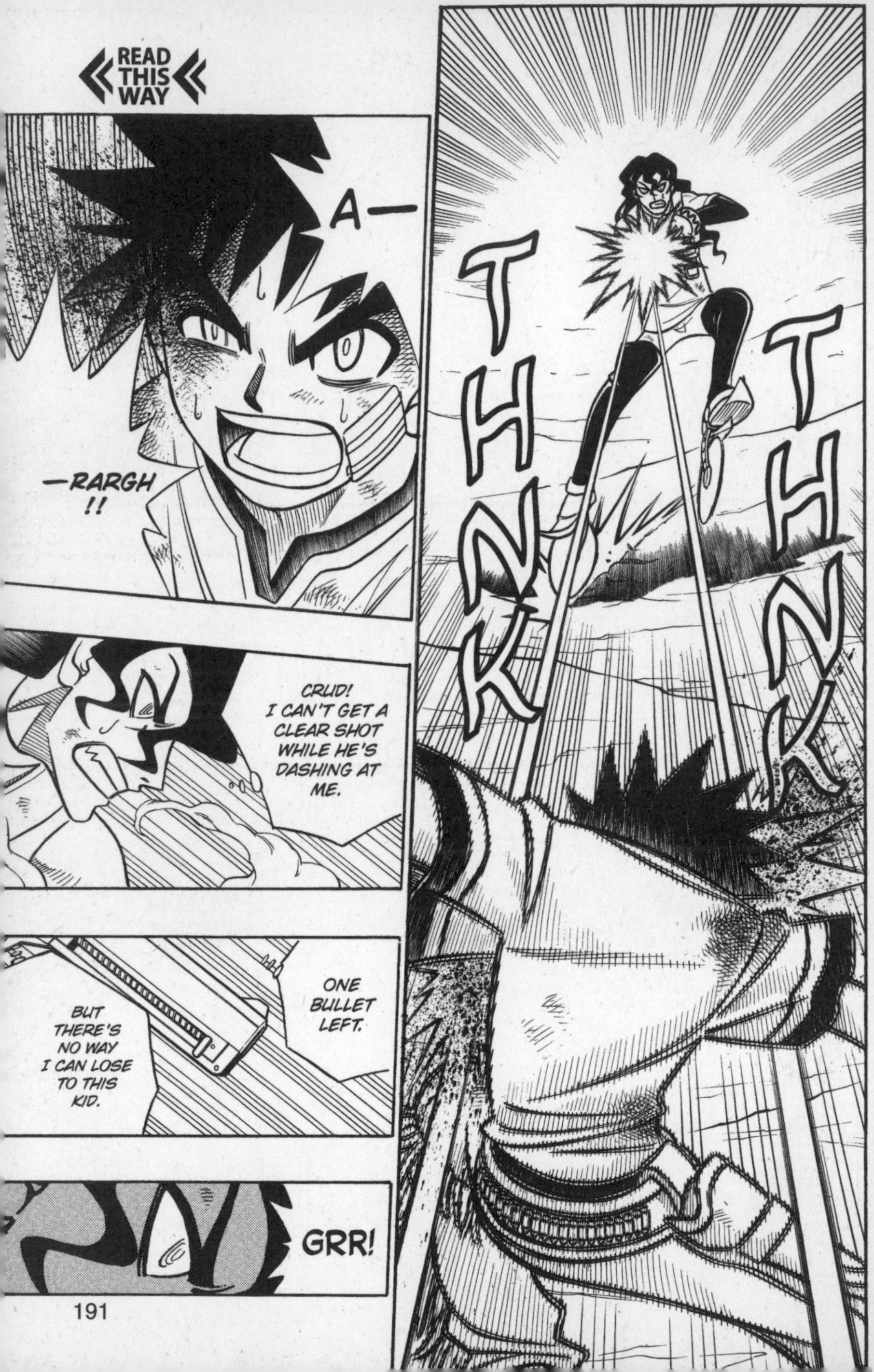
THNK
THNK
A—
—RARGH!!
CRUD! I CAN'T GET A CLEAR SHOT WHILE HE'S DASHING AT ME.
ONE BULLET LEFT.
BUT THERE'S NO WAY I CAN LOSE TO THIS KID.
GRR!

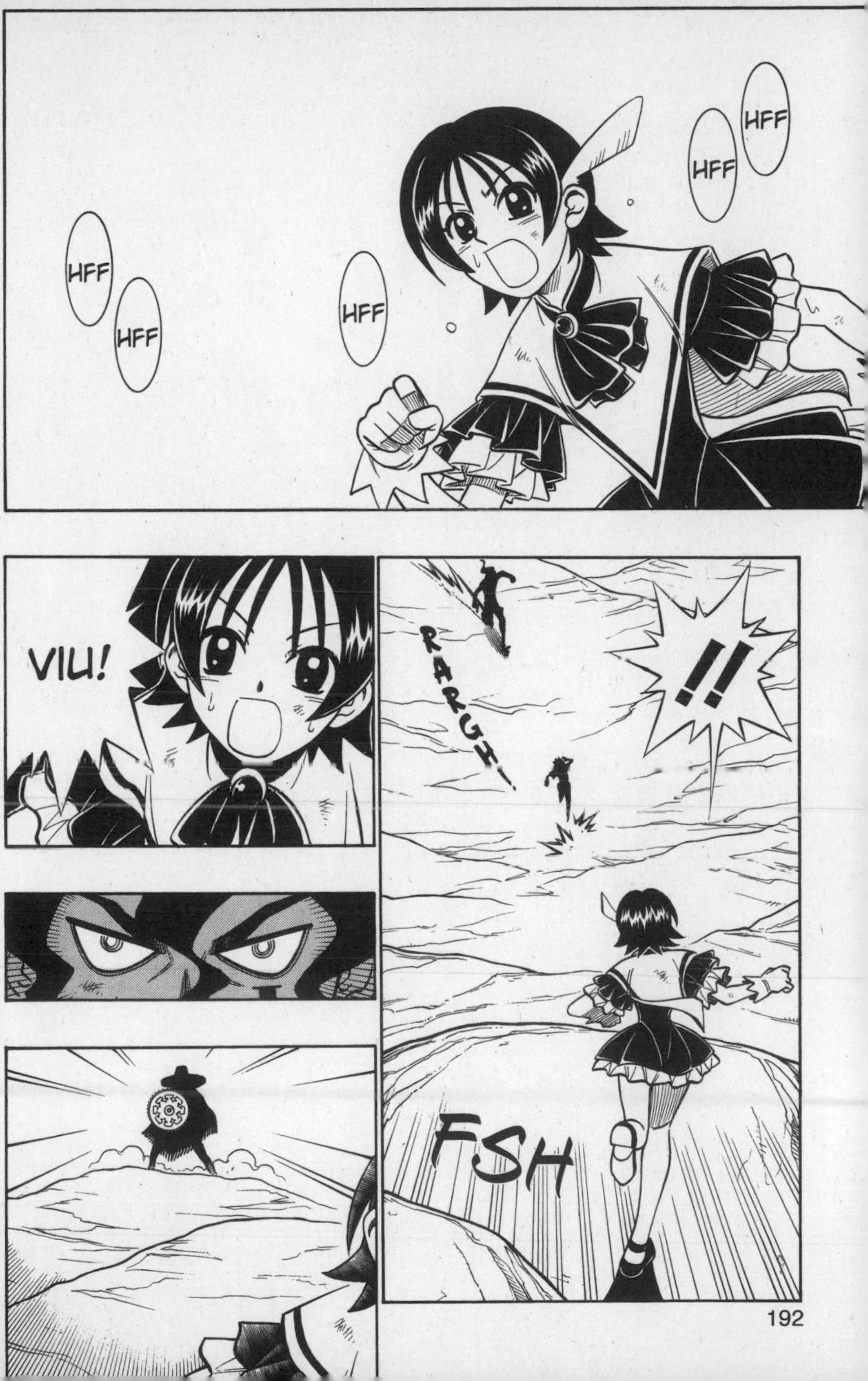
HFF
HFF
HFF
HFF
HFF
!!
RARGH!
FSH
VIU!

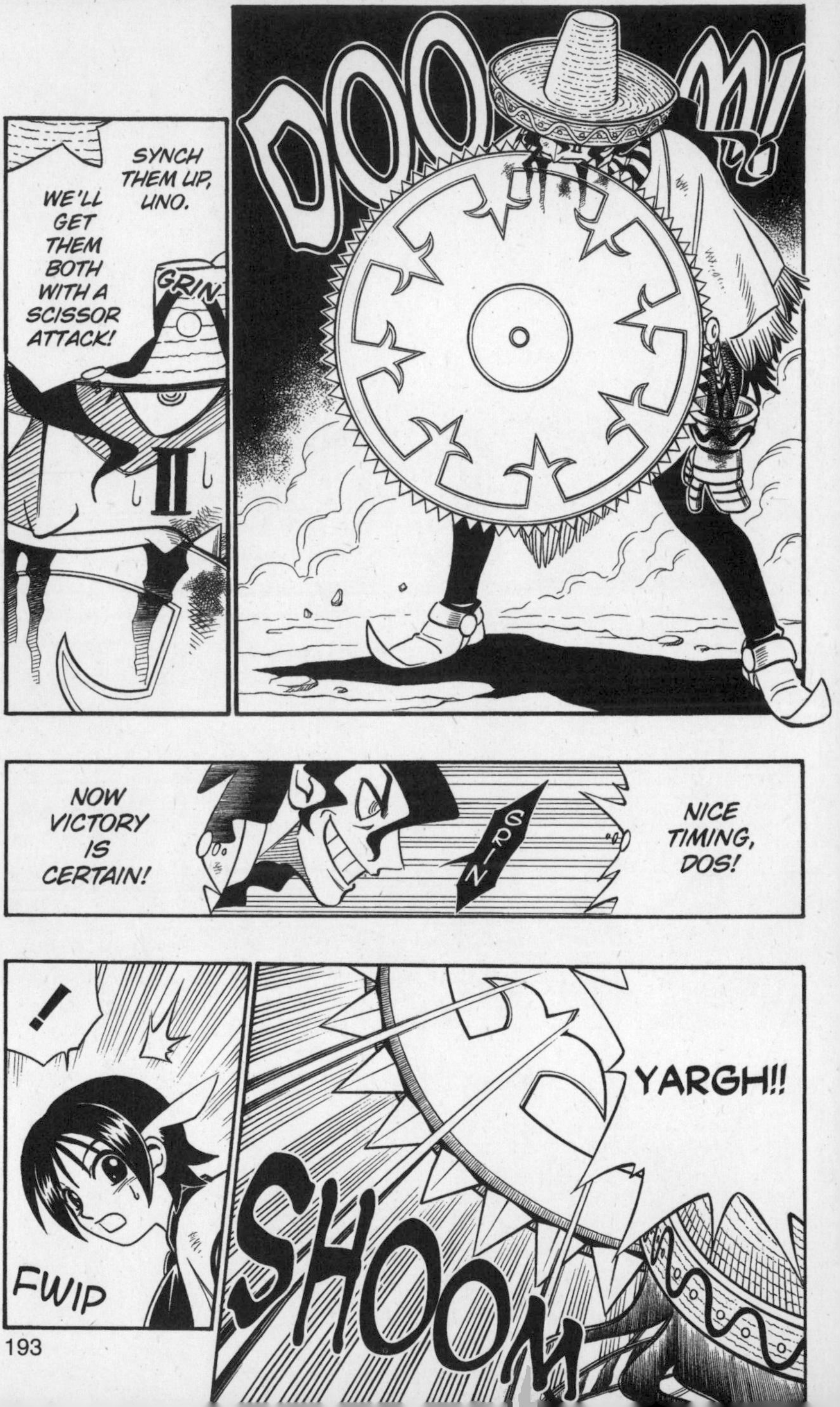
DOOOM!
SYNCH THEM UP, UNO.
WE'LL GET THEM BOTH WITH A SCISSOR ATTACK!
GRIN
NICE TIMING, DOS!
GRIN
NOW VICTORY IS CERTAIN!
YARGH!!
SHOOOM
!
FWIP

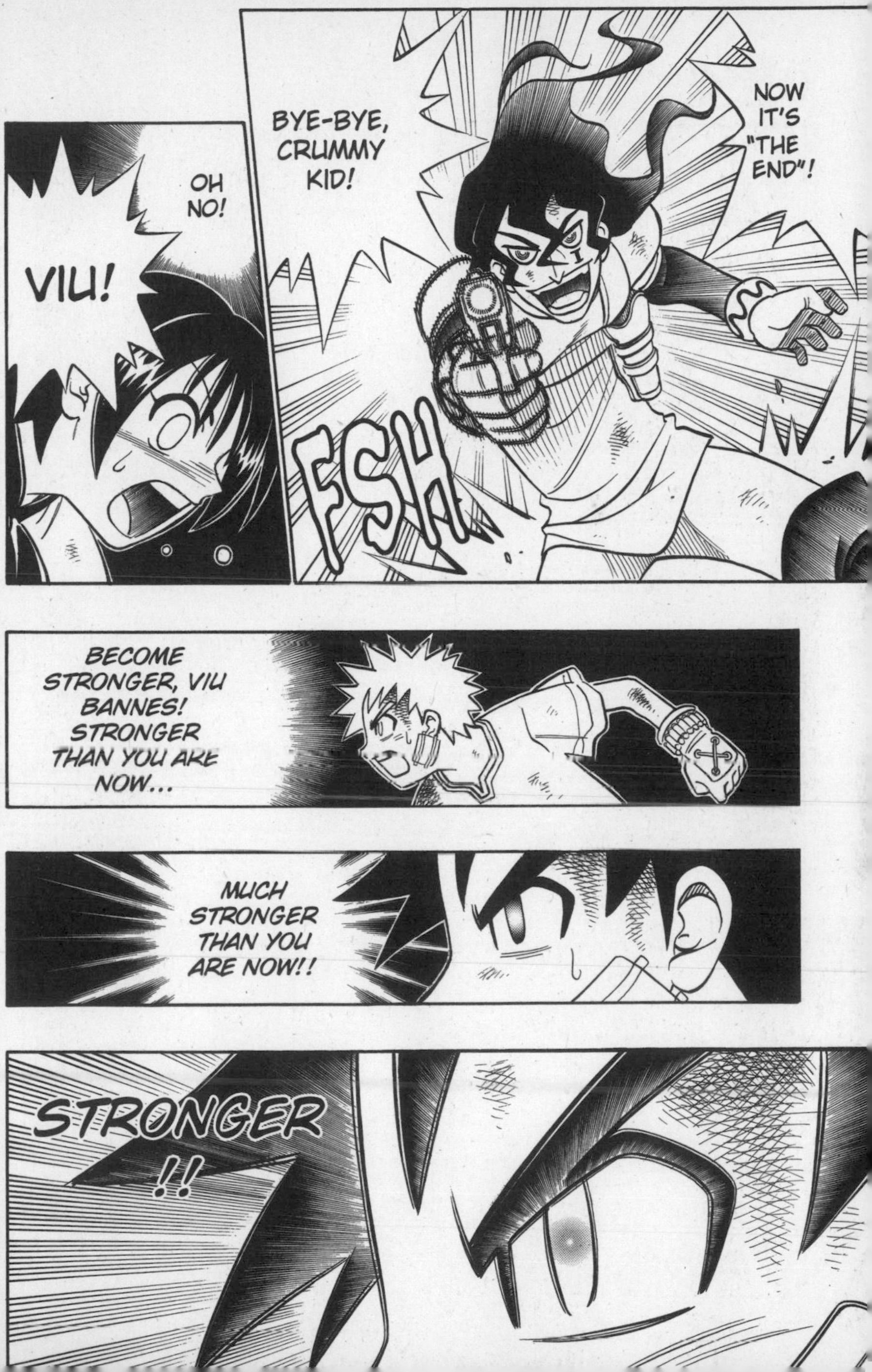
NOW IT'S "THE END"!
BYE-BYE, CRUMMY KID!
FSH
OH NO!
VIU!
BECOME STRONGER, VIU BANNES! STRONGER THAN YOU ARE NOW...
MUCH STRONGER THAN YOU ARE NOW!!
STRONGER !!

READ THIS WAY

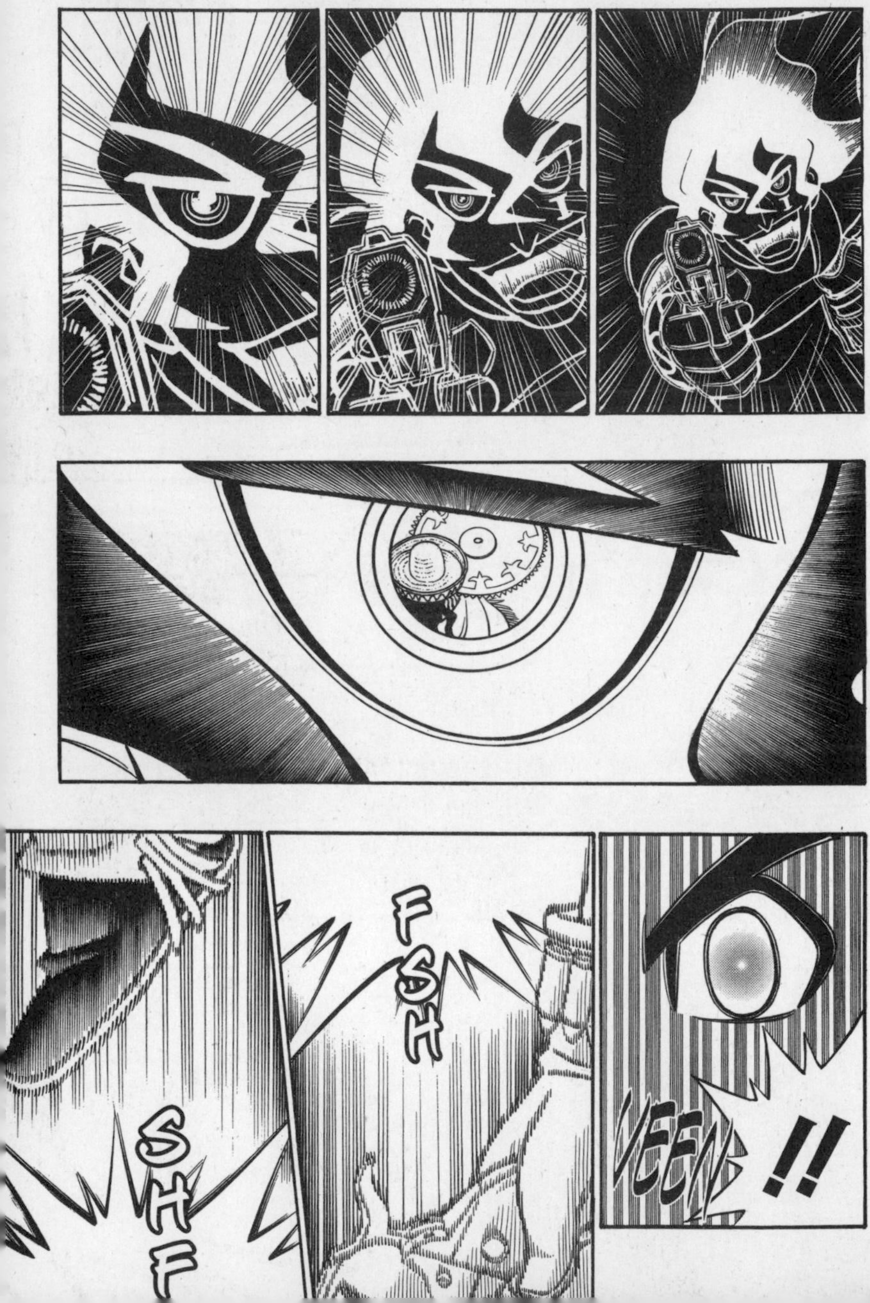
VEEN!!
FSH
SHF

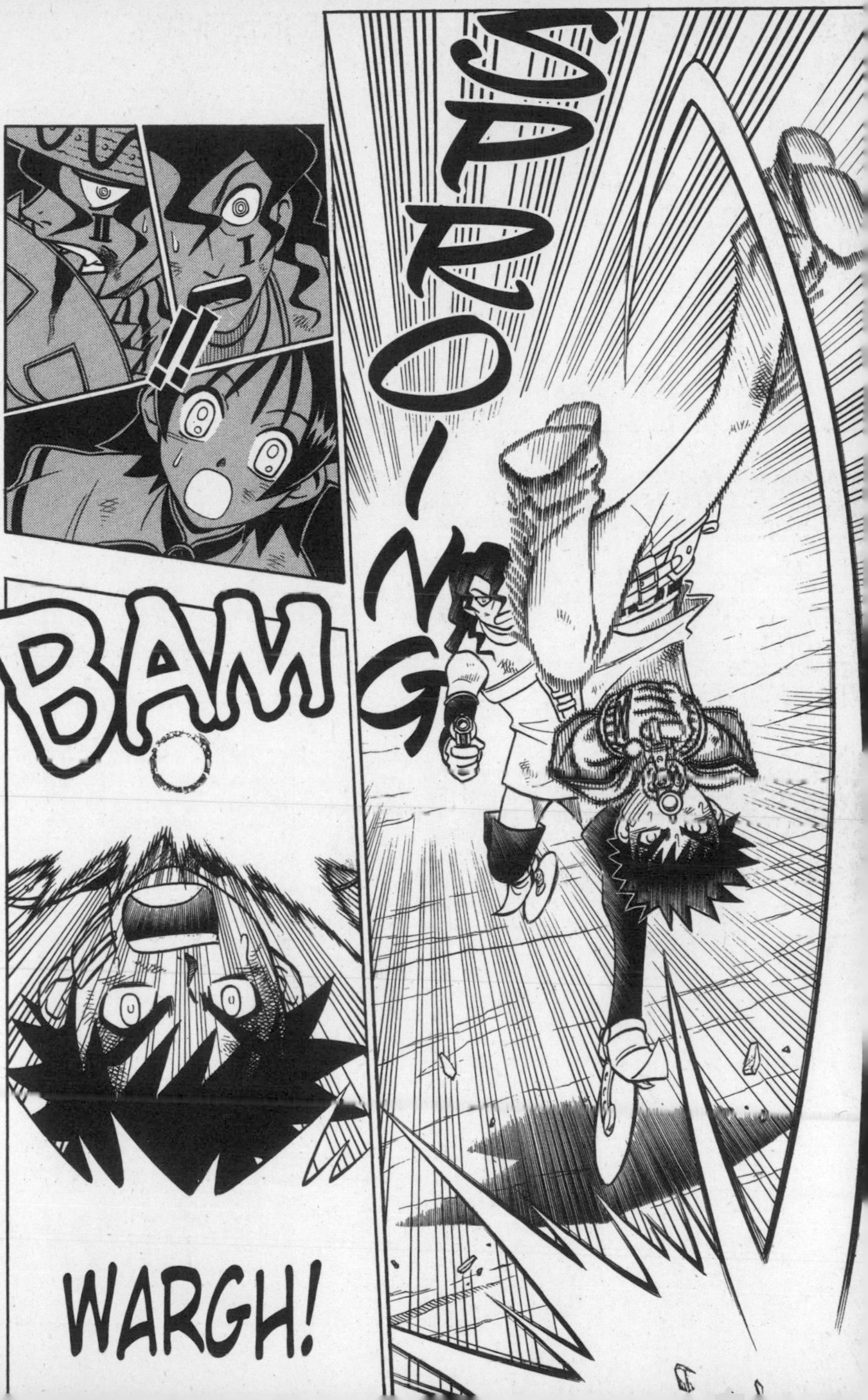
SPROING
!!
BAM
WARGH!

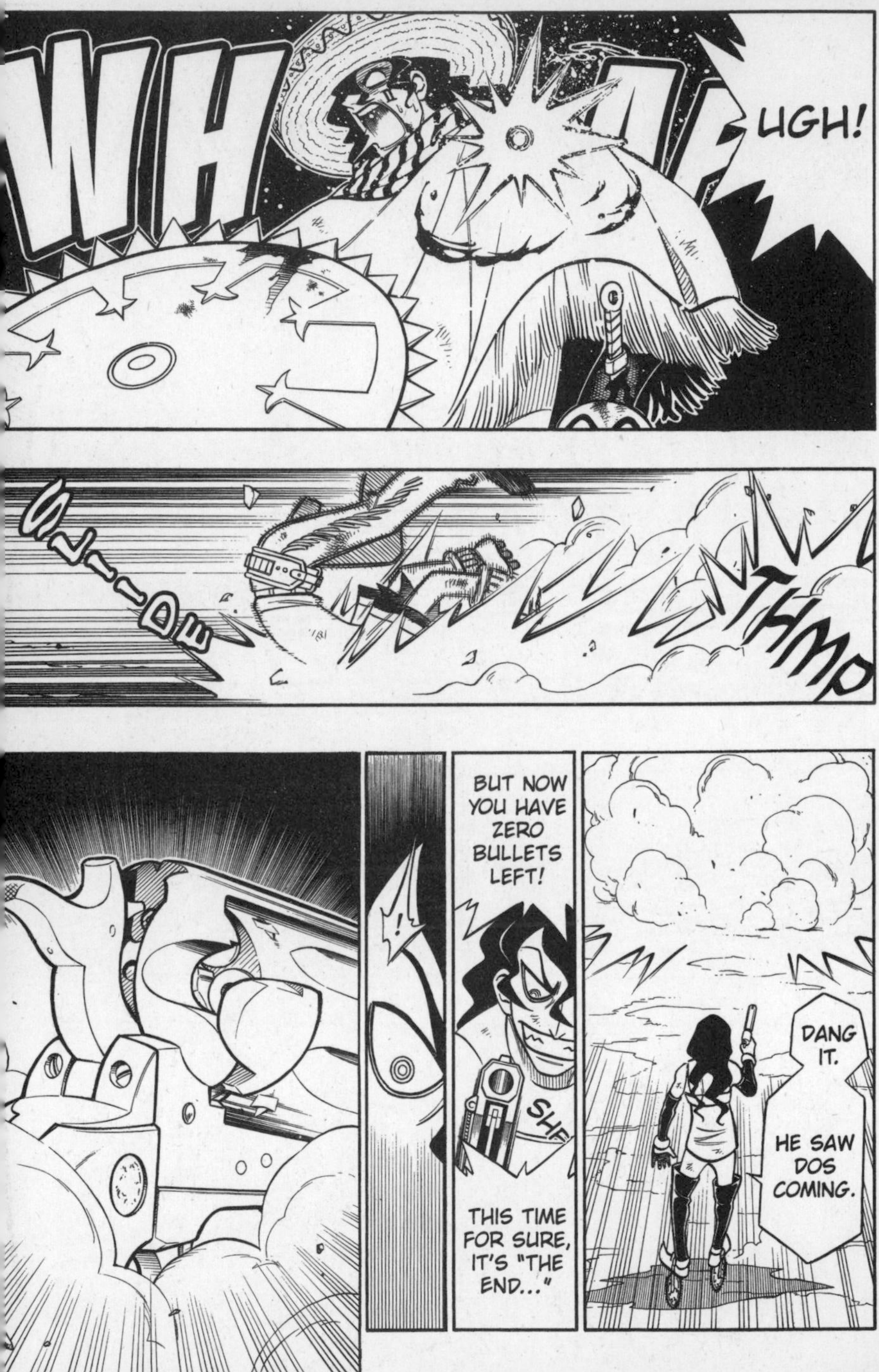
UGH!
SLI--DE
THMP
DANG IT.
HE SAW DOS COMING.
BUT NOW YOU HAVE ZERO BULLETS LEFT!
THIS TIME FOR SURE, IT'S "THE END..."

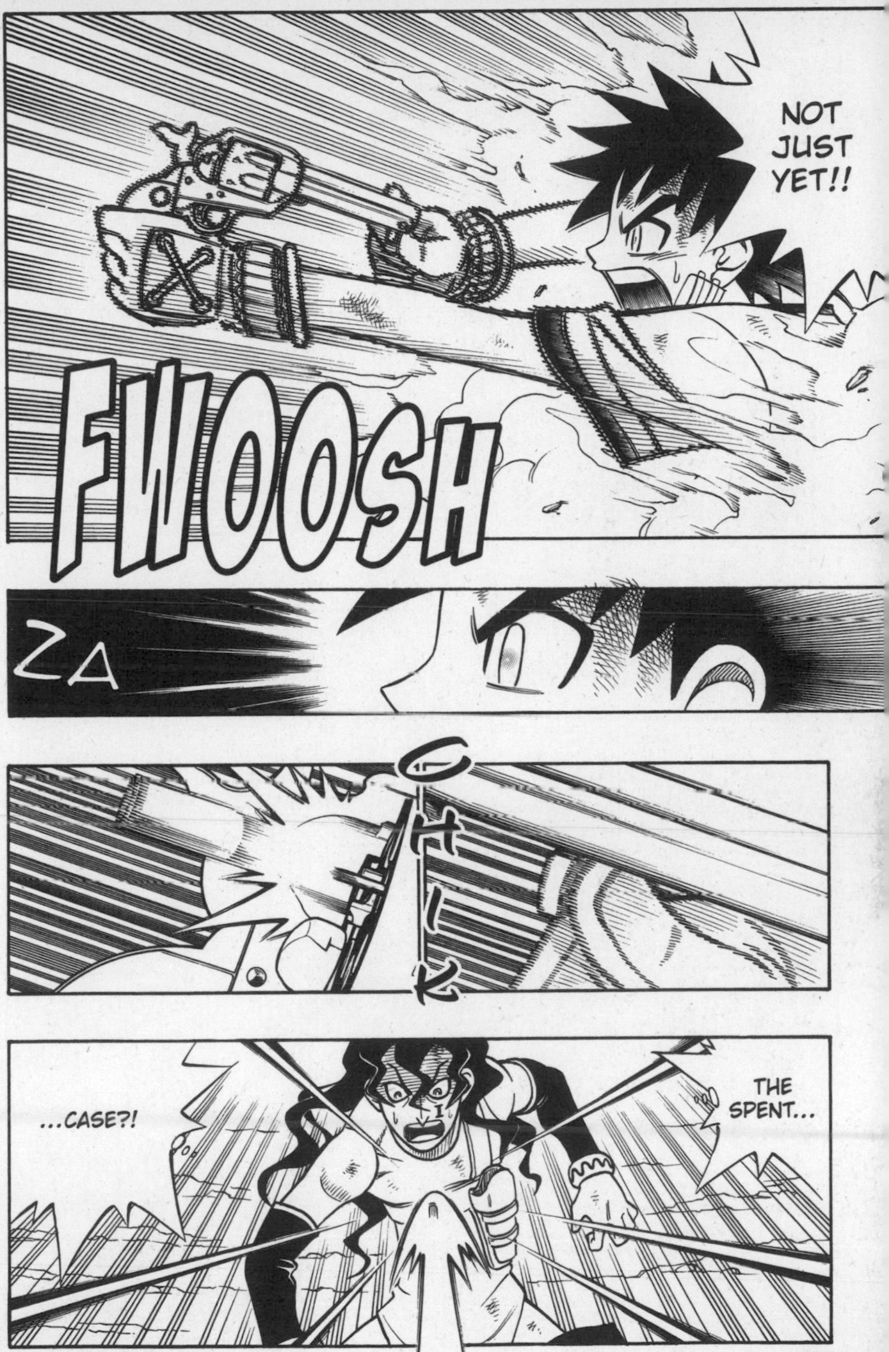
NOT JUST YET!!
FWOOSH
ZA
CHIK
THE SPENT...
...CASE?!

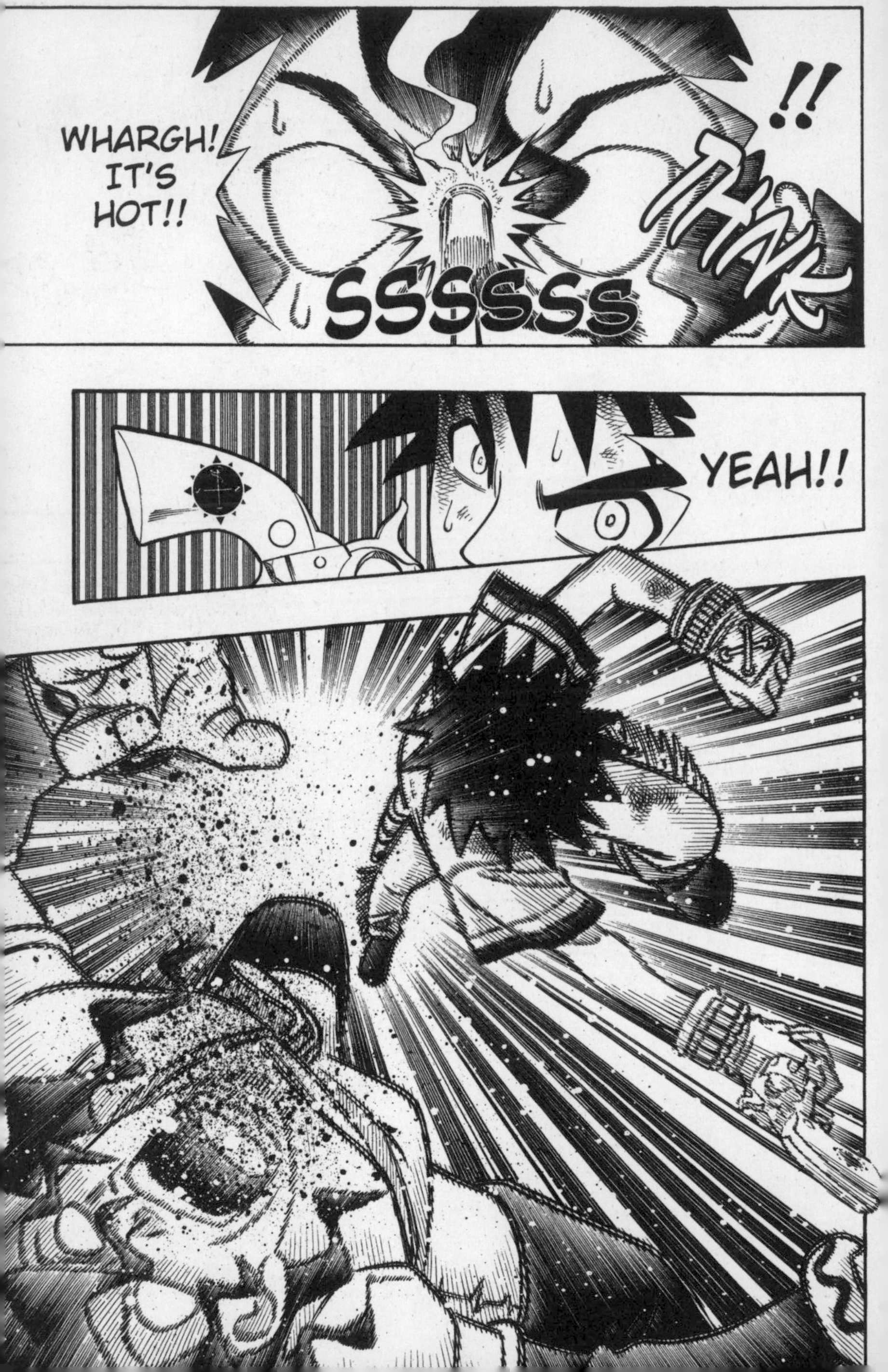
!!
TINK
WHARGH! IT'S HOT!!
SSSSSS
YEAH!!

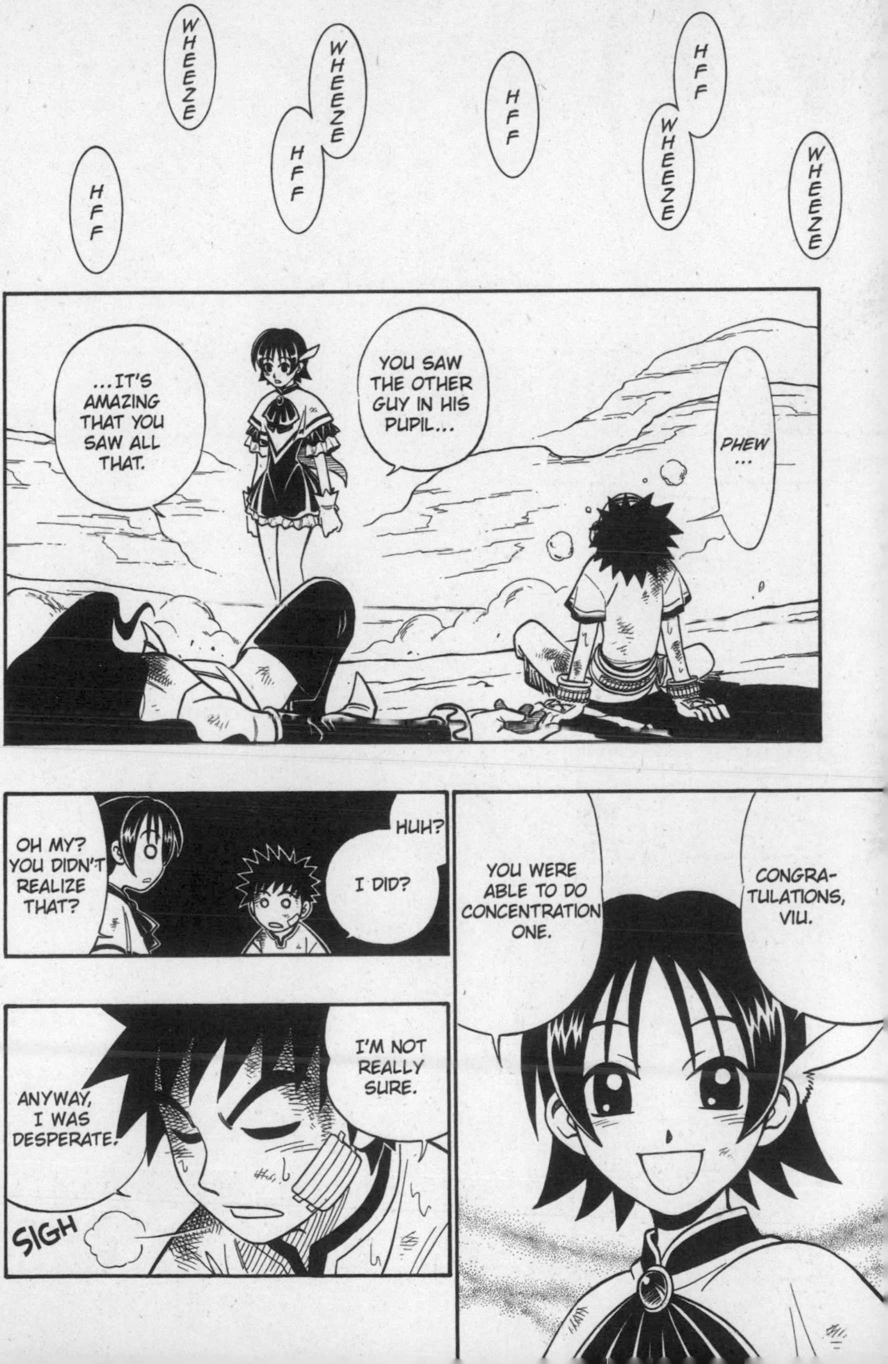
WHEEZE
HFF
WHEEZE
HFF
WHEEZE
HFF
WHEEZE
HFF
PHEW...
YOU SAW THE OTHER GUY IN HIS PUPIL...
...IT'S AMAZING THAT YOU SAW ALL THAT.
CONGRA-TULATIONS, VIU.
YOU WERE ABLE TO DO CONCENTRATION ONE.
HUH?
I DID?
OH MY? YOU DIDN'T REALIZE THAT?
I'M NOT REALLY SURE.
ANYWAY, I WAS DESPERATE.
SIGH

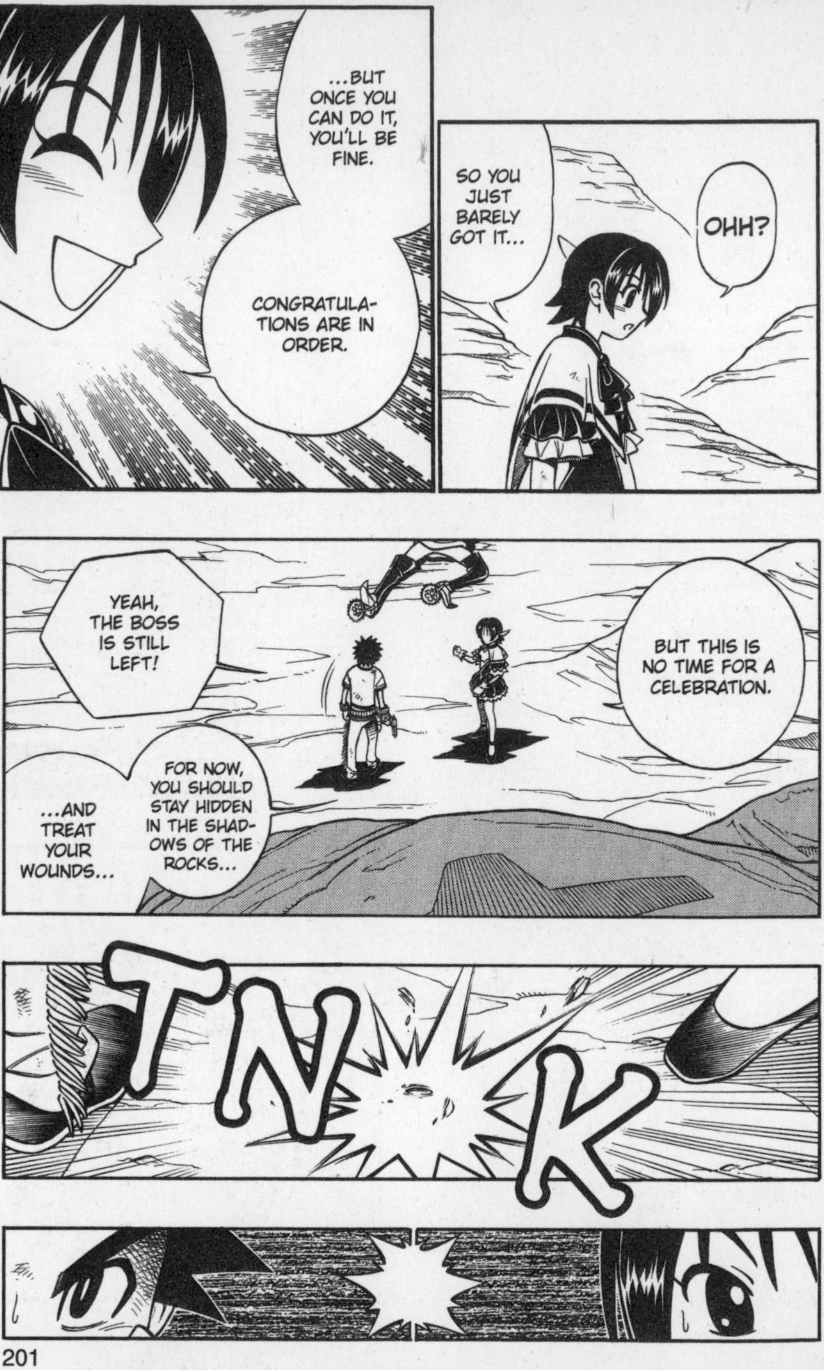
OHH?
SO YOU JUST BARELY GOT IT...
...BUT ONCE YOU CAN DO IT, YOU'LL BE FINE.
CONGRATULA-TIONS ARE IN ORDER.
BUT THIS IS NO TIME FOR A CELEBRATION.
YEAH, THE BOSS IS STILL LEFT!
FOR NOW, YOU SHOULD STAY HIDDEN IN THE SHAD-OWS OF THE ROCKS...
...AND TREAT YOUR WOUNDS...
TNK

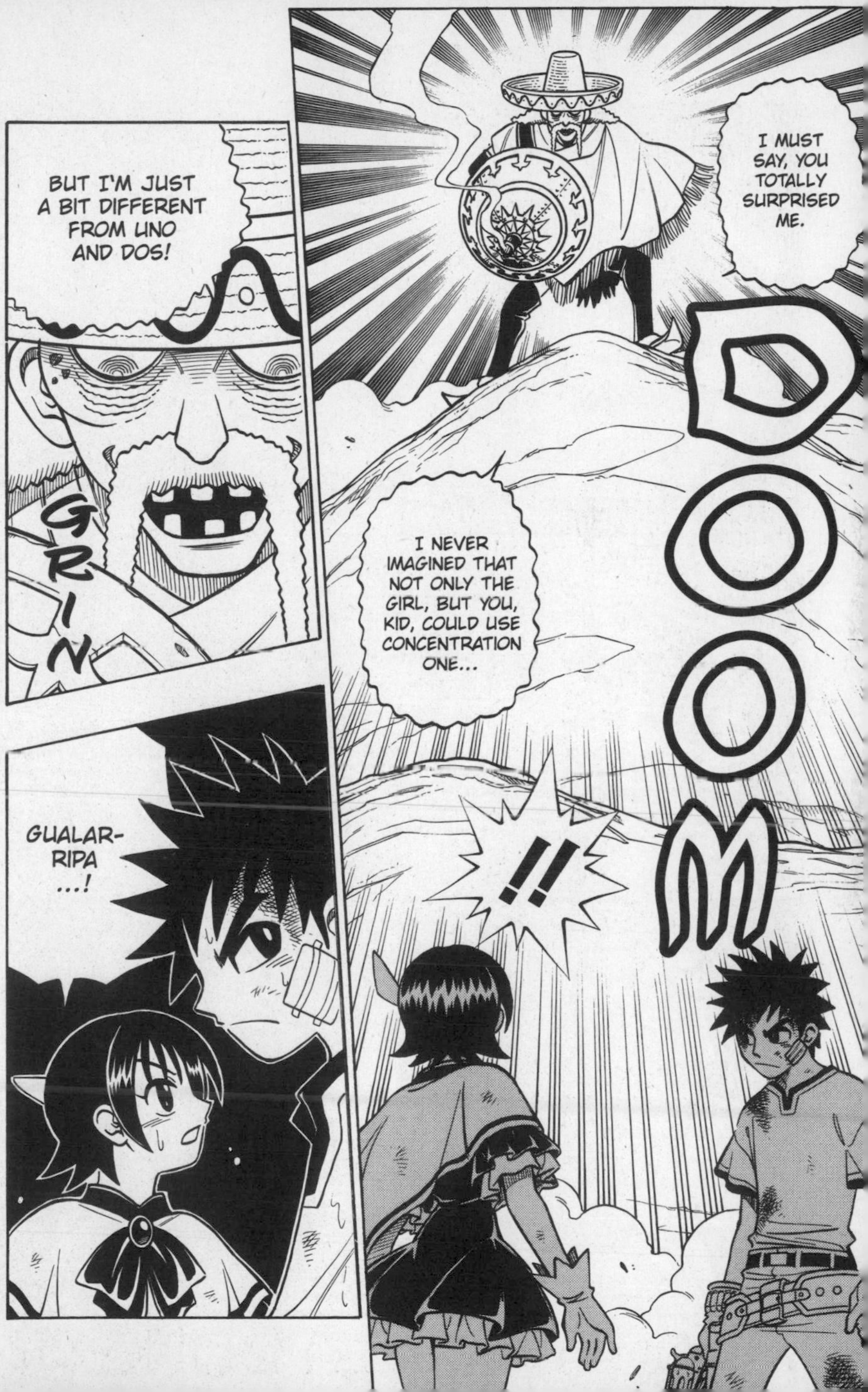
I MUST SAY, YOU TOTALLY SURPRISED ME.
DOOOM
I NEVER IMAGINED THAT NOT ONLY THE GIRL, BUT YOU, KID, COULD USE CONCENTRATION ONE...
!!
BUT I'M JUST A BIT DIFFERENT FROM UNO AND DOS!
GRIN
GUALAR-RIPA ...!

# CHAPTER 18

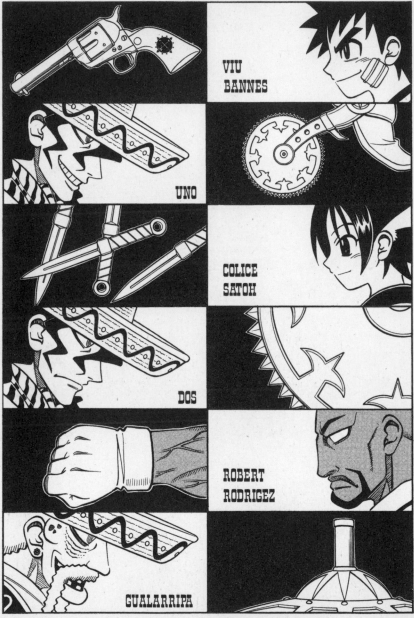

VIU
BANNES

UNO

COLICE
SATOH

DOS

ROBERT
RODRIGEZ

GUALARRIPA

# MUCH MUCH STRONGER

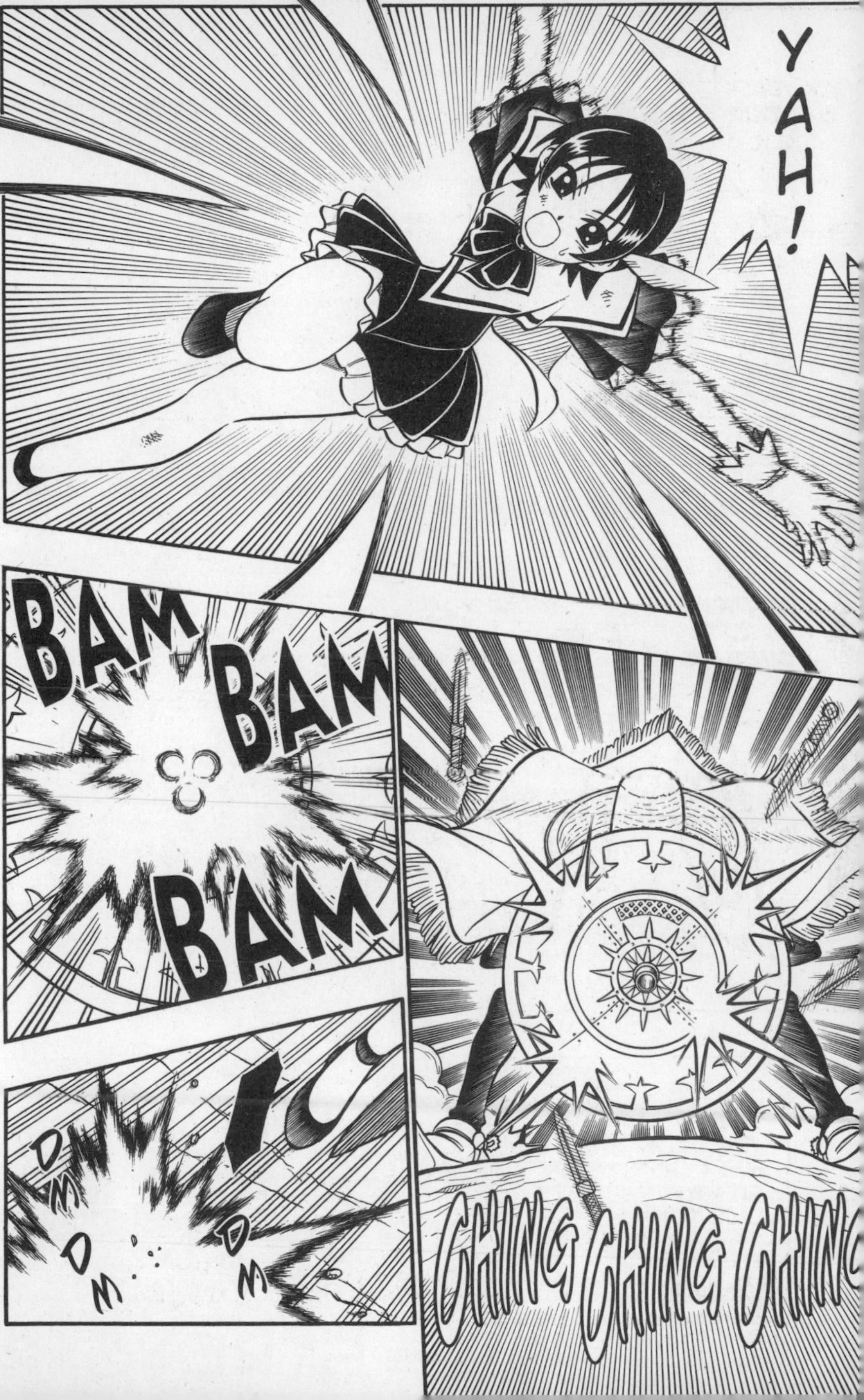
YAH!
CHING CHING CHING
BAM BAM BAM
DM DM DM

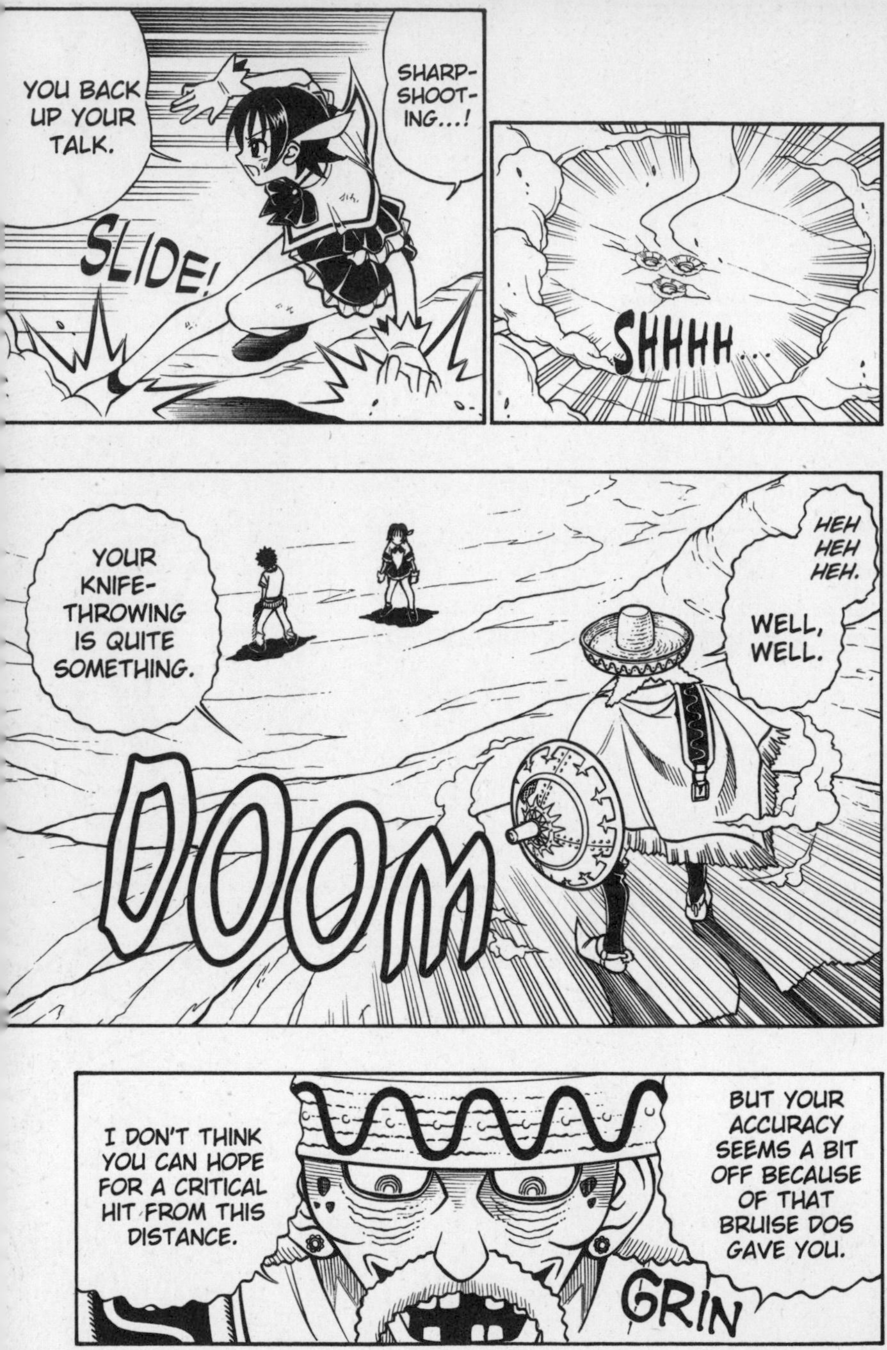
SHHHH...
SHARP-SHOOTING...!
YOU BACK UP YOUR TALK.
SLIDE!
HEH HEH HEH.
WELL, WELL.
YOUR KNIFE-THROWING IS QUITE SOMETHING.
DOOM
BUT YOUR ACCURACY SEEMS A BIT OFF BECAUSE OF THAT BRUISE DOS GAVE YOU.
GRIN
I DON'T THINK YOU CAN HOPE FOR A CRITICAL HIT FROM THIS DISTANCE.

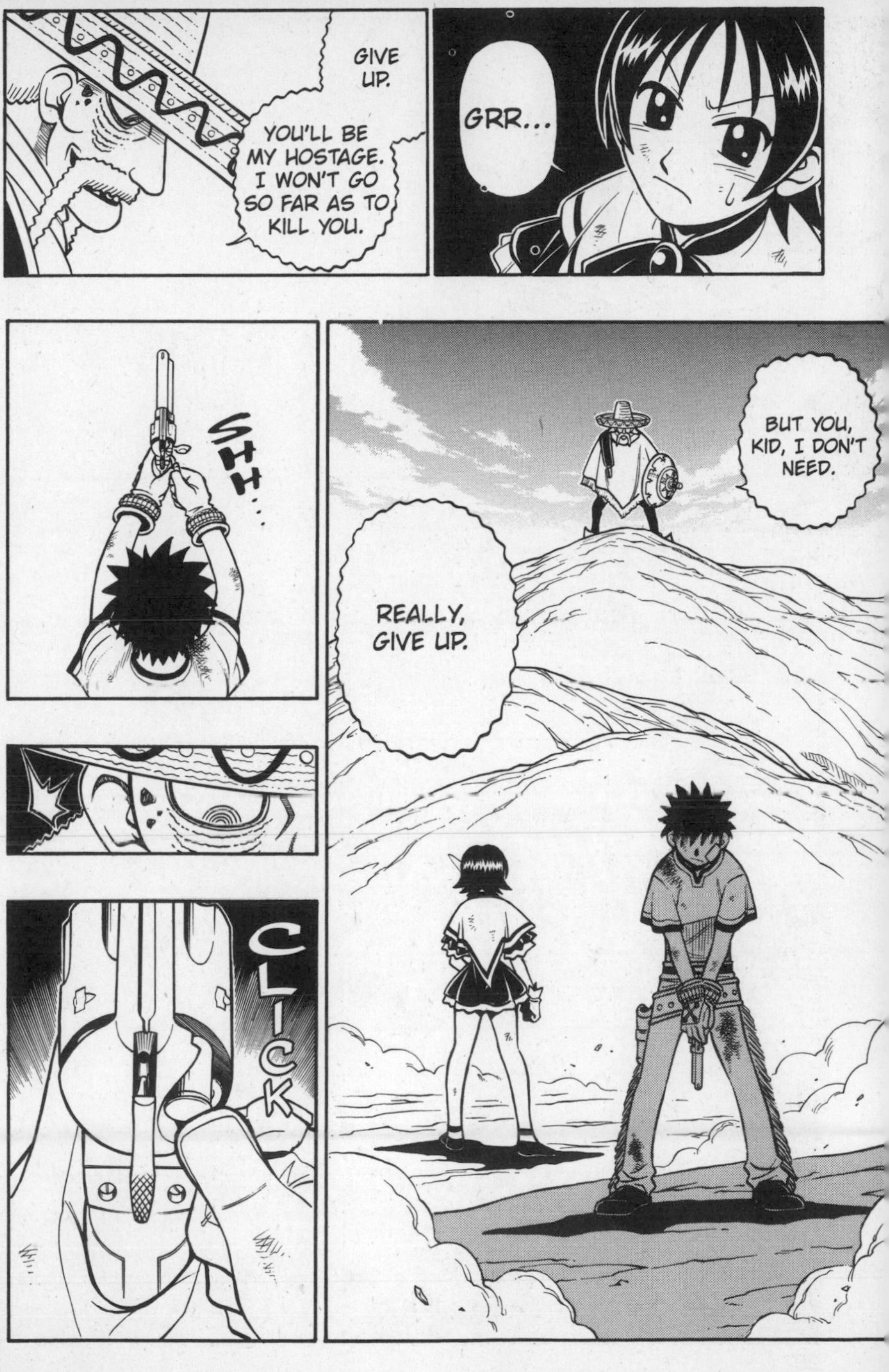
GRR...
GIVE UP.
YOU'LL BE MY HOSTAGE. I WON'T GO SO FAR AS TO KILL YOU.
BUT YOU, KID, I DON'T NEED.
REALLY, GIVE UP.
SHH...
CLICK

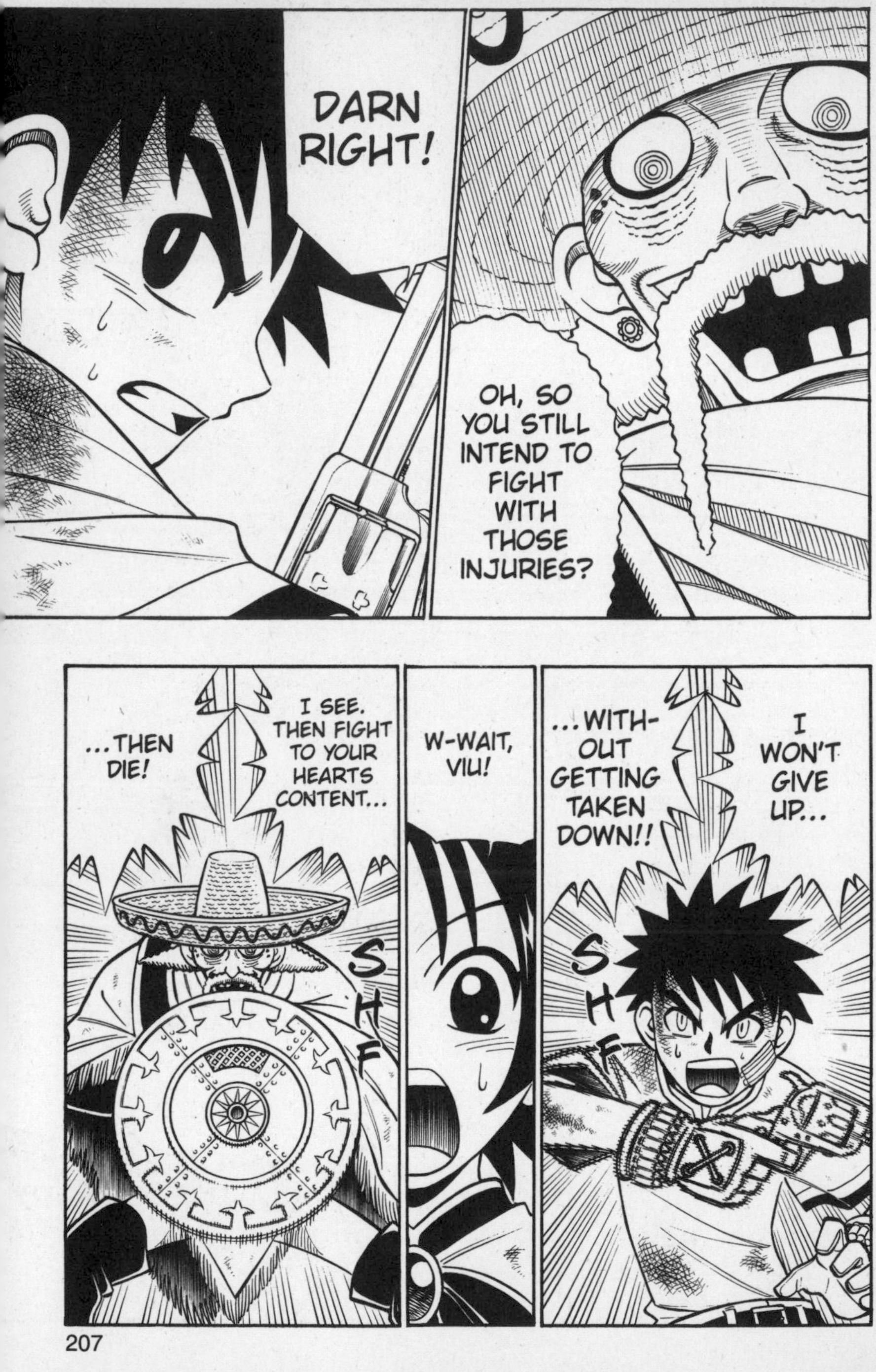
OH, SO YOU STILL INTEND TO FIGHT WITH THOSE INJURIES?
DARN RIGHT!
I WON'T GIVE UP...
...WITH-OUT GETTING TAKEN DOWN!!
SHF
W-WAIT, VIU!
I SEE. THEN FIGHT TO YOUR HEARTS CONTENT...
...THEN DIE!
SHF

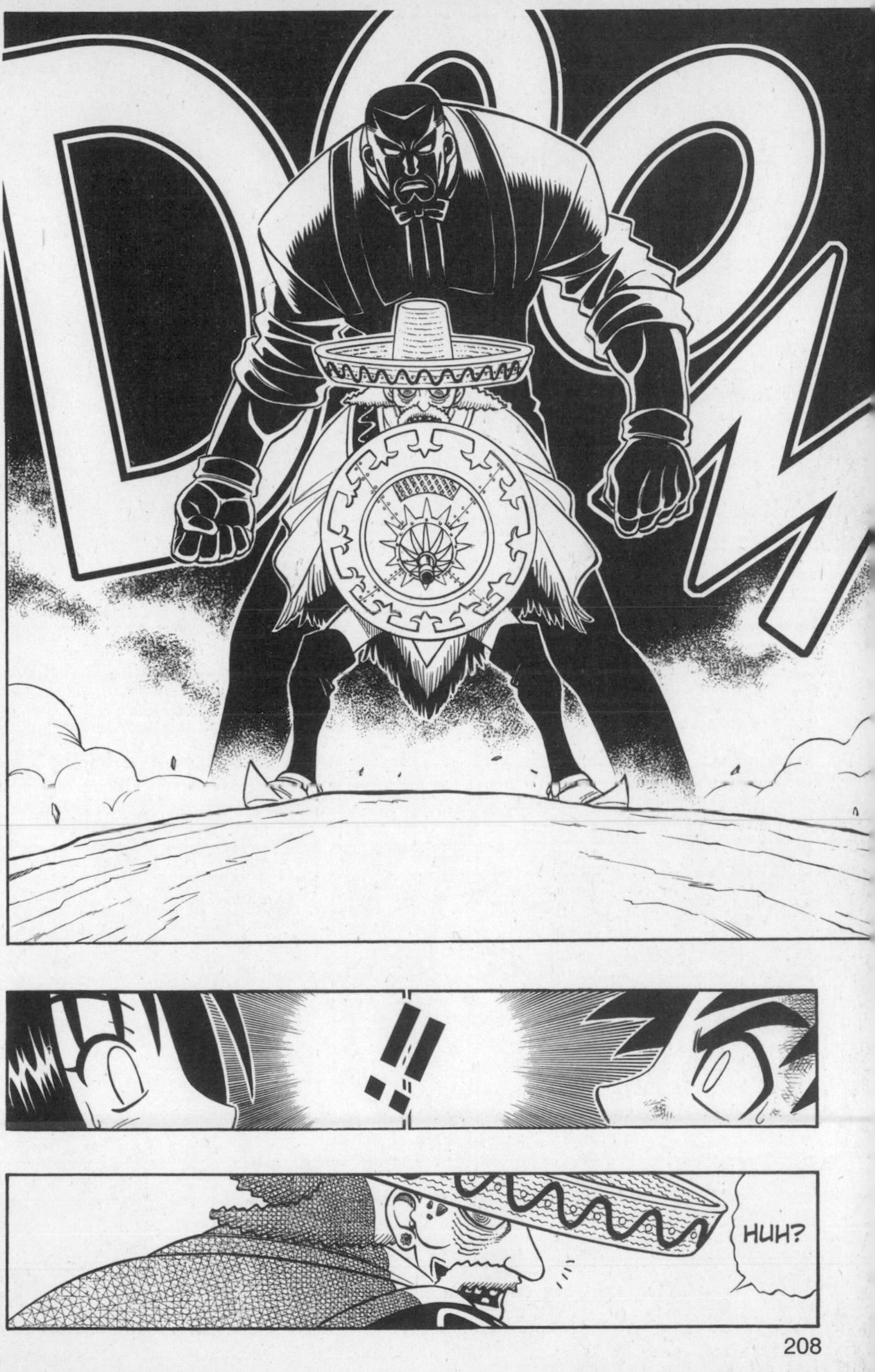
!!
HUH?

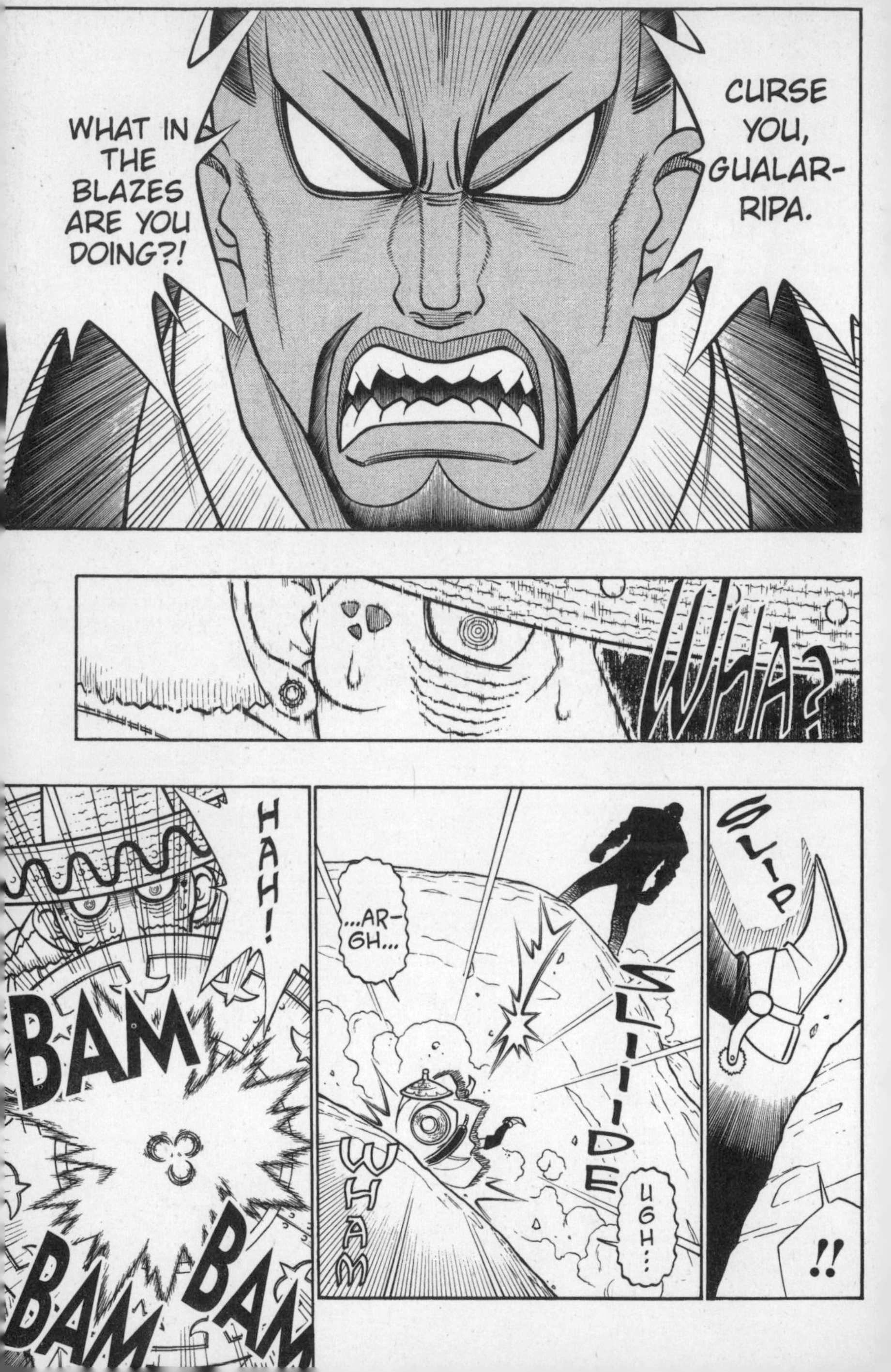
CURSE YOU, GUALAR-RIPA.
WHAT IN THE BLAZES ARE YOU DOING?!
WHA?
SLIP
!!
...AR-GH...
SLIIIDE
UGH...
WHAM
HAH!
BAM
BAM
BAM

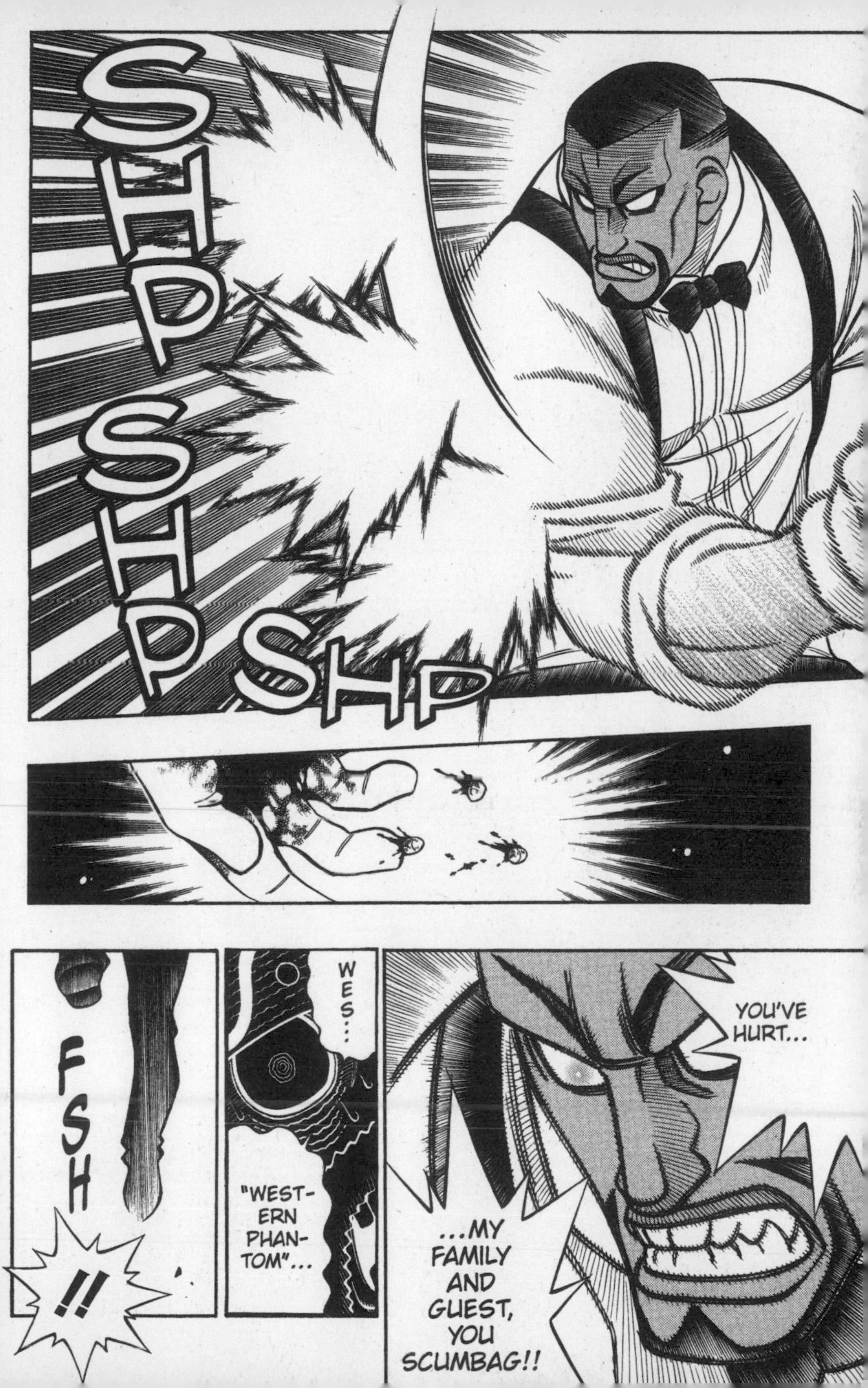
SHP SHP SHP SHP
YOU'VE HURT...
...MY FAMILY AND GUEST, YOU SCUMBAG!!
WES...
"WEST-ERN PHAN-TOM"...
FSH
!!

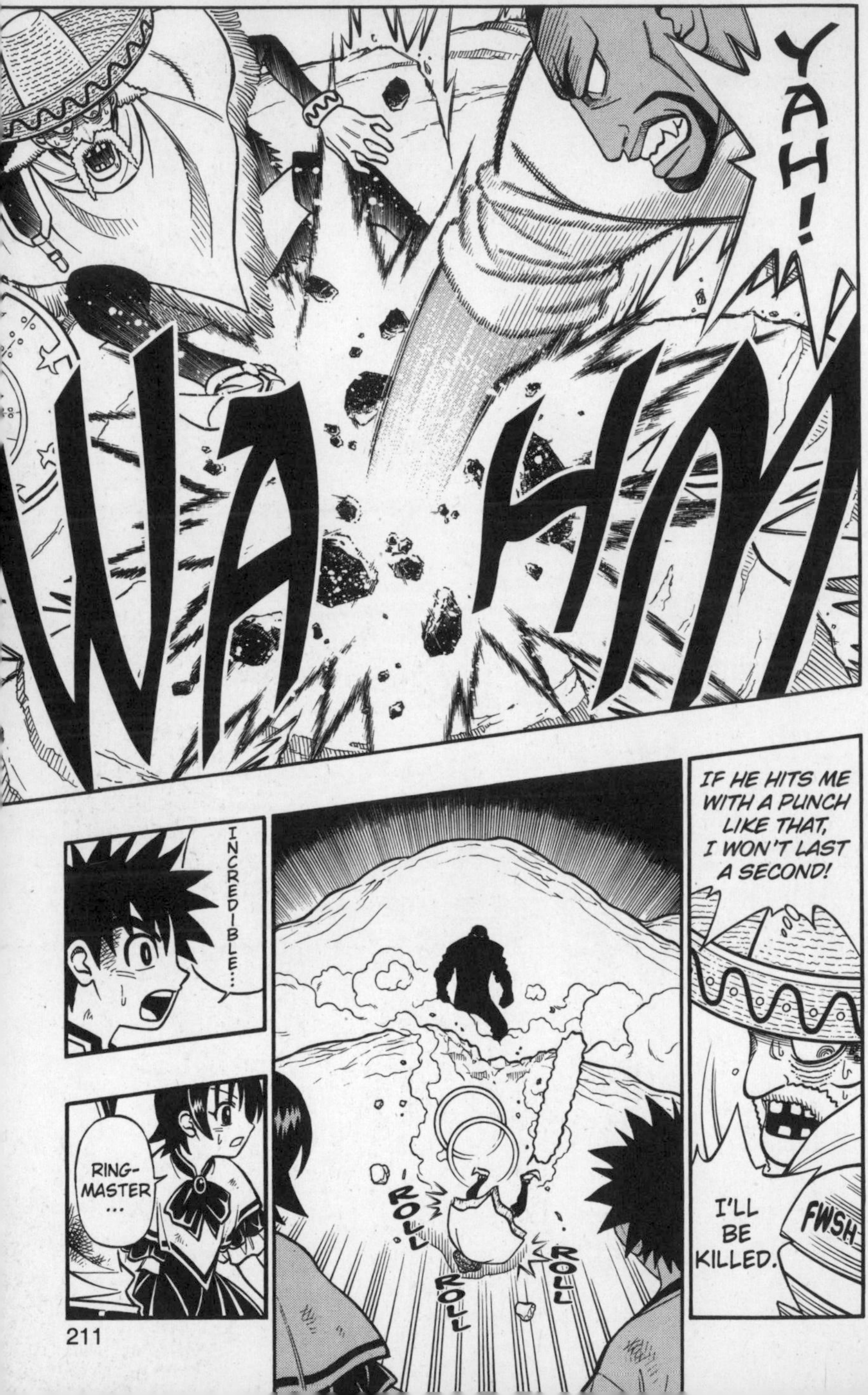
YAH!
IF HE HITS ME WITH A PUNCH LIKE THAT, I WON'T LAST A SECOND!
I'LL BE KILLED.
FWSH
ROLL
ROLL
ROLL
INCREDIBLE...
RING-MASTER...

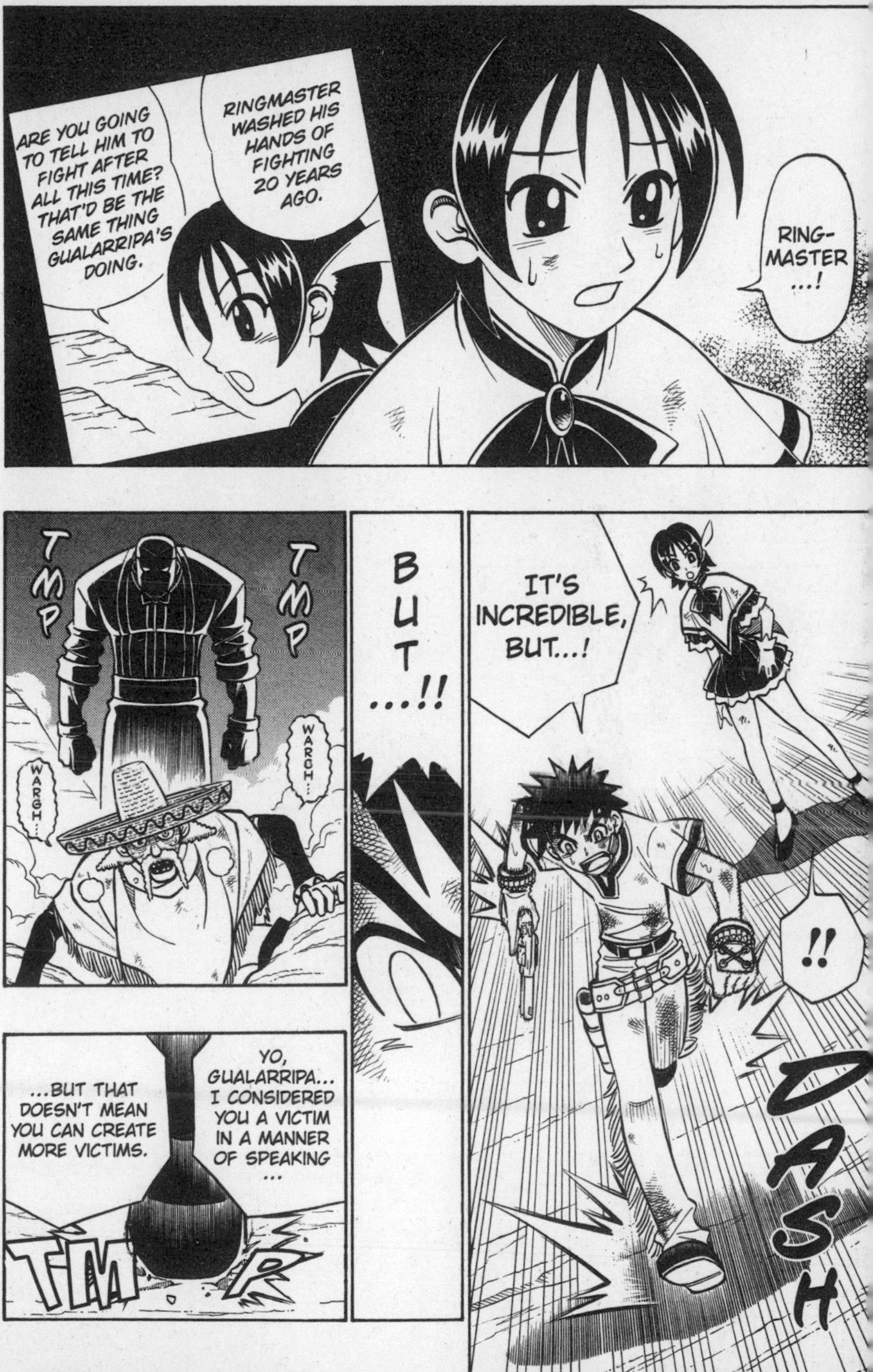
RING-MASTER ...!
RINGMASTER WASHED HIS HANDS OF FIGHTING 20 YEARS AGO.
ARE YOU GOING TO TELL HIM TO FIGHT AFTER ALL THIS TIME? THAT'D BE THE SAME THING GUALARRIPA'S DOING.
IT'S INCREDIBLE, BUT...!
!!
DASH
BUT ...!!
TMP
TMP
WARGH...
WARGH...
YO, GUALARRIPA... I CONSIDERED YOU A VICTIM IN A MANNER OF SPEAKING ...
...BUT THAT DOESN'T MEAN YOU CAN CREATE MORE VICTIMS.
TMP

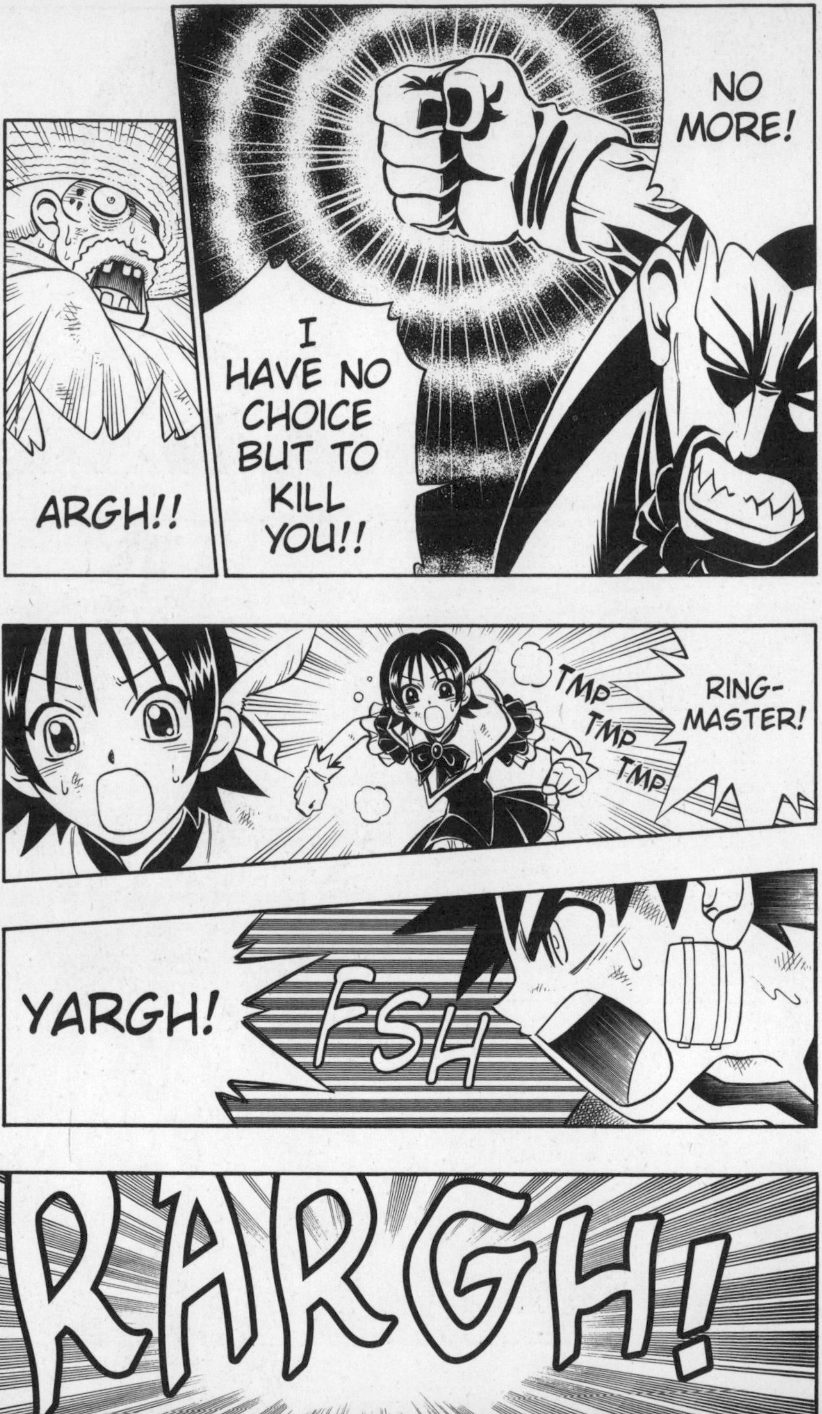
NO MORE!
I HAVE NO CHOICE BUT TO KILL YOU!!
ARGH!!
RING-MASTER!
TMP TMP TMP
FSH
YARGH!
RARGH!

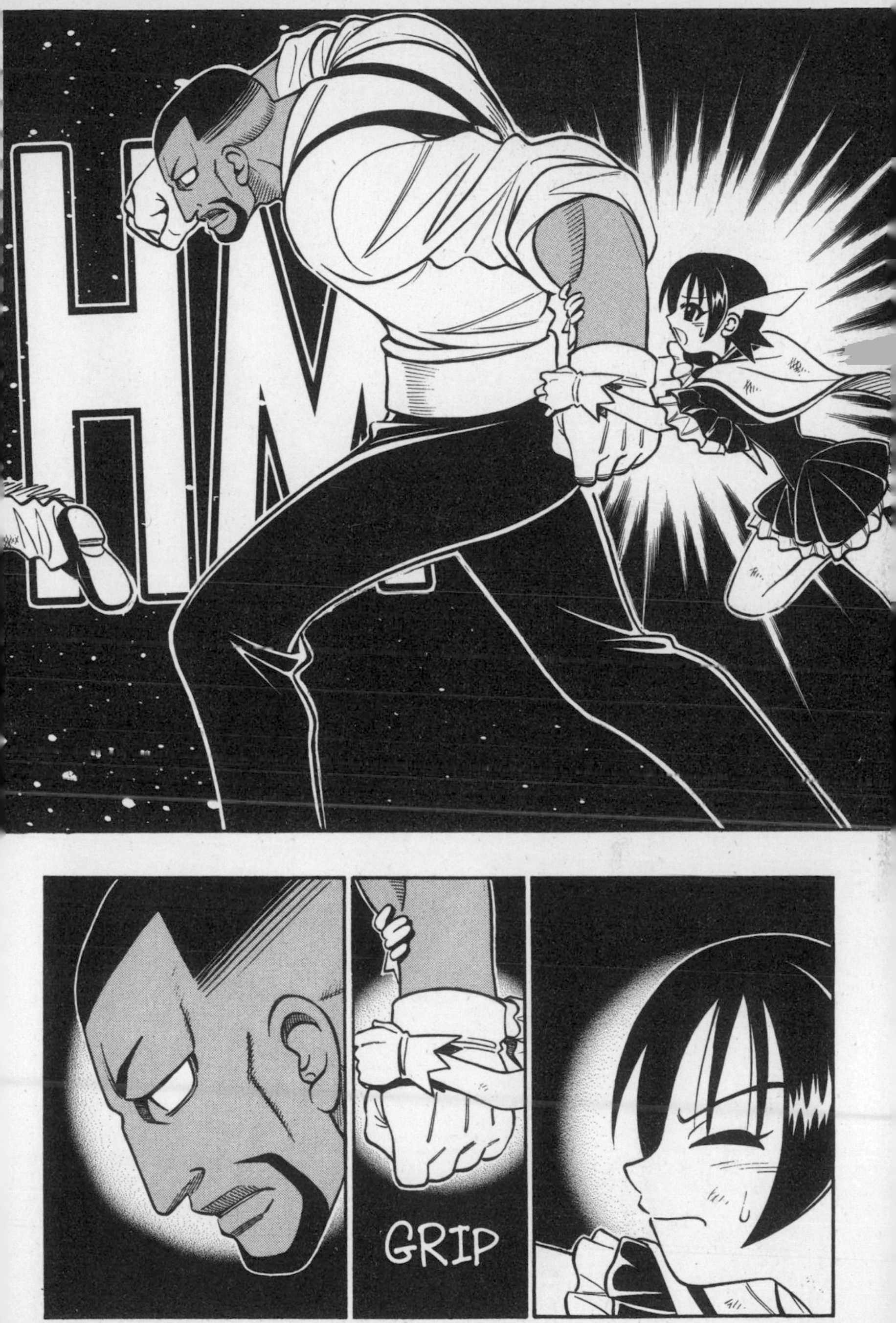
HM
GRIP

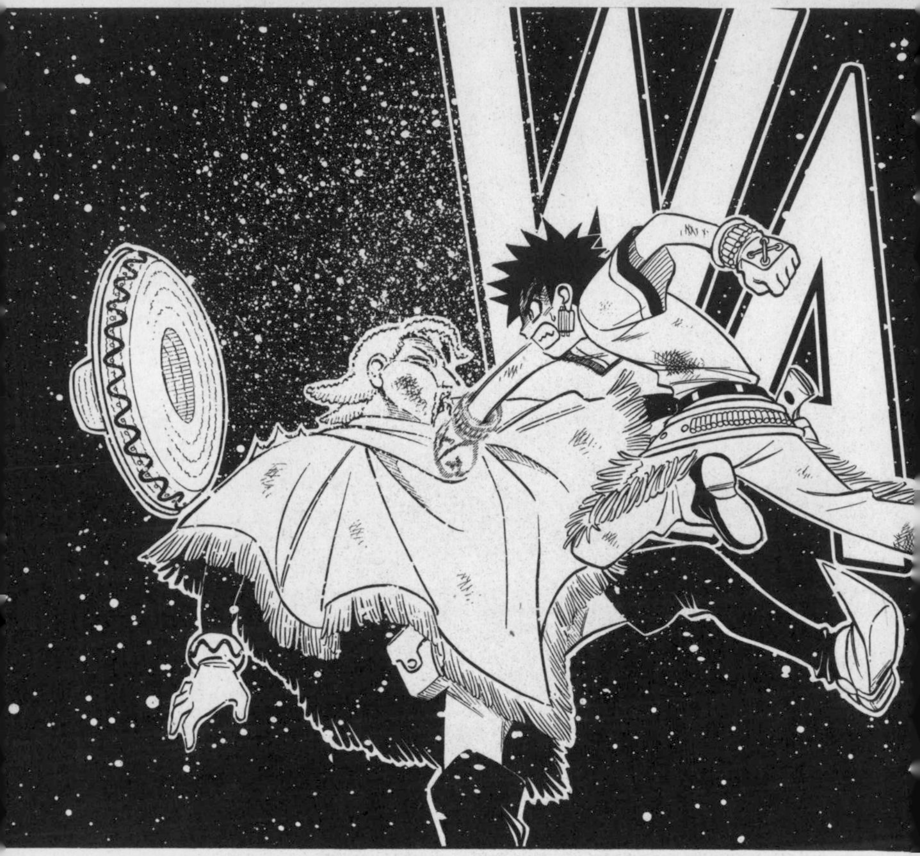

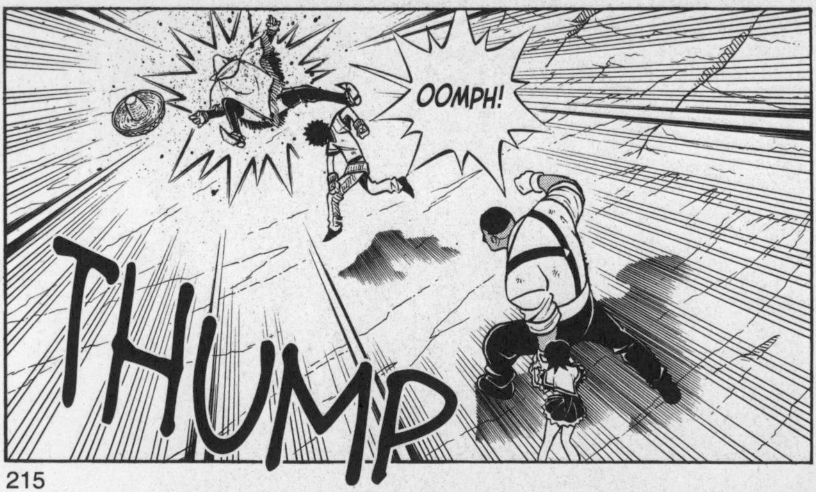
OOMPH!
THUMP

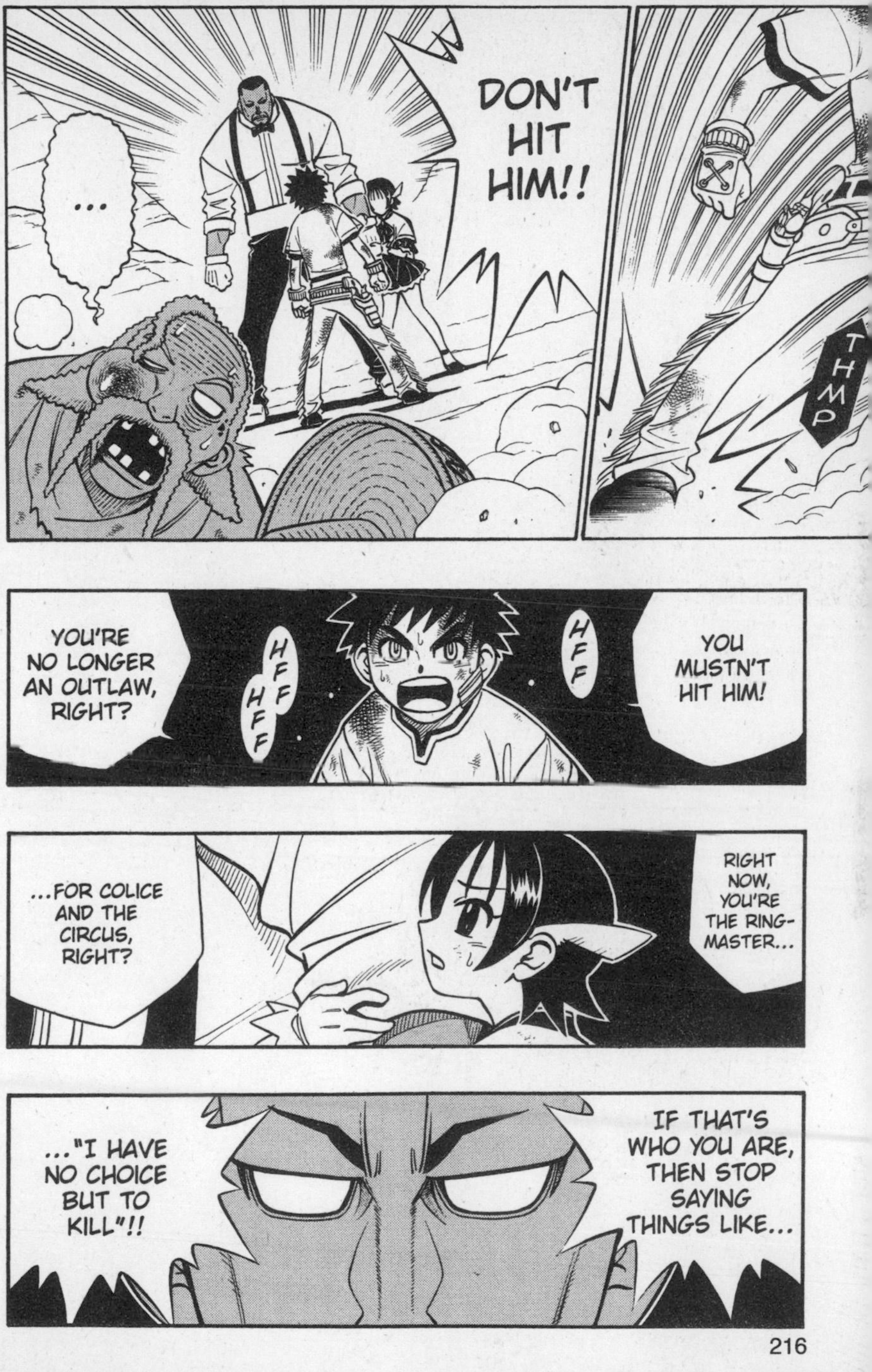
THMP
DON'T HIT HIM!!
...
YOU MUSTN'T HIT HIM!
HFF
HFF HFF
YOU'RE NO LONGER AN OUTLAW, RIGHT?
RIGHT NOW, YOU'RE THE RING-MASTER...
...FOR COLICE AND THE CIRCUS, RIGHT?
IF THAT'S WHO YOU ARE, THEN STOP SAYING THINGS LIKE...
..."I HAVE NO CHOICE BUT TO KILL"!!

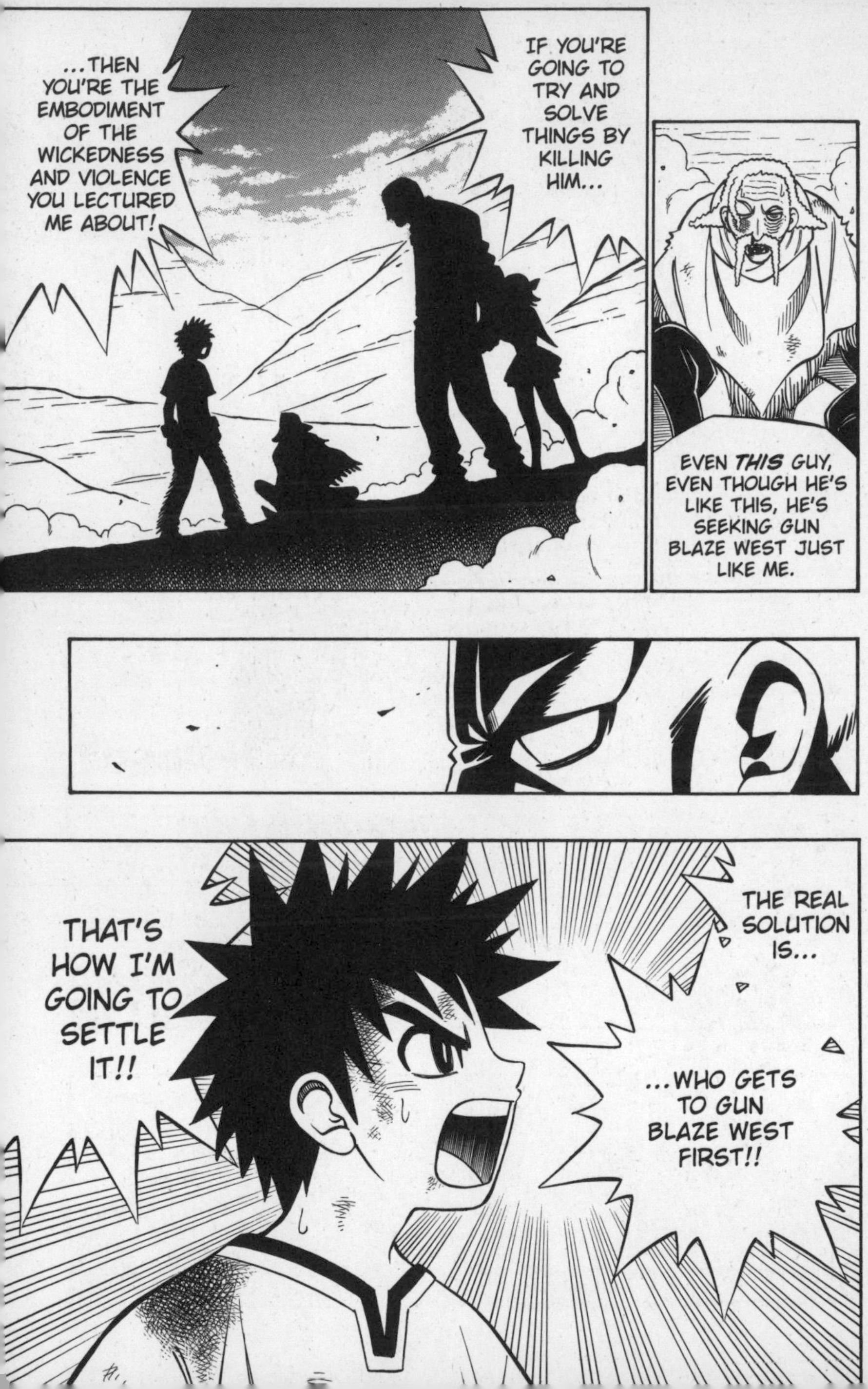
EVEN *THIS* GUY, EVEN THOUGH HE'S LIKE THIS, HE'S SEEKING GUN BLAZE WEST JUST LIKE ME.
IF YOU'RE GOING TO TRY AND SOLVE THINGS BY KILLING HIM...
...THEN YOU'RE THE EMBODIMENT OF THE WICKEDNESS AND VIOLENCE YOU LECTURED ME ABOUT!
THE REAL SOLUTION IS...
...WHO GETS TO GUN BLAZE WEST FIRST!!
THAT'S HOW I'M GOING TO SETTLE IT!!

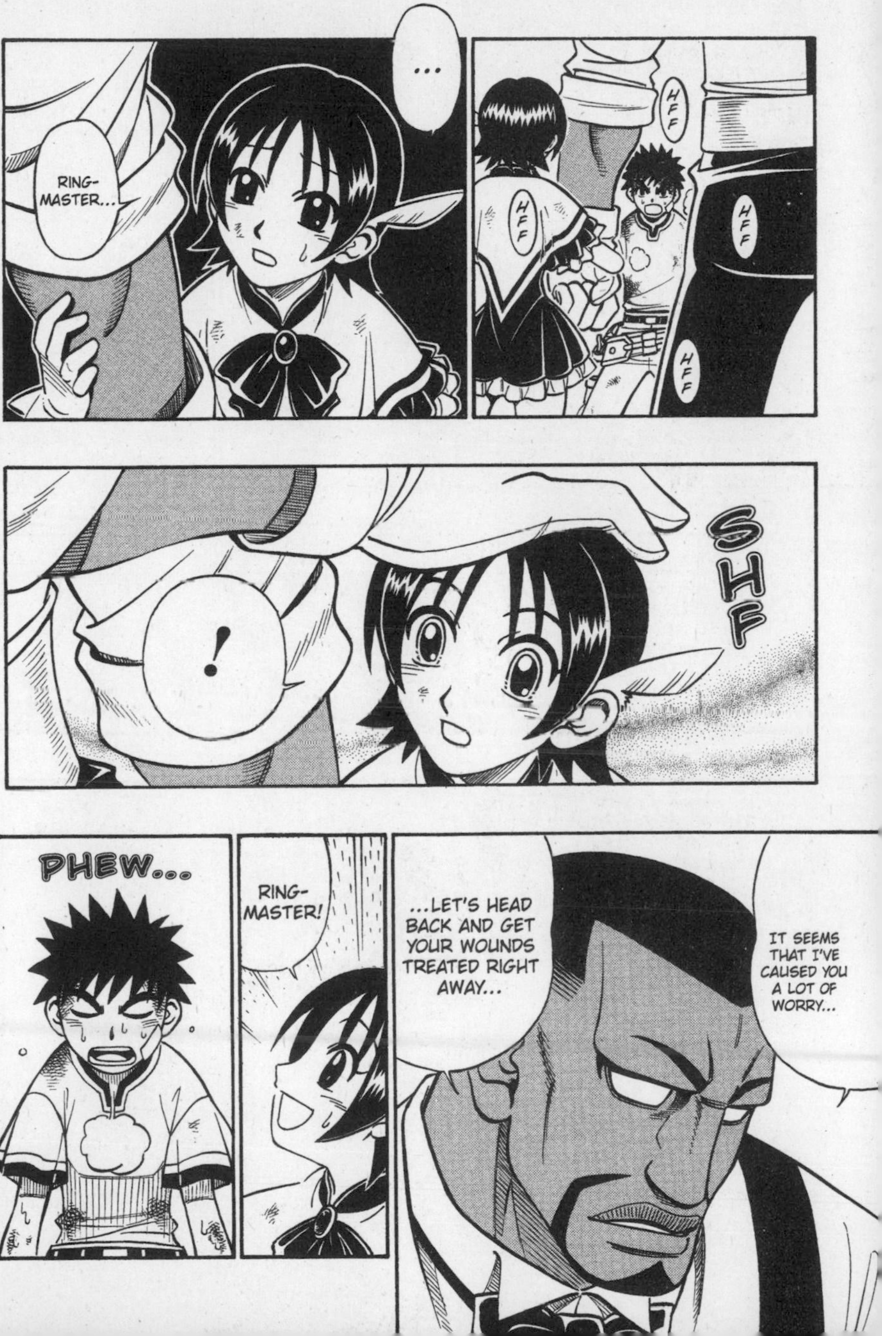
HFF
HFF
HFF
HFF
...
RING-MASTER...
SHF
!
IT SEEMS THAT I'VE CAUSED YOU A LOT OF WORRY...
...LET'S HEAD BACK AND GET YOUR WOUNDS TREATED RIGHT AWAY...
RING-MASTER!
PHEW...

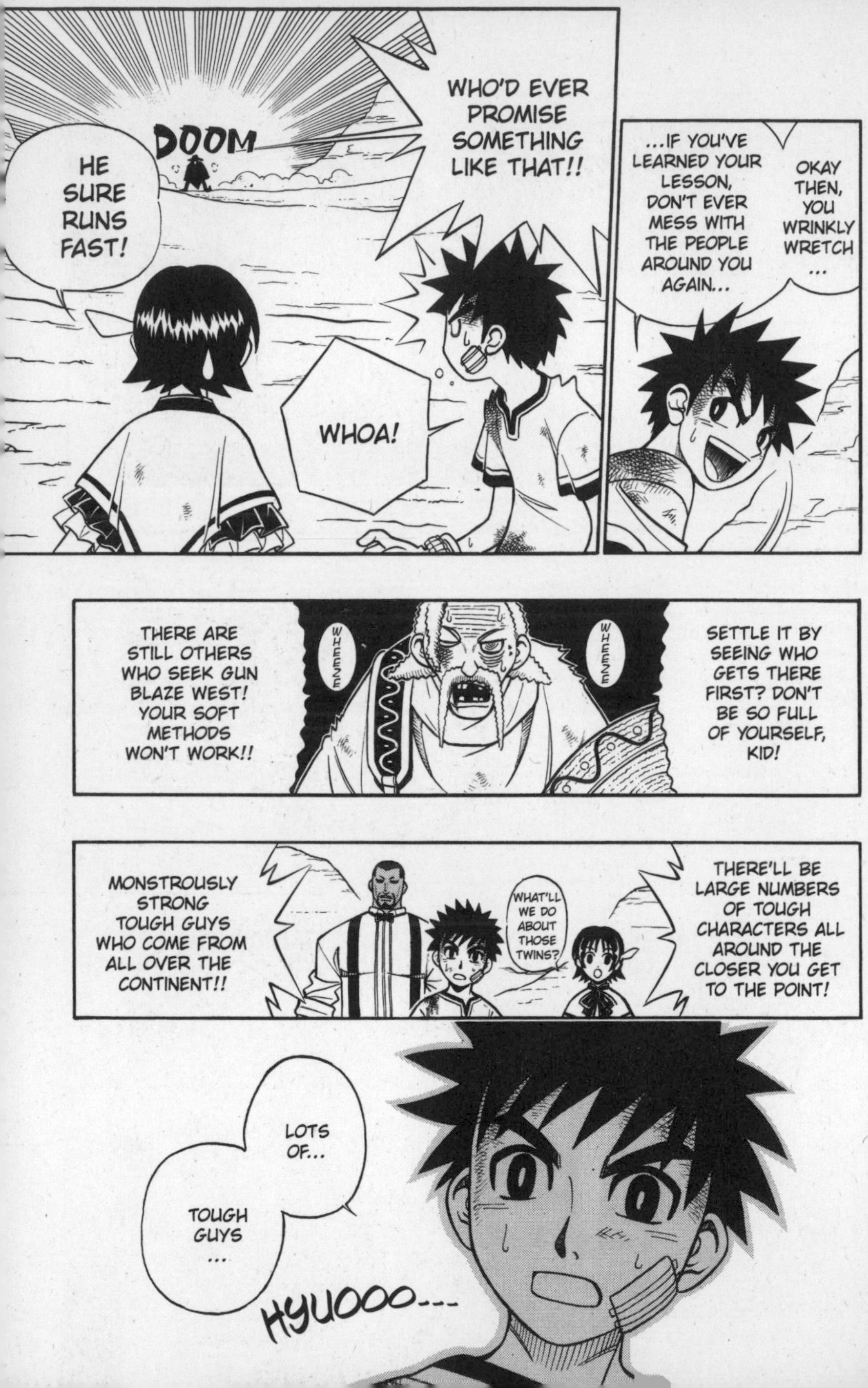
OKAY THEN, YOU WRINKLY WRETCH ...
...IF YOU'VE LEARNED YOUR LESSON, DON'T EVER MESS WITH THE PEOPLE AROUND YOU AGAIN...
WHO'D EVER PROMISE SOMETHING LIKE THAT!!
DOOM
WHOA!
HE SURE RUNS FAST!
SETTLE IT BY SEEING WHO GETS THERE FIRST? DON'T BE SO FULL OF YOURSELF, KID!
WHEEZE
WHEEZE
THERE ARE STILL OTHERS WHO SEEK GUN BLAZE WEST! YOUR SOFT METHODS WON'T WORK!!
THERE'LL BE LARGE NUMBERS OF TOUGH CHARACTERS ALL AROUND THE CLOSER YOU GET TO THE POINT!
WHAT'LL WE DO ABOUT THOSE TWINS?
MONSTROUSLY STRONG TOUGH GUYS WHO COME FROM ALL OVER THE CONTINENT!!
LOTS OF...
TOUGH GUYS ...
HYUOOO...

IN OKLAHOMA
ROAR!
BUTLER, HOW IS OUR PROGRESS?
TOOOT!
WE'RE RUNNING A LITTLE LATE.
ARE YOU IN A HURRY, BARON?
NO. AS LONG AS WE MAKE IT BY THE DEADLINE.
AFTER ALL, RUSHING IS FOR THE PETTY...
...AND NOT IN MY NATURE.
IN TENNESSEE
ROAR!
WHEEZE
HFF
WHEEZE
HEY, HANG IN THERE, LEADER.
JUST A LITTLE FURTHER TILL THE POINT.
DMM...
WEREN'T YOU THE ONE WHO SAID YOU WANTED TO BE ABSOLUTELY THE FIRST ONE THERE, J.J.?

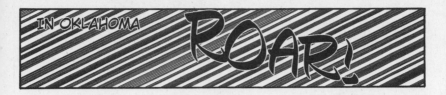

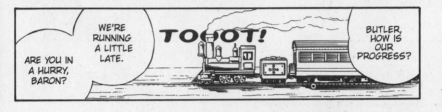

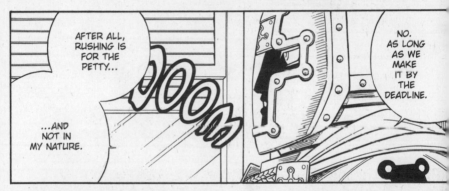

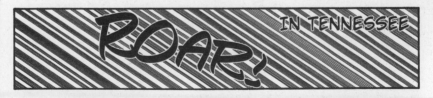

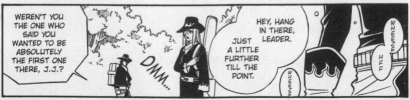

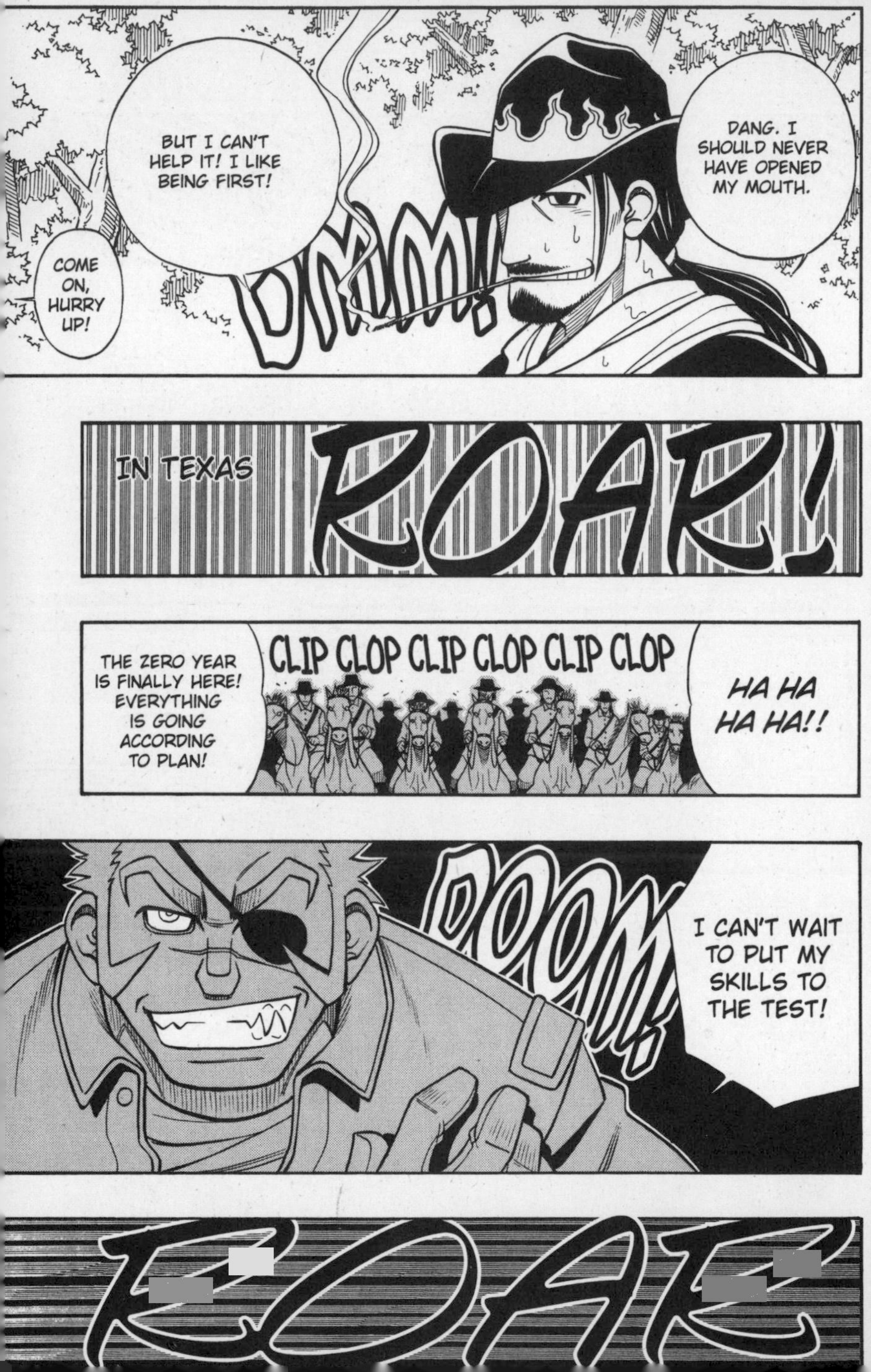
DANG. I SHOULD NEVER HAVE OPENED MY MOUTH.
BUT I CAN'T HELP IT! I LIKE BEING FIRST!
COME ON, HURRY UP!
ROAR!
IN TEXAS
HA HA HA HA!!
CLIP CLOP CLIP CLOP CLIP CLOP
THE ZERO YEAR IS FINALLY HERE! EVERYTHING IS GOING ACCORDING TO PLAN!
I CAN'T WAIT TO PUT MY SKILLS TO THE TEST!
ROAR

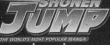

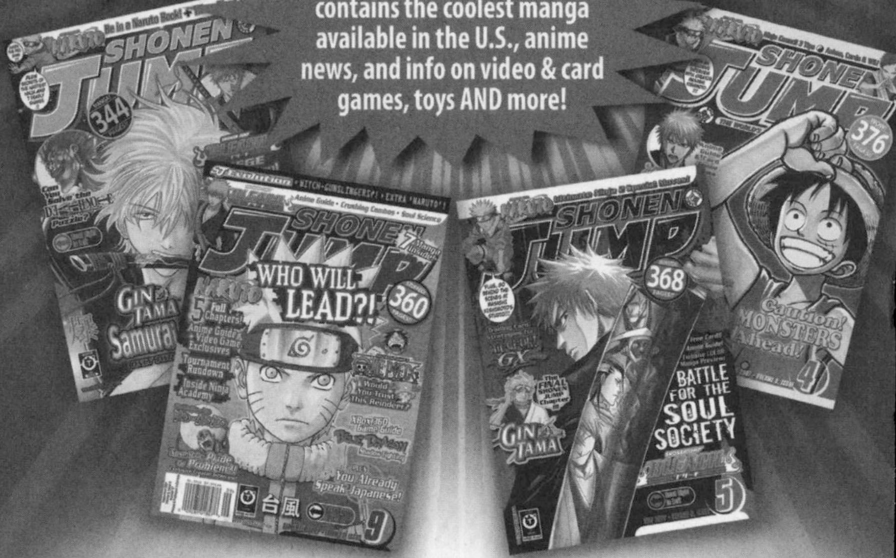

# Save 50

*JUMP*

THE WORLD'S MOST POPULAR MANGA

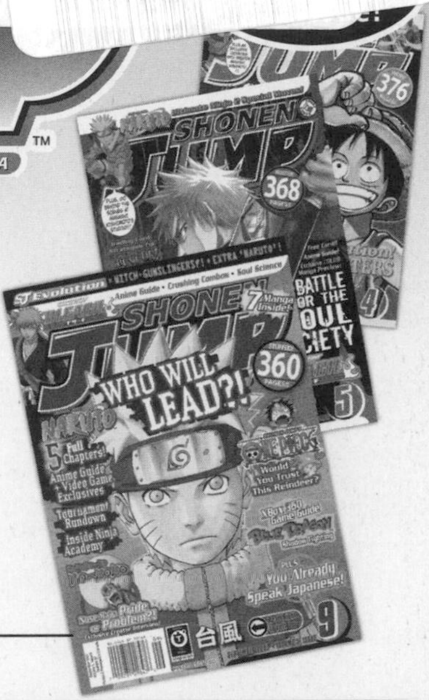

**Each issue of SHONEN JUMP contains the coolest manga available in the U.S., anime news, and info on video & card games, toys AND more!**

☑ **YES!** Please enter my one-year subscription (12 HUGE issues) to **SHONEN JUMP** at the LOW SUBSCRIPTION RATE of **$29.95!**

NAME

ADDRESS

CITY                    STATE         ZIP

E-MAIL ADDRESS                              P7GNC1

☐ MY CHECK IS ENCLOSED (PAYABLE TO SHONEN JUMP)  ☐ BILL ME LATER

CREDIT CARD:     ☐ VISA     ☐ MASTERCARD

ACCOUNT #                              EXP. DATE

SIGNATURE

CLIP AND MAIL TO ➡

SHONEN JUMP
Subscriptions Service Dept.
P.O. Box 515
Mount Morris, IL 61054-0515

Make checks payable to: **SHONEN JUMP**. Canada price for 12 issues: $41.95 USD, including GST, HST and QST. US/CAN orders only. Allow 6-8 weeks for delivery.

BLEACH © 2001 by Tite Kubo/SHUEISHA Inc. NARUTO © 1999 by Masashi Kishimoto/SHUEISHA Inc.
ONE PIECE © 1997 by Eiichiro Oda/SHUEISHA Inc.

RATED
T
FOR
TEEN
ratings.viz.com